RESPONDING TO LITERATURE

A STEP-BY-STEP GUIDE FOR STUDENT WRITERS

D1309202

RESPONDING TO LITERATURE

A STEP-BY-STEP GUIDE FOR STUDENT WRITERS

John Sheridan Biays, Jr.
Broward Community College

Carol Wershoven
Palm Beach Junior College

McGRAW-HILL BOOK COMPANY

New York   St. Louis   San Francisco   Auckland   Bogotá   Caracas
Colorado Springs   Hamburg   Lisbon   London   Madrid   Mexico
Milan   Montreal   New Delhi   Oklahoma City   Panama   Paris
San Juan   São Paulo   Singapore   Sydney   Tokyo   Toronto

This book was set in Times Roman by Better Graphics, Inc.
The editors were Emily Barrosse and Jack Maisel;
the cover was designed by Fern Logan
the production supervisor was Diane Renda.
R.R. Donnelley & Sons Company was printer and binder.

Cover painting ''The Disc'' by
Fernand Leger provided by
Nimatallah/Art Resource.

RESPONDING TO LITERATURE:

A Step-by-Step Guide for Student Writers

1 2 3 4 5 6 7 8 9 0 DOCDOC 8 9 3 2 1 0 9 8 7

ISBN 0-07-005160-7

See Acknowledgments on page 474.
Copyrights included on this page by reference.

LIBRARY OF CONGRESS
Library of Congress Cataloging-in-Publication Data

Biays, John Sheridan.
    Responding to literature: a step-by-step guide for student writers / John Sheridan Biays,
  Carol Wershoven.
      p.   cm.
    ISBN 0-07-005160-7
  1. English language—Rhetoric.   2. Criticism—Authorship.
  3. Report writing.   4. Literature—Study and teaching.
  I. Wershoven, Carol.   II. Title.
  PE1479.C7B5   1988   87-27976
  808'.0668—dc19   CIP

ABOUT THE AUTHORS

John Sheridan Biays, Jr. and Carol Wershoven teach at Broward Community College and Palm Beach Junior College, respectively. Between them, the authors hold five graduate degrees in English and curriculum. Biays stays active writing feature stories for popular publications and developing instructional material for composition, literature, and interdisciplinary courses. Wershoven is the author of *The Female Intruder in the Novels of Edith Wharton* (Associated University Presses, 1983) and a number of scholarly articles for journals and critical collections. She has developed innovative courses in women's studies and film as literature.

For this husband-wife writing team, *Responding to Literature* is a culmination of their 34 years' combined teaching experience. They have taught every level from college freshmen to university seniors, from remedial writing to honors seminars. As teachers, they have seen the need to emphasize process as well as product in the teaching of writing; as writers, they have designed this text to meet that crucial need.

For our parents:
Virginia Langshaw
and John Sheridan Biays,
and Rosa De Raedemaeker
and William Wershoven

CONTENTS

PREFACE

Responding to Literature: A Step-by-Step Guide for Student Writers is an extensive guide and workbook that can be used as a companion to any literature anthology or as a supplement for any course where writing about literature is required. This book is designed to give students additional practice in effective writing, for it emphasizes the importance of reading critically, developing thesis statements, selecting appropriate supporting detail, and planning essays through detailed outlines and drafts.

The text evolved from our many years of teaching composition and literature courses. College freshmen are usually introduced to the rhetorical modes during their first semester of college English. However, when they progress to an introductory literature course (or a second semester literature-based composition course), anxiety often develops. We discovered that many students could not merely be told *how* to write about literature; they needed to work through the process in manageable steps, just as they had done in their expository writing course. Process, we learned, is crucial to the end products of improved writing and analytical skills. Our book, then, is a collection of explanations, examples, and activities that enable student writers to understand and enjoy literature by writing about it, clearly and competently.

To provide instructors with as many options as possible, the explanations in the book are purposely simple. Instructors will, most likely, supplement them with their own lectures and through the apparatus in literature anthologies. Throughout our book, the material on structured essays is complementary and overlapping, and instructors can use sections of the text in any order they choose. Some instructors may skip exercises entirely; some may have students work through exercises as a basis for class discussions and workshops; some may use them to generate ideas for in-class writing assignments. We trust that the scope of the book will enable instructors to select, modify, and develop exercises to suit their individual specifications.

The focus of our book is a thematic approach—we have structured each section of the text (short story-drama-poetry) to culminate in a complete critical analysis. Our goal is two-fold: to improve students' writing ability while showing them how analysis can lead to reintegration and a deeper understanding of a work. We recognize that there are many valid approaches to teaching writing about literature; thus, we have tried to incorporate enough varied material so that each pedagogical and theoretical position can find something of value.

Responding to Literature: A Step-By-Step Guide for Student Writers is a book we wrote for students—a step-by-step guide for the intimidated student along with ample exercises and approaches for the initiated student. It is also a book for teachers; we share what has worked in our teaching experiences in hopes that it may supplement your own classroom strategies.

For their useful criticisms and suggestions throughout the development of the manuscript, we would also like to thank Thomas A. Duff, Seton Hall University; William Hamlin, University of Missouri; John M. Hansen, Catonsville Community College; Jeffery Helterman, University of South Carolina; Nancy G. Hume, Essex Community College; Richard H. Lerner, City Colleges of Chicago; Russ McGaughey, Humboldt State University; Spencer Olesen, Mountain View College; Marie Saunders, Central State University; and Robert Weiss, West Chester University. We would also like to thank all the people at McGraw-Hill who helped to bring this book to completion.

Many people at McGraw-Hill were involved in the complex tasks of developing, revising, and editing this comprehensive book. We are extremely grateful to Emily Barrosse, College Division editor, for recognizing the need for our book; Charlotte Smith, developmental editor, for providing ongoing support and valued suggestions; Jack Maisel, senior editing supervisor, for meticulously reviewing and designing the text; and to Nancy Myers, College Division representative in southeast Florida, for her thorough professionalism in serving as our liaison to McGraw-Hill's New York headquarters.

John Sheridan Biays, Jr.
Carol Wershoven

INTRODUCTION

People can read literature in as many different ways as they live their lives. Some people let life flow over them, passively allowing encounters with others and events to stream by, never questioning, reacting only minimally, seeing their world in one dimension. Some people barely live at all; for them, life is a movie they observe with only grudging interest. They become distanced from their own lives, not really a part of life.

Others dive into that flow of life, for they ask questions about what they see and about what happens. They attempt to understand life; their central question is "What does it mean?" Such people try to find some structure to the events of their lives; they try to discover the reasons behind peoples' actions, or they try to anticipate and plan for the future by assessing the past. They see life on more than one level, for not only do they observe, but they also try actively to interpret and even to involve themselves in life. They are not merely reactors, but actors, analysts, evaluators.

Those who read literature can choose similar alternatives. A person can read passively, allowing the accumulated words to glide by, seeing only the surface. Or a person can question, interpret, connect, relate—he or she can analyze. A person can ask of literature not only "What does it say?" but "What does it mean?" and even "How does it mean it?"

To answer such questions takes thought, a certain kind of challenging thought, the same kind you use when you examine the events and people in your life. This kind of thinking is, of course, not easy or automatic, but in both reading and living, it provides special rewards. Only by penetrating the surface of both the text of literature and the text of your life can you discover answers to the one question that dominates both literature and life: "What does it mean?"

In the following exercises, you will be practicing new ways to develop a certain kind of thinking; some of these exercises will be very simple, but others will be more challenging. You will be asked to write your thoughts, and the writing assignments will require you to use the different ways of developing an idea that are used in writing other kinds of essays. That is, when you write a plot summary of a story, you will be writing a *process analysis*; when you describe the characters, you may be writing a *comparison/contrast*. You may be asked to *classify* a character or a literary work, and, in studying a character's motives, you will be developing a *causal analysis*. In all of your written assignments you will be supporting your ideas by using *examples* and *illustrations*.

Each exercise is directed towards one goal: to help you see. Seeing is developing insight, developing the ability to make connections, distinguishing patterns, and discerning meaning. Like living life, reading and writing about literature takes discipline, energy, and skill. But, like living life, the more you involve yourself in the process, the more you receive from it.

PART ONE

THE SHORT STORY

PLOT

READING THE STORY FOR PLOT

Reading a short story with understanding depends, first of all, on comprehending what *happens* in the story. The events, or happenings, of the story form a plot line.

The plot line of a story consists of the events which describe some specific conflict and its outcome. Since a short story is *short*, the events given to you will not be very numerous or complicated. Most stories will contain the same pieces of one pattern, although these pieces may be placed in different sequences. The typical pattern for the plot of a short story is shown in the accompanying diagram.

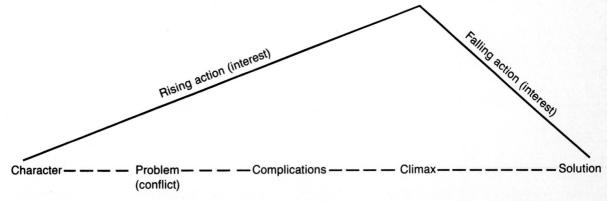

A short-story writer knows that he or she must draw the reader into the story very quickly. A good description of a scene may interest the reader for a short time, but very soon the reader must meet a person, a *character*.

And, after the reader meets this character and gets to know the person somewhat, something else must happen very quickly. The character must encounter a problem, a *conflict* of some kind. That problem may be represented by another character, or by a situation, a natural force, or even some aspect of the first character's personality.

In literature, *the character faced with a conflict or dilemma* is called the *protagonist*. You may have heard this type of character called the *hero*, but this term may not be most appropriate since it can mean good or moral, and very often the main character in a short story is neither. Edgar Allan Poe's protagonists may be murderers; other protagonists may be fugitives from justice, thieves, or revolutionaries. Such characters are faced with conflicts but are not necessarily good, so it is more accurate to think of them as protagonists than as heroes.

Whatever represents the conflict that faces the protagonist is called the *antagonist*. In literature, a typical conflict involves one person struggling against another:

Man vs. man
protagonist vs. antagonist

In certain stories, or in television or film, such typical conflicts are the detective against the criminal, the sheriff against the gunslinger, the soldier on the front lines against the soldier on the opposition, the child against the parent, or the husband against the wife. Regardless of the conflict, people are usually striving to achieve some goal while struggling against some obstacle or obstacles.

There are other typical conflicts:

Man vs. society
(a character may rebel against society's restrictions, for example)
Man vs. nature
(a character may have to fight an animal, a hurricane, or a hard winter, for example)
Man vs. the machine
(a modern character may match wits with a computer, or may lose a job to technology, for example)
Man vs. himself/herself
(a person may have to struggle against some part of his or her personality or character, for example, an addiction to alcoholism or the manifestation of an irrational fear)

Or, a conflict may occur between the protagonist and several different antagonists. Whatever the conflict in a short story may be, you can be sure that you will be introduced to it soon, or your interest in the story will not build.

Shortly after a conflict is introduced, another series of steps must be taken to maintain and heighten the reader's interest in the story. Conflict itself must become tangled; incidents and scenes must *complicate* the conflict, or draw it out and build it up, so that the reader begins to wonder what will happen next and how it will turn out.

In typical stories, the fugitive may elude the detective several times, or the outlaw may threaten the sheriff and almost (but not quite!) shoot him down. At any rate, tension (and reader interest) builds through these complications until the reader reaches *the highest point of tension* in the story—the *climax*. At this point, the reader is indeed asking, "How will all this turn out?" or "How will it end?" If you are watching a drama on television, the climax is the point at which you *never* change the channel.

As soon as the reader knows the outcome, or as soon as the major question is resolved, the climax of the story is passed and the *solution* (sometimes called the *denouement*) part of the story begins. Here you see *all the loose ends of the story tied up*; that is, you find out what will happen to the fugitive who has been apprehended. Or, in a murder mystery, you may find out how the detective solved the puzzle. Since this part of the story answers no major questions, reader involvement and interest begin to fall, and the writer soon ends the story.

Most short stories and most dramatic television series contain all the pieces of the plot line described above; however, not all stories present these pieces in the same order. A story may begin with the solution and *flash back* to the introduction of character and conflict; or it may begin in the middle with a complication of the conflict and a later flashback to the beginning; or a part of a plot line may be missing—a story may end right at the climax, leaving the reader to imagine the solution. Sometimes the events in the story may be jumbled, but if you look very carefully the major pieces of the plot will be evident. And if you find a story where very little seems to be happening, you may have to look within—you may be dealing with a story in which the protagonist is his or her own antagonist.

To intensify the plot, and to make the reader involved in its outcome, writers often use a literary technique known as *foreshadowing*. Foreshadowing is *a hint of events to come*; if a story is well-written, you should be able to give it a second reading and find several hints of what comes later.

WHY PLOT IS IMPORTANT

The first step toward understanding a story is to determine its plot by observing what happens and noting the structure of incidents in some developing pattern involving a protagonist and his or her conflict. Once you understand what a story *says*, you can better understand what it *means*.

There are several reasons why you must concentrate on plot, and one important reason is that, in writing about a short story, you may have to write a short *plot summary*.

WRITING THE PLOT SUMMARY

The plot summary is useful if

1 Your readers are unfamiliar with the story you are discussing, for example, if each student in a class has been assigned individual short stories for outside reading and class reports. A well-written plot summary will enable you to focus on key incidents, utilize transitional devices, and feel confident if called upon to present your summary to the class.

2 You want to mention key events and identify key characters *early* in a long essay; then you don't have to interrupt the rest of your essay for explanations of events or identifications of characters.

To help you write a plot summary, try the exercise that follows.

EXERCISE: PLOT SUMMARY PRELIMINARIES

Select a story from the list below or use one assigned by your instructor. Read it carefully—twice. On the first reading, try to obtain an overall sense of what happens in the story. On the second reading, concentrate on identifying who it happens to (the protagonist), who or what stands in the protagonist's way or presents a conflict (the antagonist), and the key incidents of the plot.

"The Catbird Seat"—James Thurber
"The Magic Barrel"—Bernard Malamud
"The Necklace"—Guy de Maupassant
"Odor of Chrysanthemums"—D. H. Lawrence
"The Killers"—Ernest Hemingway
"The Open Boat"—Stephen Crane
"Quality"—John Galsworthy
"The Cask of Amontillado"—Edgar Allan Poe
"I Want to Know Why"—Sherwood Anderson
"Where Are You Going, Where Have You Been?"—Joyce Carol Oates

After you have read the story twice, complete the summary that follows.

Title of story _____

Author _____

1 Who is the protagonist of the story? _____

2 Identify the antagonist(s). _____

_____

_____

3 Quote the exact lines in the story which introduce the point of conflict.

_____

_____

_____

_____

4 Briefly, in four to eight complete sentences, list the incidents which complicate the conflict. _____

_____

_____

_____

_____

_____

_____

_____

_____

_____

5 Directly quote the section of the story which is the climax, the highest point of tension. _____

_____

_____

_____

_____

_____

6 List what loose ends are taken care of in the solution part of the story.

_____

_____

_____

7 Identify three examples of foreshadowing in the story. Quote specific lines for each; then explain what the lines foreshadow.

First quote: _____

_____

What is foreshadowed: _____

_____

Second quote: _____

_____

What is foreshadowed: _____

_____

Third quote: _____

_____

What is foreshadowed: _____

_____

If you have completed questions 1 through 6, you are ready to combine your answers into a well-written, one- or two-paragraph plot summary. (You can save the answer to question 7 for another writing assignment.) The summary follows the structure of a process essay; it describes the steps through which a story's conflict is resolved. It names and identifies important characters and describes the major events of the story. It does not explain the events; that is, it does not interpret them. The plot summary merely describes what happens.

Note: Since the purpose of this summary is merely to *highlight*, briefly, the significant events and characters, it does not need direct quotes from the story. But it's a good idea to examine the exact words of the key incidents before you write about them.

To help you write your own plot summary, *consider how you could write one for Flannery O'Connor's "A Good Man Is Hard to Find."* Here is a list of answers for questions 1 through 6, the raw material for a plot summary of "A Good Man Is Hard to Find."

1 The grandmother is the protagonist.

2 Her antagonists are The Misfit and also her false opinion of herself.

3 The conflict begins when the grandmother selfishly objects to the family's trip to Florida yet goes anyway: "The next morning the grandmother was the first one in the car, ready to go."

4 On the drive, the grandmother irritates the family with her stories about Southern traditions and her superior attitude.

She also conceals her cat in the car.

She finds someone who reinforces her attitudes when the family stops at Red Sammy's Barbecue.

She causes a car accident.

She flags down help—The Misfit—and identifies him as an escaped convict.

The Misfit and his men shoot the family—one by one.

The grandmother pleads for her life and flatters The Misfit.

5 The climax occurs when the grandmother touches The Misfit and says, "Why you're one of my babies. You're one of my own children!"

The Misfit shoots her.

6 The Misfit and his men move on.

The grandmother lies dead, her blue eyes open to the sky.

ORGANIZING THE DATA: THESIS AND TOPIC SENTENCE

With this data, you can put together a *short* plot summary. To give this plot summary a focus, you need a *thesis*, or *one sentence that summarizes the series of events.*

If you have more than one paragraph, you also need a *topic sentence* or *a sentence in each paragraph that conveys the main idea of the paragraph.*

Look back at the events of "A Good Man Is Hard to Find" and consider how you could sum them up in one sentence. Here's a *sample thesis*:

```
''A Good Man Is Hard to Find'' begins with a simple family va-

cation but ends with a nightmarish series of incidents.
```

You can start a plot summary with this *thesis*. Look again at the thesis and notice its two contrasting parts:

1 Simple family trip
2 Nightmarish incidents

So you can split the plot summary into two parts, or two paragraphs: one on the beginning of the story, which seems pretty lighthearted, and the second on the nightmarish second half of the story. *Each paragraph* should get its own *topic sentence*.

   Since the summary will be only two paragraphs long, you can begin the first paragraph with the main idea, *the thesis*, then, staying in that paragraph, move to the main point of the first paragraph only—the first topic sentence.
   The beginning of the first paragraph of the summary will look like this:

thesis sentence
```
''A Good Man Is Hard to Find'' begins with a simple family va-

cation but ends with a nightmarish series of incidents. Ini-
```
topic sentence
```
tially, the protagonist—the grandmother—and her son Bailey,

with his wife and three children, pile into Bailey's car for a

typical summer trip from Georgia to Florida.
```

To finish the first paragraph, you can add the description of events for the first half of the story.
   In the second paragraph, you can begin to discuss the events of the second half of the story. Start this paragraph with this *topic sentence*, to focus on the detail:

```
When the grandmother flags down another traveler and identi-

fies him as The Misfit, murderer and escaped convict, she

meets her main antagonist and invites tragedy.
```

Now you can add the description of events in the second half of the story to develop this paragraph.

Note: Developing a paragraph takes more than adding a couple of sentences to the topic sentence. A well-developed paragraph generally needs *at least* four sentences of relevant material to support the topic sentence.

   To review:

   You have a list of detail for "A Good Man Is Hard to Find."
   You have a thesis and two topic sentences. You can now provide a rough

outline for a two-paragraph plot summary and check to see if you have sufficient detail.

THE OUTLINE OF A PLOT SUMMARY

Thesis: "A Good Man Is Hard to Find" begins with a simple family vacation but ends with a nightmarish series of incidents.

I Initially, the protagonist grandmother and her son Bailey, with his wife and their three children, pile into Bailey's car for a typical family trip from Georgia to Florida.
  A The grandmother irritates everybody with her stories of the Old South and her superior attitude.
  B She conceals her cat in the car.
  C At Red Sammy's she finds a friend who shares her opinions.
  D She misdirects the family.
  E She causes a car accident.
II When the grandmother flags down another traveler and identifies him as The Misfit, an escaped convict, she meets her main antagonist and invites tragedy.
  A The Misfit's henchmen shoot the family members.
  B The grandmother tries to save her own life.
  C She touches The Misfit and calls him her child.
  D He shoots her.
  E He and his friends leave; she is dead.

Before you put all this data together, consider one more writing technique that will make the plot summary clear and effective—the technique of writing transitions.

TRANSITIONS FOR A PLOT SUMMARY

Transitions are *words, phrases, or even sentences that help the reader follow the connections between your ideas.* Good transitions make the difference between writing that is acceptable and writing that is exceptional.

Since a plot summary is a kind of *process* and since it traces a *sequence* of events in chronological order, it requires transitions that show time sequence.

Here is a list of words and phrases useful as *time transitions*:

In the beginning	Subsequently
First	Afterward
At first	Later
Initially	In the meantime
Right away	Suddenly
Almost immediately	While
As the story begins	During
Meanwhile	When
Second	Ultimately
At the same time	Finally
Soon after	At last

Good writing involves revision, and one of the steps of revision is checking for (and even adding) appropriate transitions.

Now you have a structure and enough detail for a plot summary; you have a choice of transitions. Take a look at how all of this material is put together into two paragraphs. Particularly note how the simple sentences of the outline are expanded with even more detail and how transitions are used.

Sample Plot Summary: Flannery O'Connor's "A Good Man Is Hard to Find"

thesis

''A Good Man Is Hard to Find'' begins with a simple family vacation but ends with a nightmarish series of incidents. Ini-

transition and topic sentence

tially, the protagonist grandmother and her son Bailey, with his wife and three children, pile into Bailey's car for a typ-

transition

ical summer trip from Georgia to Florida. As they begin the drive, the grandmother reveals her irritating qualities, rem- iniscing about the lost glories of the Old South, enjoying her superior status as a ''lady,'' and selfishly sneaking her pet

transition

cat into the car. When the family stops at Red Sammy's Bar- becue, the grandmother again regrets the loss of ''the good old days'' and of ''good men'' in her conversation with Red

transition

Sammy. Back on the road, the grandmother misdirects the family

transition

to a dirt road and, ultimately, she and her cat cause a car ac- cident.

transition and topic sentence

When the grandmother flags down another traveler and iden- tifies him as The Misfit, an escaped convict, she meets her main antagonist and invites tragedy. One by one, the family members are escorted by The Misfit's henchmen into the woods.

transition

There they are shot. Meanwhile, the grandmother tries various tactics to try to save her own life. She flatters The Misfit; she tries to bribe him, to appeal to his religious convic-

transition

tions. At last, in a moment of understanding, she touches her

```
antagonist, The Misfit, and calls him one of her ''babies.''

The Misfit recoils, shoots the grandmother, and the three

criminals move on. The old woman is left, eyes open in death,

to peer at the cloudless sky.
```

EXERCISES: PLOT SUMMARY

1 Now that you have a sample plot summary for reference, write your own plot summary.

2 As noted earlier, sometimes the pieces of the plot are in a jumbled order. Read one of the following stories, all of which have complex plots, or plots out of chronological sequence, and write a one-paragraph plot summary that puts the pieces of the plot in correct time sequence. Don't forget to use effective transitions.

Suggested Stories

"Roman Fever"—Edith Wharton
"A Rose for Emily"—William Faulkner
"The Short Happy Life of Francis Macomber"—Ernest Hemingway
"Ethan Brand"—Nathaniel Hawthorne
"An Occurrence at Owl Creek Bridge"—Ambrose Bierce

3 Dramatic television series regularly follow the plot line described in this section. Watch an hour-long episode of a dramatic television series, and, in one paragraph, summarize its plot. Identify the protagonist(s), antagonist(s), and those scenes that develop the conflict; bring it to a climax, and indicate a solution.

EXERCISE: USING TRANSITIONS

Choosing the appropriate transitions is not easy. To give you some practice, try the following exercise. Below are the topic sentence and sentences of detail for a one-paragraph plot summary of Sherwood Anderson's "Death in the Woods." The detail is in the correct time order. Use the topic sentence as the first sentence of your paragraph. Combine the remaining detail into a smoothly written paragraph, using effective transitions.

Topic sentence: The protagonist of "Death in the Woods," Mrs. Jake Grimes, is an abused wife and mother who dies as pathetically as she lived.

1 She leaves the family farm on a snowy morning.
2 She is going to town to trade eggs for some meat for her husband and son; she is desperate to feed them.
3 The big farm dogs accompany her.

4 In town, she gets some scraps from the butcher, who mutters about her cruel husband and son, her antagonists.

5 She begins the trip back to the farm.

6 It is getting dark and it is snowing.

7 The farm dogs are joined by other dogs.

8 Mrs. Grimes stops in a clearing to rest, her pack of food strapped to her back.

9 She loses consciousness as the hungry dogs circle her.

10 They take the pack of food from her body, tearing her clothes.

11 Her corpse is found by a hunter.

12 Men from town come to see her body, partly stripped, and they see the circle of dog tracks around the corpse.

13 The townsmen are awed by this sight.

14 Public opinion drives the violent Grimes men from the town.

CHARACTER

A short story may be a success or a failure depending on the strength of its characters. Consider this situation:

> You pick up the morning newspaper and read that Lee Thomas has been seriously injured playing football in the local park. You've never met Lee, so all you know about this person is what little biographical information the paper provides—age, address, etc. The story may strike you as curious, interesting, or even a little sad, but you are very slightly involved in it because you don't know the person in the story.

Consider, however, another situation:

> You pick up the morning newspaper and read that Lee Thomas has been seriously injured playing football in the local park. You are shocked and concerned because Lee was your next-door neighbor and best friend in grade school; you grew up together and even played football together. Immediately you are drawn into the newspaper story; you want to know more about the incident. You care; you are involved because you *know* the person in the story.

These two situations help to illustrate what the writers of many short stories try to do—involve the reader in the story by making the reader understand the significant characters. If a character is merely a name and some biographical information, the reader may not understand or care what happens to that character. But if the reader can learn about the character and can regard him as a real person, the reader will more likely become involved in the story.

How does a writer accomplish such a task? He or she can make a character "live" by giving a specific, detailed depiction of that character. The portrait may be revealed by showing the reader:

1 *Who the character is*. Biographical information including age, physical description, and occupation is involved here. Questions that can be answered by this kind of detail are "Who is this character?" "What does this person look like?" "How old is the character?" "What does this person do for a living?" "What kind of past has this person had?" "What is the character's family background?" and "What are the character's goals?"

2 *With what the character surrounds him or herself*. This kind of detail can reveal a great deal. In daily life, you categorize people by how they dress, what kind of car they drive, where they live, how neat or messy they are, and what objects are precious to them. You can consider the same information when you are learning about fictional characters.

3 *What the character says*. Look closely at the dialogue in the story. Consider not only *what* the character says, but also *how* he or she says it (in dialect, slang, formal English) and *to whom* he or she says it. (Is the character expressing the same feelings to different people, or is the character acting as a different person with different people?)

4 *What others say to the character and what others say or think about him or her*. Consider the reactions of others to the character, as revealed in their speech to the person. Then consider what they may say about the character when he or she is not present, or what they may think about the character.

5 *What the character does*. In a short story, all action can be significant. So whatever a character does can be crucial to the reader's understanding of that character. Consider, particularly, how the character acts toward others, but don't forget to examine how the character treats himself or herself and how the character achieves goals.

6 *Why the character does what he or she does*. Without proper *motivation* (that is, a reason for actions), a character's believability can fall apart. A good story includes, however subtly, clues as to why the characters act the way they do. These clues may be found in such elements as a character's background, education, or social position, or in a character's own words. Without motivation of character, a story can lack coherence and order; it can become a mere string of incidents.

7 *What the character thinks*. Characters not only act; they *think*. Thought is as revealing as action. When a writer brings the reader within the character's mind, the reader has the opportunity to explore the character's needs and desires, fears and conflicts, motives and goals.

When you are analyzing a short story, you will be looking carefully at two kinds of characters—protagonists and antagonists. Since these characters are the center of the conflict and of the story itself, they will get more attention from the writer. In order to understand the events of the story you must understand the people who are responsible for and who are affected by these events.

LITERARY TERMS RELATED TO CHARACTER

There are a few words that are commonly used to describe different types of characters, and you may want to use these terms in your analysis of character.

The character who is well-defined, the character you feel you know a great deal about, is a *round* character. Most often, the protagonist is a round character.

The character who is only minimally described, the person you know very little about, is a *flat* character. Minor characters, who play only a slight role in the story, are often flat, one-dimensional characters.

Think of these terms as opposites: round/flat.

The character who changes during the course of a story, that is, who grows up, learns something about himself or about life, or develops in some significant way, is a *dynamic* character. Very often, a protagonist will be a dynamic character.

The character who remains the same throughout the story, who does not grow, develop, or learn, is a *static* character. A protagonist can be a static character, for that may be the writer's point—this particular character cannot or will not change.

Think of these terms as opposites: dynamic/static

A character who is immediately recognizable because you have seen this kind of character in numerous television shows, movies, or popular literature, or because he fulfills preconceived notions of how a certain person from a certain background should act, is a *stereotype*. Creating a stereotype takes little imagination, since the stereotypical character can easily be moved from one story to another without alteration, and the reader will easily recognize him. Think, for example, of such stereotypes as the absentminded professor, the mad scientist, the peace-loving sheriff in the frontier town who is forced to use his gun, or the dumb blonde. Stereotypes are an easy way to reinforce a reader's prejudices; they rarely challenge a reader to think and analyze. Although stereotypes are often used for comic effect, they should not substitute for complex, well-defined characters in a significant conflict.

EXERCISE: DETAILS OF CHARACTER

Read one of the stories on the list below, or a story assigned by your instructor, concentrating on an overall sense of the story's events. Read it again, this time focusing on the protagonist. Then, answer the questions below. The questions are designed to help you select the detail of the story the author uses to develop a character. By concentrating on this detail, you may gain a better appreciation and understanding of the story, and may feel better-prepared to write about it. Your assigned story may not permit you to answer all of these questions (some data may be missing), but look closely into the story and do as much as the story allows.

Suggested Stories

"A New England Nun"—Mary Wilkins Freeman
"In the Region of Ice"—Joyce Carol Oates
"A&P"—John Updike
"The Country Husband"—John Cheever
"A Worn Path"—Eudora Welty
"The Darling"—Anton Chekov
"The Chrysanthemums"—John Steinbeck
"My Kinsman, Major Molineux"—Nathaniel Hawthorne
"The Blind Man"—D. H. Lawrence
"Bid Blonde"—Dorothy Parker
"Boule de Suif"—Guy de Maupassant

Short story title _____

Author _____

1 In two sentences, describe the physical characteristics of the protagonist. _____

_____

_____

_____

_____

2 Directly quote the lines from the story which gave you those characteristics. _____

_____

_____

_____

_____

_____

3 Describe the protagonist's goals, conflicts, and background (in complete sentences). _____

_____

_____

_____

_____

4 Quote the lines from the story that support your answer to question 3.

_____

_____

_____

_____

5 Describe the character's environment—that is, what kind of place he lives in, what objects he owns or values, what he wears. Write complete sentences. _____

_____

_____

_____

_____

6 Quote lines that support your description for question 5. _____

_____

_____

_____

_____

_____

_____

7 Look closely at what the protagonist says. Select three significant statements. First, quote the lines. Then briefly explain the situation when each statement is made—what is happening in the story, who the lines are said to. Then explain what each statement reveals about the character. Be careful to focus on the most significant lines you can find.

Statement 1 (direct quote): _____

_____

_____

_____

_____

Context (who the lines are said to, what is happening in the story at the time,

what the speech is in response to, what effect the speech has): _____

_____

_____

_____

_____

Significance (what the speech reveals about the protagonist): _____

_____

_____

_____

_____

_____

Statement 2 (direct quote): _____

_____

_____

_____

_____

Context: _____

_____

_____

_____

_____

_____

Significance: _____

_____

_____

_____

_____

_____

Statement 3 (direct quote): _____

_____

_____

_____

_____

Context: _____

_____

_____

_____

_____

_____

Significance: _____

_____

_____

_____

_____

_____

8 Comment on *how* the protagonist talks and what this reveals about him:

_____

_____

_____

_____

_____

9 Select one significant statement that another character makes to the protagonist. Quote the statement, explain its context (what is happening when it is said, who says it, etc.), and give its significance (what it tells us about the protagonist).

Statement quoted: _____

_____

_____

_____

_____

Context: _____

_____

_____

_____

_____

Significance: _____

_____

_____

_____

_____

10 Find something interesting that another character says about the protagonist. Quote the statement and, if necessary, explain what it tells us about the protagonist.

Quote: _____

_____

Explanation: _____

_____

_____

11 Consider the actions of the protagonist in the story. Briefly list three significant actions and explain what each tells us about the protagonist.

Action 1: _____

_____

_____

Significance: _____

_____

_____

Action 2: _____

_____

_____

Significance: _____

_____

_____

Action 3: _____

_____

_____

Significance: _____

_____

_____

12 Consider the same three actions. Give some reasons (given within the story) why the protagonist performed them. In other words, explore motivation.

Motive for action 1: _____

_____

_____

Motive for action 2: _____

_____

_____

Motive for action 3: _____

_____

_____

13 Quote a significant passage in which the protagonist's thoughts are revealed. Discuss what these thoughts reveal about him.

Quoted thoughts: _____

_____

_____

_____

_____

What the thoughts reveal about the protagonist: _____

_____

_____

_____

_____

_____

WRITING THE CHARACTER ANALYSIS ESSAY

The exercise you just completed helped you to accumulate detail about one character. Now, to write an essay of character analysis, you must sort out that detail and structure it into a coherent essay. Writing such an essay, of a fairly standard, five-paragraph length, for example, is simpler if you work through a process of selection and organization before you write.

Try working through this plan for organizing and writing a *five-paragraph character analysis*.

Step 1 Survey all the detail you have collected. Try to group that detail into clusters that reveal some similar qualities in the character.

For example, two of the character's actions and his dress and speech may reveal a person who is poor and unhappy. Other details may add up to another quality—the character may be revealed as a person used by others.

THESIS AND TOPIC SENTENCES

Step 2 After your survey, try to sum up, *in one sentence*, what the character is like. This summary sentence is the *thesis*, or the controlling idea, for your entire essay.

For example, if you were to study the character of Mrs. Jake Grimes in Sherwood Anderson's "Death in the Woods," you might begin with this thesis:

Mrs. Jake Grimes is a woman who has been denied any love or tenderness; she exists only to be used.

Step 3 Now that you have a thesis, look again at all your detail. Look carefully at those details that fit together to make one point. In this step, you need to pick and choose, to perform two functions at once—*to divide* and *to combine*. That is, you are selecting all the detail that will help support, explain, and illustrate your thesis. But you cannot write your essay merely by lumping all this detail together. Instead:

1 *Combine* detail that makes one point. It will later be gathered into one paragraph.

2 *Divide* the detail into groups; each group makes a different point.

In a five-paragraph essay, you are looking for three groups of detail, for three major paragraphs that explain and illustrate your thesis.

Look at "Death in the Woods" and the sample thesis again. Try to split the thesis up and ask some questions about it.

Thesis Part 1

Mrs. Grimes has been denied any love or tenderness.
How do you know this? What in the story tells you this? Where are the

examples? Where is the specific evidence? What in her background made her like this? Think about the answers to these questions before you write anything more.

Thesis Part 2

She exists only to be used.
Where in the story is this shown? Who uses her? Why? How does she feel about being used? What does she do about it? What finally happens to her? Again, think about the answers to these questions.

The answers to such questions can help you devise *categories*, groups of detail that can fit into paragraphs. After you have categories, with lists of detail, you can sum up each grouping with a topic sentence. For example, your categories for Mrs. Grimes might be

1 How Mrs. Grimes got into this situation
2 What she does about it
3 What finally happens to her

From the categories, you can formulate topic sentences, controlling ideas for three separate paragraphs.

Topic Sentence for Category 1

From her childhood on, Mrs. Grimes was trapped in a cycle of exploitation.

Topic Sentence for Category 2

Because she had always been brutalized by the world, she learned to expect nothing from it.

Topic Sentence for Category 3

After Mrs. Grime's death, others began to notice her value.

Now you have the bare bones of an outline for an essay. You are ready for the next step.

Step 4 Fill in the *specific detail* from the story that explains, illustrates, and supports your topic sentences. As you support each topic sentence, you are also supporting your thesis.

Your detail comes from the work you did earlier in the Details of Character exercise. It includes exact quotes, from the story, of description, significant speeches, or significant action. It also includes such detail from the story rewritten into your own words.

In compiling a rough outline of your detail, remember that you will *not* be able to use all the material you discovered by working through the earlier exercise. You will use only the most effective quotes and examples, selecting detail that is related to your topic sentences, and thus constructing a coherent outline.

A ROUGH OUTLINE

A rough outline for the central three paragraphs of a character analysis of "Death in the Woods" might look like this:

Topic Sentence 1

From her childhood on, Mrs. Grimes was trapped in a cycle of exploitation.

  1 She was an orphan.
  2 She slaved as a "bound" girl.
  3 The farmer she worked for frightened her with his lust.
  4 His wife was jealous of her.
  5 Her only escape was to another trap—marriage to a shiftless farmer, Jake Grimes.
  6 He worked her like an animal and beat her.
  7 Later, her son abused her.
  8 She lives to feed both her men and the farm animals.

Topic Sentence 2

Because Mrs. Grimes had always been brutalized by the world, she learned to expect nothing from it.

  1 To her, life is just survival.
  2 She is passive—it's her way of getting along.
  3 Even her death is passive.
  4 It is not really suicide.
  5 It is the only escape, because Mrs. Grimes does not even have happy memories to escape to.

Topic Sentence 3

After Mrs. Grimes's death, others begin to notice her value.

  1 Dead in the snow, Mrs. Grimes looks, to the townsmen, like a young girl.
  2 The men feel awe at the sight of her body.
  3 They are angry at her husband and son.
  4 Now they want to seek revenge on the Grimes men.
  5 The narrator and his brother get a mystical feeling from the sight of the dead woman.
  6 All the attention is paid too late.

Step 5 Plan your first and last paragraph. So far you have the detail and topic sentences for three paragraphs, but this process was designed, as you remember, to end in a five-paragraph essay.

There are two paragraphs left to plan—the first and the last. The first paragraph will be an introductory paragraph. It will include a *lead-in*, several sentences that lead smoothly to the thesis sentence. The last paragraph will be a concluding paragraph. It will tie all the detail back together in a subtle return to the thesis.

Consider the following options before you write the lead-in to the thesis.

WRITING LEAD-INS

Writing the lead-in to any thesis takes a certain skill. The lead-in must be a smooth and logical way of introducing your main point. Generally, the simplest way to lead into your thesis is to write several sentences of introduction and to make your thesis the last sentence in the first paragraph. There are many ways to write those introductory sentences; some suggested ways are as follows:

1 Make some general but relevant comments, about the subject matter of the thesis, that can lead to a more specific thesis.

2 Mention personal experiences or attitudes that you and the reader might share to lead to the thesis.

3 Write a few general sentences about the author that can lead to the thesis.

4 Write a few general sentences about the story that can lead to the thesis.

In each case, note how your sentences are moving from the general to the more specific; that is, you are giving the reader some time to focus on your main idea; you are preparing him for it.

You can take one thesis and lead into it in many ways. Here are four possible lead-ins to give you a sense of what an introductory paragraph can do.

Thesis for a Character Sketch of Mrs. Grimes of Sherwood Anderson's "Death in the Woods"

Mrs. Jake Grimes is a woman who has been denied any love or tenderness; she exists only to be used.

Lead-in 1   Make some general comments about the subject matter of the thesis that lead into the thesis.

The value a person places upon himself or herself is largely determined by the value others give to that person. Those who grow up loved and cherished learn to feel worthwhile and develop a healthy sense of self. Such a background of love and caring can sustain a person through periods when he or she feels unloved and insiginificant. But those who have never known love, who have never been given any human warmth, soon come to see themselves as worthless. Such an emotionally starved person is Mrs. Jake Grimes of Sherwood Anderson's "Death in the Woods," for *she is a woman who has been denied any love or tenderness; she exists only to be used.*

Lead-in 2 Mention personal experiences and attitudes you and the reader might share to lead into the thesis.

Sometimes we meet people who seem so shut off from the world and from other people that we begin to wonder how they survive. We are tempted to judge these people as hard or unfeeling because they are difficult to know. It takes insight for us to realize that such people may have grown up without the care and love necessary for human development, and to recognize that a lack of caring can permanently distort personality. Sherwood Anderson describes a closed-in, distorted personality in the character of Mrs. Jake Grimes in "Death in the Woods." *She is a woman who has been denied any love or tenderness; she exists only to be used.*

Lead-in 3 Begin with a few general sentences about the author. You may draw this information from an instructor's lecture, from introductory material in a literature anthology, or from some of your own research.

Sherwood Anderson's short stories often focus on characters we would hardly notice in real life. He writes about insignificant people, people who are often shy or unattractive, lacking in manners, confidence, or charm. Frequently, Anderson reveals the hidden value of such insignificant people, their true nature and worth. Such characters have to struggle to maintain their inner worth because the world has not given them much love or compassion. A good example of this type of character is Mrs. Jake Grimes of "Death in the Woods." *She is a woman who has been denied any love or tenderness; she exists only to be used.*

Lead-in 4 Write a few general sentences about the story.

Sherwood Anderson's "Death in the Woods" is a story about different kinds of coldness. Most of it is set in a lonely woods in winter, and the freezing weather and snow add to the chill. The inhabitants of the small town at the edge of the woods and those on the neighboring farms seem equally cold— cold-hearted, remote, and unfeeling. The chief victim of this frozen world is the story's protagonist, Mrs. Jake Grimes. She is a woman who has suffered all her life from a lack of human warmth. *She has been denied any love or tenderness; she exists only to be used.*

Now that you've taken care of the first paragraph of the essay, you can think about the last one—the conclusion.

WRITING THE CONCLUSION

The final paragraph of a short essay, the conclusion, should *not* introduce a completely new idea because there is no place in the conclusion to develop it. It should *not* flatly state, "This paper has just shown. . . ." But it should, smoothly and subtly, bring the reader back to the main idea, the thesis, of the essay. It is the final comment the writer makes, his last chance to drive his main idea home.

In the sample essay on Mrs. Grimes, the conclusion can remind the reader of the three ideas of the three main paragraphs, and then move the reader back to the thesis that summarizes them.

Three ideas

1 She grew up and lived as a thing.
2 She never fought back because she expected nothing from the world.
3 She got attention too late.

Thesis

She was denied love; she lived to be used.

A short, sample conclusion that incorporates these ideas is presented below. The key ideas are underlined for you.

Sample Conclusion for a Character Analysis of Mrs. Jake Grimes

Mrs. Grimes died as she lived—exploited, for "even after her death [she] continued feeding animal life," her sack of scraps ripped open by her dogs. Treated not as a person but as a thing, Mrs. Grimes died without expecting much or ever seeing her own value. Her tragedy is not so much the account of her death as it is the story of her life, lived without love or even respect, and of attention finally paid, too late.

OUTLINE FOR THE CHARACTER ANALYSIS

You now have the basis for five paragraphs of material about Mrs. Jake Grimes. You have a rough, partial outline. Before you go any further, try to refine that outline and incorporate the first and last paragraphs into it.

You don't need to write your lead-in into the outline. All you need for the first paragraph (on the outline) is the thesis sentence. You don't need to write your entire concluding paragraph into the outline, either. Instead, just write one sentence that indicates what your conclusion will be like.

Complete Outline for a Character Analysis of Mrs. Jake Grimes

I Thesis: Mrs. Jake Grimes is a woman who has been denied any love or tenderness; she exists only to be used.
II From her childhood on, Mrs. Grimes was trapped in a cycle of exploitation.
   A She was an orphan.
   B She slaved as a "bound" girl.

    C The farmer she worked for frightened her with his lust.

    D His wife was jealous of her.

    E Her only escape was to another trap—marriage to a shiftless farmer, Jake Grimes.

    F He worked her like an animal and beat her.

    G Later, her son abused her.

    H She lives to feed both her men and the farm animals.

III Because Mrs. Grimes had always been brutalized by the world, she learned to expect nothing from it.

    A Life is just survival.

    B She is passive; it's her way of getting along.

    C Even her death is passive.

    D It is not really suicide.

    E It is the only escape, because Mrs. Grimes does not even have happy memories to escape to.

IV After Mrs. Grimes's death, others begin to notice her value.

    A Dead in the snow, Mrs. Grimes looks, to the townsmen, like a young girl.

    B The men feel awe at the sight of her body.

    C They are angry at her husband and son.

    D Now they want to seek revenge on the Grimes men.

    E The narrator and his brother get a mystical feeling from the sight of the dead woman.

    F All the attention is paid too late.

 V Mrs. Grimes lived without love, and received attention only after death.

With an outline complete, you're ready to write. But as you write, you need to think about two things:

  1 Transitions

  2 How to use direct quotes from the story

Consider transitions first.

TRANSITIONS WITHIN AND BETWEEN PARAGRAPHS

When you worked through a plot summary, you worked on time transitions. In this essay, you will be working on another kind of transition; the links are not only *within* paragraphs but *between* them. This kind of transition requires you to use a pattern of repeated words, phrases, or ideas to keep the reader on track.

For example, if you want to stress that Mrs. Grimes was used by others, you can repeat the phrase a couple of times within one paragraph. If you are sick of the repetition, you can reinforce the idea of *used* with a synonym, like "exploited."

As you begin each new paragraph, try not to startle your reader by jumping right into a new idea. Instead, you can begin the new paragraph with a word, phrase, or idea from the paragraph you just completed. This repetition not only reinforces the last point you made; it's a way of linking that point to the new one you are about to make.

QUOTING FROM THE STORY

This analysis will require you to quote from the story to support your points.

Be sure that the *context* of what you quote is *clear*. That is, if you quote dialogue, be sure the reader is told who said it, and to whom and under what circumstances it was said. If you quote description, identify who or what is being described, and under what circumstances.

You can incorporate short quotes—pieces of the author's sentences—right into your own sentences, like this:

> To the narrator, Mrs. Grimes seems somehow transformed into ''the body of some charming young girl.''

You can incorporate a complete sentence and attribute it to a speaker like this:

> As the narrator says, ''Whatever happened she never said anything.''

If you use a long quote from the story, a quote of more than fifty words (about four typed lines), you indent the quote ten spaces from your left-hand margin, double-space it, and eliminate the quotation marks. The indentation takes the place of the quotation marks.

Be careful not to overdo the use of long quotes, or your essay will merely repeat the words of the story, and you might lose the reader's attention. Generally, short quotes integrated into your own paragraphs are better.

You will see examples of each kind of quote and transition in the character analysis of Mrs. Grimes that follows.

A Character Analysis of Mrs. Jake Grimes of Sherwood Anderson's ''Death in the Woods''

lead-in

The value a person places upon himself or herself is largely determined by the value others give to that person. Those who grow up loved and cherished learn to feel worthwhile and develop a healthy sense of self. Such a background of love and caring can even sustain a person through periods when he or she feels unloved and insignificant. But those who have never known love, who have never been given any human warmth, soon come to see themselves as worthless. Such an emotionally

thesis

starved person is Mrs. Grimes of Sherwood Anderson's ''Death in the Woods,'' for she is a woman who has been denied any love or tenderness; she exists only to be used.

topic sentence

From her childhood on, Mrs. Grimes has been trapped in a cycle of exploitation. As an orphan, she became a ''bound''

specific examples for
support

girl, legally contracted to work at slave labor for a farmer,
who terrified her with his lust, and for his wife, who frightened the girl with her jealousy. The girl's only escape from
this prison was marriage to Jake Grimes, a shiftless farmer
who beat her and expected her to work the farm alone. When the
couple's son grows up, he joins the father in abusing the
mother. They demand that she feed them, and somehow she must
also sustain the animals of the farm:

long quote for support
indented; no quotation
marks

> How was she going to get everything fed?--that was
> her problem. The dogs had to be fed. There wasn't
> enough hay in the barn for the horses and the cow.
> If she didn't feed the chickens how could they lay
> eggs? Without eggs to sell how could she get things
> in town, things she needed to keep the life of the
> farm going?

quote commented on;
short quote for support

Her life is nothing but an endless battle to meet the demands
of the animals--and men--who devour her strength and youth,
turning her into an ''old woman when she isn't even forty
yet.''

transition restated

Trapped by life, Mrs. Grimes never thinks of fighting back.

topic sentence

Because she had always been brutalized by the world, she
learned to expect nothing from it. Life, to her, is merely
survival. As the narrator says, ''Whatever happened she never
said anything. That was her way of getting along.'' Even her

detail: quotes and
examples for support

death is not a conscious suicide; it is just a surrender to

circumstances that dominate her, as events have always domi-
nated her. She dies, dreamily fading into the cold, ''softly
and quietly.'' And her dreams could have provided no escape,
for she had no happy past to dream of, ''Not many pleasant
things had happened to her.'' In dying, as in living, Mrs.
Grimes knew of no way but to give in, because she had never
seen herself as someone worth fighting to save. Deprived of
the love that teaches one she is valuable, Mrs. Grimes placed
little value on her life.

transition
topic sentence

detail

As the narrator of the story says, Mrs. Grimes was ''one of
the nameless ones,'' the insignificant ones, but, after her
death, others began to notice her, to see her value. Lying
frozen in the snow, the body of Mrs. Grimes seems somehow
transformed into ''the body of some charming young girl.'' The
townsmen who cover her body regard it with a kind of respect
and awe, and they want to avenge her mistreatment at the hands
of her husband and son. The sight of the dead woman creates a
''strange mystical feeling'' in the minds of the adolescent
narrator and his brother. Too late, someone sees the beautiful
person inside the mistreated, broken woman.

transition restated

thesis restated

Mrs. Grimes died as she lived––exploited, for ''even after
her death [she] continued feeding animal life,'' her sack of
scraps ripped open by her dogs. Treated not as a person but as
a thing, Mrs. Grimes died without ever seeing her own value.
Her tragedy is not so much the account of her death as it is the
story of her life, lived without love or even respect, and of
attention finally paid, too late.

WRITING THE CHARACTER ANALYSIS: A CHECKLIST

You've worked through the steps of a short character analysis. Now you're ready to write your own. Start with the detail of the exercise on a protagonist, character exercise one. Follow these steps:

1 Survey the detail. Group it roughly.

2 Formulate a thesis.

3 Combine and divide the detail into topic categories, and then write topic sentences.

4 Write a rough outline for the body of your paper.

5 To that outline, add a thesis statement that will come at the end of the first paragraph and a summary sentence for the concluding paragraph.

6 Write a draft, with an effective lead-in and a subtle conclusion.

7 Revise, considering transitions and effective use of direct quotes.

EXERCISE: COMPARISON/CONTRAST OF CHARACTERS

Read two short stories by the same author. Read once for a general overview; then reread them, focusing on the major characters and making some *connection* between the protagonists of the two stories.

Write a thesis which summarizes the main similarity between the two characters. In a five-paragraph paper, discuss and develop that thesis, with specific examples (including direct quotes) from both stories. Include some discussion of significant differences between the protagonists, either throughout the essay or in a separate part of the essay.

Note: You may have to read several stories by the same author before you find two with similar protagonists. Or consider the pairs suggested below:

Edgar Allan Poe—"The Black Cat" and "The Cask of Amontillado"

Nathaniel Hawthorne—"Young Goodman Brown" and "Roger Malvin's Burial"

Flannery O'Connor—"Everything That Rises Must Converge" and "Good Country People"

James Joyce—"Counterparts" and "A Painful Case"

F. Scott Fitzgerald—"Winter Dreams" and "The Last of the Belles"

TECHNIQUES IN THE SHORT STORY

All well-written stories focus not only on character and plot, but also on *techniques*—that is, on specific literary devices which can underline, intensify, and expand the story's impact and meaning. The more you become aware of these literary devices and can recognize how and why they are used, the more you can understand and appreciate a literary work.

Below is a list of some common literary techniques, with brief definitions.

COMMON LITERARY TECHNIQUES

foreshadowing: a hint of things to come

As you were told in the Section 1 of this book, foreshadowing appears quite frequently. Your enjoyment of literature can be enhanced if, as you read, you can discover hints of future events or of the outcome of the story. Sometimes you can find the foreshadowing only on a second reading, since these hints can be cleverly integrated into complex fiction.

You can find foreshadowing in description, narrative, and dialogue, and it helps to create interest and to involve the reader in the work.

irony: a contrast between what is literally stated and what the statement may mean

There are many forms of irony. Sometimes, irony is very close to sarcasm; nearly the opposite of what is said is intended. In this case, the contrast is quite obvious. In other cases, the irony is more subtle; what is stated simply has more than the one, surface meaning. In Eudora Welty's "A Worn Path," for example, there is irony in the white hunter's words to the old black woman.

When he smiles and says, "You take my advice and stay home, and nothing will happen to you," while he shoulders his gun, the reader is reminded of the words of many people warning black people to stay in their place.

Sometimes the irony, the hidden meaning, doesn't appear until you reach the end of the story, when the climax and/or subsequent events cast a new and often contradictory light on earlier statements. Flannery O'Connor's "A Good Man Is Hard to Find" uses this technique. When the grandmother of the story first sees The Misfit, she senses that his face "was as familiar to her as if she had known him all her life," and the climax of the story casts a new meaning on this line. The ironic line also hints at the story's climax; when irony involves such hints of the story's outcome, it is called *ironic foreshadowing*.

Generally, irony involves a mix of opposing meanings or emotions; a line of dialogue or a situation may be bittersweet, or an event may bring both relief and guilt.

> *symbol*: something that stands for something else

When an author uses a concrete, tangible object or scene, and that object or scene stands for *more* than itself, that author is employing symbolism. Symbolism may be hard to spot, simply because we are exposed to it daily and take it for granted.

The young girl, for example, who receives a single rose from a young man hopes she is getting more than a flower. The symbolism would not be the same if she were to receive a single tulip! For another example, brides in Western culture rarely wear red, for the color carries certain symbolic associations.

We have national symbols—the flag, the eagle, Uncle Sam—and we have commercial symbols—golden arches and small alligators on cotton shirts.

Similarly, the writer can inject meaning into his work (consciously or not) when events and objects begin to stand for more than the obvious. In "A Good Man Is Hard to Find," for example, the grandmother's navy blue, straw, sailor hat with the white violets is more than an elegant accessory. After the car accident, the hat remains pinned to the grandmother's head, but the hat is crumbling into pieces. When the grandmother watches her son being taken to his death and she pleads for her own life, she pulls off the hat brim and lets it fall to the ground. The hat may be a symbol of the grandmother's own ladylike and superior pose, a pose that is falling apart as catastrophe enters her life.

The grandmother's hat is mentioned several times in this story—a hint that it may be more than a hat. When you read, you may become aware of a repetition of an object, or of a description of a place, and such repetition may indicate a symbolic element.

> *images*: the associations an event, person, or scene may acquire through a pattern of description. The description appeals to one of our senses.

An image is less concrete and more "fuzzy" than a symbol. Like a symbol, it involves a penetration beneath the obvious, but unlike a symbol, an image is not necessarily based on something tangible within the story. That is, an image is not the rose a young girl receives; instead, it may be a series of descriptions that compares the young girl to a flower.

Very often, an image can add a new and different meaning to a character, scene, or situation. For example, a character may be described as looking like a lovely person, and her words and manners may be sweet. However, that same woman may be described, more than once, as sitting in shadow, in a small, dark area, or in a stuffy room with the windows shut. Soon, the image associated with this sweet, pretty woman becomes one of entrapment, enclosure, and suffocation. The woman does not directly symbolize a prison, but you are beginning to associate her with an image of confinement and limitation.

John Cheever uses images in a similar way in "The Swimmer." When he compares the main character, Neddy Merrill, to a summer's day, you can associate the character with the warm, pleasant season, but when he ends the comparison by stating that Neddy is particularly like the last hours of a summer's day, you may get another picture of sunset, or decline, or maybe of the afternoon thunderstorms. Through this description, Cheever adds meaning to the portrait of Neddy.

Note: When you consider and examine literary devices like foreshadowing, symbols, and images, you must always consider them within the context of the entire work: its overall plot, structure, and meaning. One concrete object may acquire wholly different symbolic meanings, depending on the context in which it is placed. A color takes on different associations and creates different images, depending on its context.

To understand this, try the next exercise on color images.

TECHNIQUES EXERCISE: COLOR IMAGES IN CONTEXT

Consider each description of the color red, and, in the space provided, jot down the associative meaning that immediately comes to your mind. That is, list what associations spring to your mind, and what you think the color *in this scene* might stand for.

1 A beautiful, dark-haired woman with expensive jewelry is wearing a red chiffon dress at a cocktail party. _____

_____

_____

_____

2 A slightly disheveled woman, wearing a red, shiny dress, stands alone at night, smoking a cigarette, beneath a lamp post on a sleazy city street. _____

_____

_____

_____

3 A red stain spreads across a man's white jacket. The man wearing the jacket is lying down. _____

_____

_____

_____

4 A red stain spreads across a white tablecloth. _____

_____

_____

_____

5 A red sun sinks on the horizon. _____

_____

_____

_____

6 A red light flashes at a crossroads. _____

_____

_____

_____

7 Dozens of small red lights hang on a green tree. _____

_____

_____

_____

_____

_____

As you examined the color red in these descriptions, you may have associated it with such diverse meanings as elegance, vice, violence, disorder, natural beauty, or decline, or with something as ordinary as a signal to *stop*. The color, then, has no *one* meaning, no one symbolic equivalent in this exercise; it must be considered as *part of a larger framework*. As you examine literary techniques, focusing on the framework, the *context* of the technique, is as important as noting the technique itself.

MORE ON LITERARY TECHNIQUES

Point of View

We all know that an event can take on various meanings, depending upon who tells us about it. Similarly, a story's meaning depends largely upon whom the writer creates to tell the story. That person or voice a writer creates to tell a story is called the *point of view*.

The study of how point of view functions in a story and of the different kinds of point of view can be both complex and fascinating. The choice of point of view is the author's choice with respect to how the reader is led into the world of the story, and thus point of view is a central element in fiction.

Below is a description of the most basic kinds of points of view, to introduce you to this technique.

omniscient point of view: the all-seeing, all-knowing storyteller

God is omniscient, a being who knows the future, who can see two scenes occurring simultaneously, read all peoples' thoughts, and interpret all events.

The omniscient point of view uses a narrative voice that can describe two or more scenes occurring simultaneously, enter the mind of more than one character, know the outcome of events before they occur, and interpret them for the reader. This point of view is godlike, for the storyteller gives us more than any one human being in real life could possibly know.

limited omniscient point of view: the point of view is restricted to what one person, usually a character in the story, could see and learn about events. This narrator can interpret only what his limited knowledge allows and can directly report only his own thoughts.

Note: Remember, however, that one person can also learn what happens in scenes he does not witness, or what others think and hear—by report.

dramatic point of view: the story is told only through a description of events; there is no interpretation and no entering the mind of any character. Imagine a movie camera set up in a room; the camera will record what happens, what is said and done. It will not interpret events; it will not tell what anyone is thinking. This is the dramatic point of view.

Generally, the more a reader has to do for himself, the more he is forced to become involved in a story. Thus, each of the points of view demands a different amount of "work" (involvement) from the reader.

Less involvement (interpreting, putting the pieces of the story together)—omniscient point of view.

More involvement (working with what a person can know and learn)—limited omniscient point of view.

Most involvement (figuring out what events mean, why characters act as they do)—dramatic point of view.

The First and Third Person Point of View

The point of view may also be labeled *first* or *third* person. This is a label taken from grammatical terms and is easy to recognize.

If the point of view of the story is a voice or character who refers to herself as "I," the point of view is the *first person*.

If the voice that tells the story refers to all the characters as "he" and "she" or by their names, and that voice does not refer to herself as "I," the point of view is third person.

Note: Just because the point of view is first person, do not be fooled into thinking that "I" is the author speaking. The "I" is a voice, a character, the author created, and the "I" may not be the most reliable of narrators.

Some Other Techniques

Sometimes individual authors become known for specific techniques which they use frequently to convey or enhance meaning.

One such common technique is the *mirror* image, or the *double*. In this technique, one character may be paired to another character so that hidden aspects of personality (in the first character) are revealed. In everyday life, for example, people often react most negatively to those traits in a person which they cannot accept as part of themselves. The writer who uses the double technique makes the connection between unrecognized aspects of one character by presenting them more openly in another character. The reader, and sometimes the character, makes the connection.

Related to the technique of the double is the technique of the *alter ego*, or *second self*. These terms, too, refer to a twin of a character, representing some aspect of his personality. For good examples of the use of literary doubles, read "The Secret Sharer" by Joseph Conrad, "Bartleby the Scriverner" by Herman Melville, "Everything That Rises Must Converge," "A Good Man Is Hard to Find" by Flannery O'Connor, or "Counterparts" by James Joyce.

Another literary technique, often associated with James Joyce's stories, is the *epiphany*, a moment of recognition or awareness on the part of the reader alone or, perhaps, on the part of a major character as well that reveals some new insight, some crucial understanding. To see how an epiphany can illuminate a story, read James Joyce's "Araby," "Clay," or "A Painful Case." In some literary analyses, this moment of epiphany may also be called a *revelation*. Moments of insight or revelation are common to stories of *initiation*, stories which trace the growth of an individual toward maturity, most often through a painful experience. The narrator of Anderson's "Death in the Woods," for example, experiences a kind of initiation. Stories of initiation are very common in American literature; "My Kinsman, Major Molineux," by Nathaniel Hawthorne, or "The Killers" by Ernest Hemingway can be considered stories of initiation.

Certain stories can be read as *allegories*; that is, they are stories in which specific characters or events, consistently and directly, stand for abstract ideas such as greed, temptation, or perseverance. There are allegorical qualities in Eudora Welty's "A Worn Path," because certain events in the main character's journey may be direct equivalents of conflicts in every person's life, and the main character herself may represent every person on earth. But, because the story does not use either the character or the journey to represent only one thing, and one thing only, the story is not completely allegorical. Rather the main character and her journey are more complex, more symbolic.

An allegory is different from a symbol in that symbols are open to a variety of interpretations; they can represent several things at one time. In allegory, an older literary form, there is more likely to be one direct equivalent to the character or scene, and that equation is maintained throughout the story. To see the use of a character in an allegorical way, read Nathaniel Hawthorne's "Young Goodman Brown" and examine the role of Brown's wife.

Another, more modern, literary technique is called *stream of consciousness*. This is an attempt to record the full flow of a character's thought processes. Such a record is *not* simply an account of what a character is thinking, but a description of how the person's mind works, through emotions, sensations, memories, fragments of thoughts—a description of what is taking place within the mind. Of course, using the stream-of-consciousness technique effectively requires special talent on the part of the writer, and deriving meaning from the technique requires concentrated attention on the part of the reader. Done well, the stream-of-consciousness technique can illuminate an inner world in a special way. The technique is frequently associated with the novels of James Joyce and William Faulkner. For an example, read "Barn Burning" by William Faulkner.

Identifying Techniques

It's a good idea to learn the definitions of the basic literary techniques so that, as you read stories, you are prepared to recognize the various techniques they use. To become familiar with literary techniques, try the following exercises.

EXERCISE: POINT OF VIEW

Go back to three stories you have already read. Re-read them, quickly. Identify the point of view: omniscient, limited omniscient, dramatic, or first person. Find lines that support your identification of the point of view. For example, to support your identification of a story as written in the omniscient point of view, quote lines that emphasize the thoughts of two characters as given by the person or voice telling the story. To support the dramatic point of view, quote a key scene that is *all* description—no interpretation, no thoughts. (Be sure the entire story is like that.)

Title of story one: _____

Author: _____

Point of view: _____

Supporting quote(s): _____

_____

_____

_____

Title of story two: _____

Author: _____

Point of view: _____

Supporting quote(s): _____

_____

_____

_____

Title of story three: _____

Author: _____

Point of view: _____

Supporting quote(s): _____

_____

_____

_____

EXERCISE: IRONY

Reread a story suggested by your instructor to gather details for this exercise, or read one from the list that follows—twice, the first time for an overall sense of the story and the second time for obtaining the detail needed to complete this exercise. Select two examples of irony. Quote each example below; then briefly explain the irony. (Note the double meaning of the lines.)

Suggested Stories

"My Kinsman, Major Molineux"—Nathaniel Hawthorne
"Everything That Rises Must Converge"—Flannery O'Connor
"A&P"—John Updike
"Roman Fever"—Edith Wharton
"The Open Boat"—Stephen Crane

Short story title: _____

Author: _____

Irony (quoted): _____

_____

_____

_____

Irony explained: _____

_____

_____

_____

Irony (quoted): _____

_____

_____

_____

Irony explained: _____

_____

_____

_____

EXERCISE: IMAGES

Reread a story suggested by your instructor and focus on the main character, or pick one of the suggested stories that follow and read it twice—the first time for an overall sense of the story and the second time for focusing in on the main character. Consider the descriptions of that character and look for images. You may consider descriptions not only of the character but also of scenes or objects to which the character is connected.

Below, give in direct quotes two examples of such images; then discuss how these images influence the reader's perception of the character.

Suggested Stories

"Quality"—John Galsworthy
"Clay"—James Joyce
"The Horse Dealer's Daughter"—D. H. Lawrence
"A Rose for Emily"—William Faulkner
"The Fall of the House of Usher"—Edgar Allan Poe

Short story title: _____

Author: _____

Image (quoted): _____

_____

_____

How image influences perception of character: _____

_____

_____

_____

Image (quoted): _____

_____

_____

_____

How image influences perception of character: _____

_____

_____

EXERCISE: SYMBOLISM

Reread a story suggested by your instructor and look for one symbol in the story, or pick a story from the following list and read it twice—a first time for an overall sense of the story and a second time to look for a symbol.

Below, first quote the lines that contain the symbol; then explain for what you think the symbol stands. You can give more than one meaning to the symbol.

Suggested Stories

"Miss Brill"—Katherine Mansfield
"Where Are You Going, Where Have You Been?"—Joyce Carol Oates
"The Chrysanthemums"—John Steinbeck
"A Hunger Artist"—Franz Kafka
"The Birthmark"—Nathaniel Hawthorne

Short story title: _____

Author: _____

Symbol (quoted): _____

_____

_____

_____

_____

What the symbol stands for: _____

_____

_____

_____

_____

_____

_____

_____

WRITING THE TECHNIQUES ESSAY

When you become familiar with how to recognize different literary techniques, you are ready to begin writing a short paper on techniques.

Try working through such a paper, a five-paragraph essay, using John Cheever's ''The Swimmer'' as the story for the analysis.

GROUPING DETAILS

Step 1 Read the story. Then reread it, underlining examples (as many as you can find) of any three of the techniques listed below:

Foreshadowing
Irony
Symbolism
Images
Doubles

Step 2 Make a list of your examples, divided into three categories (one for each kind of technique). For example:

1 Symbols for the stages of the swim
    Early afternoon: good weather, clear pools, rich owners, parties, friendliness
    Late afternoon: storm, public pool, hostile lifeguard
    Darkness: empty pool areas, hostile people or no people
2 Images of the journey and of Neddy
    Neddy like a summer's day
    A pilgrim
    Overgrown riding ring
    Drained pool
    Locked boathouse
    Locked house
3 Foreshadowing
    Sunny afternoon has clouds
    Neddy's drinking
    One hostess' remark
    Another one's gossip
    His mistress' reaction

With this list, you have the basis for a rough outline of the three central paragraphs of your essay.

Now, you must plan a paragraph for the introduction and the thesis, and a concluding paragraph.

WRITING A THESIS

Step 3 The thesis of the techniques essay should

1 Mention what specific techniques you will discuss.
2 Relate the techniques to the overall impact of the story. That is, the thesis should mention that the techniques are important to the story as a whole.

For example, try this thesis:

''The Swimmer'' by John Cheever effectively uses the literary techniques of symbolism, images, and foreshadowing to enhance and express meaning.

WRITING THE CONCLUSION

Step 4 Take your idea further in the conclusion. Try to come up with some way of concluding your essay that not only restates the thesis but takes it a little further; that is, ''How do these techniques enhance and express meaning? What meaning?''

To answer these questions, consider the impact of the entire story. Is it cheerful? Optimistic? Surprising? Does it upset you? Make you think? What feeling does the story leave you with? How did the techniques help create this feeling?

Try this concluding idea for ''The Swimmer'':

Through his subtle but consistent use of symbols, images, and foreshadowing, Cheever shows us not one afternoon but a whole life in decline.

Step 5 Write the short outline. You now have enough material for the outline. For the three central paragraphs section of the outline, you need to look at your original list of three categories of detail. Then,

1 Compose a topic sentence for each category.
2 Look at each example of technique, and not only list it but note what it means or how it works.

Here's a short outline for a techniques essay on ''The Swimmer.''

A Sample Outline

 I Introduction

  Thesis sentence: ''The Swimmer'' by John Cheever effec-

  tively uses the literary techniques of symbolism, images,

  and foreshadowing to enhance and express meaning.

topic sentence II The stages of Neddy Merrill's swim can symbolize the

  stages of his life.

A In the early afternoon he swims in sunshine, in clear
  pools, surrounded by friendly people.

B At this time his life seems happy.

C In the middle of the afternoon he encounters a storm and
  a dingy public pool with hostile lifeguards.

D His life seems less sunny.

E In the last stages of his swim he is in darkness, either
  with unfriendly people or, finally, alone.

F He is now at the last part of his life--the dark, sad
  part.

topic sentence   III The images associated with each stage of the swim empha-
                     size Neddy's sense of failure.

A Early, Neddy is compared to a summer's day.

B He is a pilgrim; he seems to have a purpose.

C Later, he is surrounded by an overgrown riding ring, a
  drained pool, and a locked boathouse.

D The images are now negative.

E Finally, he faces his locked and empty house--his empty
  life.

topic sentence   IV Throughout the story, Neddy's final confrontation with
                     his failure is foreshadowed.

A The sunny afternoon has clouds in it, foreshadowing a
  problem to come.

B Neddy drinks heavily all day, indicating a personal
  problem.

C One hostess refers to Neddy's troubles, giving a hint of
  some personal misery.

D Another gossips about how he went broke overnight, revealing more trouble.

E Neddy expects his ex-mistress to be happy to see him;

but her unfriendliness tells the reader something is

wrong.

F All these hints prepare us for the end of his swim.

topic sentence V Through his subtle but consistent use of symbols, images,

and foreshadowing, Cheever shows us not one afternoon but

an entire life in decline.

Step 6   Write a rough draft. With a short outline completed, you're ready to write a draft of a five-paragraph essay. The draft includes an effective lead-in to the thesis (to create an introductory paragraph), effective transitions within and between paragraphs, and the use of specific examples from the story to support your points. Some of these examples are direct quotes; some are not.

Be careful to make your support specific. Don't say, "There's a lot of foreshadowing of Neddy's failure when he swims." Instead, say "Neddy's failure is foreshadowed early in the story by the clouds on a sunny afternoon," or "The hostess' reference to Neddy's troubles tells us that something is wrong."

Step 7   Revise your first draft. Check it for:

Specific examples—are there enough?
Direct quotes—are they in a clear context?
Transitions—is this essay smooth?

as well as for grammar, spelling, and structure. Now you can write the final draft.

What follows is the final draft of a sample essay on techniques in "The Swimmer."

Literary Techniques in John Cheever's "The Swimmer"

lead-in   ''The Swimmer'' begins as a simple story about a man who de-

cides to spend a Sunday afternoon swimming home through his

neighbor's pools. His undertaking seems innocent enough, even

if it is somewhat silly, but soon his journey takes on a

slightly puzzling quality; and the story is not so simple. The reader, aware of certain techniques used throughout the story, begins to see the swim as more than an amusement and finds a deeper meaning. For John Cheever, author of ''The Swimmer,'' effectively uses the literary techniques of symbolism, images, and foreshadowing to express and enhance the story's meaning.

The most significant technique in the story is the use of symbols, for the stages of Neddy Merrill's swim can represent the stages of Neddy's life. For example, the first part of Neddy's swim is carefree and exhilarating, like the sunny weather. The water of the pool is a clear, light green, and the owners of the pool are rich and friendly. There are a catered party, a smiling bartender, and welcoming hosts. But, by the middle of the swim, the clouds are rising, and it storms. Neddy shivers in the cold air; and at the public pool, the water stinks of chlorine, and the lifeguards scold Neddy for swimming without an identity disk. Neddy's journey, like his life, is moving down to the third stage, where twilight and then darkness creep in, and where another hostess calls him a ''gate crasher.'' Soon the stars are out; it's cold and lonely on the last part of the swim, and Neddy is ''so stupefied with exhaustion that his triumph seemed vague.'' Has Neddy failed in his lighthearted adventure just as he failed in life? Each stage of the swim seems to be a step down, not a move to victory.

The images associated with the stages of the swim seem to emphasize Neddy's sense of failure. At first, Neddy ''might

detail

have been compared to a summer's day,'' and ''a pilgrim, an explorer, a man with a destiny.'' But, in a few moments he moves from happy social scenes to a big house that is suddenly empty, to a riding ring all overgrown with grass and its jumps dismantled. This picture of an affluent life in decay is followed by the scene of a pool that has been drained, a locked boathouse, and a house with a posted For Sale sign. By late in the afternoon the explorer has become a pitiful figure stranded in the middle of a busy highway, looking like ''the victim of foul play'' or ''merely a fool.'' And when Neddy finally makes it home, his own house is locked; like his life, ''the place was empty.'' Neddy is left to face the outcome of his journey, a life of loneliness and pain.

topic sentence

This confrontation is not unexpected, for it has been foreshadowed throughout the story. We know that something is wrong with Neddy's world because of the constant hints Cheever supplies. Even the sunny afternoon that begins the story has thunderclouds in it. Although Neddy is compared to a summer's day, the description continues with ''particularly the last hours of one,'' indicating a decline to darkness. Neddy's growing physical weakness and his growing thirst for alcohol are other signs of a problem. When one hostess says to Neddy, ''We've been terribly sorry to hear about all your misfortunes,'' and another whispers that the Merrills ''went for broke overnight,'' the questions about Neddy's situation increase. When Neddy's former mistress, who he expects will greet him warmly, rejects him and refuses to give him any more

detail

detail

money, the stage is set for the last sad scene. The dark house, the rusty garage doors, the loose rain gutter all signal a decay. Neddy's final lonely stand, in the darkness, is no surprise.

conclusion

What begins as a light story, then, soon becomes more as the reader follows Cheever's clues. Through his subtle but consistent use of symbols, images, and foreshadowing, Cheever shows us not one afternoon, but a whole life in decline. Sooner or later Neddy Merrill, like the reader, cannot ignore the hidden signs of decay.

thesis restated, related to impact of story

EXERCISE: THE TECHNIQUES ESSAY

Now that you've worked through the steps of the sample techniques analysis, you're ready to write your own.

Read a story, looking first for an overall appreciation and understanding. Then reread it, underlining examples (as many as you can) of any three kinds of techniques. Then, in a five-paragraph essay, write one paragraph on each technique you found. Each of these three paragraphs must include specific examples (some quoted) of the technique along with your explanation of and comments on the examples and how they are used. You can refer to the shorter exercises in this section for examples.

Your first paragraph must include a lead-in of several sentences. Then try this model for your thesis:

"_____" by _____
      (title of story)   (author)

effectively uses the literary techniques of _____,
                                               (first technique)

_____, and _____
  (second technique)   (third technique)

to enhance and express meaning.

Your conclusion should restate the thesis and show how techniques enhance and express the story's meaning.

EXERCISE: A SKELETON OUTLINE

Your outline for this essay should be structured like the one below. You fill in the blanks.

I Thesis sentence:

examples of the
technique explained
and discussed

II Topic sentence for first technique:

A

B

C

D

E

F

examples of the
technique explained
and discussed

III Topic sentence for second technique:

A

B

C

D

E

F

examples of the
technique explained
and discussed

IV Topic sentence for third technique:

A

B

C

D

E

F

V A concluding sentence restating the thesis and relating

the techniques to the specific meaning of the story:

Note: In writing this essay, be sure to follow the steps outlined for you in the
sample techniques essay given in this section.

THEME

IDENTIFYING THEME THROUGH CONFLICT

All the elements of a short story—characters, plot, literary techniques—are utilized for one purpose: to express a theme. The *theme* of any literary work may be defined as its *central statement*, its *focus*, its *point*. The more complex the literary work, the more likely it will contain several themes; but in a short story you should be able to concentrate on one theme.

A story's theme is, most likely, not going to be spelled out for the reader, for that would make the story boring and turn the story itself into a form of sermon or propaganda. Each reader may interpret theme somewhat differently, for literature is complex and multifaceted. On the other hand, a reader can misinterpret theme if he or she misunderstands or disregards the evidence of the story itself.

Now that you have become familiar with all the separate elements of a story, the next step is to learn how to identify theme. The easiest way to do this is to *look carefully and closely at the story's conflict and how it is resolved.* Below is a process for identifying theme:

1 Who is the story's protagonist?
2 Who or what is the antagonist?
3 What is the conflict?

    _____ vs. _____
      (what protagonist represents)   (what antagonist represents)

4 How does the conflict develop? (Trace the key scenes.)
5 How is the conflict resolved?

Consider an example: Suppose you read a story, set in the United States in the 1960s, about a young man who is about to be drafted into the army and will most likely be sent to fight in Vietnam. The young man knows that it is right to fight for his country, but he is ambivalent about the morality of this particular war.

His father, a traditional, patriotic man, urges the son to "do his duty." The father strongly supports the war in Vietnam and cannot understand why his son is hesitant to fight. So far, you have

1 A protagonist—the son and his crisis of conscience.
2 An antagonist—the father and his patriotism
3 A conflict—son vs. father or conscience vs. country.

As you read further, there are two *key scenes*—two separate incidents in which the conflict between father and son is deepened and explored. In one, the son is given a chance to flee to Canada where he will be safe from the draft, but where he will be alienated from his country and cut off from his family and friends.

In another scene, the son and the father become involved in a passionate argument over the right thing to do. The father threatens the son with a kind of emotional disinheritance if the son refuses to fight.

You now have material for step 4. Examine the key scenes and note how they develop the conflict.

4 The conflict develops into a choice between personal values and the values of home and country.

Step 5 is to consider how the conflict is resolved—how the story ends. Suppose the son chooses to reject his father and his father's traditional patriotism. He goes to Canada and, in the last lines of the story, you can see him feeling justified in his decision. He misses his family and grieves for the broken relationship with his father, but he knows he has done what he had to do.

You are now ready to move to step 6: identifying a theme. You have already identified the specific details of character and plot. Now take the specific details and widen them:

What is being represented here?
A son (who represents individual conscience) must choose between that conscience and the demands of his country (represented by his father).

What choice does the son make?
He chooses to follow his conscience.

How does the choice turn out?
Pretty well, although the son experiences regret and loss.

With these facts, you can formulate a *theme* for the story: *a one-sentence, general statement derived from the story's conflict*. Or you can formulate several themes:

The conflict between personal values and society's rules is painful, but one must follow his conscience.

A man must follow his conscience and live by a higher law than society's rules.

Those who love us can not always know what is best for us; we must determine our own values.

What you do when you look for a theme is *not* so obvious as looking for a moral, but you must search for a meaning, for some general statement you can derive from specifics. *The key is to look closely at the specifics of the conflict.* You would be incorrect in saying that the theme of our sample story is:

Everything will turn out beautifully if we only live by our inner values.

You would be wrong because certain specifics in the conflict do not support this statement; the son is not totally happy. He feels ambivalent, torn.

What if the sample story ended differently? Suppose the son went to Canada. As soon as he got there, he felt ashamed. He felt cowardly and disgraced. Every account of a soldier killed in war intensified his guilt. He began to realize that his father had been right.

Such an ending would lead you to a different theme like those that follow:

If one puts personal needs above those of his or her country, he or she will feel only failure and guilt.

One must learn to live for the good of society as a whole if he or she is to live a meaningful life.

Love of country demands that we put aside love of self.

Whatever theme you identify, it is essential that it:

1 Reflects the specifics of the story.

2 Expresses them in a general way (i.e., not "John must choose the good of America over his own personal needs.").

3 *Be expressed in a complete sentence.*

You don't say much if you say, "The theme of this story concerns moral values," or "This is a story about choices," or "The theme concerns patriotism," or "The theme is how a young man with conflicting feelings faces war."

Be careful that your expression of theme *identifies a conflict and its resolution, and draws some conclusion about the two.* Your statement of theme must be more than a word—*Choices*, or a phrase—*moral values*, or a dependent clause—"how a young man with conflicting feelings faces war." It must give the reader a clear, complete idea of the conflict of the story, its resolution, and its *meaning*.

EXERCISE: IDENTIFYING THEME

Choose any story you have already read. Reread it, concentrating on identifying the elements that will lead you to a theme. Then complete the process below.

Story: _____

Author: _____

    Step 1: Identify the protagonist: _____

    Step 2: Identify the antagonist: _____

    Step 3: Identify the conflict:

_____ vs. _____
      (what the protagonist represents)   (what the antagonist represents)

    Step 4: Identify two or more key scenes where the conflict develops significantly. Briefly describe each.

First key scene: _____

_____

_____

_____

Second key scene: _____

_____

_____

_____

Additional key scene(s): _____

_____

_____

_____

_____

_____

    Step 5: How is the conflict resolved? Briefly describe.

_____

_____

_____

_____

Step 6: In a complete sentence, write a theme for the story. Make it a general statement based on the specifics above. _____

_____

_____

_____

Now that you have learned how to identify a theme, you are ready to tackle the complete critical analysis of a short story, and your statement of theme will become the thesis of your entire paper.

THE COMPLETE CRITICAL ANALYSIS

THE BASIC PARTS

A critical analysis of a short story discusses all the separate elements—character, conflict, plot, and techniques—and unifies the discussion with a specific statement of theme. Again, you will consider *what a story says* and *what it means*.

The basic parts of a critical analysis are

   I Introduction
   Lead-in
   Thesis statement
   II Short plot summary
   III Analysis of the protagonist(s)
   IV Analysis of the antagonist(s)
   V Discussion of how the conflict develops in significant scenes
   VI Discussion of how the conflict is resolved, including identification of climax and solution
   VII Analysis of literary techniques
   VIII Conclusion

You have already written most of the separate parts of an analysis: plot summary, character analysis, analysis of techniques. You have already studied how to identify a theme.

Now, as you write each part of the complete critical analysis, you can unify your essay if you consider the following question for each section you write: "How does my discussion of protagonist (or antagonist, or key scenes, or techniques) connect to the theme?"

STRUCTURE AND CONTENT OF EACH PART

Before you write, go through the following outline more carefully so that you have a better idea of the analysis's *content and structure*.

I Introduction: The lead-in and the thesis statement.

Remember to not begin with your thesis as the first sentence of your paper. Instead, begin with several sentences of introductory material, general statements about your story or its theme. These sentences should mention both the title of your story and its author. If you wish, you can use a little background on the author (if you make it relevant) for your lead-in.

All these general statements are to be used as a smooth transition to your *thesis statement*: a one-sentence statement of theme. Remember that in order to arrive at a theme, you must examine the conflict between the protagonist and antagonist and its resolution. This means that *formulating a theme requires a great deal of preliminary thinking and analysis.*

This theme becomes the focus of your essay. That is, the rest of your paper provides different kinds of detail supporting your statement of theme, explaining why you believe that statement best sums up the story. Be aware that sometimes the theme of the story can best be expressed by a direct quote from the story itself.

II Plot summary

This is a *brief* description of what happens in the story. Assume the reader has not read the story you are analyzing, identify the main characters by name (so you don't have to do it, obtrusively, later), and briefly chart the events.

This is *not* the place to interpret what happens in the story; you are not to be concerned here with what the story means. All you want to do is tell the facts. Keep the plot summary short. For a short story, write no more than two paragraphs; one is even better. There should be little need to quote from the story in this section.

III Analysis of the protagonist

Every story involves someone vs. someone (or something) else, some protagonist vs. some antagonist. In this section, write a character analysis of the protagonist. What is this person like and how do we know it? Liberal use of specific examples and quotes from the story is appropriate here.

Try not to be too concerned (yet) with what the protagonist *does* during the story; try to focus on *what he is like as the story begins*. You may, of course, need to use specific examples of the protagonist's actions to describe him, but don't rehash the entire plot, and avoid discussing the climax and other key scenes. This section of your essay may be more than one paragraph.

IV Analysis of the antagonist

Now describe who or what the protagonist is up against. Depending on the story, there may be several antagonists to discuss here. Consider them all. Again, specifics from the story are necessary here. If you have a protagonist who is his or her own antagonist, save that part of his or her personality which creates the conflict, the "bad side," or the part that is his or her own worst enemy, for the antagonist section of your essay. This section of your paper may be more than one paragraph.

V Discussion of how the conflict develops in significant scenes

In this section describe and interpret the conflict, as it begins and as it becomes complicated. *This section is different from the plot summary*. The plot summary quickly skims the whole story, with no interpretation. The plot summary gives a panorama; the conflict section focuses only on those scenes which introduce or intensify the story's main conflict and does *not* skim those few scenes. You must consider carefully what light each scene casts on the developing conflict. Obviously, in this section you need to provide quotes, cite specific examples, and interpret. You need to consider what both the protagonist and antagonist do, and what each action means. This section of your paper should be more than one paragraph. In fact, it's a good idea to write a separate, developed paragraph for each key scene of the conflict. Try to focus each paragraph with a *topic sentence* that sums up *how the scene develops the conflict*.

VI Discussion of how the conflict is resolved, including identification of climax and solution

Trace the conflict right through to its climax and solution (if there is one). Identify what you think is the highest point of tension (climax), in the story, and the "tying up of loose ends" part (solution). Remember, how a conflict is resolved is a significant determiner of theme. Specific details and quotations are appropriate to this section, too. This section may be more than one paragraph, depending on the degree of complexity of the climax and solution of your story.

Note: Careful analysis of the *key scenes* (scenes developing and resolving the conflict) of a story is not easy. Since a short story *is* short, you will probably find yourself referring to scenes you've already mentioned earlier in your paper. You may feel that you are repeating the plot summary. You won't be if, in this section, you analyze the incidents of the story in terms of how they complicate the conflict and reveal the theme. To be sure you understand the difference between plot summary and analysis of key scenes, take a look at the *sample analysis of the key scenes* of Flannery O'Connor's "A Good Man Is

Hard to Find'' *right after this discussion of the outline*. Study it; then compare it to the plot summary of the same story included in Section 1, page 14.

VII Analysis of literary techniques

This is the place to identify those literary techniques which enhance and express the story's theme. That is, it is not enough just to mention techniques the story uses. You must tie them in to the story's point. If there is foreshadowing, what is being foreshadowed and why? How are images used to develop theme? Quotes citing specific examples of techniques are important here.

Beginning writers tend to gloss over this part of the essay. If you consider the story carefully and reread it for literary techniques, you will probably find a great many of them. And, if you think about these techniques, you can most likely see their role in the overall structure and meaning of the story. You should write more than one paragraph on techniques. An easy way to group the techniques is to write one paragraph, for example, on foreshadowing; another on images.

VIII Conclusion

This is easy. Briefly recap the points you have made earlier about characters, conflict, and techniques. Then slide smoothly into a restatement of your theme, in different words.

A few cautions: This paper is very much like a traditional research paper. When you want to support or develop a point in a traditional research paper, you cite a fact or an authority. In this paper, when you want to support or develop a point, cite a specific detail from the story. Give an example from the story or quote a line or two.

Just be sure that your quotes are put in context. That is, you must in some way identify what is being said or done, when, and by whom. And, as in all good writing, the quote must be incorporated so that it makes grammatical sense.

The hardest part of revising this paper may be linking each section to the next one. Your final paper should not include roman numerals or subheadings. Instead, careful transition sentences can link each part of the paper to the other parts. And overall unity will be achieved if you *keep your theme in mind, throughout the analysis*.

The outline discussed above should give you some sense of "what goes where" in your analysis. Because you may be using certain key lines or scenes as examples more than once, you may worry that your paper is becoming repetitive. The major concern will probably be that your plot summary, key scenes, and climax sections are too similar. They won't be, if you remember:

The plot summary skims through events without interpreting them. This section is used to familiarize the reader with the facts of the story.

The conflict, climax and solution sections focus on a few key scenes and interpret them in depth.

To give you a better sense of how to write a critical analysis, study the samples that follow:

1 An analysis of the key scenes of "A Good Man Is Hard to Find" to compare to the earlier plot summary of the story
2 A sample outline for a complete critical analysis of Eudora Welty's "A Worn Path"
3 A sample critical analysis essay on Eudora Welty's "A Worn Path"

Sample Analysis of the Key Scenes of Flannery O'Connor's "A Good Man Is Hard to Find"

topic sentence	The conflict of ''A Good Man Is Hard to Find'' begins when
	the grandmother and her family begin their trip. As they pile
first key scene	into the car, we see the contrast between the grandmother's
	illusions about herself and the reality. When the grandmother
	cautions her son about speed traps and chatters to her bored
specific detail analyzed	grandchildren, she thinks she is helpful; actually she is an-
	noying. Her comments about ''the cute little pickaninny'' and
	her story about the watermelon and the foolish black servant
	reveal not her superior status but her racism and lack of un-
	derstanding of poverty and discrimination. Above all, her
	white organdy—and—lace collar and cuffs, her straw hat and ar-
	tificial violets reveal her need to see herself as a lady
	superior to those around her.
transition, topic sentence	Her sense of superiority is reinforced by her conversation
	with Red Sammy, the restaurant owner who also feels he is bet-
second key scene	ter than most of the world. The two commiserate over the state
specific detail analyzed	of the universe as Sammy complains, ''These days you don't
	know who to trust,'' and the grandmother agrees that people
	''are certainly not nice like they used to be.'' This pair

flatter one another by dividing the world into an exclusive group of good people and a far—larger group of degenerates. Of course they believe they are members of the small group. In reality, Sammy is fat, dirty, and lazy, and, like the grand—mother, blind to his own faults.

transition,
topic
sentence

third key
scene

detail
analyzed

climax

climax
analyzed

The grandmother's faults are soon brought home to her when, through her misbehavior, the family car is wrecked, and the family confronts The Misfit. At first, the grandmother, thinking only of saving herself, tries to flatter The Misfit into sparing her. Over and over, she reassures him that he is a good man; if she can bring him up to her level, if she can admit him into her exclusive club of superior people, he will not be her murderer. As she hears the gunshots that kill her family, she uses flattery, then an appeal to The Misfit's religious values, but nothing works. Her calling on Jesus sounds more like a curse than a prayer. Soon desperate, she even denies her own faith; to placate The Misfit, she is ready to concede that maybe Jesus ''didn't raise the dead.'' This self—styled ''good'' person is revealed as selfish and faithless, ready to do or say anything to save her life.

In the climactic scene, the grandmother, having run out of tactics, must finally face herself. Rather than try to raise The Misfit to what she believed was her level, she must in—stead understand that her moral stature is as low as his. When she reaches to touch The Misfit and murmurs, ''Why you're one of my babies. You're one of my own children!'' she finally sees the connection between his wickedness and her own. He is not a good person, but neither is she.

solution

Does the grandmother realize her own selfishness too late? She dies with her eyes open wide, her face ''smiling up at the cloudless sky.'' But we are not sure what she sees. In the mo-

topic
sentence

ment before death, perhaps she truly saw herself. And perhaps that vision saved not her life, but her soul.

Sample Outline for a Critical Analysis of Eudora Welty's "A Worn Path"

I Thesis statement: In the struggle and ultimate triumph of Phoenix, we see that with love, courage, and perserverance we can overcome whatever life inflicts upon us and can attain our goals.
II The plot of "A Worn Path" centers on one day of frustration and triumph.
    A The story begins in early morning in the country outside Natchez.
    B As Phoenix walks, she faces her own weakness and, also, some obstacles in nature.
    C She then faces a white hunter.
    D Nearly reaching her goal, she forgets what the goal is.
    E Finally getting the medicine for which she came, she begins her return trip.
III Phoenix Jackson is a complex character.
    A She seems to be a pitiful person.
        1 She is old and small.
        2 She is a poor black woman.
        3 She is in a difficult situation.
        4 She is often afraid, tired, disoriented, and discouraged.
    B Yet Phoenix is a figure to be admired, not pitied.
        1 She has strength, humor, dignity.
        2 Her determination gets her across a frightening creek.
        3 She can laugh at a threatening dog.
        4 She maintains her dignity in front of a white hunter.
        5 She is not too proud to ask for help (tying her shoes) to maintain a dignified appearance in town.
IV Phoenix faces several antagonists.
    A One of Phoenix's antagonists is her aging body.
        1 It's a long journey for an old person.
        2 She fights time in two ways.
        3 She has much ground to cover in one day.
        4 She does not have long to live.
    B There are antagonists in the environment and in society.
        1 There are the weather, the countryside and the city streets and stairs.
        2 There are animals.
        3 There are people.
    C Phoenix's mind can also be her enemy.
        1 She daydreams.
        2 She forgets her purpose.
       3 In the doctor's office, she loses her memory.
V The antagonists change as the scenes change.
    A At first, Phoenix's enemy is nature.

       1 She struggles up a hill.

       2 She catches her dress on thorns.

       3 She crosses a log bridge.

       4 She confronts a scarecrow.

   B Her second obstacle, as she moves toward town, is humankind.

       1 A white racist hunter with a gun threatens her.

       2 He advises her to go home.

       3 He misunderstands the serious purpose of her trip.

       4 He aims his gun at her.

       5 His words reflect a racist attitude.

   C In this scene, Phoenix also faces her own guilt and fear.

       1 She has stolen a nickle.

       2 She thinks she is caught.

       3 Yet she is brave and defiant, especially when the hunter mocks her.

       4 Her attitude represents the bravery of many black people.

   D Phoenix's mind and other people are again problems when Phoenix is in the doctor's office.

       1 An intolerant attendant attacks Phoenix when her memory fails her.

       2 She is mocked.

       3 Finally, a kind nurse helps her.

       4 She remembers her goal.

VI Phoenix, in the climax, gets the medicine and something more.

   A Remembering for what she came, she is able to ask for it.

   B She also gets another nickle.

   C She will use it to buy a gift for her grandson.

   D She has achieved her goal, and something extra—another chance to show her love—has been given to her.

VII Two clusters of images and symbols reinforce the idea that love and courage are powerful qualities.

   A The first cluster of images compares Phoenix to a bird.

       1 Her cane taps like a bird chirping.

       2 Her name is a mythical bird's name.

       3 Like the mythical phoenix, Phoenix Jackson endures.

   B Phoenix Jackson is also connected to someone holy; she is even connected to Christ.

       1 Her skin has a golden color.

       2 Like Christ, she does not live to please herself but lives for others.

       3 A "charity case," she represents spiritual love.

       4 The story is set at Christmas, Christ's birthday, and Phoenix, like Christ, is a giver.

VIII Phoenix can overcome all that fate throws in her path and, with her courage and charity, she can continue to travel the "worn path" of human struggle and triumph.

A Sample Critical Analysis: "A Worn Path"

lead-in

Eudora Welty's ''A Worn Path'' is a moving account of the

winter journey of Phoenix Jackson, an old black woman deter-

mined to get to town. As the story progresses, Phoenix
encounters many obstacles but she overcomes them all, for she
possesses certain qualities that enable her to endure and

thesis statement achieve. In the struggle and ultimate triumph of Phoenix, we
see that with love, courage, and perseverance, we can overcome
whatever life inflicts upon us and can attain our goals.

topic sentence   The plot of ''A Worn Path'' centers on one day of frustration and triumph. The story begins in the country, in the
early morning, as Phoenix begins her long walk to Natchez. On

plot summary   her way, Phoenix must fight her own weariness as well as the
natural obstacles--cold weather, thorny bushes, hills,
streams. She encounters a white hunter who both threatens and
assists her. Finally, when Phoenix is within reach of her
goal, her old age and exhaustion cause her to forget her initial purpose. But at last she reaches the end of her journey:
in the doctor's office she gets the medicine her grandson
needs to survive, and she can, triumphant, begin the trip
home.

transition   The story of Phoenix's journey is enriched by the complex
characterization of Phoenix herself, the protagonist of the

topic sentence   tale. Initially described as ''very old and small, an old
protagonist   Negro woman with her head tied in a red rag,'' Phoenix seems to
detail   be a pitiful character. She is frail, poor, and elderly. She
must struggle through a piny woods and up hills, and she must
be careful not to cut herself on a barbed-wire fence because
there is no money to pay for doctor's fees. Phoenix is often
afraid, disoriented, discouraged, and tired in the course of
her journey.

topic sentence
protagonist, continued

Despite Phoenix's old age, poverty, and physical weakness, she is a figure to be admired, not pitied. Each negative character trait is countered by a positive trait, by her inner strength, her humor, her dignity. Phoenix's inner determination, for example, gets her across the creek so that she can congratulate herself, saying, ''I wasn't as old as I

detail

thought.'' Her humor prompts her to laugh at herself when a threatening dog causes her to fall into a ditch; she can describe herself as ''Lying on my back like a June-bug waiting to be turned over.'' And Phoenix knows how to maintain her dignity. Confronted by a white man who advises her to give up her long trip and refuses to take it seriously, she remains firm: ''I bound to go to town, mister. . . . The time come around.'' Even after a tiring walk through the woods, she is mindful of the dignity of appearance. She is not too proud to ask another to tie her shoes, since her old bones will not allow her to bend to do it herself. She asks this favor so she will be appropriately dressed for town.

topic sentence
antagonist

On her travels, Phoenix faces several antagonists. Old, tired, and vulnerable, Phoenix's aging body is, of course, one of her greatest obstacles. She is fighting her old age in at-

detail

tempting a journey that would exhaust a younger person. She is, in two senses, fighting time——her age and her need to cover much ground in one day. ''The time getting all gone here,'' Phoenix notes as the sun moves higher in the sky. Her remark applies to both the day's goal and her time of life.

topic sentence
antagonist, continued

There are other antagonists on the journey, natural elements like the cold December weather, the hills, the creeks and fields to be crossed. The city streets to walk and the stairs to climb present other problems. There are animals to fear——the big dog which threatens her and the hunter's dog—— and people to fear, too——like the hunter himself.

And within Phoenix is another antagonist, for an old woman's mind can wander, and she can daydream, or even forget why she made her journey in the first place. Just as she has finally reached her destination, Phoenix momentarily forgets her mission: ''It was my memory had left me. There I sat and forgot why I made my long trip.'' Overcoming the obstacles of environment, Phoenix must also overcome the obstacles within.

Whatever the obstacle, internal or external, Phoenix over- comes it. The conflict of this story traces the steps to Phoenix's ultimate achievement, and the antagonists change as the scenes change. At first, her enemy is nature. Her path takes her up a hill, and she hesitates. ''Seem like there is chains about my feet, time I get this far.'' But she climbs. She frees her dress from the thorny bush. Eyes shut, balancing with her cane, she marches across the solitary log that bridges a creek. Crossing a withered cotton field, she con- fronts a scarecrow that she mistakenly takes for a ghost and, realizing her silly blunder, she laughs and dances.

After a wild dog pushes her into a ravine, she faces a new obstacle: man. A white hunter, complete with gun and hunting dog, comes to her aid, but his assistance carries with it both racism and an implied threat. Lifting Phoenix free of the ditch, the hunter advises her to go home. When she insists that she must go on, he trivializes her mission and treats her

Margin annotations:

detail

topic sentence
antagonist, continued

detail

transition

topic sentence

conflict

first key scene

detail

topic sentence

second key scene

detail

like a child. ''I know you colored people! Wouldn't miss going to town to see Santa Claus!'' Then, in what he perceives as a joke, he aims his gun at Phoenix, but she does not flinch. His final words to Phoenix describe an attitude not only toward her but toward the ''journey'' of all blacks to a better life: ''You take my advice and stay home, and nothing will happen to you.''

second key scene, continued

This scene is particularly threatening to Phoenix because, in this encounter, she has sinned and she is guilty and afraid. She has cleverly stolen a nickle dropped by the hunter and, when he raises his gun, she thinks he has caught her. True to her character, she is brave and defiant. Asked, ''Doesn't the gun scare you?'' she responds, ''No, sir. I seen plenty go off closer by, in my day, and for less than what I done.'' Like the hunter's words, Phoenix's words describe a conflict larger than her personal one.

topic sentence

People again present a problem when Phoenix at last arrives at the doctor's office, and Phoenix is again her own enemy

third key scene

here. When Phoenix's memory briefly fails her, she is attacked by an impatient and intolerant attendant. ''Speak up, Grandma. . . . What's your name? We must have your history, you

detail

know.'' The woman calls her a ''charity case,'' and only the kindness of a nurse spares Phoenix further abuse. As the old woman falters, the nurse offers her a seat and explains that Phoenix regularly comes for the medicine that keeps her grandson alive. And then Phoenix remembers her purpose. ''My little grandson, he sit up there in the house all wrapped up, waiting by himself. . . . We is the only two left in the world. He suf-

fer and it don't seem to put him back at all. . . . He going to
last. . . . I remembers so plain now, I not going to forget him
again, no, the whole enduring time.''

topic sentence

She and the child will endure. Phoenix gets the life-sus-
taining medicine she came for, and, in the solution of the

climax and solution

story, she gets even more. With the stolen nickle and the gift
of an additional five cents from the attendant, Phoenix has
another opportunity to give. Out of her enduring love, she

detail

will take the ten cents, and, she explains, ''I going to the
store and buy my child a little windmill they sells, made out
of paper. He going to find it hard to believe there such a
thing in the world.'' Protected by her enormous love, Phoenix
gets what she came for, and she is given something extra,
something that will bring love and happiness to the child when
she returns home.

transition to techniques

Throughout the story, the power of Phoenix's love is empha-
sized by Welty's use of literary techniques. Two clusters of
images and symbols related to the protagonist stress the
strength of love and courage in a person's life.

topic sentence

The first cluster of images connected to Phoenix compare
her to a bird. The noise of her cane tapping is ''like the

one technique

chirping of a solitary little bird,'' and Phoenix's name is

detail

the name of a mythical bird, a bird which is reborn from its
own ashes, a bird which does not die. This association with
the bird of mythology is important, since Phoenix Jackson,
too, endures and does not surrender to death.

And a further connection can be made. The phoenix is sometimes associated with Christ, who died and was reborn. And

topic sentence

Phoenix Jackson is also connected to someone holy, like Christ. For example, her skin has ''a golden

second technique

color . . . underneath,'' with her cheeks ''illuminated by a yellow burning under the dark.'' It is as if a halo surrounded her. Phoenix is, of course, a sinner but, like Christ, she lives so others (in her case, her grandson) may live, so she is

detail

a symbol of enduring love. As the attendant says, she is a ''charity case,'' but charity can mean love for others. Eudora Welty reinforces the associations of Christ, love, and endurance by setting the story in the Christmas season—Christ's birthday, a time when love is expressed through giving. And as Christmas ends the old year, the new year begins. Life, like Phoenix and her love, endures.

conclusion

A symbol of love and giving, Phoenix lives so that her grandson, utterly dependent on her, can live. She is able to manage any conflict that fate throws into her path, and, with her courage and charity, she can continue to travel the ''worn path'' of human struggle and survival.

EXERCISE: THE COMPLETE CRITICAL ANALYSIS

Now write your own critical analysis of a short story. Select one of the stories listed below or one assigned by your instructor. Be sure to use the Critical Analysis section of this book as a guideline.

Suggested Stories

Joyce Carol Oates: ''Four Summers,'' ''In the Region of Ice,'' ''Where Are You Going, Where Have You Been?''
John Cheever: ''The Country Husband''
William Faulkner: ''Dry September,'' ''The Bear,'' ''Barn Burning,'' ''A Rose for Emily''
James Joyce: ''Araby,'' ''Counterparts,'' ''Clay,'' ''A Little Cloud,'' ''A Painful Case''

Frank O'Connor: "First Confession," "My Oedipus Complex," "Guests of the Nation," "The Drunkard"

Stephen Crane: "The Open Boat," "The Blue Hotel"

Flannery O'Connor: "Revelation," "Good Country People," "Everything That Rises Must Converge"

Dorothy Parker: "Big Blonde"

Ernest Hemingway: "The Killers," "A Clean, Well-Lighted Place," "The Snows of Kilimanjaro"

Albert Camus: "The Guest"

Jean Paul Sartre: "The Wall"

Guy de Maupassant: "The Necklce," "Boule de Suif"

Anton Chekov: "Gooseberries," "The Darling"

Edgar Allan Poe: "The Fall of the House of Usher," "The Cask of Amontillado," "Ligeia," "The Black Cat"

Nathaniel Hawthorne: "Rappaccini's Daughter," "Ethan Brand," "Wakefield," "My Kinsman, Major Molineux," "Young Goodman Brown"

F. Scott Fitzgerald: "Babylon Revisited," "Winter Dreams," "The Last of the Belles"

Edith Wharton: "Roman Fever," "The Other Two"

Willa Cather: "Paul's Case"

Henry James: "The Beast in the Jungle," "Europe"

D. H. Lawrence: "The Rocking Horse Winner," "The Horse Dealer's Daughter," "Odor of Chrysanthemums"

PART TWO

TWO

DRAMA

SOME INTRODUCTORY TERMS

Almost all plays are written to be performed, so if you merely read a play, you can miss much of its impact. Nevertheless, with some imagination and concentrated involvement, you can read a play and experience its power and delight in its entertainment.

Plays are, of course, very different from short stories. Writers of short stories can convey information through narrative, description, and dialogue. Playwrights must focus almost exclusively on *dialogue* as a means of transmitting the facts and meaning of the play. The dialogue must serve many functions. It must tell about the *action* of the play: it must establish what significant events happened before the play began (set the scene), it must clarify what is happening in the present (describe conflicts), and it must move the story along (develop and resolve conflicts). It must tell about the *characters* of the play: it must provide information about the character speaking, about the character(s) listening, and about the characters not present. It must explore the relationships of the characters. In addition, dialogue must provide insight into the kind of world the characters inhabit. And it must convey the meaning of the play.

All these functions place heavy demands on the dialogue. Some plays have a narrator, or a person (or persons) functioning like a narrator, but in most cases, it is through the dialogue of the characters that the reader must approach the play. And the reader must be attentive to the subtle meanings of the dialogue: he or she cannot skim it as if it were small talk.

In one sense, the reader of a play has an advantage over the audience of a play in his or her ability to focus on the dialogue. The reader, dealing only with the printed page, is not subject to the divided demands of watching the performance while listening to the all-important dialogue. And the reader, unlike the audience, can go back over the dialogue, can reread the lines, reacting, evaluating, analyzing, as he or she reads.

When you read a play, be aware that the playwright has another, less significant way to convey information to the reader of a play. This way is through the *stage directions*. When a play is actually staged, these directions are clues (to the director) as to how the scenery should look, what lighting should be used, what music or other sound is needed, and how the characters should look, move, and speak. The audience sees the director's translation of the stage directions in the actual production.

But, in the case of the stage directions, the reader of the play again has a certain advantage over a member of the audience, for a director can vary in his or her interpretation of the stage directions, or, in some cases, the playwright may have included requirements in the stage directions which are difficult to convey on stage. If, for example, a stage direction calls for a character to look "concerned about the futility of an existence he is ready to end," whether this look can be conveyed depends on the director and the actor. But the reader of a play reads the actual directions; the reader sees things the audience of an actual production may only guess at. Since stage directions can contain material important to understanding a play, they, like the dialogue, should be read carefully.

The following exercises are designed to heighten your awareness of the importance of dialogue and stage directions. An increased awareness can develop your understanding and appreciation of drama.

**EXERCISE: THE IMPORTANCE OF DIALOGUE
IN A KEY SCENE—*ANTIGONE***

To increase your awareness of the significance of dialogue, do the following exercise. Read the first scene of *Antigone*, from the entrance of Antigone and Ismene to their exit. Then, supply the details (drawn from the dialogue of that scene) that support the general statements below. Put the detail in sentences. In each list of detail, include at lest one direct quote from the scene.

Note: This careful gathering of evidence is a way of approaching a study of several aspects of a play: character, conflict, key scenes.

I The first scene of *Antigone* tells us a great deal about a recent conflict in Antigone and Ismene's lives.

Detail A: _____

Detail B: _____

Detail C: _____

Detail D: _____

Direct quote from scene: _____

_____

II The first scene tells us about a new conflict developing between Antigone and Ismene, based on a decision Antigone has made.

Detail A: _____

Detail B: _____

Detail C: _____

Detail D: _____

Direct quote from scene: _____

_____

III The first scene reveals Antigone's character.

Detail A: _____

Detail B: _____

Detail C: _____

Detail D: _____

Direct quote from scene: _____

_____

IV The first scene reveals Ismene's character.

Detail A: _____

Detail B: _____

Detail C: _____

Detail D: _____

Direct quote from scene: _____

_____

V The relationship between Antigone and Ismene is revealed in the scene.

Detail A: _____

Detail B: _____

Detail C: _____

Detail D: _____

Direct quote from scene: _____

_____

EXERCISE: THE IMPORTANCE OF DIALOGUE
IN A KEY SCENE—ANY PLAY

Select any play you have read, and select one significant scene, with a minimum of characters in it (it does not have to be the first scene). Review the scene, and then supply the detail (drawn from the dialogue of the scene) that supports the general statements below. Put the detail in sentences. Include at least one direct quote from the scene for each list of detail. Depending on your scene, you may not be able to supply all the detail to support all the statements, but do as much as you can.

Note: This careful gathering of evidence is a way of approaching a study of several aspects of a play: characters, conflict, key scenes.

I The scene tells about conflicts that occurred earlier.

Detail A: _____

Detail B: _____

Detail C: _____

Detail D: _____

Direct quote from the scene: _____

_____

II The scene introduces and/or develops a conflict.

Detail A: _____

Detail B: _____

Detail C: _____

Detail D: _____

Direct quote from the scene: _____

_____

III The scene reveals aspects of one speaker's character.

Detail A: _____

Detail B: _____

Detail C: _____

Detail D: _____

Direct quote from scene: _____

_____

IV The scene reveals aspects of a second speaker's character.

Detail A: _____

Detail B: _____

Detail C: _____

Detail D: _____

Direct quote from scene: _____

_____

V The scene tells about relationships between characters.

Detail A: _____

Detail B: _____

Detail C: _____

Detail D: _____

Direct quote from scene: _____

_____

EXERCISE: STAGE DIRECTIONS

To develop an awareness of the importance of stage directions, select a play you have read, preferably one written in the late nineteenth or early twentieth century, since such plays tend to have detailed stage directions. Review the play, paying particular attention to the stage directions. Then, in a short essay (500 words), do two things: *analyze* what information is contained in the stage directions (how do the directions help establish setting, characterization, motivation, mood?), and *discuss* how these directions could best be carried out in an actual production, if you were staging the play. Would the play, for example, require elaborate scenery, costumes, lights? Is there anything in the stage directions that would be difficult to convey? Is there anything in the directions you would ignore?

DRAMATIC CONVENTIONS

Enjoying drama, whether you are watching or reading a play, requires you to use your imagination, to enter the world of the play. To do so means to approach the play with a certain open-minded, accepting attitude, an attitude that allows you to become a part of the drama and to get everything you can from it. This attitude of acceptance is sometimes called *suspension of disbelief*, a willingness to enter the world of the play.

Such an open attitude is particularly important because each play has its own *dramatic conventions*, techniques of the theater common to a particular kind or period of drama. In the twentieth century, the most familiar conventions are probably the dramatic conventions of late nineteenth and early twentieth century plays, conventions designed to add an element of realism to the staging of plays. These conventions may have become so familiar and so accepted that you take them for granted. For example, when you think of the setting of a play, you may automatically think of a scene set in a typical living room with realistic furniture. But this "realistic" room has one whole wall cut away, for it is part of the convention of the *three-sided stage*, a convention familiar to you.

Plays from different historical periods have different dramatic conventions. Shakespeare, for example, made brilliant use of the *soliloquy*: an actor, alone on stage, thinking out loud. Many plays use the *aside*, in which a character speaks "aside" to another character, or directly to the audience, yet other characters on stage do not hear the words. A *stage whisper*, which can be heard in the last row of the theater, is another convention. A convention of both Greek and Elizabethan drama was the *performance of all roles by male actors*. In certain contemporary plays, the reader or audience must accept a *nonrealistic staging*, complete with rapid, often puzzling flashbacks, dreams, visions, or scenery that lurches and sways.

The conventions of each play should not prevent you from appreciating it. As you read further in drama, you will become more familiar with the various conventions of the various periods of the theater. By acknowledging them and by accepting them, your involvement in the plays will be enhanced.

THE STRUCTURE
OF A PLAY

If you've ever seen a play performed, you know it is essential that, very early in the play, *you know what is going on*. You need to know when and where the scenes are taking place, the relationships of the characters to one another, what happened to the characters *before* the play began, and what is happening to them now. If you are lost, if you are confused, if you cannot follow these "facts" of the play, you will become frustrated, and you may leave the world of the play.

This early part of the play, which *tells you what is going on*, is called the *exposition* part. The first act of a long play is usually expository—that is, it must explain things to you and involve you in the story. As is true of the entire play, the success of the exposition part depends on the dialogue and stage directions.

EXERCISE: EXPOSITION

Read the first act of a long play (three to five acts) you have never read before. In a short paper (500 words), discuss how this act is used as exposition. Consider how it tells you:

1 What happened before the play began.
2 Who the characters are.
3 Their relationships to one another.
4 What the conflicts of the play will be.

Make sure that your points are supported by specific examples and quotes from the play.

102

Then, react to the first act: Does the information it provides intrigue you and make you want to read on? Is the exposition confusing, and do you feel frustrated?

CHARACTERS AND CONFLICT

Like the short story, plays have

1 A protagonist: the character(s) faced with a conflict
2 An antagonist: the character(s) or element(s) that represent the conflict.

Fairly early in the play, the protagonist and antagonist are introduced, and the point of conflict is revealed. Soon, as in the short story, the conflict becomes *complicated* in key scenes, and the tension builds. When the play reaches its highest point of tension, its moment of greatest conflict, and you ask "What will happen?" or "How will this all turn out?" you are at the *climax* of the play. And, as in the short story, the loose ends of the conflict are pulled together in the *solution* or *denouement* section. Reading a play, then, you should search for this pattern. Ask yourself:

Who is the protagonist?
Who (or what) is the antagonist?
Where is the point at which the conflict begins?
What scenes complicate the conflict?
What is the climax?
How is the conflict resolved?

As you answer these questions, you are collecting the specific facts needed to determine a *theme* for the play. As in the case of the short story, the theme can be derived from the facts of the conflict. Again, *the theme is a general statement, a one-sentence expression of the point, the central idea, of the play.* And, as in the case of the short story, your interpretation of the facts of the play may differ from another person's interpretation. Thus, you may come up with a different theme. Both your interpretation and someone else's may be valid, as long as both are based on the facts, the specific parts of the play. You use the *specifics* of the play to arrive at a *general* statement of theme.

EXERCISE: CHARACTER IN KEY SCENES—
ANTON SCHILL IN *THE VISIT*

Characters involved in significant conflict, protagonists and antagonists, deal with conflict in a series of dramatic scenes. To understand how character is revealed and developed in key scenes, do the following exercise.

Read Durrenmatt's *The Visit*. Then go back, and reread the first act, from the beginning *up to* the entrance of Claire Zachanassian into Gullen. Then reread the end of the second act, when Anton Schill goes to the train station to escape the town. As you reread, focus on the character of Anton Schill: What is he like in the early part? What is he like in the crucial scene at the train station? Has he changed? If so, how?

Then, supply the detail from these two scenes that support the general statements below. Put the detail in sentences. Use at least one direct quote from the scene in each list of detail. This focus on the details of the scene is a way of analyzing both character and the development of conflict in key scenes.

I As the play opens, Schill is ready to flatter and manipulate Claire to obtain her wealth.

Detail A: _____

Detail B: _____

Detail C: _____

Direct quote from scene: _____

_____

II His memories of the love affair are pleasant; he admired Claire.

Detail A: _____

Detail B: _____

Detail C: _____

Direct quote from scene: _____

_____

III He is dishonest about his part in the end of the affair and ready to accept others' dishonesty in their flattery of him.

Detail A: _____

Detail B: _____

Detail C: _____

Direct quote from scene: _____

_____

IV At the railroad station, Schill is terrified of the townspeople.

Detail A: _____

Detail B: _____

Detail C: _____

Direct quote from scene: _____

_____

V He is pitiful in his cowardice and fear.

Detail A: _____

Detail B: _____

Detail C: _____

Direct quote from scene: _____

_____

VI Then, suddenly, Schill becomes a new person.

Detail A: _____

Detail B: _____

Detail C: _____

Direct quote from scene: _____

_____

EXERCISE: CHARACTER IN KEY SCENES—ANY PLAY

Focusing on one significant character as he or she appears in two significant scenes is one way to explore character and conflict in a play. To develop your ability to select the details that reveal character and conflict in key scenes, do the following exercise.

Select any play you have read, and review two key scenes that involve one important character. As you review, focus on what each scene tells about that character and his or her conflicts. Then, in complete sentences, create general statements that summarize the traits and attitudes of the character in each of the scenes. Below each general statement, list (in sentences) the details of the scene that support your general statement. In each list of detail, include one direct quote from the scene.

Traits and Attitudes of Character in Early Scene

I Trait/attitude one: _____

_____

Detail A: _____

Detail B: _____

Detail C: _____

Direct quote from scene: _____

_____

II Trait/attitude two: _____

_____

Detail A: _____

Detail B: _____

Detail C: _____

Direct quote from scene: _____

_____

Traits and Attitudes of Character in Later Scene

III Trait/attitude one: _____

_____

Detail A: _____

Detail B: _____

Detail C: _____

Direct quote from scene: _____

_____

IV Trait/attitude two: _____

_____

Detail A: _____

Detail B: _____

Detail C: _____

Direct quote from scene: _____

_____

EXERCISE: IDENTIFYING THEME

To help you arrive at a theme statement for a play, try this exercise, which focuses on identifying those elements that can lead you to a theme.

Review any play you have read, concentrating on identifying the protagonist, antagonist, conflict, and key scenes that develop the conflict—the elements that will lead you to a theme. Then, complete the process below.

Play: _____

Author: _____

   Step 1: Identify the protagonist(s): _____

   Step 2: Identify the antagonist(s): _____

   Step 3: Identify the conflict:

_____ vs.
(what the protagonist represents)

_____ .
(what the antagonist represents)

   Step 4: Identify two or more key scenes in which the conflict develops significantly. Briefly describe each scene.

First key scene: _____

_____

_____

Second key scene: _____

_____

_____

Additional key scene(s): _____

_____

_____

_____

_____

_____

   Step 5: How is the conflict resolved? Briefly describe: _____

_____

_____

_____

Step 6: In a complete sentence, write a theme for the play. Make it a general statement based on the specifics you have noted.

Theme: _____

_____

GREEK TRAGEDY AND ITS INFLUENCE

The history of Western theater began thousands of years ago in one of the theater's golden ages, the period of Greek drama. From this period come not only standards of what a tragedy should be, but concepts of what a comedy should contain. The golden age of Greek theater is called the classical period, since the plays of this time became the *classics*, the standard by which to compare other, later works.

If only because so much later drama is influenced by Greek theater, you need to understand its characteristics. Greek tragedy initiated dramatic techniques and elements that are still used today as they continue to influence countless playwrights. Understanding the characteristics of Greek theater will help you to appreciate the classics, works that survive today because they present conflicts and themes relevant to any time period.

Greek tragedy evolved from religious rituals that stressed the sacrificial nature of human life and the inevitability of death. Tragedy, then, is concerned with the pain of human existence, and with attempts to deal with that pain. It pits the individual against forces so large as to be invincible: against destiny, chance, the gods; and yet it convinces the audience of the nobility of such an uneven struggle. It pits the individual against a part of himself or herself and yet convinces us to admire the person who contributes to his or her own destruction. It is a drama of contradictions, puzzles, and riddles, for it focuses on the eternal questions of how one must live in a world of suffering, how one can act freely in a world circumscribed by limitations of self and fate. Perhaps because it poses no easy answers to these enduring questions, tragedy, in its richness, depth, and complexity, has endured and has evoked some deep response from each new generation.

Tragedy fascinated a great thinker of its own time. The philosopher Aristotle was also an early student of literary theory. In a work called *The Poetics*, he carefully examined existing Greek tragedies to see what common elements helped create their impact and convey their meaning. The following terms that can be applied to an analysis of Greek tragedy are mainly derived from Aristotle's work in *The Poetics*.

A tragedy, in dramatic terms, is much more than a play with a sad ending. That is, in order to be classed as a tragedy, a play must first be *serious in theme* and must focus on a *tragic hero* (a term which can apply to a male or female character). The following must be true of the hero: During the play, the hero's situation must change from good to bad; he or she must experience a shift in circumstances that is a dramatic one. That shift is called the *tragic reversal*.

So that the reversal has the greatest impact, the hero must be *of high position* (king, princess, military leader) so that he or she falls far—from one of the highest in the land to one of the lowest.

So that the audience cares about the hero, he or she must be *essentially a good person*. If the hero were essentially wicked and fell, the audience would feel he or she deserved to fall and would neither sympathize with the hero nor think very deeply about the play. Instead, the hero must be someone whose basic goodness leads the audience to question his or her seemingly disproportionate suffering, and thus to question the meaning of suffering in the world.

Yet although the hero must be essentially a good person, his or her suffering cannot be presented as entirely unfair, arbitrary, or accidental. The character's fall must, in large part, be brought on by the character's own action, by an exercise of *free will*. Fate (destiny, chance, accident, coincidence, the work of the gods, anything beyond a person's control) can help bring on the fall, but there must also be an element of free will involved, or the fall is pathetic, not tragic.

As you consider the above specifications, you may form a question: What would a good person do that is so awful it could bring on a tragic fall? The answer reveals the beauty and complexity of tragedy, for the hero is not perfect; he or she is not a saint. The hero is, like the audience, very human, and, like all people, has flaws. In particular, the hero has one *tragic flaw* (the Greek word for this is *hamartia*) that brings on the fall. This flaw may be greed, or ambition, or jealousy, or anger, or a desire for revenge. Quite often in the Greek plays, the flaw is an incredible arrogance, an overwhelming egotism that blinds the hero to reality, a flaw the Greeks called *hubris*. Since the Greeks believed strongly in the power of their gods, the hero is often punished by the gods when arrogance causes him or her to insult the gods or violate their laws. In this way, the existence of the gods is confirmed by the hero's fall. The gods' involvement in the hero's life shows that the gods do exist and that life is not just a series of accidents. Human actions have consequences; human life has meaning in another world, the world of the gods, when the gods can punish humans.

As the gods punish the hero, a paradoxical movement often takes place. The hero who fell because of some inner flaw, perhaps through pride, is now humbled by pain, reduced to the nothingness of an outcast or obliterated in death and yet is, at the same time, made more noble. The hero finds new values and new identity in suffering and is raised, in spirit, to a higher plane. Facing his or her error, the hero rises in the fall.

The self-confrontation necessary to acknowledge one's flaws is another common element in Greek tragedy. At some point, the hero must admit to his or her flaw. This point in the drama is called *the recognition*.

Another central moment, when the hero's situation shifts, decisively, from good to bad, is called the *tragic reversal*. Smaller reversals may foreshadow the major one; for example, certain actions intended to bring good, instead bring evil.

There are also certain conflicts (and related symbols and images) that recur in Greek tragedies. They include:

Fate vs. free will: Throughout a Greek tragedy, a character's situation will often be blamed on fate; that is, the hero or others will deny that the hero is responsible for what happens to him or her. The gods, or chance, will instead be blamed. Often, the role of fate will, indeed, be great, but remember: *Without some exercise of free will on the part of the hero, there can be no tragedy.*

Blindness vs. sight: People can become so blinded by ego that they can no longer see reality, and this blindness may, indeed, afflict the proud characters of Greek tragedy. Blindness and sight (including blind characters who can "see" more of the reality than the sighted ones) are prominent images and symbols in the language of tragedy, for they enhance an important theme.

Ignorance vs. knowledge: Ignorance is a kind of blindness, and ignorance can prevent people from acting the way they would if they had knowledge of certain things.

When the audience possesses knowledge that the hero (or another character) does not, there is a situation filled with *dramatic irony*. And when ignorance limits the characters' choices, it restricts their freedom. And in the connection between ignorance, blindness, and lack of freedom, you can see how all these conflicts—fate vs. free will, blindness vs. sight, and ignorance vs. knowledge—may be linked in the complexity of one play.

One other term linked to Greek tragedy is a significant one: *catharsis*. Catharsis is an experience which the audience undergoes; it is *the release of emotions* which the tragedy brings on. As the audience watches a good man fall, it feels a mix of emotions: *pity* for the hero and *terror* both for him and for itself. For if sorrow and pain can come so suddenly to an important and powerful person, it could happen in anyone's life.

Greek tragedy builds to this catharsis, to this release of emotions, and it is important to understand that the catharsis is a healthy, cleansing experience for the audience. The catharsis is a shared expression of human emotion, an outpouring of compassion and an acknowledgment of the deepest fears—a release that keeps people in touch with their own human feelings.

Perhaps the most puzzling quality of tragedy is the essential optimism of its view of the world. For thousands of years, audiences have sought, and critics have analyzed, the *positive experience of tragedy.*

Tragedy pays tribute to ideals. That is, it ultimately presents the world, not in its shabby reality, *not as it is, but as it should be.* It shows characters who believe in something enough to die for it, who make choices based on ideals; it shows the gods concerned enough about the individual man to punish him when he is wrong or to offer him spiritual rewards when he is noble. Tragedy, above all, is set in a world where events have meaning, where there is some moral order, where the individual man matters and can affect the world, and where a spiritual force cares about that world.

DRAMATIC CONVENTIONS OF GREEK TRAGEDY

You were already introduced to one convention of Greek tragedy—all the roles were played by men. There are certain other conventions of Greek tragedy.

Masks

Greek dramas were often staged in huge amphitheatres, before crowds of thousands. The acoustics were excellent, but the size of the theater made it hard for some in the audience to see the expressions on the actors' faces. To intensify these expressions and to convey them to a large audience, masks were worn by the actors.

Death and Violence

Although the plots of Greek tragedies are filled with violence and death, the Greeks did not believe in actually depicting the acts of death and violence on stage. Rather, such scenes are described as having taken place elsewhere, the descriptions being enough to stimulate the imagination and convey the sense of horror and doom.

The Greek Chorus

In Greek tragedy, there is a group of characters (fifteen members) who speak in unison and who have a leader (called Choragos) who says certain lines alone. The action of the play develops through an alternating pattern of a dramatic scene and a choral recitation. The chorus, which evolved from the groups of singers and dancers used in ritual religious dramas, moved in a slow and graceful dance as it recited its lines, the first part of the chorus chanting the *strophe* part of the recitation, the second part chanting the *antistrophe.*

The members of the chorus represent a contingent of townspeople, often respected citizens, who are present in the key scenes of the play as well as in choral interludes. The chorus functions in several ways:

1 It provides exposition.

2 It reacts to and evaluates the actions of the main characters as concerned observers would.

3 It provides interludes (when the main characters are offstage) of commentary, plot summary, and plot advancement.

4 It makes important theme statements.

Because the chorus fills such important functions, you must pay particular attention to its lines in the play. Often, it's the chorus that states the message of the play most carefully, or that foreshadows that message.

The Unities

Greek drama observed the rules of the three unities:

Unity of time: Although the play may make extensive reference to past events, the action of the play takes place in one day.

Unity of plot: A tragedy focuses on one plot.

Unity of place: The settings of the play are limited to those places a character could travel in one day.

The unities obviously unify or "tighten up" the tragedy. The concentration on one plot intensifies that plot; the complete reversal of a man's status in one short day increases the impact of the fall, as does the sense of suffocation created by a limited setting.

Greek tragedies can be analyzed like any other literary work. They, too, contain a protagonist (the hero) involved in a conflict with an antagonist, and the resolution of that conflict conveys some meaning. And the foreshadowing, irony, images, and symbols of the play enhance that meaning. Tragedies express themes, and careful analysis reveals these themes.

EXERCISE: THE CHORUS

This exercise will increase your awareness of the functions of the chorus. To do the following, first read either *Oedipus Rex* or *Antigone* by Sophocles. Below, use direct quotes from the play to show the chorus fulfilling each function.

1 The chorus provides exposition.

Direct quote: _____

_____

_____

_____

_____

_____

2 The chorus reacts to and/or evaluates the actions of the main characters.

Direct quote expressing such reaction and/or evaluation:

_____

_____

_____

_____

3 The chorus provides interludes (when the main characters are offstage) of commentary or plot summary, or plot advancement.

Direct quote showing the chorus commenting on events, or summarizing them, or explaining what happened between scenes: _____

_____

_____

_____

_____

_____

4 The chorus makes theme statements.

Direct quote of a theme statement: _____

_____

_____

_____

EXERCISE: DRAMATIC MOMENTS

This exercise will familiarize you with significant elements of Greek tragedy; it requires that you have already read *Oedipus Rex* or *Antigone*. Using specific lines from the play (direct quotes), identify these dramatic moments:

Moment of recognition: _____

_____

_____

_____

_____

Moment of reversal: _____

_____

_____

_____

_____

Find a line or lines which contain an example of dramatic irony: _____

_____

_____

_____

_____

_____

EXERCISE: THE TRAGIC HERO

This exercise will help you to recognize the characteristics of the tragic hero. It requires that you have already read *Oedipus* or *Antigone*. Select one character from either play who you think fits the qualifications of the tragic hero. Then supply the evidence required below.

_____ meets many of the requirements for a tragic hero.
(character's name)

1 He/she is basically a good person, with good intentions.

Evidence (a direct quote from the play): _____

_____

_____

_____

Evidence (an explanation in your own words of how the lines above show goodness or good intentions): _____

_____

_____

2 He/she has a tragic flaw, which is _____.

Evidence (a direct quote from the play): _____

_____

_____

Evidence (an explanation in your own words of how the lines above reveal the flaw): _____

_____

_____

3 The hero's fall is at least partly caused by his/her own free will.

Evidence (a direct quote from the play): _____

_____

_____

Evidence (an explanation in your own words of how the lines above indicate the exercise of free will): _____

_____

_____

4 The hero's situation is drastically changed during the play.

Evidence of initial situation (a specific detail from the play that describes the hero's status; attitude of others toward the hero): _____

_____

Evidence of situation at end of play (a specific detail from the play that describes the hero's status; attitude of others toward the hero): _____

_____

ANALYZING CHARACTER IN DRAMA

The analysis of a central character in a play is a common writing assignment when you study drama. To write this kind of essay, you need to focus on the same components of literary analysis you do for any essay about literature: a clear and manageable thesis, a clear structure organized around topic sentences developed by specifics from the literature, an effective conclusion.

When you write about a character in Greek tragedy, you might find it helpful to review the qualities of the tragic hero as a way of approaching the assignment. That is, consider, first of all, whether the character to be analyzed meets the requirements of the hero: Is he or she a good person—of high rank? Does he or she fall far? Is his or her fall due in some measure to a tragic flaw? etc. This approach may help you to organize your essay.

To answer the above questions, you will, of course, have to delve back into the play and find specific examples and direct quotes from the play. This material will be the supporting detail that makes up most of your essay. After you organize it into categories, you can form topic sentences for each category. Then you can compose a thesis sentence that sums up the character to be discussed. Make sure that sentence is one you can support, in detail, throughout your essay.

EXERCISE: ANALYZING CREON IN *ANTIGONE*

Write a short character analysis of the character of Creon in *Antigone*. To do this, first reread the play, looking for specific lines and incidents that reveal Creon's character. Underline these lines and examples as you read. Creon may be considered the protagonist of the play, so, as you read, you can be looking for character traits that fit Creon into the mold of the tragic hero.

Keep in mind that you will have to write a thesis statement that sums up the character and that can be supported by detail from the play.

After you have reread the play, you will need to write a complete outline of your essay, with a clear, workable thesis and with topic sentences (for each paragraph) that summarize some aspect of Creon's character as it is revealed in the play.

To get you started, here is a partial outline of such an essay.

EXERCISE: COMPLETING A SAMPLE OUTLINE

This outline contains a thesis sentence and topic sentences for each major part of a character sketch of Creon. It also contains one section of detail developing one topic sentence.

To complete the outline, fill in the remaining detail. Use the direct quotes and examples from the play you noted as you reread. When you come to the concluding paragraph, be sure to restate your thesis (in new words). Write your detail in complete sentences.

Partial Outline for a Character Analysis of Creon in Antigone

I Lead—in

    Thesis statement: Although Creon genuinely cares for the city he rules, his inflexibility, shown in his refusal to listen to counsel, leads to his tragic fall.

topic sentence

II Initially, Creon sincerely tries his best to restore order to a troubled, war—torn Thebes.

    A As he calls the elders of the city to him, Creon stresses his love for the city.

sentences of detail

    B This love is more important to him than his love of friends.

direct quotes supporting topic sentence

    C He says, ''no enemy of the state/Could be my friend'' since ''Our country bears us all securely onward,/And only while it sails a steady course/Is friendship possible.''

    D His edict also shows that he is willing to place love of country above another love——love of family.

    E When he decrees that his own nephew's body is to be left unburied, he is showing that obedience to law is more important than duty to family.

    F Creon is faced with a kingdom in chaos, so he chooses to ''guard the greatness of the city'' by imposing harsh laws with no exceptions.

sentences of detail

G He truly believes that both the leader and his people should place the common good above personal good.

direct quotes

H He says that ''whoever/Feels in his heart affection for his city/Shall be rewarded both in life and death.''

I Creon, in his edict about Polyneices, is trying to live up to his own definition of a good man.

III But his efforts show a rigidity of belief; he places too much stress on obedience to his will.

sentences of detail

A

B

direct quotes
supporting topic
sentence

C

D

E

F

G

topic sentence

IV Creon, insulted by the rebellion of a girl, refuses to understand her motives; he refuses to listen to her side of the conflict.

A

sentences of detail

B

C

direct quotes
supporting topic
sentence

D

E

F

G

topic sentence

V Creon is equally resistant to the good counsel of his own
son, Haemon, who tells him what the people of Thebes are
too afraid to say.

A

sentences of detail

B

C

direct quotes
supporting topic
sentence

D

E

F

G

topic sentence

VI Even the blind prophet, Tiresias, cannot convince Creon that he must open his mind and change his ways.

A

sentences of detail,

B

C

D

direct quotes
supporting topic
sentence

E

F

G

topic sentence

VII Eventually, Creon must confront his own mistakes and change his ways, but he does so too late.

A

sentences of detail

B

C

direct quotes
supporting topic
sentence

D

E

F

G

concluding paragraph   VIII Although Creon, in part, blames fate for his suffering,

he must face his own role in bringing disaster to himself

and the city.

add three to   A
five sentences of detail

B

C

restate thesis   D
sentences in different
words

E

Once you have written a complete, organized outline, you can write the rough draft of the character analysis. In the draft, you can begin to combine some of the short sentences of detail into smoother sentences; you can begin thinking about effective transitions within and between paragraphs. You can write an effective lead-in to your thesis sentence, mentioning the name of the play and its author. Later, you can revise that draft, preparing the final essay.

EXERCISE: ANALYZING ANTIGONE

Many readers think that Antigone is the protagonist, of *Antigone*. Considering her as the protagonist, write a short (about 500–750 words) analysis of Antigone. Construct your own outline first.

COMPARING AND CONTRASTING IN A CHARACTER ANALYSIS: ANTIGONE AND ISMENE

One effective way to analyze character is to compare and contrast two characters in the same literary work. Such a comparison contrast can be the basis for an entire essay, or it may be a part of a larger essay.

Whether you write an entire essay of comparison and contrast or use this technique as part of an essay, you must keep your comparison/contrast *clear, smooth, and logical. Appropriate transitions* will help you to do this. These transitions (words, phrases, or sentences) signal a major point of comparison/contrast without announcing it.

Of course, before you consider transitions, you must select the detail that will be connected. The first step in writing any comparison/contrast is gathering that detail from the work to be discussed.

Below, detail from Antigone is grouped into two lists: similarities (comparisons) between Antigone and her sister Ismene, and differences (contrasts) between them. First, take a good look at these lists. Then, examine the paragraphs that follow them, paragraphs that combine the detail, with *transitions*.

List 1: Similarities between Antigone and Ismene

Antigone and Ismene share a family history of tragic events.
Their father Oedipus killed his father and married his mother.
Their mother Jocasta hanged herself.
Their brothers killed each other in civil war.
Children of incest, they feel they are doomed and alone in the world.
As Antigone says to Ismene, "I cannot imagine any grief/That you and I have not gone through."
Antigone reverences the dead and the laws of the gods.
Ismene reverences them also, saying, "They mean a great deal to me."
Antigone loves her family, saying, "It is my nature to join in love."
Ismene, too, loves her family; for example, she tells Antigone, "What do I care for life when you are dead?"

List 2: Differences between Antigone and Ismene

Antigone is very strong-willed.

Of her act of rebellion, she says, "Creon is not strong enough to stand in my way."

Ismene is weak; she says, "I am helpless. I must yield to those in authority."

Ismene is also a realist, saying, "Impossible things should not be tried at all."

Antigone is the idealist, saying, "I am doing only what I must" and, if her attempt is a failure and leads to death, "It will not be the worst of deaths—death without honor."

Antigone is willing to act and live and die alone; she is independent.

Ismene needs others—for approval and support.

Ismene is ready to share the blame for Antigone's crime because she is afraid to go on living without her sister.

Sample Comparison and Contrast Paragraphs

After you gather detail, you can organize it into smooth paragraphs. To do so, you need

1 To focus the detail with a topic sentence that summarizes the point of the paragraph.

2 To insert effective and appropriate transitions that show readers the links between ideas.

Below is a paragraph comparing Antigone and Ismene. Compare it to the original list and notice the topic sentence and the transitions.

topic sentence

transitions underlined

Antigone and Ismene share a tragic family background and a love for family and religion. Both women suffered when their father Oedipus realized he had killed his father and married his mother. Jocasta, the sisters' mother, killed herself, and their brothers killed each other in civil war. Children of incest, the two feel they are doomed and alone in the world. As Antigone says to her sister, ''I cannot imagine any grief/That you and I have not gone through.'' The two are also united in a love for their family and in reverence for religion. Antigone reverences her dead parents and brothers; her act of rebellion is an act of respect for her brothers and also for the gods. Similarly, Ismene says of the gods, ''They mean a great deal to me.'' Like Antigone, who says, ''It is my nature to join in love,'' Ismene is a loving person. Her love for her sister is seen in her words to Antigone, ''What do I care for life when you are dead?'' <u>The two sisters are linked</u> in bonds of love and sorrow.

Now take a good look at the sample paragraph contrasting Antigone and Ismene. Again, note the topic sentence and the transitions, and compare this paragraph to the original list of detail it was written from.

topic sentence

transitions underlined

<u>The essential differences between Antigone and Ismene are the differences between a strong and a weak personality and can be seen in their reactions to Creon's edict.</u> When Creon decrees the desecration of her brother's corpse, Antigone is very strong-willed, saying, ''Creon is not strong enough to stand in my way.'' She will defy his law and bury her brother. <u>In contrast</u>, Ismene is fearful and weak, for she feels ''helpless--I must yield to those in authority.'' Ismene's fear makes her a realist; she believes that ''Impossible things should not be tried at all.'' Antigone, <u>on the other hand</u>, is not so fearful of consequences and is an idealist, saying she is doing ''only what I must.'' <u>Unlike</u> her sister, Antigone is not concerned with the impossibility of succeeding in her attempt to bury her brother. If it fails and leads to her death, ''It will not be the worst of deaths--death without honor.'' In burying her brother, Antigone is not afraid of acting alone; she is independent. <u>But</u> her sister needs others for approval and support. Thus, while Ismene's realistic fears of the consequences keep her from sharing in Antigone's crime, her fear of loneliness makes her want to share Antigone's punishment. Ismene is afraid of living alone after Antigone's

death, again showing the difference between her and her

stronger sister.

Using Transitions in Comparison/Contrast

As you can see, certain words and phrases work well as transitions when you want to compare or contrast. Here are two short lists.

Transitions for Comparing (showing likenesses)

Like _____,
Just as _____, so, too, _____
Similarly
Likewise
Also
Both
The two share
They are united in
Not only _____ but also _____

Transitions for Contrasting (showing differences)

Unlike
In contrast
But
However
On the other hand
While _____,

EXERCISE: COMPARISON/CONTRAST PARAGRAPHS

Now that you've seen sample comparison/contrast paragraphs, try your own. The following are two lists of detail from *Antigone*. The first list can be the basis for a comparison paragraph; the second can be used to write a contrast paragraph.

Be aware that neither list has a topic sentence to focus the detail. You need to *write a topic sentence for each list, to focus your paragraph*. Also, *remember to use appropriate transitions*.

List 1: Similarities between Creon and Antigone

Creon loves his family.
Antigone loves her family.
Creon places love of the state above love of family.

Antigone places love of the gods above love of living family members.
The chorus says Antigone is "headstrong, deaf to reason! She has never learned to yield."
Tiresias tells Creon, "You should be able to yield for your own good."
Creon later says he has been "rash and foolish."
Haemon tells his father, "It is not reason never to yield to reason."
His words apply to Creon.
The words echo the Chorus' judgement of Antigone.

List 2: Differences between Antigone and Creon

Creon values the laws of the state above everything else.
He says, "Anarchy, anarchy! Show me a greater evil!"
Antigone believes that a law like the King's is not valid if it violates religious laws.
She says Creon's law "was not God's proclamation."
Creon believes no religious honor is due a dead enemy like Polyneices.
Antigone believes "these honors are due all the dead."
Creon eventually admits his errors, saying, "I have been rash and foolish."
Antigone dies believing she is right.
She goes to the cave, saying, "I have done no wrong./I have not sinned before God."
Creon changes his attitudes during the course of the play.
Antigone remains constant in her beliefs.

A Note on Comparing and Contrasting

The examples and exercises just presented all group similarities and differences into separate paragraphs.

This division is one way to compare and/or contrast. But you can also combine similarities and differences within the same paragraph, as long as your structure and transitions are logical and clear.

By the same principle, an entire paper of comparison/contrast need not be split in half, with similarities in one half, differences in the other half. You could also split the essay another way: You could discuss one character in the first half, the second character in the second half. In each case, you would, of course, have to tie the two halves together in both the introduction and conclusion of the essay.

Another way to structure a comparison/contrast essay is to combine the things compared throughout. This is called a point-by-point structure. Here you organize by a point (or topic) that relates to both things compared. Directly below, you'll see more about the point-by-point structure.

Worth remembering here is that *the structure you choose for comparing and contrasting is up to you: pick what works best for your topic, what seems logical and easy to follow.*

EXERCISE: COMPLETING A SAMPLE COMPARISON/CONTRAST OUTLINE

Below is a skeleton outline for a complete short essay comparing and contrasting Antigone and Ismene. It follows a *point-by-point structure*. That is, it is organized around topics relevant to both characters being analyzed. As you find the detail to develop the topic sentences of the outline, you'll find you may be combining similarities and differences in the same paragraph (if both similarities and differences help support the topic sentence).

In this skeleton outline, you have

Thesis sentence
Topic sentences
One list of detail to develop one topic sentence.

You fill in the rest by giving examples and direct quotes from the play.

Sample Outline: Comparing/Contrasting Ismene and Antigone
Point-by-Point Structure

I Thesis statement: While both Antigone and Ismene are capable of great love, the objects of that love and their ways of expressing love reveal sisters who are very different.

II As the play begins, the sisters reveal that each cares deeply for the other and each is unafraid to trust the other.

A They meet to share their grief over their recent loss of two brothers and to remember earlier losses.

B Antigone's first words in the play call Ismene ''dear sister.''

C Antigone is close enough to Ismene to confide her plans for rebellion.

D Antigone explains to Ismene that she feels compelled to do ''only what I must.''

E Ismene is close enough to her sister to challenge her deepest beliefs, saying, ''Impossible things should not be tried at all.''

F The sisters cannot understand one another, but they do love one another.

III While they love one another and also their family, the sisters differ in what else they value.

A

B

C

D

E

F

Each sister expresses her deepest values in her own way:
Antigone, through activity; Ismene, through submission
and surrender.

A

B

C

D

E

F

VI Ultimately, both sisters prefer death to a life they feel
is intolerable.

A

B

C

D

E

F

VII Antigone and Ismene are women trapped in a world of pain, sustained by deep love, reacting to conflict in different ways.

WRITING ABOUT TECHNIQUES IN DRAMA

Many of the techniques used in short story can be used in drama as well. Playwrights use the same techniques of foreshadowing, images, symbols, and irony that authors of short stories use. They may also rely on such techniques as dramatic irony and, as in the case of the short story, techniques are used to enhance and underscore theme.

In *Antigone*, for example, there are many images (patterns of description) related to inflexibility or rigidity. These images are connected to both Creon and Antigone, thus linking the characters in this pattern of description. If you consider why these images are associated with both characters, you may discover another link between the images and the theme: things (and people) that are inflexible can break easily at the first assault; they do not bend in conflict. Rigid people do not give in to others' pressure; they do not open themselves to others' advice. Both Creon and Antigone, inflexible people, rigid in their attitudes, are broken in the play.

Similarly, *Oedipus* relies on many images of blindness and sight, ranging from a character who is physically blind but who "sees" the future, to accusations that Oedipus cannot or will not see, to Oedipus' physical blindness after he has "seen" his crime. Since blindness can be connected to ignorance, and since this play is about one man's insistence on *knowing*, at whatever cost, you can again see a linking of image, character, and theme.

EXERCISE: IMAGES IN *ANTIGONE*

To familiarize yourself with recognizing techniques in a play, do this exercise. It requires that you have already read *Antigone*.

Survey *Antigone*, looking for specific lines that contain images of rigidity, inflexibility, or stubbornness related to either Antigone or Creon. Place these lines, as supporting evidence, below the general statement provided. (The general sentence connects these specific images to a significant theme of the play.) Then put each quote in context, explaining who says the lines, to whom, and/or about whom, and at what point in the play are they said.

General statement: Images of rigidity and inflexibility, connected to both Antigone and Creon, link the two in their dangerous refusal to bend or take counsel in times of conflict.

Example (direct quote from the play): _____

_____

_____

Context: _____

_____

Example (direct quote from the play): _____

_____

_____

Context: _____

_____

Example (direct quote from the play): _____

_____

_____

Context: _____

_____

EXERCISE: IMAGES IN *OEDIPUS*

To familiarize yourself with recognizing techniques in a play, try this exercise. It requires that you have already read *Oedipus*.

There are many images of sight and blindness in Oedipus. Survey the play, looking for lines that contain images of seeing or blindness (physical or emotional, deliberate or fated). Then use these lines as support for the general sentence below. (The general sentence links images to an important theme in the play.) Then put each quote in context, explaining who says the lines, and to whom, and/or about whom, and at what point in the play are they said.

General statement: Images of sight and blindness in *Oedipus* underscore one of the play's major concerns—the power and danger of seeing and knowing.

Example (quote from the play): _____

_____

_____

Context: _____

_____

Example (quote from the play): _____

_____

_____

Context: _____

_____

Example (quote from the play): _____

_____

_____

Context: _____

_____

WRITING A TECHNIQUES ESSAY

You can, with sufficient detail, write a short essay concentrating on the techniques of a play. To do so, be sure that your thesis links the use of these techniques to a specific theme of the play, and choose the specific examples of techniques so that they focus on reinforcing that theme.

EXERCISE: OUTLINING THE TECHNIQUES ESSAY

To help you get started on a short techniques analysis, you may want to complete the outline below, modifying it as your essay requires.

I Thesis statement: In _____, the techniques of
(name of play)

_____, _____, and
(first technique)   (second technique)

_____ help to reinforce the drama's theme
(third technique)

that _____.
(state theme in a complete sentence)

II _____ is used frequently and helps to _____.
(first technique)

_____.
(show how it relates to theme)

give examples,   A
including direct quotes,
of the techniques in   B
the play and relate to
theme   C

                         D

                         E

                         F

III _____ also enhances the idea of
(second technique)

_____.
(state theme—different words)

                         A

specific details of   B
technique, including
direct quotes, related   C
to theme
                         D

                         E

                         F

IV A third literary technique, _____, under-
(name it)

scores the theme of the play.

A

specific details of
technique, including
direct quotes, related
to theme

B

C

D

E

F

conclude: put thesis in
new words

V The use of _____, _____, and
(first technique)   (second technique)

_____ significantly develop the play's cen-
(third technique)

tral theme of _____ .
(Use a phrase here if you wish.)

WRITING A COMPLETE CRITICAL ANALYSIS OF TRAGEDY

Having examined character and technique, you are now ready to try a complete critical analysis of the play as a whole. You can analyze any Greek tragedy (or any play at all) using the same structure we used to write a critical analysis of a short story. Briefly review that structure:

1 The focus of your analysis is the *theme*, the *central idea* of the play. That idea must be expressed in a sentence, and that sentence becomes the *thesis statement* for your entire essay.

Remember that there is more than one possible theme for a literary work, and be aware that any theme statement that can be *adequately supported by evidence* from the play itself should be acceptable. The key to a good essay is presenting the facts of the play as support for your thesis. So, to explain and support your thesis, you must *look closely* at the characters, the conflict and its resolution, and the literary techniques.

2 After you introduce your essay and state your thesis, write a *short plot summary* (no more than two paragraphs) so that you won't be forced to identify characters and key incidents throughout the rest of the essay. The plot summary should not include interpretation of events; it requires little or no quotation from the work itself. It merely relates the sequence of events and the characters involved in these events.

3 Analyze the *protagonist(s)* of the play. In this section, discuss what the main character, faced with a conflict, is like. Support your points with specific references to the actions of the play. Quote liberally to develop your ideas. This section of your analysis will probably be longer than one paragraph.

4 Write a similar analysis of the *antagonist(s)* (who—or what—represents the conflict) of the play. Be aware that some aspect of the protagonist can act as the antagonist, and that there can be more than one antagonist. Again, use the specifics of the play for support, and quote freely. This section will probably be longer than one paragraph.

5 Trace and examine the *key scenes* of the play that *develop the conflict* between the protagonist and antagonist. This section is not the same as the plot summary: a plot summary *tells* the reader (very briefly) what happened; the key scenes analysis *shows* the reader how and why things happened, and what events mean in relation to theme. As a general rule, try to write *one developed paragraph* for each scene, and look for:

a scene in which the conflict begins
at least two scenes that complicate and develop the conflict
the climactic scene (In a tragedy, examine this scene to see if it includes a recognition and reversal.)
a scene that ties up loose ends and perhaps contains a theme statement.

In this section of your essay, you should be quoting, commenting on, and analyzing dialogue and action. This is the longest section of your analysis.

6 Identify and analyze the literary techniques that enhance the theme of the play. Try to write a paragraph on each separate technique; develop the paragraph with specific examples of the technique, and explain how that technique is related to the central ideas of the play. Look for symbols, images, foreshadowing, irony, and write developed paragraphs on at least two techniques. Quote freely and comment on the significance of the quotes.

7 Write a conclusion that *smoothly moves the reader from the parts of your analysis back to the whole*: the thesis statement. Restate that thesis in different words.

EXERCISE: COMPLETING A SAMPLE OUTLINE

To help you write the complete critical analysis, here is a partial outline for a complete critical analysis of *Antigone*. You will need to add the detail to this outline before you write the essay. This partial outline gives you the thesis, the topic sentences, and some transitions.

I Lead–in

transition sentence—
use as first sentence in
plot summary

 Thesis statement: An inflexible man can destroy himself and others.

II <u>Antigone</u> is the story of a man whose good intentions are not enough to save him from his arrogance.

A is topic sentence for
first paragraph of
plot—it will be the
second sentence in the
paragraph

1–6 are sentences of
plot summary

 A As the play begins, Creon, ruler of Thebes, must re–store order to a city racked by civil war.

  1

  2

  3

  4

  5

  6

B is topic sentence
for second paragraph
of plot summary

1–6 are sentences of
plot summary

 B Although others try to advise Creon of his error, he refuses to listen.

  1

  2

  3

  4

  5

  6

topic sentence for
analysis of protagonist

III Creon, the play's protagonist, is essentially a decent and caring family man and a dedicated ruler.

 A

sentences for one
paragraph of detail

B

C

D

E

F

G

topic sentence for
analysis of antagonist

IV But Creon is also his own worst enemy, for he is stubborn
and proud.

A

sentences for one
paragraph of detail

B

C

D

E

F

G

transition to key
scenes—**V** is the first
sentence, **A** the
second in the
paragraph. **A** is the
topic sentence for the
first key-scene
paragraph.

V In several key scenes, Creon's inability to grow and
change his attitudes bring him to his destruction.

A Antigone's act of rebellion infuriates Creon because
he perceives it solely as a threat to his authority.

1

sentences for one
paragraph analyzing
this scene

2

3

4

5

6

topic sentence for
second key scene

B Creon mistakes Haemon's concern for his father, thinking it is childish disobedience.

add sentences for one
paragraph of analysis

1

2

3

4

5

6

topic sentence for third
key scene

C Creon doesn't want to believe Tiresias's prophecy be-

cause it challenges his own attitudes and actions.

1

add sentences for one
paragraph of analysis

2

3

4

topic sentence for
climax

VI Finally, when it is too late, Creon sees the tragic con-

sequences of his own stubborn refusal to change and

adapt.

A

add sentences for one
paragraph of analysis

B

C

D

E

F

transition sentence to
techniques—**A** is the
topic sentence and the
second sentence of the
paragraph

VII The tragic consequences of man's inflexibility are rein-

forced through the play's images of rigidity and

foreshadowing of disaster.

A Images of inflexibility are connected to both Creon

and Antigone.

1

sentences of detail and analysis of images	2
	3
	4
	5
	6

topic sentence for paragraph on foreshadowing   B A sense of disaster is created through many references to the future and through warnings that good judgment and counsel are essential to man's happiness.

	1
sentences of detail and analysis of foreshadowing	2
	3
	4
	5
	6

restated thesis—work it smoothly into a concluding paragraph   VIII In its portrait of a decent man brought down by his own rigidity, _Antigone_ shows us the destructive force of the closed mind.

FROM OUTLINE TO ESSAY

Below is a sample critical analysis of *Antigone*. It follows the structure of the outline that preceded it. Note how the key ideas of the outline are developed through the use of specific details. Note also the use of transitions and the incorporation of direct quotes in the essay.

A Sample Critical Analysis of *Antigone*

lead-in

Most people admire a certain character trait often called <u>backbone</u>, an ability to stand by one's principles and to remain firm in one's beliefs in the face of criticism and conflict. While this trait may often be considered a virtue, an excess of such firmness can be dangerous, when firmness becomes inflexibility. This danger is demonstrated in the conflicts of <u>Antigone</u>, particularly in the character of Creon. Creon, a ruler with strong, deep beliefs, becomes rigid in abiding by his beliefs. As he clings to attitudes and be-

thesis

comes increasingly inflexible, he falls. And in his fall, we see that an inflexible man can destroy himself and others.

plot summary

<u>Antigone</u> is the story of a man whose good intentions are not enough to save him from his arrogance. As the play begins, Creon, ruler of Thebes, must restore order to a city racked by civil war. On one side of the conflict were Creon's forces, including his nephew Eteocles; on the other side, a group led by Creon's nephew Polyneices. In the battle, the brothers, Polyneices and Eteocles, killed one another. When the war is

plot summary

over and Creon is victorious, he decides to reassert his authority and restore order by calling for a full religious burial for Eteocles but forbidding any burial service for the rebel Polyneices. By issuing an edict against the burial of Polyneices, Creon is violating his city's religious beliefs, placing his law against the law of the gods. His edict is challenged by his niece, Antigone, sister of Eteocles and Polyneices, who feels that the laws of the gods and her love of her brother make it imperative for her to bury her brother. Antigone openly defies Creon's edict and is brought before him. Creon sentences her to die.

The consequences of Creon's actions are drastic. Although others try to advise Creon of his error, he refuses to listen. When Antigone tries to convince Creon that the laws of the gods have a higher value than his law, he becomes infuriated. Instead of heeding her argument, he accuses Antigone's sister Ismene of conspiracy in the crime. When Creon's son Haemon (who is engaged to Antigone) tries to warn Creon that his edict is unpopular with the people, Creon accuses his son of disloyalty and weakness. When Tiresias, the old blind prophet, warns Creon of the penalties of such a stubborn defiance of the gods, Creon accuses Tiresias of treason. Finally, when Tiresias predicts doom for Creon, Creon becomes afraid. He buries Polyneices and then goes to free Antigone. But he is too late: Antigone has hanged herself, Haemon first tries to kill his father and then kills himself, and Creon's wife, Eurydice, kills herself. Creon is left alone and broken.

transition

The story of Antigone is tragic not only because of these events, but because the man at the center of them is not a villain. Creon, the play's protagonist, is essentially a decent and caring family man and a dedicated ruler. He has been a father to his nieces, Antigone and Ismene, raising them as princesses, and allowing one to become betrothed to his son.

topic sentence

protagonist

As a ruler, he cares deeply for the stability of his city, placing the common good above all other considerations. He declares that ''Our country bears us all securely onward/And only while it sails a steady course/Is friendship possible.'' His decision to defile the body of Polyneices is made out of a passion for justice, for he believed Polyneices was ''Eager to drink deep of his kindred's blood,/Eager to drag us off to slavery.'' The traitor must be punished to demonstrate Creon's promise that the wicked never shall be awarded ''more approval than the just.'' In a country divided and bloodied, Creon seeks to restore peace and law, a noble ambition.

transition topic
sentence

antagonist

antagonist

But while Creon may have good intentions, he is also his own worst enemy, for he is stubborn and proud. We see his quick anger and rigidity surface when he first receives news that an unknown person has tried to bury Polyneices. When the chorus speculates, fearfully, that perhaps the gods attempted the burial, Creon is infuriated, calling the chorus ''old'' and ''senseless.'' He refuses to heed their suggestion that his edict is wicked, but instead creates a paranoid rationale for the act of disobedience, claiming that enemies have bribed the guards to bury the body. He declares that it is ''Inconceivable!'' that the gods should disapprove of his decree, thus linking his wishes to the gods' decisions, as if he were on the level of the gods. He even accuses the guard who informs him of the crime of being the criminal, and when the man talks of Creon's misjudgment, the words introduce a major theme of the play. Creon will continue to make the wrong judgments because he will not change his mind--or open it.

transition

In several key scenes, Creon's inability to grow and change his attitudes bring him to his destruction. In the first of these scenes, Antigone's act of rebellion angers Creon be-

topic sentence

cause he perceives it solely as a threat to his authority. He

first key scene

calls Antigone ''insolent,'' ''an evil-doer/Who, caught red-handed, glorifies the crime.'' He will not listen to her explanation for her act: her reverence for the gods, her love for both her brothers. He thinks only that ''if she . . . goes unpunished, I am no man--she is.'' Creon is as much angered by Antigone's open and unashamed attitude as he is by the act itself.

transition

Creon is next infuriated by a plea from his son. When Haemon

topic sentence

tries to get Creon to change his mind, Creon mistakes Haemon's concern for his father, thinking it is childish disobedience.

second key scene

Haemon hints that ''Some other's thought, beside your own, might prove/To be of value.'' He warns that the people of the city fear Creon and admire Antigone's bravery and virtue, and he warns that the man who believes he alone is right ''will be found/Empty when searched and tested.'' ''Let yourself change,'' he begs. But Creon's reaction is to call Haemon a ''woman's slave'' and to ask, angrily, ''Are men as old as I am to be taught/How to behave by men as young as he?'' He refuses to listen to his son.

transition

In a third encounter with someone who tries to advise him,

topic sentence

Creon again reacts angrily. Creon doesn't want to believe Tiresias's prophecy because it challenges his own attitudes

third key scene

and actions. Creon prefers to charge Tiresias with greed and treachery rather than heed his warning that ''you stand upon

the brink of ruin.'' This time, he refuses to listen to an <u>old</u>
man, not a young one, and again Creon speaks impulsively and
defensively. But, in this encounter, Creon finally begins to
recognize his error. He is fearful of Tiresias's power, acknowledging, ''never has he foretold/Anything that proved
false concerning Thebes.'' If Tiresias is indeed telling the
truth, Creon must change his stubborn course, or he is doomed.

topic sentence

climax

    Finally, when it is too late, Creon sees the tragic
consequences of his stubborn refusal to change and adapt. As
he carries the body of his son and hears of Eurydice's suicide, Creon admits, ''My folly slew my wife, my son./I know
not where to turn mine eyes./All my mistakes before me rise.''
He has lost a son who tried to kill him before turning the
sword on himself, he has lost a wife who died cursing him. he
has lost his niece, he has lost the respect of the city. He
wants only to die, for he has recognized the ''folly''--the
stubborn refusal to change--that destroyed him and those he
loved.

transition

topic sentence

**one technique—
images**

    The tragic consequences of such inflexibility are rein-
forced throughout the play by images of rigidity and
foreshadowing of disaster. Images of inflexibility are connected to both Creon and Antigone. Creon, confronting his
disobedient niece, warns her that self-willed people are
''the first to come to grief.'' ''The hardest iron,'' he
claims, ''Baked in the fire, most quickly flies to pieces,''
and the most unruly horse can be broken by ''a touch of the
curb.'' He cannot see that Antigone mirrors him in her stubbornness. Even when his son warns him not to be ''over-

rigid,'' Creon refuses to change. He cannot see himself in Haemon's analogy of trees that yield, surviving a winter flood, but those resisting perishing ''root and branch.'' Creon thinks of his city as ''tossed/By a tempestuous ocean,'' but he does not head Haemon's words that ''the mariner who never slackens/His taut sheet overturns his craft.''

transition topic sentence

second technique— foreshadowing

There are other warnings. A sense of disaster is created through many references to the future and through warnings that good judgment and counsel are essential to man's happiness. Early in the play, after Creon has first sentenced Antigone to die, the chorus notes that a good man can be deceived, that ''to one/Whom the gods madden, evil . . . Seems good.'' Haemon tells his father that the greatest gift the gods have sent to man is the gift of reason, but Creon continues to act irrationally. Tiresias tells Creon that ''Stubborn self-will incurs the charge of folly,'' but not until Tiresias predicts utter disaster for Creon does Creon become fearful and flexible. ''To yield is bitter,'' Creon says, ''But to resist, and bring/A curse upon my pride is no less bitter.''

foreshadowing

transition

conclusion

The curse comes, because Creon changes too late. He closed his mind to counsel for too long, and therefore he lost all that gave his life meaning and purpose. Although he was initially motivated by a genuine concern for his people, Creon allowed his rigid pride to doom him and those nearest to him. In its portrait of a decent man brought by his own rigidity, Antigone shows us the destructive force of the closed mind.

EXERCISE: AN ALTERNATIVE CRITICAL ANALYSIS OF *ANTIGONE*

While the sample outline and essay focused on Creon as the protagonist of *Antigone*, an alternative approach might be to write a critical analysis focusing on Antigone as the protagonist. You can use the same structure for the essay, beginning with a theme statement, then writing a short plot summary, analyzing protagonist and antagonist, then analyzing the meaning of key scenes, discussing techniques, and pulling it all together in a conclusion.

EXERCISE: THE ENDURING CONCERNS OF *ANTIGONE*

Greek tragedy is still read today for many reasons. One of these reasons is that it raises timeless questions and addresses conflicts common to many cultures. *Antigone*, for example, voices concerns not only of its time but of our own, such as the:

proper role of man in society
proper relationship of parent to child
divided loyalties of family members
demands of conscience vs. those of country
role of a good leader
role of religion in government

Write an essay (500 words or more) exploring how the play deals with one or more of these concerns, and then draw parallels between the topics as explored in the play and as reflected in twentieth century life.

THE INFLUENCE OF GREEK TRAGEDY

The power of Greek tragedy is evident not only in the survival of the plays themselves, but in the influence of the form on subsequent drama. In other historical periods, tragedy, based largely on the dramatic principles described by Aristotle, flourished. The most significant of these periods is the late Renaissance, the age of Shakespearean tragedy.

Shakespeare does not duplicate the form and conventions of Greek tragedy; he violates the unities often by using double plots (as in *King Lear*) and setting scenes in places distant from one another (as in *Othello*). His plays do not use an alternating rhythm of scene and chorus; instead, the action in a Shakespearean tragedy shifts from dramatic event to dramatic event, balanced occasionally by short moments of comic relief. In his use of the aside and the soliloquy, Shakespeare often heightens the sense of dramatic irony. Iago's soliloquies in Othello, for example, draw the audience into his net of evil to witness the calculated destruction of a good man.

While Shakespeare may modify the conventions of tragedy, he, like his Greek predecessors, is concerned with the fall of a good but flawed man, and his works, like the earlier plays, show us a world where ideas matter and are even worth dying for.

The influence of Greek tragedy continued, appearing in seventeenth-century France and the neoclassical age, particularly in the works of Jean Racine. Elements of tragedy appear in twentieth century plays, for the conflicts of man against fate or against himself or herself, the classic themes and questions, contain enduring appeal. Today some believe that tragedy cannot be written in our time, when many feel the individual is helpless and insignificant in a world without faith or meaning. Yet others, like Arthur Miller in *Death of a Salesman*, explore the contemporary tragedy of the ordinary man confronting his destiny and recognizing his flaws. While modern man may have lost the world view of the great ages of tragedy, he has not lost the universal desires and fears that fill tragedy, and so the form lives on in the early plays themselves and in those elements of later plays that borrow from the heritage of tragedy.

EXERCISE: MODERN PLAYS AND GREEK TRAGEDY

Although many believe that modern plays cannot fulfill all the requirements of Greek tragedy, a number of modern plays do utilize many of these elements. Read one of the plays listed below, or one assigned by your instructor, looking for ways that it uses the elements of Greek tragedy.

Then, in a comparison paper, discuss the elements of the modern play that are similar to those of Greek tragedy. And also discuss what purpose the similarities serve. That is, how do the characteristics of Greek tragedy add to the meaning of the modern play?

Your thesis statement should include two parts:

1 State the fact that the modern play is similar to Greek tragedy in many ways.

2 Summarize how the elements of Greek tragedy enhance the theme of the modern play.

For example, here is a sample thesis statement for a comparison essay on Greek tragedy and *Desire Under the Elms*: The elements of Greek tragedy present in *Desire Under the Elms* help to reveal the timelessness of the conflicts between fathers and sons.

Suggested Plays

Eugene O'Neill—*Desire Under the Elms*
Arthur Miller—*Death of a Salesman, A View From the Bridge*
Jean Anouilh—*Antigone*
Jean-Paul Sartre—*The Flies*

COMEDY—THE CLASSIC FORM

THE COMIC APPROACH

Like Greek tragedy, classic comedy evolved from religious rituals. But while tragedy grew from those rituals that stressed the inevitability of sacrifice and death, comedy grew from a celebration of life and growth. But both forms, tragedy and comedy, do more than present a story to entertain. They both show the world in a new light, challenging the audience to better understand that world. These two types of drama differ, however, in their approaches to such a challenge.

An eighteenth-century writer, Horace Walpole, drew an interesting distinction when he said, "The world is a comedy to those that think, a tragedy to those who feel." The difference he noted embodied a crucial distinction of attitude. It is a *difference of distancing*. As the audience follows the destiny of the tragic hero, it moves close to the character, becoming *emotionally involved*. As the audience enters the world of comedy, it steps back, becoming *amused observers*. In a tragedy, the audience feels pity for the suffering hero and shares the hero's pain; in a comedy, the audience may be more critical of the foolishness of the characters, an attitude that pulls the audience away from identification.

Tragedy explores the confrontation of the lone individual with his or her destiny and inner failings, a noble and serious struggle. Comedy presents people in conflict with their society or with their own foolishness, and the struggle has the potential to be equally difficult and serious. Yet the comic resolution is a triumph of life, not death, of *harmony* and *regeneration*.

Specific differences between comedy and tragedy may help to make their essential difference clearer. Tragedy involves a *reversal*, a movement of the protagonist *from security or happiness to pain*. Comedy, too, involves a reversal, but it is a *movement from frustration to success*. The *recognition* of tragedy becomes, in comedy, a *discovery* that helps the characters to avoid disaster: a revelation of mistaken identities, a resolving of misunderstandings. In addition, the passing of time works in opposing ways in the two dramatic forms. In the tragedy, *time becomes an enemy*, as pain comes inevitably or time runs out; in comedy, time is a friend, for there is a sense that enough time will resolve all conflicts. As time runs out in tragedy, the play ends in death and thus celebrates the meaningful death. As enough time elapses in a comedy, the play ends in reconciliations, in unions, in renewal.

A most significant difference between the forms involves their views of the ideal and the real. If classic tragedy *presents an ideal*, one worth dying for, or one the gods will uphold against man's violations, classic comedy *focuses on the real*. That is, classic comedy contrasts people's elevated notions, of themselves, of others, of institutions, with the way things and people really are.

In comedy, there is a *deflation of an elevated ideal*. Many characters in comedy are *types*, types the audience may recognize and laugh at because the characters' inflated opinion of themselves is so much at odds with the way others see them. The lovers of a comedy may be separated not because their families are at war over some great issue, or because the lovers themselves share a serious internal conflict, but because a greedy father wants his daughter to "marry money," or because the lovers are sulking over a silly quarrel.

In the classic comedy form, which evolved from the Greeks, through Shakespeare's comedies and on into the neoclassic period, there is often a love plot, maybe even a plot involving two pairs of lovers. But surrounding the plot is the real atmosphere of the comedy—the wit, irony, sarcasm, farce, slapstick—which exposes the world of the play for what it really is.

With such an emphasis on the split between the ideal and the real, comedy quite naturally often focuses on the disparity between *appearance* and *reality*. Characters, for example, are often something different from what they appear to be; plots hinge on mistaken identity, on concealed characters overhearing conversations, on hidden relationships. Language teases with puns and other double meanings. Things and people in comedy may not be what they appear to be; characters are rarely noble, but are more frequently all too human. Yet society, in its tolerance, makes room for most of the foolish and the flawed, and people find their place. Comedy teaches that there are ways to live, particularly with others, as well as things to die for.

In its stress on the reality of what life is, comedy most markedly differs from tragedy. Some people believe that, with its commitment to ideals and its belief in the capacity of the individual to reach for the ideal, tragedy is a more optimistic form. For although comedy can make an audience laugh or smile, it provokes amusement at people's vices: silliness, or egotism, or greed, or lust, or duplicity. It can create a vision of a world of fools, and, although it may end "happily," it may do little to stimulate a belief in the possibilities for human development.

Tragedy, on the other hand, may leave the audience drained, shaken by the misery it has witnessed. But it also shows the individual reaching beyond the ordinary, striving for a higher meaning and purpose in life. And, although the individual may be defeated and destroyed, the striving is genuine, even great.

Whichever form of drama you prefer, it is worth noting that both tragedy and comedy are visions of the same world, one where people are imperfect and disaster may come at any time. Both are attempts to express the endless conflict between things as they are and things as they could be.

EXERCISE: CHARACTERS AS TYPES—*TARTUFFE*

Comedy often contains characters who are easily recognizable types, that is, characters who represent follies or traits or quirks that many people might possess. Comic types often include the clever servant, the vain young man, the foolish lovers, the impulsive son or daughter, the clever manipulator. To develop your ability to recognize such types and to increase your awareness of their role in comedy, try the following exercise.

Read *Tartuffe*, concentrating on the character types you can recognize as you read. Then identify what *type* each of the following might be, that is, what universal traits of the character help to categorize him or her. Write a sentence identifying the type for each character, and then write one or two sentences of detail from the play supporting your classification of the character.

Below is a sample to get you started.

Orgon: Orgon is, in many ways, a typical harassed husband and father. Evidence: His daughter doesn't want to marry the husband he has selected for her, his wife deceives him by trying to keep unpleasant information from him, his son argues with him over his sponsorship of Tartuffe. He thinks his only friend in all the family troubles is Tartuffe, and this man is at the center of all Orgon's problems.

Damis (classify as a type): _____

_____

Evidence: _____

_____

Mariane (type): _____

Evidence: _____

_____

Valère (type): _____

Evidence: _____

_____

Dorine (type): _____

_____

Evidence: _____

_____

_____

EXERCISE: CHARACTERS AS TYPES—ANY COMEDY

To familiarize yourself with how characters who represent certain common human traits are used as types in comedy, try the following exercise.

Consider any comedy you have read and select three characters in it as examples of types. You may look for such types as the foolish husband, the sly manipulator, the angry father, the deceitful wife, the impulsive son or daughter, the clever servant, the vain young man; but many other types are also used in comedy. For each character, supply the information below.

Title of play: _____

Author: _____

Name of character 1: _____

Type: _____

Evidence (one or two sentences of detail from the play justifying and explaining your classification):

_____

_____

_____

Name of character 2: _____

Type: _____

Evidence: _____

_____

_____

Name of character 3: _____

Type: _____

Evidence: _____

_____

_____

EXERCISE: CHARACTERISTICS OF COMEDY

Many classic comedies contain such plot devices as mistaken identity, misunderstandings, last-minute rescues, concealed characters, and overheard conversations. To increase your awareness of such comic elements, review any classic comedy you have read, looking for as many of the devices listed below as you can find. For each one, give the specifics of how it is used, that is, what scene it appears in, what characters are involved, etc.

Play: _____

Author: _____

Mistaken identity (act and scene): _____

What character's identity is mistaken? _____

By whom? _____

Misunderstanding (act and scene): _____

What characters are involved in a misunderstanding? _____

_____

What is misunderstood? _____

_____

Concealed character (act and scene): _____

Who is concealed and why? _____

_____

_____

Who knows about the concealment? _____

Who doesn't? _____

Overheard conversation (act and scene): _____

Who is overheard? _____

Who overhears? _____

What impact does this scene have in moving the plot forward?

_____

_____

Last-minute rescue (act and scene): _____

Who is rescued? _____

By whom? _____

Is the rescue a complication of the plot or the climax?

_____

_____

EXERCISE: CHARACTERS—IDEAL VS. REAL

The comic difference between ideals and reality is often revealed through a play's characters. To appreciate how characters can be used to express this difference, do the following exercise.

Consider any comedy you have read, and select one character who appears to meet an ideal but is, in reality, a different person. Support your selection by providing at least one piece of specific evidence (detail, examples, direct quotes) from the play for each point. If you choose *Tartuffe*, for example, you might begin by saying that Orgon at first appears to be a good father, one who wants material and spiritual happiness for his daughter. Then you might say that Orgon is later revealed to be a foolish man more concerned with his own obsessions than with his daughter's needs. Then you would support your statements with specific evidence from the play.

Then consider a second character from the same play, one who, at some point in the play, admits that he is not the person he thought he was. Again, supply at least one piece of specific evidence from the play for each point you make.

Play: _____

Author: _____

Part 1: A character who at first appears to be _____

_____
(describe the ideal the character seems to represent)

is _____.
(character's name)

Evidence: _____

_____

It is soon clear that _____ is actually
(character's name)

_____
(state the more realistic assessment of this character)

_____.

Evidence: _____

_____

Part 2: A character who must recognize that he is not the person he/she

thought he/she was is _____.
(character's name)

At first, this person thought of himself or herself as _____

_____
(state the idealized self-assessment)

_____.

Evidence: _____

_____

Eventually this character must recognize his or her shortcomings:

_____

(state the more realistic self-assessment)

_____

Evidence: _____

_____

EXERCISE: THE REAL WORLD OF COMEDY

To further study the conflict of the ideal and the real, read one of the comedies below, or one suggested by your instructor. Instead of focusing on the plot, write a short paper that discusses the real world the play exposes. That is, by analyzing specific conflicts and characters, and by citing specific scenes and dialogue, explain which of man's follies are displayed for your amusement.

Suggested Plays

Shakespeare—*Much Ado About Nothing, As You Like It, A Comedy of Errors, A Midsummer Night's Dream, Twelfth Night*
Molière—*Tartuffe, The Misanthrope, The Imaginary Invalid*
Jonson—*Volpone*
Sheridan—*The School for Scandal, The Rivals*

EXERCISE: COMPLETING THE SAMPLE OUTLINE—*TARTUFFE*

To help you get started, here is a partial outline of such an essay on *Tartuffe*. Read the play twice—once for an overall sense of the play, a second time concentrating on the real world of the play; and then fill in the details of the outline below before you write your essay. Below are the thesis, topic sentences, and some transitions.

I Lead–in

Thesis statement: Both the characters and conflicts in

Tartuffe reveal a society that fails to live up to its own

standards.

transition to topic
sentence **A**
(put both in same
paragraph)

II Orgon considers himself a good father and a sensible man,

but his actions show that he is neither.

A Although he thinks he is a loving father, Orgon places

his own desires above the good of his children.

1

details of support from
the play

2

3

4

5

6

7

topic sentence

B Although Orgon thinks he is an intelligent and sensible

man, Tartuffe easily fools and manipulates Orgon.

1

2

details of support from
the play

3

4

5

6

7

transition sentence to
topic sentence **A** (put
both in same
paragraph)

III The lovers of the play, Mariane and Valère, consider them—

selves faithful and true, but they are also silly and

petty.

A When an obstacle comes between them, Valère reacts with

more vanity than love.

1

details of support from
the play

2

3

4

5

6

7

topic sentence

B Mariane, her pride wounded, also reacts foolishly to

the same threat.

1

details of support from
the play

2

3

4

5

6

7

transition sentence to
topic sentence **A**

IV Tartuffe's success and growing power reveal how people

who say they value piety can mistake the appearance of

piety for the real thing.

topic sentence

A Two characters are fully conned by Tartuffe.

1

supporting detail from
the play

2

3

4

5

6

7

topic sentence   B Others, who also say they value piety, see Tartuffe as a hypocrite, but they are not too concerned about his deception——until it threatens their well——being.

1

supporting detail from the play   2

3

4

5

6

7

topic sentence   C Tartuffe's hypocrisy is more powerful than the vague ideals of the other characters, so he nearly destroys them all.

1

supporting detail from the play   2

3

4

5

6

7

restated thesis—work into a smooth concluding paragraph   V Ultimately, the play reveals a world that needs more common sense and less high-flown idealism.

OTHER KINDS OF DRAMA AND WAYS TO WRITE ABOUT THEM

TYPES OF DRAMA

As you may have guessed, it is impossible to classify all plays into neat little categories. The traditional classifications of tragedy and comedy are only points of departure from which the variety of plays of subsequent historical periods evolved.

As the original types blended and changed, *tragicomedy* emerged, as did a multitude of other kinds of drama. As time passed, the conventions of drama, too, changed. Before the nineteenth century, drama did not attempt to create the illusion and detail of the real world and real people. In Shakespeare and Molière's time, for example, the setting of the play was not designed to be a duplication of an actual place. Only in the late nineteenth century did the *realistic* play, with elaborate, authentic-looking sets and costumes and realistic dialogue, come into prominence. Playwrights like Ibsen and Shaw wrote elaborate stage directions indicating the symbolic importance of the environment in the conflict of the play, and an extreme form of realism, *naturalism*, stressed the power of heredity and environment in determining a person's fate. Elements of naturalistic drama are evident in the plays of such writers as Strindberg and O'Neill.

In the twentieth century, there was a rebellion against realism: theater became innovative and experimental. Modern plays may deliberately challenge the audience's traditional dramatic expectations with such techniques as rapidly shifting scenes, slide projections, thematic use of music, bizarre dialogue, intrusive or garish lighting effects. New kinds of drama, like *theater of the absurd* or *expressionist drama*, may challenge traditional forms of theater as they challenge traditional attitudes and values. As modern plays explore a world where the individual appears alienated from self, from others, from God, these plays may utilize new techniques to express a deeper, felt reality. They delve into a reality of the emotions, of the inner life. Such plays may employ dreams, visions, or memories to explore how the individual experiences events, not to duplicate them.

Whatever type of play you are reading, it is not as important to be able to categorize it as it is to be able to appreciate and understand it. If you can enter the world of the play, by accepting its conventions, you can become involved in its conflict. If you can derive some meaning from that conflict, you will gain more than if you can "type" a play that confuses or bores you.

OTHER WAYS TO WRITE ABOUT DRAMA

If you are asked to write a critical essay about a play (of whatever historical period), you can focus on any one or a number of literary elements within the play. That is, your approach can be any one of the approaches already suggested, or it can be a combination of approaches. As always, you must unify your essay with a thesis statement, and, if your thesis is not a statement of the theme, it must relate your analysis of some literary element to the theme of the play.

Remember, too, that the more specifics you can give from the play—details of incidents, explanations of scenes and their meaning, exact quotations and paraphrased references—the more convincing and developed your analysis will be.

Below are the kinds of questions you may use to analyze a play:

1 Write a detailed character analysis of the play's protagonist. What is this person like? What are his goals, dreams, struggles, strengths, weaknesses? How is his character revealed? Through his words and actions? Through how others perceive him and react to him? What are his motives? How does the protagonist change during the course of the play? How are these changes revealed in the key scenes of the play? What does the protagonist learn? Again, remember to connect the protagonist's role and characterization to the overall themes of the play. (For examples of this kind of essay, see our analysis of Mrs. Jake Grimes in Sherwood Anderson's short story, "Death in the Woods," or of Creon in the play *Antigone*.)

2 Write a detailed character analysis of both the protagonist and antagonist, considering the questions listed in the previous item, and, again, link these two characters (protagonist and antagonist) in conflict, to the play's themes. You may also want to structure this essay as a comparison/contrast essay, comparing and contrasting the protagonist and antagonist on some basis related to the play's themes. (For an example, see the comparison/contrast of Antigone and Ismene.)

3 Consider the specific dramatic techniques used in the play. These techniques may include foreshadowing, irony, symbolism, images, dramatic irony, or other techniques central to the work. Structure your analysis around a thesis relating the techniques to the overall themes of the play, and then divide the major segments of the essay into paragraphs describing how each technique enhances and explores theme. Again, specific examples, including direct quotes, are essential here. (For examples, see our techniques analysis of the short story "The Swimmer" and our sample outline for a techniques essay in the drama section of this book.)

4 Consider what dramatic conventions are a part of the play, and then consider how and why they are used. The dramatic conventions may range from the use of a chorus or narrator, to asides and soliloquies, to a very detailed and realistic stage set, to a highly unrealistic setting. Focus your essay around a thesis relating the conventions to the overall themes of the play, and then divide the essay into segments describing how each of the conventions enhances or explores theme. Specific examples from the play are essential to the essay.

5 Trace the developing conflict of the play as it is revealed in key scenes of the play. To do this, you may need to begin with a brief plot summary and a brief character analysis of the protagonist and antagonist. Then you should discuss, in detail, those scenes that complicate the conflict, up to and including the climax of the play and its solution. Since conflict is a specific demonstration of a more general theme, you should be able to link conflict to theme in your thesis.

As you analyze key scenes, remember that specifics (details, direct quotes) are needed for development of your ideas. (For an example of a short plot summary, see our summary of the short story "A Good Man Is Hard to Find"; for an example of how to develop a paragraph analyzing a key scene, see our analysis of the key scenes of "A Good Man Is Hard to Find.")

6 Write a complete critical analysis of a play. To review, your outline for such an essay should include the elements below.

I Lead-in
   Thesis statement: a one-sentence statement of theme
II Short plot summary—no more than two paragraphs.
   Identify important characters, briefly skim events.
III Character analysis of the protagonist(s)
IV Character analysis of the antagonist(s)
V Tracing and interpreting of key scenes of the conflict
VI Identification and interpretation of the climax and solution
VII Analysis of specific literary techniques and relating of them to theme
VIII Conclusion relating all the elements discussed above to a restatement of the thesis

Remember to unify the essay by noting, in each section of your analysis, how each part of the play connects to its theme. To give you an example of a complete critical analysis, a complete critical analysis of *The Visit* by Friedrich Duerrenmatt follows.

A Critical Analysis of *The Visit* by Friedrich Duerrenmatt

lead-in

The Visit challenges us with a series of questions: How far
will man go to achieve prosperity? How is revenge different
from justice? Does mercy have any place in the administration
of justice? Above all, The Visit questions our definition of a
human being by showing men tempted to reject their humanity.

thesis statement

Ultimately, in the character and conflicts of Anton Schill,
the play demonstrates that to be truly human, a man must accept responsibility for his acts and must face their
consequences.

plot summary

The play begins with one big question, when Claire
Zachanassian, who grew up in the town of Güllen and who is now
the richest woman in the world, returns to her childhood home.
Since Claire left Güllen, many years earlier, the town has
fallen into poverty and despair. Everyone waits for Claire's
arrival and asks, ''Will she save us?'' Güllen hopes to benefit from Claire's philanthropy and relies on Anton Schill,
Claire's former lover, now a Güllen storekeeper, to convince
her to be generous.

plot summary

When Claire arrives, she makes the townspeople an offer beyond their dreams––and beyond nightmare. They will receive
millions. There is only one condition, the nightmare element
of the offer. In return for the money, they must kill Anton
Schill. Claire wants revenge on the lover who, years earlier,
drove her, pregnant with his child, from the town and forced
the destitute girl into prostitution. At first the people of
Güllen are indignant at the cruelty of Claire's offer. They
refuse. But soon they are tempted by the promise of wealth,

and they rationalize that, after all, Claire deserves to see justice done. They find it easy to blame Schill and to disguise their greed as a hunger for justice. Eventually, they kill Schill and achieve material prosperity.

protagonist

Anton Schill, the victim of the story, at first seems deserving of the town's contempt. He is ready to use Claire to get money for the town, for, as the Burgomaster tells Schill, ''we depend entirely on you'' to manipulate Claire into saving Güllen. In return, he has been promised the position of mayor, and he is flattered into believing he is loved and admired by all. Schill seems to feel no guilt whatsoever about his earlier cruelty to Claire; when asked why they never married, he merely shrugs, ''Life came between us.'' Although he abandoned his pregnant lover for the wealthier Mathilde, the storekeeper's daughter, he fully expects Claire to have forgotten or forgiven his sins.

antagonist

But Schill's former lover is now his enemy; she has come for vengeance. While Schill still thinks of Claire as an easily manipulated child, she is now a hard and fierce woman, ''with a face as impassive as that of an ancient idol.'' Like the goddess of revenge, she has already destroyed the judge and the false witnesses Schill used to drive her from Güllen. Now she wants to complete her retribution, and she has the power to do so. While Schill has become a small-town failure, Claire has survived the death of her baby, has prospered through eight marriages, has gained earthly power and riches on a fantastic scale. In her ability to survive plane crashes and car accidents, she seems indestructible. In her reduction of people to

''things'' she can buy, she seems terrifying. She is ready to
use the entire town of Güllen as the instrument of her vengeance.

second antagonist

Güllen is only too ready to fulfill Claire's desire. While
at first the people object to the viciousness of the deal,
they are soon tempted by promises of wealth. The broken people
of a broken town do not particularly want to commit murder,
but they do want the money that will come with Schill's death.
Unlike Claire, they do not openly seek Schill's death, but
eventually they accept it as a necessary means to a greater
good—prosperity. As the mayor tells Schill, ''God knows the
lady has every right to be angry with you.'' Soon the town convinces itself that ''we'll really have to do something! And
not because of the money—But out of ordinary human decency.''

first key scene

Schill's enemies, his lover and his fellow townsmen, make a
man out of him. At first he finds it hard to recognize the town
as his enemy, because he believes they will refuse Claire's
offer. At first he is merely appalled by Claire's hatred, asking, ''Why are you doing this? It was all dead and buried,''
and he still refuses to accept his own guilt. He believes the
mayor's initial reaction to the offer, ''We may be poor but we
are not heathens.'' He believes he is safe.

second key scene

But soon Schill recognizes the town as his enemy. When the
people of Güllen enter Schill's store and buy luxuries on
credit, he becomes suspicious. He soon realizes that they plan
to pay for their purchases with the price on his head.
Panicked, he runs to the Policeman for protection, but the
Policeman is wearing new shoes and drinking expensive beer.

The Burgomaster, too, offers no help; he is smoking expensive cigars and has a new typewriter. Even Schill's Pastor, who advises Schill to ''Put your trust in heaven, my friend,'' has bought a new church bell. At this point, no one wants to be Schill's executioner; they want the fruits of his death but want to evade responsibility for it. They use the escape of Claire's pet panther as a pretext for carrying guns. Maybe Schill can be shot, in the confusion, by accident. Or maybe Schill will run away, so they will not have to kill him. The Pastor pleads with Schill, ''Do not tempt us further into the hell in which you are burning. Go, Schill. . . . ''

climax

Schill's reaction to this murderous greed is a cowardly desire to flee. In terror, he runs to the train station, but he is afraid to board the train, thinking the townspeople will push him onto the tracks. Suddenly, on his knees in panic, Schill rises to become a man. When a truck driver offers him a ride out of town, to safety, Schill's personal conflict reaches its climax. With a new dignity and courage, he refuses to run away. Facing his accusers, he gets to his feet, saying, ''This is my town. This is my home. . . . I've changed my mind. I'm staying.''

solution

Schill remains courageous throughout the last act of the play. Given the chance to reveal Claire's deal to the press and thus to save his life, Schill refuses. His courage forces the town to actively seek his death. The people try one more evasion of their own responsibility; they ask Schill to commit suicide, calling it the ''path of honor.'' Schill's refusal reveals his own growth and Güllen's degeneration:

long direct quote:
indented 10 spaces
from left margin, no
quotation marks

You've put me through hell, you and your town. You were my friends, you smiled and reassured me. But day by day I saw you change—your shoes, your ties, your suits, your hearts. If you had been honest with me then, perhaps I would feel differently toward you now. I might even use that gun you brought me. For the sake of my friends. But now I have conquered my fear. Alone. It was hard, but it's done. And now you will have to judge me. And I will accept your judgment. For me that will be justice. How it will be for me, I don't know.

Güllen is thus forced to act to get its money, and the people, acting as a group and again avoiding individual responsibility, kill Anton Schill. The real tragedy is not the death of the newly heroic man; it is the corruption of the town. The teacher, one of Güllen's last ethical men, reveals this moral decay: ''I wish I could believe that for what they're doing . . . they will suffer for the rest of their lives. But it's not true. In a little while they will have justified everything and forgotten everything.'' With Schill dead, Güllen, dead inside, prospers. And Claire, satisfied, takes the body of her lover away to her home, in a strange gesture of love.

techniques

The growth of Schill's humanity and the contrasting destruction of the townspeople are underscored through Duerrenmatt's use of several literary techniques. He contrasts the human with the nonhuman in several ways. The play is full of animal images. Claire was once a kitten; Schill in youth is a panther, but later he is a grey and soft panther. Claire's blind servants are ''dogs,'' and the names of her attendants, Bobby, Kobby, and Lobby, are pets' names. People in the play are also referred to in less than human ways. For example, many characters in the play are more types than individuals: they are The Athlete, The Pastor, The Doctor. Claire is often referred to as a witch, and her power to survive and to control others makes her seem superhuman, a goddess. Only Schill, in his moral growth, becomes more than an animal, and, in his weakness, less than a god. He is a human being.

conclusion   As a human, he must face his flaws. The play stresses the need to face reality, not evade it, by contrasting the hypocrisy of the town with the truth voiced by the two characters, Schill and Claire. Evil as she may be, Claire speaks the truth. She openly declares her hatred; she refuses the lying flattery of the mayor's reception for her. She never resorts to evasion. By the end of the play, her honesty has forced Schill to become honest, and thus to become a man. Schill's growth from self-deceived coward to honest human being is thus the center of the play. It is a moral development rewarded only by death, but Anton Schill does not die like an animal. He is no longer the fleeing pet panther. At the end, Schill faces justice--as a man.

EXERCISE: MORE ON *THE VISIT*

There are many other approaches to a critical analysis of *The Visit*. You might want to consider the town of Güllen as the protagonist, or devise a theme about the meaning of justice, or about what it means to be a *human* being.

EXERCISE: CLASSIC TRAGEDY AND *THE VISIT*

The Visit, a modern play, contains certain echoes of Greek tragedy, demonstrating, once again, the enduring power of the classics. In a short essay, consider those elements of *The Visit*, including characters, conflicts, and theme, that can be linked to similar elements in Greek tragedy. Among the elements you might want to consider are the:

Conflict of a person confronting inescapable pain
Use of the townspeople of Güllen as a chorus
Image of Claire as a figure of relentless fate, a goddess
Emerging nobility of a person through suffering
Observance of any of the unities
Use of a recognition scene
Use of a reversal scene or scenes

Use specific evidence from *The Visit* to support your points.

THREE

POETRY

People often find poetry to be the hardest form of literature to analyze, perhaps because their earliest experiences with poetry stressed appreciation rather than understanding. Many can remember sitting in a grade school classroom, listening to the teacher read a poem, then hearing the instructor ask, "Now, isn't that beautiful?" Very often, students sat in such a class, knowing they were expected to feel something about the poem, and afraid to admit they had no idea what the poem even said. After a few experiences like that, people can develop a lasting aversion to poetry.

True appreciation of a poem demands, first, a disciplined approach to understanding it. As with any other literary form, you must first understand *what a poem says* and *how it says it* before you can begin to appreciate what it means.

This section will stress a step-by-step approach to analyzing poetry, to eliminate the bewilderment and confusion so often associated with the form.

Each step will be discussed separately; then all the steps can be integrated into a complete and extensive critical analysis incorporating these elements:

Theme
Ideas
Emotions
Literary techniques
Style
Critique

As with the short story and the drama, the emphasis will be on recognizing how each part of a poem contributes to its expression of theme, and that theme will become the thesis of the analysis essay.

HOW POETRY IS DIFFERENT FROM OTHER LITERARY FORMS

Common sense tells you that a poem is different looking than a short story or novel. It's often short, and the grouping of words and lines is not neatly bunched into paragraphs, but often into clusters of lines called *stanzas*. Some people think that all poetry rhymes at the end of each line, but not all poetry rhymes. All poetry does, however, contain some kind of rhythm, a beat of some kind, because *poetry is a blend of sound and meaning.*

This blend is a challenge to the reader; all the techniques of poetry are combined to challenge the reader's imagination. More than any other literary form, poetry forces the reader to become involved in the work, to think and feel—if he or she is to derive anything from the poem. Thus, reading the poem is in itself a creative act, one that may require you to call on your own experiences, reading, imagination, and spontaneous reactions in order to be drawn into the poet's world.

Poetry challenges you because it makes startling and unusual connections between things you might never, otherwise, associate. These connections are called *figurative language*.

Take a look at one, two-line poem and see how the connections are made:

The apparition of these faces in the crowd
Petals on a wet, black bough.

That's the poem. So—now what?

First, be sure you understand the dictionary meaning of the words the poem uses. Look up the following in a good dictionary.

Apparition: _____

_____

_____

Bough: _____

_____

_____

Now, try to insert the dictionary (denotative) meaning of these words into the lines of the poem:

The unexpected appearance of these faces in the crowd.
Petals on a wet, black tree limb.

Now consider the connotative meanings of the words in the poem. The connotative meaning is not the dictionary definition; it is rather the kind of emotional associations you can make with specific words. To dig for connotative meaning, you have to dig into memory and imagination, to "free associate" words, feelings, ideas.

Let's look at "petals." Petals are the parts of the blossom of a plant or tree. What colors are petals? Pretty colors: white, pink, yellow, lavendar, peach. . . . Petals don't last long; flowers don't bloom long; petals drop off the stem; they might cling, wet, to the stronger limbs of a wet tree.

Let's look at "apparition." An apparition, the dictionary tells you, is not only a sudden or unexpected appearance. It is also something supernatural, a phantom, a ghost.

Keeping all these associations in mind, look at the title of that two-line poem, and now see if, knowing the title (a giveaway!), you can see the possible connection the poet, Ezra Pound, is making.

Title: "In a Station of the Metro."

The metro is the underground, the subway. Think about the connection.

In the subway station, faces (apparitions, phantoms, ghosts) suddenly appear in the crowd. They are like petals (fragile, pretty, vulnerable) clinging to a wet, black tree limb.

Question: In a subway station, what is long and black and shiny (and thus looks wet)? *Answer*: The train.

So, put it all together.

People in the crowd suddenly appear, seeming almost supernatural, almost nonhuman.
They are vulnerable, clinging to the shiny black train.

You can go further:

People and flowers are connected.
People and flowers are both living things, a part of nature.
Trains are mechanical, not living things.
Yet the people seem somehow more (or less) than human—ghosts.
And the train is compared to a tree branch, stronger than, supporting, the fragile human beings.

What is the poem saying about men, machines, and nature? There is no one answer. There are several answers. But to arrive at any answer, you have to *understand the figurative language*, to *follow the poet's connections*. It's a challenge, but meeting that challenge can be satisfying and can widen your perceptions of the world.

As the above example indicates, *the first and most crucial step in analyzing a poem is knowing what it says*. After you know what it is about, you can interpret what it means in a number of ways. But if you are wrong about what the poem says, because you have not understood the actual words of the poem, the entire analysis will be wrong. That is, if you decided that "In a Station of the Metro" was about ghosts selling bouquets of black flowers in a forest, you would have a hard time justifying this interpretation with the *evidence* of the words of the poem. You would have to ignore the word "metro" in the title; you would have to ignore the implied comparison of people to flowers; and you would be injecting a "sale" into the poem. Only by dealing with the *facts* of the poem can you approach the poem successfully.

We stand behind our mice.

Microsoft® Mouse Limited Lifetime Warranty.

Microsoft warrants to the original purchaser that this Microsoft Mouse (also referred to as "Product") is free from defects in materials and workmanship and will perform substantially in accordance with the Product documentation for the life of the Product. This Limited Lifetime Warranty does not apply to the software or disks that accompany the Microsoft Mouse, which are covered by the Microsoft License Agreement. THIS PRODUCT IS INTENDED FOR SALE IN THE USA ONLY. IF YOU RESIDE OUTSIDE THE USA, THEN MICROSOFT PROVIDES THIS PRODUCT "AS IS" WITHOUT WARRANTY OF ANY KIND. If failure of the Product has resulted from accident, abuse, or misapplication, Microsoft shall have no responsibility under this Limited Lifetime Warranty.

Purchaser's Exclusive Remedies.

During the first two (2) years after purchase, your exclusive remedy for a defective Microsoft Mouse shall be, at Microsoft's option, either (a) repair or replacement of the Product that does not meet this Limited Lifetime Warranty or (b) return of the purchase price. After the initial two (2) year period, your exclusive remedy shall be the repair or replacement of the Microsoft Mouse upon your payment of a $25.00 handling fee. In order to obtain warranty service, you must first contact Microsoft Product Support at (206) 882-8089. If Product Support is unable to solve the problem, you will be asked to call Microsoft Customer Service at (206) 882-8088 to obtain a return authorization number. Then return the Product, with a copy of your proof of purchase, to Microsoft at the following address:

   Customer Service Department
   Attention: Hardware Repair
   Microsoft Manufacturing
   21919 20th Ave. S.E.
   Bothell, WA 98021

You are responsible for the cost of shipping the Product to Microsoft. Microsoft is responsible for the cost of returning the repaired or replacement Product to you. Repair parts and replacement Product will be either reconditioned or new.

Disclaimer of Other Warranties.

The above are the only warranties of any kind, express or implied, including but not limited to the implied warranties of merchantability and fitness for a particular purpose, that are made by Microsoft on this Microsoft product. No oral or written information or advice given by Microsoft, its dealers, distributors, agents, or employees shall create a warranty or in any way increase the scope of this limited lifetime warranty, and you may not rely on any such information or advice.

Limitation of Liability.

Neither Microsoft nor anyone else who has been involved in the creation, production, or delivery of this product shall be liable for any direct, indirect, consequential, or incidental damages (including without limitation damages for loss of business profits, business interruption, loss of business information, and the like) arising out of the use of or inability to use this product even if Microsoft has been advised of the possibility of such damages. Because some states do not allow the exclusion or limitation of liability for consequential or incidental damages, the above limitation may not apply to you.

Miscellaneous

This Limited Lifetime Warranty shall supercede any inconsistent warranties contained in the Microsoft License Agreement. This Limited Lifetime Warranty is governed by the laws of the State of Washington. Should you have any questions concerning this Limited Lifetime Warranty, or if you desire to contact Microsoft for any reason, please write to:

Microsoft Customer Sales and Service
16011 N.E. 36th Way
Box 97017
Redmond, WA 98073-9717

THIS LIMITED LIFETIME WARRANTY GIVES YOU SPECIFIC LEGAL RIGHTS. YOU MAY HAVE OTHERS, WHICH VARY FROM STATE TO STATE.

0988 Part No. 04529

THE IDEAS OF THE POEM

The first step in analyzing a poem is gathering the ideas of the poem. It begins with a paraphrase of every idea the poem expresses. The word "idea" is important, because, to understand what a poem says,

> Don't paraphrase to the end of the line!
> Paraphrase to the end of an idea.

Ideas often run over two, three, or four lines. Identifying ideas demands that you use a dictionary so that you can begin with the correct denotations of words. Then you can *transform the language of the poem into your own words,* into your *paraphrase*.

If you can successfully accomplish this step in poetry analysis, half the battle is over. Then you can begin to "associate," to play with the connotations of words, to consider what the poem *means*.

To be sure you understand this crucial first step, try the following exercises. Remember:

1 Paraphrase to the end of the thought, not to the end of the line.
2 Sentence structure in a poem is not always the order used in prose.

Hint: For each sentence used in the poem, look for the main verb. Then move it to where it would be in a conventional sentence.

EXERCISE: PARAPHRASING

Each of the following is part of a poem. Paraphrase each selection. Use a dictionary if you have *any* doubt what a word means.

For this exercise, do not consider what complexity of interpretation the lines may conceal; just "translate" into simple English what the lines say.

1 That age is best which is the first,
    When youth and blood are warmer;
But being spent, the worse, and worst
    Times still succeed the former.

(From "To the Virgins, to Make Much of Time" by Robert Herrick.)

Paraphrase: _____

_____

_____

_____

_____

2 My mother bore me in the southern wild,
  And I am black, but O! my soul is white;
  White as an angel is the English child,
  But I am black, as if bereaved of light.

(From "The Little Black Boy" by William Blake.)

Paraphrase: _____

_____

_____

_____

_____

_____

3 If thou must love me, let it be for naught
  Except for love's sake only. Do not say
  'I love her for her smile—her look—her way
  Of speaking gently—for a trick of thought
  That falls in well with mine, and certes brought
  A sense of pleasant ease on such a day—
  For these things in themselves, Beloved, may
  Be changed, or changed for thee—and love, so wrought
  May be unwrought so.

(From "Sonnets from the Portuguese," Number 14, by Elizabeth Barret Browning.)

Paraphrase: _____

_____

_____

_____

_____

_____

_____

4 Ah, love, let us be true
   To one another! for the world, which seems
   To lie before us like a land of dreams,
   So various, so beautiful, so new,
   Hath really neither joy, nor love, nor light,
   Nor certitude, nor peace, nor help for pain;
   And we are here as on a darkling plain
   Swept with confused alarms of struggle and flight,
   Where ignorant armies clash by night.

(From "Dover Beach" by Matthew Arnold.)

Paraphrase: _____

_____

_____

_____

_____

_____

_____

5 A narrow Fellow in the Grass
   Occasionally rides—
   You may have met Him—did you not—
   His notice sudden is—

The Grass divides as with a Comb—
A spotted shaft is seen—
And then it closes at your feet
And opens further on—

(From "A Narrow Fellow in the Grass," Number 986, by Emily Dickinson.)

Paraphrase: _____

_____

_____

_____

_____

_____

_____

_____

_____

_____

EXERCISE: COMPLETE PARAPHRASE OF A POEM

Paraphrase the complete poem below:

Richard Cory

Edwin Arlington Robinson

Whenever Richard Cory went downtown,
We people on the pavement looked at him:
He was a gentleman from sole to crown,
Clean favored, and imperially slim.

And he was always quietly arrayed,
And he was always human when he talked;
But still he fluttered pulses when he said,
"Good morning," and he glittered when he walked.

And he was rich—yes, richer than a king—
And admirably schooled in every grace:
In fine, we thought that he was everything
To make us wish that we were in his place.

So on we worked, and waited for the light,
And went without the meat, and cursed the bread;
And Richard Cory, one calm summer night,
Went home and put a bullet through his head.

_____

_____

_____

_____

_____

_____

_____

_____

_____

_____

_____

_____

EXERCISE: PARAPHRASING SHAKESPEARE'S SONNETS

At some point, in some class, you will be required to read poetry written by Shakespeare or his contemporaries. You can panic when you are confronted with language that looks jumbled and words that you've never seen before. Or you can approach the poetry with a few rules in mind, and you can make some sense of it.

Rule 1   Read to the end of the thought, *not* to the end of the line.

That time of year thou mayst in me behold
When yellow leaves, or none, or few, do hang
Upon those boughs which shake against the cold,
Bare ruined choirs, where late the sweet birds sang.

In the above passage from Shakespeare's Sonnet 73, the thought runs all the way from the first word, "That," to the last, "sang." If you try to make sense out of each line by itself, you will become very confused and may miss the thought entirely. Instead, try transforming the language into modern English, working through to the *end of the thought*.

That time of year you can in me see
When yellow leaves, or no leaves, or a few, hang
On the tree limbs that tremble against the cold,
Like empty, decrepit rows of a church's choir,
Where lately the birds sang.

Rule 2   Rearrange the sentence structure, *looking for where the verb belongs*, so you can understand the lines. Try it with the same lines:

You can see (in me) the time of year
When yellow leaves, or no leaves, or a few, hang
On the tree limbs that tremble against the cold,
Like the empty decrepit rows of a church choir,
Where the birds were lately singing.

What time of year is it when the trees are nearly bare of leaves and it's cold? Autumn. Or winter. What is the speaker saying? "When you look at me, you see that I am like autumn."

Rule 3   Don't let the language defeat you. "Thee" and "thou" just mean "you," so why make these words into monsters? Transform verbs like "mayst" into "may." Most editions of Shakespeare's poems have footnotes that explain difficult words or phrases. Use the footnotes. And, if you need to, use a good dictionary. The effort will be worth it.

To develop your skills in reading Shakespeare's poetry, try this exercise, which requires you to work through a paraphrase of the remaining lines of Sonnet 73.

The following is the complete sonnet. Read it several times, trying to get an overall sense of the poem's meaning, then looking for how the lines are grouped into thoughts.

Sonnet 73

William Shakespeare

That time of year thou mayst in me behold
When yellow leaves, or none, or few, do hang
Upon those boughs which shake against the cold,
Bare ruined choirs, where late the sweet birds sang.
In me thou see'st the twilight of such day
As after sunset fadeth in the west;
Which by and by black night doth take away,
Death's second self that seals up all in rest.
In me thou see'st the glowing of such fire,
That on the ashes of his youth doth lie,
As the deathbed whereon it must expire,
Consumed by that which it was nourished by.*
  This thou perceiv'st, which makes thy love more strong,
  To love that well which thou must leave ere* long.

   * "Consumed by that which it was nourished by" can mean destroyed, put out, by the ashes of the same fuel that once fed the flame.
   * ere = before

1 Consider the following group of four lines as one idea, and paraphrase them.

In me thou see'st the twilight of such day
As after sunset fadeth in the west;
Which by and by black night doth take away,
Death's second self, that seals up all in rest.

Paraphrase: _____

_____

_____

_____

_____

Now, summarize the lines. The speaker of the poem says the "you" of the

poem (the "thou") can compare the speaker to _____.

  2 Consider the next four lines as one idea, and paraphrase them.

In me thou see'st the glowing of such fire,
That on the ashes of his youth doth lie,
As the deathbed whereon it must expire,
Consumed by that which it was nourished by.

Paraphrase: _____

_____

_____

_____

Now, summarize the lines. The speaker of the poem says the "you" of the

poem can compare the speaker to _____.

3 Consider the last two lines of the poem, and paraphrase them.

This thou perceiv'st, which makes thy love more strong,
To love that well which thou must leave ere long.

Paraphrase: _____

_____

_____

(*Note*: Be sure to think about what "This" refers to in the last two lines.)

EXERCISE: A COMPLETE
PARAPHRASE—SHAKESPEARE'S SONNET 116

You can work through the same process of paraphrasing, using the same basic rules, for any of Shakespeare's sonnets. Try a complete paraphrase of this one, Sonnet 116. First, read it several times, to get an overall sense of the poem's meaning. Then look for how the lines are grouped into thoughts. After reading it several times, write a complete paraphrase, transforming the language into modern English. Be careful to consider every line; don't skim over anything, as you may skim over some part of the poem essential to understanding the entire poem's meaning.

Sonnet 116

William Shakespeare

Let me not to the marriage of true minds
Admit impediments. Love is not love
Which alters when it alteration finds,
Or bends with the remover to remove:
Oh, no! It is an ever-fixed* mark,
That looks on tempests* and is never shaken;
It is the star to every wandering bark,*
Whose worth's unknown, although his height* be taken,
Love's not Time's fool, though rosy lips and cheeks
Within his bending sickle's compass* come;
Love alters not with his brief hours and week,
But bears it out even to the edge of doom.
　If this be error and upon me proved,
　I never writ, nor no man ever loved.

* ever fixed = stationary, not moving
* tempests = storms
* bark = ship
* height = altitude
* his = Time's
* compass = the area covered by a swing of the sickle, or jurisdiction, or power

FROM PARAPHRASE TO PARAGRAPH

Now that you have a good idea of how to extract the facts from a poem, you can begin to concentrate on what those facts mean. And then you can begin to consider how to communicate that interpretation of ideas in essay form.

Look again at the poem you paraphrased, "Richard Cory." It tells a story, but, obviously, that story has some deeper meaning.

Who tells the story?

The townspeople, of a small town, it seems. It seems to be a small town because everybody seems to know Cory; and he greets the town's individuals. This isn't typical of city life.

What is the attitude of the people to Cory?

Admiration: he was "a gentleman from sole to crown"; he "glittered" when he walked; he "fluttered pulses" just by saying "good morning" so there is awe there, too. And there is envy: "we thought that he was everything/To make us wish that we were in his place."

What is Cory like?

Rich: "richer than a king." A true aristocrat: "admirably schooled in every grace."

What is the relationship of Cory to the townspeople?

He is distant: he "fluttered pulses," "glittered when he walked." The townspeople feel inferior: they are "on the pavement" looking up at him. They even seem surprised that he is "human" when he talks.

What happens?

The townspeople are discontented; they wish they were Cory. They go without "meat" (can this stand for anything?) and curse the "bread" (any connotations?) they have and wait for "light" (connotations?). And Richard Cory, the ideal, kills himself.

Writing the ideas section of your essay is easy, if you remember to consider all the facts, make references to the specifics of the poem, and quote parts of it, and effectively combine interpretation and paraphrase. That is, you are now moving from a translation of the words of the poem into a consideration of what meaning those words convey. Try to incorporate your ideas and the quotes from the poem, smoothly, into clear sentences. It's also a good practice to write one paragraph of paraphrase for each separate stanza, so that you consider each line carefully.

To give you some idea of how to move from paraphrase to paragraphs, you can look at the following sample paraphrase/interpretation of ideas for "Richard Cory" on the following pages.

Sample Paraphrase/Interpretation of Ideas for "Richard Cory"

The speaker of ''Richard Cory'' speaks for the people of a small town, and he begins by describing the citizens' interest in Cory. Whenever Cory came to town, those below him in rank, the ''people on the pavement,'' looked at him. He was in every way a gentleman, clean-cut, handsome, aristocratically slender.

But, the speaker continues, Cory did not flaunt his status; he was always ''quietly arrayed,'' and ''human when he talked.'' Still, a mere ''good morning'' from Richard Cory could set peoples' hearts racing because they were in awe of him. He seemed to glitter as he moved among them.

Not only was Cory handsome and fine; he was rich and gen-teel, ''admirably schooled in every grace,'' knowing all the social graces, a true aristocrat. Yet this seeming perfection and the townspeople's lack of money, social background, and social skills created a distance between Cory and the others.

They saw him as a model of what they had been denied: ''we thought that he was everything/To make us wish that we were in his place.''

The townspeople remained stuck in their rut, waiting for the ''light,'' perhaps for the hope of better times. Seeing Cory, who has so much, they were discontented, for they had to do without the luxuries of life (''the meat'') and they were dissatisfied with what they did have (they ''cursed the bread''). The final lines of the poem reveal another person's hidden pain, for Richard Cory, so quietly dazzling, went home and put ''a bullet through his head.'' The ideal man, the model for the townspeople, is finally revealed as a person different from others' fantasies of him.

quoted lines of poem run together in a paragraph are separated by a slash

DERIVING A THEME— LEAD-IN AND THESIS

Once you have gathered the ideas, the facts, of the poem, and have derived some meaning from them, you are ready to find the poem's *central idea*, its *theme*.

The theme of the poem is, as in the case of a short story or play, its *point*. In your analysis of any poem, the theme will be the thesis of your essay and, as in the case of short stories or plays, *there is no one correct statement of theme. Whatever statement of theme you develop*, however, *must be based on the facts of the poem*. The ideas of the poem (like the emotions it expresses, and its literary techniques, both to be discussed later) all relate to, support, enhance, and expand on the poem's theme.

The theme should be *stated in one complete sentence* and should be a general statement based on the specifics of the poem. Here are some possible theme statements for "Richard Cory," all derived from the ideas of the poem:

Difference from others, even if caused by a person's superiority, can create extreme loneliness for the person.

Caught up in our own pain, we fail to see the anguish in others.

It is foolish to envy others, for we cannot see their secret pain.

Appearances and material differences can separate a man, keeping him alone and often unhappy.

These are only some of the possible themes you can perceive in "Richard Cory." You can, no doubt, see others.

INCORPORATING THEME INTO YOUR ESSAY

At the beginning of your discussion on poetry, you were given an overview of the format for writing a complete critical analysis of a poem. You have just learned how to write the two most crucial sections, the theme and ideas sections. You may have noticed that, although the analysis essay begins with the section on theme, you first considered how to plan the section on ideas. The preparation for writing the essay worked backwards, for a simple reason: *you can't find a central idea, a theme, until you have first found all the ideas*. So, in planning your essay, look first for all the ideas, then go on to consider the central idea, the theme.

The actual analysis essay itself, however, opens with a paragraph on theme, then goes on to support the theme by discussing the specific ideas of the poem. Just as you have done for other essays, you would *begin* this essay, not with the theme as your first sentence, but *with a lead-in*. That is, write several sentences of introduction that move smoothly toward your theme statement.

Below is a sample first paragraph for an analysis of "Richard Cory." Note how it moves through lead-in to theme.

Sample First Paragraph for "Richard Cory"

lead-in

Edwin Arlington Robinson's ''Richard Cory'' contrasts the discontented, frustrated lives of small-town people with the seemingly successful and wealthy existence of their hero, Richard Cory. As the ordinary men compare their daily grind of denial with the glitter of Cory's world, they envy him. But, as the poem reveals, their envy is foolish. For Richard Cory's final action reveals a different person from the towns- people's image of him, a person who has been suffering in

thesis

secret. The poem's final lines indicate that <u>people who are caught up in their own pain fail to see the anguish in others</u>.

After such an introductory paragraph which contains a thesis statement, you can go on to the ideas section—the paraphrase/interpretation part.

Note: When you first approach a poem, looking for ideas and theme, read it over several times. Don't worry if you can't make much sense of a poem on a first reading. If everything in the poem was clear to you on a casual reading, it would hardly be poetry; it would be the kind of verse that belongs on a greeting card! The deeper you get into the poem, the more you will see in it.

Sometimes, one or two lines within the poem summarize its theme quite well. You might wish to quote these lines, and then comment on them as your statement of theme.

EMOTIONS IN THE POEM

This is a somewhat shorter part of your analysis and demands that you go back through the poem again, this time looking for what emotions are expressed within the poem. Don't look for what emotions the poem evokes in you; look for the often complex blend of emotions contained in the poem itself. A love poem, for example, may contain more than an expression of love. There may also be tinges of jealousy, or mistrust, or anger, or possessiveness.

If you think a certain emotion is being expressed, find the lines (in the poem) that convey that emotion. To give you some practice in identifying emotions, try the following exercise.

EXERCISE: IDENTIFYING EMOTIONS

Look at "Richard Cory" again. It is not enough to say this is a *sad* poem. Instead, find the lines that reveal the following emotions.

Admiration: _____

_____

_____

Awe: _____

_____

_____

Discontent: _____

_____

_____

Envy: _____

_____

_____

Hope of better things: _____

_____

_____

Despair: _____

_____

_____

Once you've identified the emotions by looking closely at the words of the poem, you are ready to incorporate this material into the next section of your essay. You write a paragraph or two analyzing the mix of emotions, using specific quotes to support your points. Here is a sample of such a section:

Sample Emotions Section for "Richard Cory"

paragraph on emotions of town

As Robinson contrasts the idealized Cory perceived by the town with the real man, he attributes a range of emotions to both the ordinary people and the extraordinary man. The town, for example, is in awe of Cory; he is so far above those ''on the pavement'' that a few words from him can set pulses to

detail from poem

fluttering. They admire his manners, his money, and his clean, slim appearance. And, of course, they envy him and wish to be him: ''we thought that he was everything/To make us wish that we were in his place.'' He has what they do not have, and he is what they cannot be. They feel unhappy with what they do have—''the bread'' they curse, and they wait only for something better, some ''light'' in their dark lives.

paragraph on emotions of Cory

Cory, on the other hand, begins as an enigma. We cannot, at first, be sure what he feels. He is always so quiet, so polite,

detail from poem

so gentle, that he seems utterly in control of his existence. Not until the end of the poem, in Cory's suicide, do we, like the town, see the hidden despair.

In writing the emotions section, you will be repeating lines you've used before and citing details from the poem you've referred to before. That is acceptable, since poetry must concentrate ideas, emotions, images, and sound patterns into condensed, highly charged language.

IDENTIFYING LITERARY TECHNIQUES

In this section of the analysis, you are looking for the specific literary techniques the poet uses in expressing theme. This section focuses on the figurative language of the poem, on how it conveys meaning.

Begin by asking, "What is the tone of this poem?" Is it a light, humorous tone? Sarcastic? Serious? Bitter? Dramatic? Understated? Didactic (directly pointing out a lesson)? Tone is like tone of voice; it implies a great deal.

Then you need to *examine every line* of the poem to discover how figurative language, symbols, images, imagery, and other poetic devices are used within the poem. To do this, you must familiarize yourself with the terms described below.

The most basic and common poetic device, the essence of figurative language, is the metaphor. A metaphor is a comparison between two things that are not alike.

Not a metaphor: She is an elegant woman.
A metaphor: She is a rose in bloom.

Sometimes the comparison is more subtle. When you're angry, you may say, "I'm fuming." You are comparing yourself to a fire. Smoke is not literally coming out of your body. Or, if a room is overheated, you may say "It's an oven in here." You are comparing the room to an oven.

When a metaphor uses "like" or "as" in the comparison, it is a simile, a special kind of metaphor.

Similes: She is like a rose in bloom.
　　　　　He is greedy as a pig.

When a comparison gives human qualities to the nonhuman (nature, animals, or things), it is a kind of metaphor called *personification*.

Note that the nonhuman must be given human qualities, not vice versa.

Not personification: The boy was a snake in his habits.
Personifications: The flowers smiled at me.
　　　　　　　　The garden was dressed in its best.

There are many other literary techniques used to convey or enhance meaning.

Something that stands for something else is called a *symbol*. Something concrete (tangible) in the poem may stand for something abstract. A sunset may stand for death, or a rose may be a symbol of perfect love, or a journey may represent the transition from life to death.

Be careful: a symbol begins with something concrete in the poem, and that concrete object or scene becomes symbolic when it means more than itself. To determine what a symbol stands for, look at how it fits into the context of the whole poem. For example, a flower may represent either an expression of love, or a beautiful life that ended early, depending on the context of the poem.

Images are recurring words or descriptions related to some pattern developing in the poem. For example, in "Richard Cory" there are regal images connected to Cory. He glitters, he is richer than a king; the man is described as a gentleman not from head to foot, but from sole to *crown*.

Imagery, on the other hand, is a pattern of words that appeals to one of the senses. *Visual imagery* helps us see something—it may relate to colors, to light and dark, to words related to a glow, or flame, or shadow. Sound imagery may include references to noises such as sighs, cries, loud noises, or to quiet and silence. *Tactile*, or *touch*, *imagery* may be related to the feel of things—textures, heat, or cold. *Taste* and *smell imagery* are less frequently used, but occasionally clusters of words can appeal to one of these senses.

Allegory is an older technique in which an abstraction, an idea, is represented by something concrete. For example, patience may be represented by a character in the poem called Patience. In allegory, the representation is extended at some length through the poem. Allegory is different from symbolism because allegorical elements have a more fixed and limited equivalent, and the allegory is extended throughout the poem, often to teach some lesson.

Alliteration is the repetition of the initial sound of words, either within one line, or over two or more.

Alliterations: Tyger, tyger, *b*urning *b*right

　　　　　The *S*oul *s*elects her own *s*ociety—
　　　　　Then—*s*huts the door—

A *paradox* is an apparent contradiction that is actually true, perhaps on another level of meaning.

Paradoxes: One man's meat is another man's poison.

　　　　　Death shall be no more; Death, thou shalt die.

Irony is language in which the implied meaning is different from the literal meaning.

Irony: we thought that he was everything
        To make us wish that we were in his place.

(Here the irony of the lines becomes clear later in the poem.)

An *allusion* is a reference in the poem that requires knowledge of events, people, places, etc., outside the poem itself. For example, there may be a reference to a literary character, "I am not Prince Hamlet," or to history and culture, "the glory that was Greece," or to a nursery rhyme, "Here we go round the prickly pear." These are only some of the most common poetic techniques and devices. There are many more, and your instructor may want to discuss some of them with you. These, however, are enough to get you started on the literary techniques section of your essay.

To do a good job in this section of your essay, you must become expert at recognizing the various literary techniques. For practice, try the following exercise.

EXERCISE: LITERARY TECHNIQUES

1 Write the exact words of the simile in the lines below:

I hear a Fly buzz—when I died—
The Stillness in the Room
Was like the Stillness in the Air—
Between the Heaves of Storm—

(From "I heard a Fly buzz—when I died—"
poem 465 by Emily Dickinson.)

Simile: _____

_____

_____

2 Write the exact words of alliteration in the lines below:

A snow-drop spider, a flower like a froth,
And dead wings carried like a paper kite.

(From "Design" by Robert Frost.)

Alliteration: _____

_____

Now find another figure of speech in the same lines: _____

_____

_____

_____

_____

3 In the following, find two examples of personification and one simile.

We have given our hearts away, a sordid boon!
The Sea that bares her bosom to the moon,
The winds that will be howling at all hours,
And are up-gathered now like sleeping flowers,
For this, for everything, we are out of tune;

(From "The World Is Too Much With Us" by William Wordsworth.)

Personification: _____

_____

_____

_____

Simile: _____

_____

_____

4 Find the metaphor in the following:

Little Lamb, who made thee?
Dost thou know who made thee?
Gave thee life and bid thee feed,
By the stream & o'er the mead;
Gave thee clothing of delight,
Softest clothing wooly bright;

(From "The Lamb" by William Blake.)

Metaphor: _____

_____

_____

5 Find the imagery in the following, and identify what kind (sight, sound, touch, etc.) it is. There is more than one kind. Write the words of the poem for each kind of imagery.

And we are put on earth a little space
That we may learn to bear the beams of love;
And these black bodies and this sunburnt face
Is but a cloud, and like a shady grove.

(From "The Little Black Boy" by William Blake.)

Imagery: _____

_____

_____

_____

_____

Now, go over the same passage and find a metaphor, a simile, and an example of alliteration.

Metaphor: _____

_____

Simile: _____

_____

Alliteration: _____

_____

6 As a final check, go back to "Richard Cory." Identify all the literary techniques you can find in the poem.

After you've identified the literary techniques of the poem, you can write about them—in clear, smooth, organized paragraphs. Try to organize this section of your paper by focusing each paragraph on a different technique, or, if there's not enough for a paragraph on each technique, by grouping several techniques under an appropriate topic sentence that connects them. Take a careful look at the sample paragraphs on literary techniques in "Richard Cory."

Sample Paragraphs on Literary Techniques in "Richard Cory"

topic sentence

The impact of Robinson's poem is heightened by his use of poetic techniques. One of the most effective techniques is the use of irony, an irony developed by contrasting the town's image of Richard Cory with the reality later exposed. To the townspeople, Cory is associated with regal images; he is a

detail from the poem

gentleman, not from head to foot, but ''from sole to crown,'' richer ''than a king,'' and he ''glittered,'' ''imperially slim,'' like someone royal and dazzling, when he walked downtown. They are surprised that he is even ''human'' when he talks, an ironic statement, because they fail to see the human suffering that conflicts with their image of Cory. And, ironically, seeing only the royal image of the man, they wish they were ''in his place.''

Other techniques reinforce this contrast. There is the

topic sentence

metaphor of a hero who can set one's blood to racing (''he fluttered pulses''). In a sight image, Cory ''glittered'' in light, while the townspeople ''waited'' for their own ''light,'' perhaps a symbol of the happiness they feel deprived of. Symbolically, they hate what they have (they ''cursed the bread'') and must do without what they feel they need (they ''went without the meat''). Sound imagery builds the tension of the poem, with its hidden and open miseries; in the beginning, any sound is soft. Cory is ''quietly'' arrayed; there are the quiet beat of fluttering pulses, the curses of the discontented people, and ''one calm summer night.'' But then there is the loud, climactic sound of a gunshot.

topic sentence

There is a frequent use of alliteration, another technique related to sound, as well. There is, for example, the repetition of the ''p'' of ''We people on the pavement looked at him,'' connecting the speaker to the streets. There is much use of the ''w'' and ''th'' sounds in lines such as ''in fine, we thought that he was everything/To make us wish that we were in his place.'' Through such sound devices, as well as through sight imagery, symbols and images, the poet enhances his contrast between a town's illusions and its sudden awaking to reality.

RECOGNIZING STYLE

In this section, you are asked to discover the *meter* and *rhyme* scheme of the poem, those parts of the poem that emphasize its sound, as well as to comment on the overall style of the poem.

When you are examining the overall style of the poem, consider the level of language and sentence structure of the poem. Does the poet use deceptively simple language to express complex ideas? Or are both the language and the ideas comparatively simple to grasp? Is the sentence structure complicated, is the language elevated and formal?

Meter is the *rhythm* of the poem, its pattern of sound. Remember, poetry is a combination of sound and meaning, so very often there is a *deliberate and consistent sound pattern* (meter) which you can identify. This pattern will often focus on one of four basic forms:

- '   *iambic*: one short (unstressed), one long (stressed) syllable
' -   *trochaic*: one long (stressed), one short (unstressed) syllable
- - '   *anapestic*: two short (unstressed) syllables, one long (stressed) syllable
' - -   *dactyllic*: one long (stressed) syllable, two short (unstressed) syllables

To understand how to find the meter of the poem, you have to think back to elementary school, when you were required to put the accent mark on the correct syllables in words. The accent mark is the stressed or *long* mark in meter; the unaccented syllable gets the unstressed or *short* mark.

Start by putting the marks on the words below:

midget	rental	Christmas
insane	regret	propose

If you did this correctly, you'll notice that the three words on the first line across all start with an accented (long) syllable followed by an unstressed (short) syllable. They are trochaic in meter. The three words on the next line across all begin with an unstressed syllable and then have a stressed syllable. This is the short-long, or iambic, pattern. When you analyze the meter of a poem, you *look at the words as they form a pattern for an entire line.*

Let's look at the line below:

Follow it utterly.

Look at *each* syllable. Mark as either short or long.

Fóllow̄ ī́t útter̄ly.

What sound pattern (of the four possibilities) do you see?
Dactyllic.
How many groupings of dactyllic meter? (We call each grouping a foot.)
The line has two feet of dactyllic meter.

Hint: If you are having trouble deciding what syllable of a word is stressed, try to mark out your own name. You'll find you know how to accent it. Try to say the word a different way; you'll see there is a definite way to stress a syllable.

If you are having trouble dealing with the entire line of a poem, start in the middle of the line, with a two-or-three-syllable word you are sure you know how to accent, and work back.

Let's do another line:

And we are put on earth a little space,

Mark it:

Ān̄d we̋ ār̄e pút ōn eár̄th ā líttl̄e spáce,

It's iambic. Count how many clusters.

Ān̄d we̋/ ār̄e pút/ ōn eár̄th/ ā lít/ tl̄e spáce,

When you are working out the meter of a poem, try several different lines from different parts of the poem. Pronounce the lines, and focus on multisyllable words you know how to pronounce. Remember to *mark each syllable.*

If you try lines from different parts of the poem, you may notice that the author writes one line in one meter, and another line in a different meter. If you find this is the case, or if you notice an extra syllable at the end of a line, just say so in your style section. It is worth noting that any variation or abrupt change in meter may well be connected to the poem's ideas: the poet may switch rhythm when he wants to stress a point. Some poems have a rhythm, but it is not at all regular. If you discover this, say so in your style section.

In this section of your essay, support your identification of meter by marking out the lines of the poem (at least two lines), marking the meter and dividing the clusters into feet.

For more practice in identifying meter, try the following exercise.

EXERCISE: IDENTIFYING METER

Mark out the meter (and count the feet) in the following lines of poetry.

1 Then be not coy, but use your time;
And while ye may, go marry;

(From "To the Virgins, to Make Much of Time" by Robert Herrick.)

The first line has _____ feet of _____ meter.
The second line has _____ feet of _____ meter and an extra syllable.

2 Marks of weakness, marks of woe.

(From "London" by William Blake.)

The line has _____ feet of _____ meter and an extra syllable.

3 What immortal hand or eye
Could frame thy fearful symmetry?

(From "The Tyger" by William Blake.)

The first line has _____ feet of _____ meter and an extra syllable.
The second line has _____ feet of _____ meter.

4 Now try these lines from "Richard Cory":

We people on the pavement looked at him
And he was always human when he talked
So on we worked, and waited for the light

Each line has _____ feet of _____ meter.

COMPLETING THE SECTION ON STYLE: RHYME SCHEME

Finding the rhyme scheme is the next step in the style section, and rhyme scheme is very easy to identify.

1 Look at the last word of the first line of the poem. Put an "A" next to it.

Whenever Richard Cory went downtown,   A

2 Look at the last word of the second line. Does it rhyme with the last word of the first line? No? Give it a "B."

We people on the pavement looked at him;   B

3 Look at the last word of the third line.

He was a gentleman from sole to crown,

"Crown" rhymes with the last word of the first line. So give it the same letter "A" as "town" has.

He was a gentleman from sole to crown,   A

4 Look at the last word of the fourth line.

Clean favored, and imperially slim.

Mark it "B" because it rhymes with the last word of the second line.

Beginning to get the hang of it? You can say that the rhyme scheme of the first stanza is A, B, A, B.

Whenever Richard Cory went downtown,   A
We people on the pavement looked at him;   B
He was a gentleman from sole to crown,   A
Clean favored, and imperially slim.   B

Go back to "A" to mark the rhyme scheme for each stanza.

And he was always quietly arrayed,   A
And he was always human when he talked;   B
But still he fluttered pulses when he said,   A
'Good morning,' and he glittered when he walked.   B

(You have to stretch "said" a little to get to rhyme with "arrayed.")

Now that you know how to recognize and analyze the elements of style, you are ready to incorporate them into a paragraph. Check the following example.

Sample Style Paragraph for "Richard Cory"

The style of ''Richard Cory'' expresses the poem's meaning

simply and clearly. The language is easily understood, and the sentence structure uncomplicated. Robinson writes his poem in lines of five feet of iambic meter. For example,

mark out two lines

We péo ple on the páve ment looked at hím;

no example needed

And he was rích--yes, rích er than a kíng--

The rhyme scheme of each stanza is consistent and simple; it is A, B, A, B.

CRITIQUE

This is the last section of your critical analysis. It should include

1 Your personal evaluation of, and reaction to, the poem.

2 A conclusion that ties together everything about the poem that you've just said.

The critique may also include some researched background on the poet and poem, if your instructor requires it. This background should *not* be a standard description of when the poet was born and when the poet died, etc. (usually lifted from the nearest encyclopedia), but material that mentions some common themes, or conflicts, or topics the poet is often concerned with, and how these themes, etc., are relevant to the poem you've been discussing.

Examine our sample critique of "Richard Cory" for suggestions on how to end your essay.

Sample Critique Section for "Richard Cory"

```
    Conveying its ironic message through simple language,

''Richard Cory'' is an effective poem. It expresses an emotion

that many of us feel: envy for those we think lead happier

lives than we do. And it reveals the foolishness of such envy

and the secret pain and sorrow in an individual's life.
```

This theme of the individual in isolation is common to the
work of Edwin Arlington Robinson. Many of his poems, such as
''Miniver Cheevy,'' ''Mr. Flood's Party,'' and ''Bewick
Finzer,'' describe individuals who cannot fulfill their
dreams or who consider themselves failures.

Robinson, an American poet who wrote in the late nineteenth
and early twentieth centuries, explores the inner lives of
such individuals, people who face defeat and who still try to
maintain some moral values. His work challenges us to look
beneath the surface of others' lives and to look within
ourselves as well. If we do so, we may, like the townspeople of
''Richard Cory,'' attain some insight into what a ''happy''
life truly involves.

THE COMPLETE ANALYSIS

A CHECKLIST

Using "Richard Cory" as an example, you have just worked through all the steps of preparing a critical analysis of a short poem. Briefly review the sections of that analysis.

  I Introduction
    A Lead-in
    B Thesis: a one-sentence statement of *theme*.
  II Ideas—a careful paraphrase/interpretation of all the ideas and expressed in the poem.
  III Emotions—a discussion of the emotions expressed within the poem.
  IV Literary Techniques—identification and discussion of the figurative language, imagery, symbols, and other techniques of the poem that use language to enhance meaning.
  V Style—a brief discussion of style and identification of meter and rhyme scheme, the techniques that focus on sound.
  VI Critique—your reaction to the poem, some background (if needed), and a conclusion

So that you can examine the sections of our analysis as they are combined to form a unified essay, what follows is an essay combining all the pieces of the "Richard Cory" critical analysis. Note that you have to add transitions between sections when they are needed, and use this sample as a model for your own work.

A Critical Analysis of "Richard Cory" by Edwin Arlington Robinson

lead-in

Edwin Arlington Robinson's ''Richard Cory'' contrasts the discontented, frustrated lives of small—town people with the seemingly successful and wealthy existence of their hero, Richard Cory. As the ordinary men compare their daily grind of denial with the glitter of Cory's world, they envy him. But, as the poem reveals, their envy is foolish. For Richard Cory's final action reveals a different person from the towns—people's image of him, a person who has been suffering in secret. The poem's final lines indicate that people who are caught up in their own pain fail to see the anguish in others.

theme

ideas

The poem begins by describing Cory as he appears to others. The speaker of ''Richard Cory'' speaks for the people of a small town, and he begins by describing the citizens' interest in Cory. Whenever Cory came to town, those below him in rank, the ''people on the pavement,'' looked at him. He was in every way a gentleman, clean—cut, handsome, aristocratically slender.

ideas

But, the speaker continues, Cory did not flaunt his status; he was always ''quietly arrayed,'' and ''human when he talked.'' Still, a mere ''Good morning'' from Richard Cory set people's hearts racing because they are in awe of him. He seems to glitter as he moves among them.

ideas

Not only is Cory handsome and fine; he is rich and genteel, ''admirably schooled in every grace,'' knowing all the social graces, a true aristocrat. Yet this seeming perfection and the townspeople's lack of money, social background, and social skills create a distance between Cory and the others. They see him as a model of what they have been denied: ''we thought that he was everything/To make us wish that we were in his place.''

The townspeople remain stuck in their rut, waiting for the ''light,'' perhaps for the hope of better times. Seeing Cory, who has so much, they are discontented, for they must do without the luxuries of life (''the meat''), and they are dissatisfied with what they do have (they ''cursed the bread''). The final lines of the poem reveal another person's hidden pain, as Richard Cory, so quietly dazzling, goes home and puts ''a bullet through his head.'' The ideal man, the model for the townspeople, is revealed as a person different from others' fantasies of him.

As Robinson contrasts the idealized Cory perceived by the town with the real man, he attributes a range of emotions to both the ordinary people and the extraordinary man. The town, for example, is in awe of Cory; he is so far above those ''on the pavement'' that a few words from him can set pulses to flutter. They admire his manners, his money, and his clean, slim appearance. And, of course, they envy him and wish to be him: ''we thought that he was everything/To make us wish that we were in his place.'' He has what they do not have, and he is what they cannot be. They feel unhappy with what they do have—the ''bread'' they curse, and they wait only for something better, some ''light'' in their dark lives.

Cory, on the other hand, begins as an enigma. We cannot, at first, be sure what he feels. He is always so quiet, so polite, so gentle, that he seems utterly in control of his existence.

ideas

emotions

emotions

Not until the end of the poem, in Cory's suicide, do we, like
the town, see the hidden despair.

literary techniques The impact of Robinson's poem is heightened by his use of
poetic techniques. One of the most effective techniques is the
use of the irony, an irony developed by contrasting the town's
image of Richard Cory with the reality later exposed. To the
townspeople, Cory is associated with regal images; he is a
gentleman, not from head to foot, but ''from sole to crown,''
richer ''than a king,'' and he ''glittered,'' ''imperially
slim'' like someone royal and dazzling when he walked downtown. The people are surprised that he is even ''human'' when
he talks, an ironic statement, because they fail to see the
human suffering that conflicts with their image of Cory. And,
ironically, seeing only the royal image of the man, they wish
they were ''in his place.''

literary techniques Other techniques reinforce this contrast. There is the
metaphor of a hero who can set one's blood to racing (''he
fluttered pulses''). In a sight image, Cory ''glittered'' in
light, while the townspeople ''waited'' for their own
''light,'' perhaps a symbol of the happiness they feel deprived of. Symbolically, they hate what they have (they
''cursed the bread'') and must do without what they feel they
need (''went without the meat''). Sound imagery builds the
tension of the poem, with its hidden and open miseries; in the
literary techniques beginning, every sound is soft. Cory is ''quietly'' arrayed,
there is the quiet beat of fluttering pulses, the curses of
the discontented people, and ''one calm summer night.'' But

then there is the loud, climactic sound of a gunshot.

There is a frequent use of alliteration, another technique related to sound, as well. There is, for example, the repetition of the ''p'' of ''We people on the pavement looked at him,'' connecting the speaker to the streets. There is much use of the ''w'' and ''th'' sounds in lines such as ''In fine, we thought that he was everything/To make us wish that we were in his place.'' Through such sound devices, as well as through sight imagery, symbols and images, the poet enhances his contrast between a town's illusions and its sudden awakening to reality.

style

The style of ''Richard Cory'' expresses the poem's meaning simply and clearly. The language is easily understood and the sentence structure uncomplicated. Robinson writes his poem in lines of five feet of iambic meter. For example,

We péo ple on the páve ment loóked at hím;

And he was rích--yes, rích er than a kíng--

style

The rhyme scheme of each stanza is consistent and simple; it is A, B, A, B.

critique

Conveying its ironic message through simple language, ''Richard Cory'' is an effective poem. It expresses an emotion that many of us feel: envy for those we think lead happier lives than we do. And it reveals the foolishness of such envy and the secret pain and sorrow in an individual's life.

critique

This theme of the individual in isolation is common to the work of Edwin Arlington Robinson. Many of his poems, such as

''Miniver Cheevy,'' ''Mr. Flood's Party,'' and ''Bewick Finzer,'' describe individuals who cannot fulfill their dreams or who consider themselves failures.

critique

Robinson, an American poet who wrote in the late nineteenth and early twentieth centuries, explores the inner lives of such individuals, people who face defeat and who still try to maintain some moral values. His work challenges us to look beneath the surface of others' lives and to look within ourselves as well. If we do so, we may, like the townspeople of ''Richard Cory,'' attain some insight into what a ''happy'' life truly involves.

EXERCISE: WRITING THE COMPLETE CRITICAL ANALYSIS OF A POEM

You are now ready to write your own critical essay analyzing a poem. Select a short poem, perhaps from the list of suggested poems below, or one suggested by your instructor. Structure your essay according to the steps and sections we have discussed.

Suggested Poems

William Blake—"The Tyger," "The Little Black Boy," "A Poison Tree," "The Chimney Sweeper" (from either *Songs of Innocence* or *Songs of Experience*), "London," "The Garden of Love"

Emily Dickinson—"Because I Could Not Stop for Death," "A Narrow Fellow in the Grass," "My Life Closed Twice," "After Great Pain," "The Soul Selects Her Own Society"

Robert Frost—"Design," "Nothing Gold Can Stay," "Stopping By Woods on a Snowy Evening," "Provide, Provide"

Edwin Arlington Robinson—"Miniver Cheevy," "Reuben Bright," "The Mill," "Cliff Clingenhagen," "Luke Havergal"

William Shakespeare—"Sonnet 18," "Sonnet 29," "Sonnet 73," "Sonnet 116," "Sonnet 130"

John Donne—"Death, Be Not Proud," "Song—Go, and catch a falling star," "The Good Morrow"

Robert Herrick—"To the Virgins, to Make Much of Time"

Richard Lovelace—"To Lucasta, Going to the Wars," "To Althea, From Prison"

William Wordsworth—"The World Is Too Much With Us"
Percy Bysshe Shelley—"Ozymandias"
Alfred, Lord Tennyson—"Crossing the Bar"
Walt Whitman—"When I Heard the Learned Astronomer"
Matthew Arnold—"Dover Beach"
Thomas Hardy—"The Man He Killed"
Wilfred Owen—"Dulce et Decorum Est"
W. H. Auden—"The Unknown Citizen"
Dylan Thomas—"Do Not Go Gentle Into that Good Night"
Countee Cullen—"Yet Do I Marvel"

OTHER WAYS TO WRITE
ABOUT A POEM

The analysis explained in this section is a good approach to writing about short poems; obviously, if you are writing about a poem that is considerably longer, you may not be able to study each element of a poem in such detail. Or you may be required to focus on a more limited topic—to examine just one part of a poem. In either case, you still need to know the *facts* of a poem—what it says and how it says it—if you are going to understand it. You still need to consider its theme, ideas, emotions, literary techniques, and style. That is, you still need to understand how each part of a poem relates to its whole, even if you are going to focus on just one part of it. And you can tie any analysis of part of a poem together with a critique.

An alternative way to analyze a poem, short or long, is to study any one of its parts. You might study

1 Ideas—trace how the poet makes his point through the progression of statements the poem makes. You might even focus on just one section of a very long poem.

2 Emotions—examine the complexity of emotions in a poem.

3 Literary techniques—consider the figurative language and other techniques used in the poem. Or focus on one or two major, recurring techniques, such as the metaphors or symbols in a poem.

4 Style—examine how meter, rhyme, language, and sentence structure are used.

In limiting your topic like this, you must still be careful to give *specific evidence* (direct quotes and examples) from the poem. And you should show how any part of the poem connects to, and enhances, its whole—its *theme*.

242

PART FOUR

THE BASICS
OF LITERARY RESEARCH

All of the sample essays shown earlier in this book could be enhanced by literary research. But the key word is "enhanced," for remember that *whenever you are required to write a literary research paper, the basics of the paper should come from your ideas*. A literary research paper should *not* be a "cut and paste" collection of statements, paraphrased or quoted, from other people. The framework of the paper and its thesis should be yours, and unless the assignment calls *only* for a survey of available research on the topic, most of the ideas of the paper should be yours as well.

The literary research paper, like other research papers, uses the work and words of others (carefully attributed to those "others") to support points *you* have determined. This type of paper is *not a book report*; *not a biography of the author* whose work you are analyzing.

Most often, it is *a literary analysis supported by two kinds of material*:

1 Specific examples from and references to the literary work (poem, story, etc.) you are analyzing

2 Interpretative comments (criticism) from literary scholars.

SELECTING A TOPIC

Before you can begin gathering the material for a literary research paper, you need to narrow your search by selecting a topic for writing. How much choice of topic you will have depends largely on your instructor's assignment. But, whatever margin of choice you are given, keep in mind that the sooner you can *focus* on a topic and *limit* it to manageable proportions, the easier your work should be.

Your instructor may be very specific in your assignment: you may be asked to write a complete critical analysis of a specific play, or to analyze the figurative language in a specific poem. In such cases, you have been given a narrow focus, and your topic is already limited. However, you may find it helpful to narrow it further, perhaps to concentrate on the metaphors in a specific poem, or to select a precise and specific theme for a complete critical analysis rather than to speculate about a number of possible themes.

If the guidelines given by your instructor are wide, you should narrow them yourself. If you are assigned an essay on any play by a specific author, focus, first, on a specific play, and then check with your instructor as to whether your essay can concentrate on one aspect of the play—one character, or several literary techniques—or whether your essay should be a complete critical analysis incorporating discussion of many aspects of the work.

If you are given a wide range of choice and are expected to narrow your topic, one way to do so is to consider some of the topics discussed earlier in this book. You might write a character analysis, or an analysis of key scenes, or of techniques, for example. However you go about selecting a topic, remember that the sooner you can limit your topic, the sooner you can limit your search for relevant material.

FINDING LITERARY CRITICISM

If you have been working through the exercises and assignments in this book, you are familiar with the first kind of material you need for a literary research paper. You know that, to find specific examples, details, and quotations from a literary work, you must read and reread that work, concentrating on finding the appropriate material. It's the second kind of material, the literary criticism, that may be new to you.

When your instructor asks you to research the criticism of a story or poem or play, he or she is not asking you to find material that merely attacks or praises the work. *Criticism* in this new sense means *analysis and interpretation*, explanation of an author's work, themes, characters, conflicts, and techniques.

Such criticism can be found in a number of places, from books to journals, through research. Before you begin to research, however, it is a good idea to have some concept of what you are looking for. Before you begin your research, it's best to

1 Focus on a specific work, or works.

2 Focus on a limited topic.

3 Determine a possible thesis and rough (very rough!) outline for your paper—you can use any of the structures given in this book.

4 Determine how much critical research is required for the assignment. Does the assignment require you to write your own analysis, supplemented by three or four critical sources? Or does the assignment require you to use a wide selection of critical opinion on the topic, limiting the inclusion of your own ideas? Most literary research papers require some blend of your own insight

and of scholarly opinion; most students new to this kind of paper tend to go overboard on the criticism at the expense of their own insight.

RESEARCH IN BOOKS

After you know what you are looking for, and have decided on a focus (tentative thesis and structure) for your essay, you can look for critical material in a number of places.

1 Use the card catalogue. Don't look just in the author catalogue. That will give only books *by* your author. Look up your author in the subject catalogue. It will give you books *about* your author—his life *and* work.

2 Particularly try to find collections of essays on your author. Each chapter in such collections will give you an essay (on your author's work) by a different person, so you will find a wide spectrum of opinion under one cover.

3 If you're lucky, you may also find collections of essays on one specific work (novel, play, even a long poem) by your author. And, even if that work is not the one you are writing about, the collection may be worth examining; it may contain discussions about recurring themes, subject matter, or techniques central to all the work of your author.

4 Check, also, introductions, forewords, or afterwords (written by scholars) to works by your author. These, too, can be valuable sources of criticism.

5 Many classics are also issued in "critical editions." That is, after the text of the work (by your author) is printed, under the same cover a collection of critical essays is included. Critical editions are another valuable source for you.

6 Use the bibliographies of all the sources above to lead you to other books and articles about your author. Use the bibliographies in encyclopedia or literary digest entries about your author to lead you to more sources. (*Warning*: *Do not* try to construct a research paper on the basis of what you find in various encyclopedias or "student guides." These sources may have been sufficient in your middle-school book reports, but now you are capable of using better sources.)

7 Your library's reference section also contains many other guides to books and articles. These guides are a good place to start your research; they can identify the books and articles you need to find.

RESEARCH IN PERIODICALS

The most effective way to find articles on your author's work is to become familiar with the *MLA Index*. This is the most comprehensive guide to periodicals (often called journals) about literature and language. The full name of this index is *The Modern Language Association International Bibliography of Books and Articles on the Modern Languages and Literatures.*

This index is easy to use and covers just about everything written about an author. From 1921 to 1955, the *MLA Index* covered all literary criticism written by Americans; since 1955, it has indexed literary criticism by scholars of all countries.

Early volumes of the index cover a number of years in one volume. Today the index is published each year and requires more than one volume for each year. To use the index, all you have to know is the *country of origin of your author* (Is he British? American?) and *the time period in which he wrote* (eighteenth century? twentieth?). Then go to the index for any year that is appropriate (be careful—nothing will be written about your author in the years before he was born!) and look up the right country and time period, within that country's listings. Your author's name will be indexed there, in alphabetical order. Beneath his name will be a list of all the articles and books written about your author in the year covered by the volume.

Other indexes and digests can help you to locate valuable books and articles. *Contemporary Literary Criticism* and *Book Review Digest*, for example, contain short excerpts of articles and essays. *Contemporary Literary Criticism* excerpts critical studies; *Book Review Digest* includes excerpts from reviews of books in the year the books were published. The *Humanities Index* lists articles from over 200 scholarly journals; the *Essay and General Literature Index* indexes both articles and books.

Note: If you are not sure how to read the entries in the *MLA Index* or any other index, always check the first pages of the index. They almost always provide a guide. The *MLA Index*, for example, abbreviates the names of the journals, and you may not be able to guess the names of the journals. The key to the abbreviation is in the front of each volume, as is an explanation of how to read each part of an entry.

Finding Journals and Articles

Not all libraries put all their journals in one central area. Instead, the journals are scattered throughout the enormous university libraries you may have to deal with. How do you find these journals? Each journal may be shelved, *according to its call number*, just like the books are. So your first step in finding a specific article in a specific journal is to *consult the serials (periodicals) listings* in your library to find the journal's call number. Write that number down, and then find your journal, among the books.

You may also find that your library is storing most of its periodicals on *microfilm*. Again, you can find the appropriate reel of microfilm (which contains the journal article you need) by knowing, first, the call number of the journal you are looking for (microfilm is also stored by call number), and second, the volume, date, article title, pages, etc. of the journal issue you need.

Once you familiarize yourself with using a microfilm reader, you will find the process automatic. In addition, you will appreciate microfilm because, unlike articles stored in their original journal forms, microfilm cannot be ripped out of the journal and stolen. With microfilm, you are assured that, at the end of your search, you will find what you are looking for.

TAKING NOTES

Now that you know where to look, you can save yourself time by looking (and taking notes) in an orderly fashion.

1 As you come across the name of an article or book you want to look up, write it on a 3 × 5 index card. Use a separate card for each article or book. On that card, put the same information you will need for your Works Cited section (a new name for what used to be the Bibliography part of your paper).

2 To save time, put this information in correct Works Cited form now. Below are the correct forms for a variety of books and articles.

BOOKS

Book by one author

Millgate, Michael. William Faulkner. New York: Capricorn, 1971.

Book by two (or three) authors

Houk, Annelle S., and Carlotta L. Bogart. Understanding the Short

   Story. New York: Odyssey, 1969.

If the book has three authors, the third author's name would also be listed, first name and then last name.

More than three authors

Blum, John M. et al. The National Experience. New York: Harcourt

   Brace, 1963.

Book whose introduction you are using

Brightfield, Myron F. Introduction. Mary Barton. By Mrs. Gaskell.

   New York: Norton, 1958. v—xiii.

Use this same form for *Afterwords*, *Prefaces* or *Forewords*.

An article you are using that you found in a collection in a book

Wilson, Edmund. ''Justice to Edith Wharton.'' Edith Wharton: A

   Collection of Critical Essays. Edited by Irving Howe. Englewood

   Cliffs: Prentice—Hall, 1962. 19—31.

ARTICLES

Article that gives you a complete date—day, month, and year, or month and year

Wilson, Edmund. ''William Faulkner's Reply to the Civil Rights

   Program.'' The New Yorker, Oct. 23, 1948: 106—17.

(If your article has both a complete date and a volume number, drop the volume number and write the date.)

Article that gives you a volume number but only an incomplete (year) date

Forrey, Carolyn. ''The New Woman Revisited.'' <u>Women's Studies</u> 2

   (1974): 37—56.

An article that gives you a volume, and a number of the issue, and an incomplete (year) date

Billigheimer, Rachel. ''The Eighth Eye: Prophetic Vision in

   Blake's Poetry and Design.'' <u>Colby Library Quarterly</u> 22.2

   (1986): 93—110.

In this entry the volume is 22. It is followed by a period and then the number is given. The number is 2.

Notice a few things about this form:

- Everything is double-spaced, even the lines within each entry. This won't matter much on your cards, but it will in your paper.
- The first line of each entry starts at the margin. All other lines for the entry are indented five spaces.
- There are no roman numerals.
- There are no p's for page.
- The names of publishers are abbreviated—not Capricorn Books but Capricorn.

If you write each source, in correct form, on a card as you discover the sources (in the card catalogue, indexes, etc.), you will save yourself time preparing your Works Cited page later. Once you've listed your sources on cards, you can begin the next step—finding these sources.

3 Check the library to see which of the sources you need are available. Don't forget to write down the call number of all the articles you are looking for. If the library doesn't have several sources you've listed on cards, don't throw the cards away. You may be able to find these sources at another library.

4 Gather your sources. If you are using a book, survey it for a few minutes before you begin to focus your reading. Check the table of contents and the index for the sections of the book most relevant to your topic.

Then attack the appropriate section(s). And, whether you read a section of a book or an article, *skim the entire selection before you take a single note.* If you don't skim first, but take notes as you read, you may find yourself copying or paraphrasing entire paragraphs, lots of them. Then you may discover that the final paragraph of what you are reading sums up, beautifully, everything you have just spent an hour taking notes on. In addition, you may need to read an entire selection before you can follow the logic and understand the components of its argument.

5 Take notes on the biggest index cards you can find: 4 × 6 or 5 × 8. At the top of the first card for a new source, list all the publishing information (title, author, date, etc.). Subsequent cards for the same source can include some coded abbreviation of this data, for your own use later.

6 Be generous with the note cards. Leave big margins. Leave one or two lines between separate but related points from the same source. Start a new card each time you find a new point, unrelated to earlier notes. Visually, the notes will be easier to work with later if they are not crammed together.

7 Your notes should do two things: first, record specific comments (analysis and interpretation) the author makes, and second, briefly trace the overall structure of the author's analysis, so that the specific material you have recorded fits the context of the larger argument/interpretation.

8 Your notes should include three things: first, a paraphrase of criticism, second, direct quotes, and third, summaries. Whenever you feel the author's language can be simplified without loss of impact or meaning, paraphrase the language—put it into your own words. Whenever you feel the point is stated most effectively in the author's own words, retain the language. You can always paraphrase quotes later. Whenever you feel a lengthy explanation can be summarized, summarize it.

If you record direct quotes, make sure you put quotation marks around them, and copy them *exactly*. Whether your notes are direct quotes or paraphrases or summaries, write down, beside each note, the exact page(s) from which it comes.

9 What kind of material are you looking for? It depends. It depends on your topic. If your paper is about imagery in two of Robert Frost's poems, you are looking for analysis of the images in the specific poems, or references to and analysis of the imagery common to all Frost's poems, or analysis of themes common to Frost (remember, you always relate specific techniques to overall themes). If your paper is a wider analysis of protagonist, antagonist, conflicts, themes, and techniques in some literary work, you are looking for any material about these parts of the work you are analyzing. You are also looking for material on typical themes, characters, conflicts, and techniques in the author's work.

You may find the author you are researching has written about his or her own work; that is, the author has commented on how it was written or what he or she intended to do. You can use such material, which may come from the author's essays, prefaces, speeches, notebooks, or letters.

10 How many notes do you need? The general rule is: it's better to have too much than too little. "Just enough" is probably too little. If your final paper uses every note you took, most likely you've forced the notes into your essay without much regard for their relevance. Assembling a good paper usually means discarding some of your research in favor of something more appropriate.

THE OUTLINE

You started your research with a rough outline. After you've taken quite a few notes, you can revise and develop that rough outline.

Before you begin to revise, check your original thesis. Is it one you can handle, based on the research you are accumulating? Or do you need to change it? Could it be clearer? Sometimes, comparing your thesis to the direction your research is pointing can lead you to a clearer, more precise thesis.

After you have looked over the rough outline, take your note cards and start sorting them, deciding which notes will be appropriate in which section of your paper. Reviewing and sorting your notes will help you to add detail to your essay.

Now you can begin to develop your outline, adding to each section specific detail from the literary work you are analyzing. For example, if you are working on a critical research paper of a short story, add the specifics of the story (examples, direct quotes) to the outline. You can add these specifics in some abbreviated, coded form that works for you.

Then decide where each critical note will best fit into your outline. Mark each spot (coded by the author's name and a page) on the outline, and mark it also on the note card (coded by the outline's section number and letter). This may seem like a time-consuming process, but it has several benefits. It allows you to quickly determine which section of your paper will need more specifics, either from the work itself or from the critics. Then you can look for those specifics, with a precise focus. The process also divides one large chore (writing a draft of an essay that incorporates both the critics and the details of the literary work) into small, manageable pieces. As you write each section of your paper, you can deal *only* with the note cards marked for that section. You can look *only* at the details from the work relevant to that section. They are all listed on your outline. You do not have to shuffle through masses of torn notebook paper, in panic and desperation.

When you have assembled a detailed, specific outline, incorporating your sources, the worst part of your assignment is over. Writing the paper will now be easier and smoother than you would believe!

To give you a sense of what the outline should look like, take a look at the following sample outline, with critical sources and detail from the literary work coded within it. This is an outline for a critical analysis of a short story. The structure of the outline follows the pattern discussed in the Short Story section of this book.

Sample Outline for a Critical Research Essay on Edith Wharton's "The Eyes"

coded reference to
critic

I Lead—in——Lewis 288

Thesis statement: Through the narrator's own account of

the phantom eyes, we realize that one can hide his evil

actions from himself——but only for a time.

plot

II The structure of ''The Eyes'' is somewhat complicated.

A The story begins by describing an evening's conversa-

tion at Culwin's home.

1 Culwin is noted for his dinners and conversation.

2 Seven guests tell ghost stories.

3 Most of the guests depart.

4 The narrator and Phil Frenham, Culwin's young

friend, remain.

5 Culwin is asked to tell a ghost story.

6 He becomes the narrator.

B Culwin, years earlier, was twice haunted by a pair of

eyes.

1 First the eyes appeared when he planned to marry his

cousin Alice.

2 He proposed out of pity, not love.

3 The eyes left when he broke the engagement.

4 Three years later, the eyes appeared when he selfishly deceived Gilbert Noyes.

5 He let Noyes believe Noyes had creative ability.

6 The eyes leave when Culwin sends Noyes away.

7 On the night he tells the story, Culwin understands
the eyes.

protagonist
III The eyes came to Culwin because he is evil inside.

A Inside and outside are different

B He is good natured and charming outside.

C He encourages young, talented men.

coded quote from story
D He is not very involved in life (''detached observer''
41), but he is not actively bad.

E He and his friends believe he is distant but basically
good.

IV A The hidden evil is subtly shown.

antagonist

coded quotes from story
B There is a ''spacious'' (42) home, but it is ''cold''
(41).

C His heart is also cold.

coded quotes from story
D He has no deep feelings (''all men superfluous'' 42)

E He encourages young men to manipulate them (''experimentation'' 42).

coded reference to critic
F Wharton thinks this is wicked. Brown——19.

G His good intentions have bad results.

key scenes
IV We must consider Culwin's actions before each appearance
of the eyes, and his subsequent reactions, to understand
Culwin.

coded quote from story

    A Just before the eyes first appear, Culwin feels vir-

      tuous (''self-righteousness'' 46).

coded reference to
critic

      1 He has proposed to Alice, thinking he is saving her,

        Nevius——98.

coded quote from story

      2 Then the eyes appear (''vicious security'' 48).

      3 Culwin can't connect them to his selfishness.

      4 He isn't learning.

key scene

    B When the eyes appear again, he deceives himself again.

      1 He can't see what he's doing to Noyes is selfish.

coded quote from story

      2 Now the eyes are ''vampires'' (56).

coded reference to
critic

      3 He doesn't see his sins. Wolff——102.

climax

VI In the climax, Culwin sees his evil in Frenham's reaction

    to his story.

    A Frenham hides his face in his hands.

    B He realizes how Culwin uses people.

    C First Culwin misunderstands.

coded quote from story

    D Then he sees himself in a mirror (''hate'' 61).

techniques

VII Culwin's realization is intensified by several symbols

    and images.

    A The eyes are a symbol of evil.

coded quotes from
story

      1 Culwin has ''nice'' (41) eyes when young.

      2 Now, in old age, Culwin has ''red'' eyes in a ''bark''

        (41) face.

      3 There is contrast to innocent people's eyes——Alice

        (''wholesome'' 49), Noyes (''blissful'' 55).

    B There are other images of Culwin that foreshadow his

      evil.

coded quotes from
story

       1 He is an ogre (''juicy'' 42).

       2 He is a gnome (''cowered'' 43).

       3 He is a ''tortoise'' (43).

       4 These are hints he is not human.

conclusion

    VIII Through the eyes, Culwin faces his lack of humanity.

THE DRAFT

INCORPORATING RESEARCH

Once you have a good, complete outline, writing the rough draft is not too difficult. The purpose of the draft is to combine your ideas, evidence from the work you are analyzing, and critics' ideas—in a clear, logical structure. A challenge you will face in writing the draft is making clear exactly what ideas are yours and what ideas come from someone else. That is, you must avoid plagiarism.

PLAGIARISM

You may think you know what plagiarism is, but let's review the meaning of the word. *Plagiarism is passing off the work, words, or ideas of another person as one's own.* What this definition means is:

1 Anytime you use more than three exact words from another writer, or even one key term from another writer, you must put the words in direct quotes and cite the source. "Cite" means give credit to the source of the words, to whoever wrote them first.

2 Anytime you take another person's words and change them into your own words, but keep the other person's ideas (that is, paraphrase or summarize), you must cite the source.

3 Even if you have an idea and find that somebody else had it first, you must cite that "somebody else."

Does this mean that you will be citing quite a bit? Probably, if your essay calls for much research. But keep in mind that if three or four sentences *in a row, in your paragraph*, all come from the same place, you do not have to cite each sentence separately.

In your paper, you must eliminate any plagiarism. *You must give credit (cite) where credit is due.* Fortunately, the new MLA format for internal citation makes it very simple to cite.

THE NEW WAY TO CITE SOURCES

With the new format, almost nothing gets a traditional footnote at the bottom of the page or notes at the end of the essay. The only footnotes you *may* need are explanatory footnotes, which add information, definitions, or comments not essential to the paper itself.

In all other instances, you use the *internal citation*. Here's all you need, *within the paper*: a name and a page.

If you are citing a critic, whether with a *direct quote* or a *paraphrase*, your internal citation looks like this:

Direct Quote

Hippolyte Taine believes that all Dickens's characters belong to two groups: ''people who have feelings and emotions, and people who have none'' (331).

Paraphrase

According to Hippolyte Taine, Dickens's characters can be divided into those who feel and those who do not (331).

Summary of a Long Passage, Retaining the Main Idea but Eliminating the Detail

Hippolyte Taine contrasts two groups of characters in Dickens, roughly split between those with emotions, who are also natural, intuitive, often poor and powerless, and those without emotions, who are sophisticated, intellectual, often rich and powerful (331—332).

All other information, traditionally put into the footnote and bibliography (the name of the book, the place of publication, publisher, date of publication) now go into the Works Cited section, in the form we showed you earlier.

Note that *the author's name is most often worked right into your own sentences. Occasionally* you can put both the author's name and the page in parenthesis, like this:

```
Dickens's characters can be divided into those who feel and

those who do not (Taine 331).
```

But try to avoid this way of citing. It creates a choppy style for your essay and is particularly distracting when you write a direct quote. The reader reads the statement but has no idea who made it until he or she comes to the end of it. Instead, try to think of smooth ways of working the author's name into your sentence. Use phrases like

According to _____	_____ continues
As _____ explains,	_____ describes
As _____ says,	_____ believes that
_____ comments that	_____ notes

Note also that the period for the sentence comes *after* the parenthesis, not before. And note that "p" for "page" is not used; just the page number.

Use your common sense in internal citations. Give the reader enough information to find the work in Works Cited. That is, if you are using *two works by the same author*, a name and a page won't be enough. You will have to *give the name of the specific work* (either in your sentence or in parenthesis) to distinguish it from the other work by the same person.

If you are citing an article that is *unsigned (no author)*, then use the name of the article instead.

If you are *quoting a writer quoted by somebody else*, make sure the reader can find the reference in Works Cited. For example, if F. R. Leavis quoted George Santayana, and you want to quote Santayana, you still have to make it clear where you found Santayana—in Leavis's article. So, you write

As George Santayana says, "When people say that Dickens exaggerates, it seems to me that they can have no eyes and ears" (Leavis 346).

In your Works Cited section, you list the Leavis article. That's where you found Santayana's words.

If your critical research paper focuses on only one novel, play, short story, or poem, you need cite *only* the page if the context makes it clear you are quoting that *one literary work*. When you make reference to the events or dialogue of the work, but *do not quote anything directly, you do not have to cite at all*—not even a page.

Note that this is the *only* material (it is somewhat like a paraphrase) that comes from a source and that needs no citation.

Citing a direct quote from Melville's "Bartleby" in a paper on "Bartleby"

```
Bartleby's most characteristic response, when he is asked to
```

```
change his routine in any way, is ''I would prefer not to''
```

```
(202).
```

No citing for an unquoted reference to some detail of "Bartleby" in a paper on "Bartleby"

```
When the narrator makes an unscheduled visit to his office on
```

```
a Sunday, he learns that Bartleby is living in the office.
```

These unquoted references to the details of the literary work you are analyzing are the *only* instances when you do not have to cite another's material.

If your analysis considers two or more literary works, by the same author, be sure the context of each quotation indicates which work is being quoted. If that is not clear, you must cite the work's name as well as the page. As in any essay, whether it uses critical research or not, you must be careful to put quotes from a literary work into some comprehensible context. *Not*:

> The narrator of "Bartleby" often takes the easy way out. " 'Poor fellow!' thought I, 'he means no mischief; it is plain he intends no insolence; his aspect sufficiently evinces that his eccentricities are involuntary' " (203).

But instead, a context:

> The narrator of "Bartleby" often takes the easy way out. For example, when Bartleby refuses to verify copies of documents, the narrator attempts to excuse him rather than be forced to fire him. " 'Poor fellow!' thought I, 'he means no mischief; it is plain that he intends no insolence; his aspect sufficiently evinces that his eccentricities are involuntary' " (203).

If you are going to use a *long quotation*, either from a literary work or from a critic, you must *follow a new format*. Indent the quote *ten spaces on the left margin*, but keep your usual right-hand margin. *Double-space* the quote; *do not* put quotation marks around it. And, with long quotes, the period comes *before* the parenthesis. A long quote is considered anything *over fifty words or four typed* lines.

AVOIDING LONG QUOTES AND TRANSFORMING THEM

Try to avoid using a number of long, indented quotes. If you use such quotes too often, your paper becomes a cut-and-paste job, a collection of other people's words. There are several ways to avoid a string of long quotes.

1 You can paraphrase the quote completely. For example, you can take the quote below and put it in your own words, retaining all the ideas.

Direct quote:

> The sense of suffocation that so many Wharton characters endure was
> Wharton's birthright, for her childhood in rich, aristocratic old New York of

the 1860s provided her not with the money to buy new and varied experiences, but with the limiting shelter of privilege. Money and rank meant only imprisonment in an exclusive cage where the main topics of conversation were food, fashion, and good form, and where one's day was filled with visiting, dining, and gossip about the select few in one's set.

(From *The Female Intruder in the Novels of Edith Wharton*, by Carol Wershoven, p. 17.)

Paraphrase:

According to Carol Wershoven, Wharton knew, firsthand, the sense of imprisonment she describes in so many of her characters. Her own childhood in the wealthy upper class of New York in the 1860s was a restricted one. Although she was rich, she was denied many experiences. Instead, she grew up trapped in a privileged routine of social activities and gossip about one's set. In this group, the major interests were fine food, proper style, and correct behavior (17).

Note the internal citation.

2 You can also avoid a long quote by breaking it up: quote some of it, paraphrase some of it. This way, you can keep the shorter quote(s) within the regular paragraph format of your paper.

Long quote:

The societies that Wharton writes about are ones in which money is the supreme good, and thus the source of power. Women in these worlds can achieve access to great wealth only through association with a male—hence they have no direct power. While their functions might include the formation and upholding of certain superficial and unimportant customs and traditions, no conventional woman in Wharton's novels makes any important rules for her world; she is merely expected to live by them.

(From *The Female Intruder in the Novels of Edith Wharton*, by Carol Wershoven, p. 15.)

Part direct quote, part paraphrase:

In the societies Wharton writes about, Wershoven says, women have no real power. Since money is the source of power in these environments, women can gain power only indirectly, through a connection to a rich man: a father, or lover, or spouse. Women may be allowed to develop and maintain "certain superficial and unimportant customs and traditions," but no woman who conforms to society's standards "makes any important rules for her world; she is merely expected to live by them" (15).

Note the internal citation; note that the second citation to an author requires only the last name.

3 You can quote only the essential part of the material. Indicate what you've omitted with an *ellipsis* (. . .). If you've omitted the end of a sentence or an entire sentence, you will have a fourth period in the ellipsis, for the period you omitted.

Direct quote:

This pattern, which emerges in too many of the novels to be casual or accidental, always contains one type of character, which I will call the female intruder. This intruder may be defined as the woman who is in some way outside of her society; she is different from other women, whether because of her background or lack of social status or because she has violated some social taboo.

(From *The Female Intruder in the Novels of Edith Wharton*, by Carol Wershoven, p. 14.)

Direct quote cut with ellipsis:

Wershoven says that ''This pattern . . . always contains one type of character . . . the female intruder. This intruder may be defined as the woman who is in some way outside of her society . . . because of her background or lack of social status or because she has violated some social taboo'' (14).

Note the internal citation.

3 If you want to use the main idea of a long passage but do not need to include every detail of the passage, you can summarize a long quote. That is, you can reduce the quote by concentrating on its central idea and then put that idea in your own words.

Long quote:

The intruders bear a close relationship to their creator as well, for their endless struggle to maintain some sense of self that threatens an intolerant society is a struggle that Edith Wharton, from her own experience, understood well. The pattern of Wharton's life parallels the conflicts she wrote of so frequently in her novels, and the pain, rejection, and isolation with which Edith Wharton lived most of her life provided her with a special identification with those female characters who suffer and grow as she did.

(From *The Female Intruder in the Novels of Edith Wharton*, by Carol Wershoven, p. 17.)

Summary:

Edith Wharton's personal conflicts, suggests Wershoven, mirrored those of her intruder characters (17).

Note the internal citation.

With these four options, you should be able to avoid too many long quotes in your essay. So that you become more comfortable with using these options, do the exercise that follows.

EXERCISE: PARAPHRASING, SUMMARIZING, AND DIRECT QUOTES

To develop your skill at incorporating research, try this exercise. Follow the directions for each section below.

1 Paraphrase the following quotation, retaining all the material it contains. Also include a correct internal citation.

Faulkner's preoccupation with the South in the great majority of his novels seems a product less of his will than of his environment; for Faulkner, as a Southerner intensely aware of the past of his own region and of his own family, the South was not merely an obvious subject for his fiction but, fiercely and inescapably, the inevitable subject.

(From *Faulkner*, by Michael Millgate, p. 4.)

Paraphrase: _____

_____

_____

_____

_____

_____

_____

_____

2 Take the following direct quote, paraphrase some of it, quote some of it. Your quote(s) should be short enough so that the passage can be retained within the standard paragraph format of your paper. Also use internal citation correctly.

The commonest charges brought against Faulker were that he lacked political awareness or a social conscience, that he wilfully obscured by unnecessary displays of technique what were essentially simple stories and situations and, above all, that he was a cynical exploiter of violence, cruelty and perversion for their own sakes.

(From *Faulkner*, by Michael Millgate, pp. 103–104.)

Paraphrase/quote: _____

_____

_____

_____

_____

_____

_____

_____

_____

_____

_____

3 Take the following quote, retain (in quotes) what is most important, indicate (by ellipsis) what is omitted. Cite correctly.

Oxford and Jefferson are exactly the same distance from Memphis in exactly the same direction, and many features of the two towns coincide—down to the position of the Confederate monument which plays such an important part on the last page of *The Sound and the Fury*—but it is impossible to say categorically that Jefferson *is* Oxford.

(From *Faulkner*, by Michael Millgate, p. 3.)

Quote/ellipsis: _____

_____

_____

_____

_____

_____

_____

_____

4 Look again at the direct quote in item 3. This time, summarize it. Cite correctly.

Summary: _____

_____

_____

MORE ON THE DRAFT

After you are familiar with the different ways of incorporating research into your paper, you can begin writing your draft. Write an *entire* draft before you worry about revision, so that you have a sense of the whole paper. If at all possible, *type the draft*. Typing will help you identify errors at a glance, give you a better sense of the length of your paper, and lead to a more organized, coherent final copy.

As you write, *refer (often!) to your outline*. Are you following it? And *keep your thesis in mind*. Are you supporting it, or wandering from the subject?

In the initial draft, don't be too concerned with your introduction, transitions, or conclusion. Don't expect them to be perfect the first time. This is a first draft. Don't spend too long on any one section of the paper. Get it all down. You can revise later. Sometimes "worrying over" the exact words for the introduction or the perfect transition becomes an excuse for not going any further.

As you introduce research into your paper, be sure your draft indicates where it comes from. This will save time later.

WORKS CITED

After you've written the first draft of the paper, draft the Works Cited section. This section used to be called the Bibliography. Now it is a list of all the works you referred to (either with a direct quote or a paraphrase) in your paper. You also cite the source in which the literary work you are analyzing appears. The list of cited works is given in alphabetical order—alphabetized by the authors' last names. If there is no author for a particular work, alphabetize the title of the article or book. If you alphabetize the source cards you used to start your research, weeding out the sources you didn't use, completing the list of Works Cited is easy.

A sample Works Cited page is included at the end of this discussion. Look it over, and use it as a model for your own work.

EDITING THE ROUGH DRAFT

When you have completed your initial rough draft, put it away for awhile—for one day, if possible. Then, when you reexamine it, you can look at it with a fresh point of view, almost like a stranger. In this review, consider:

Content: Does this essay *say anything of your own*? Or is it just a summary of other peoples' research and interpretation? Are all the interpretations you make supported by specifics from the work you are analyzing?

Structure: Is the thesis precise? Does all the material in your essay relate to the thesis? Is there any material that wanders off the subject? Are the paragraphs developed sufficiently? Does the paper begin with an interesting lead-in? Is the conclusion effective?

Style: How smooth are the transitions within paragraphs? How smooth are the transitions between paragraphs? Is this paper easy to read? Is it easy for the reader to follow the points you are making? Is the word choice appropriate (not too informal, not too elevated)?

Mechanics: Is the punctuation correct? Is the spelling (particularly of the names of authors and titles) correct? Are all direct quotes copied exactly? Are internal citations and cited works punctuated correctly?

Citations: Is there a citation for everything that needs to be cited? Are the entries in the Works Cited section complete? Is the internal citation clear, complete, and smooth?

If the final copy of your essay is to be superior in content and style, the rough draft will be revised extensively. A few students think the purpose of a rough draft is to "write the paper out" once, so that they can then notice one or two little things that need to be corrected before the final copy is prepared. These students submit a final essay nearly identical to their draft. They are often disappointed with their final grade for their papers because they are unaware thay have missed a crucial step in writing a successful essay: revision. Moving from the rough draft to the final paper takes concentration and effort; you may have to revise entire sentences, combine other sentences, add new sentences, add paragraphs, delete sentences or paragraphs, move sentences, shift paragraphs. You will have to add transitions, cut wordiness, check each line for grammatical errors. You may even have to work through one or two more drafts before you move on to the final copy.

The payoff for all this revision, of course, is a quality essay. To a reader, that final copy may look like it was simple to write—because it is clear, smooth, logical. *All your work at revision is done so that your reader does not have to work*, so that your point is so well-expressed and so convincingly presented it appears simple. It's hard to make it look so easy.

PREPARING THE FINAL COPY

Instructors differ in their requirements for the final copy of a research paper, so the most important rule to remember is, *check with your instructor* on the specifications for the paper. Some instructors want you to include a copy of your outline; others do not. Some want you to include the course number and section on the title page; others require only the name of the course.

There *are* several guidelines you can follow in preparing your final essay:

1 Unless you have some extraordinary reason preventing it, you should type the final paper.

2 The entire manuscript is double-spaced, including indented long quotes and the Works Cited page.

3 One-inch margins on all sides are generally acceptable.

4 Page numbers go in the upper right-hand corner of each page.

5 A title page generally includes the title of your essay, your name, the date you submit the essay, and the course it is written for.

Note: Most instructors will not mind a few proofreading corrections for spelling, transposed letters, punctuation, or corrections written in on your final review of the manuscript. Most instructors regard such corrections as a sign of your attention to detail. But extensive written correction can look sloppy, and first impressions do matter.

What follows is a sample critical research paper. This sample essay uses a minimum of literary research, to show you that you can write a paper based largely on your own analysis and still use literary research for a little support. Your instructor may require you to use more extensive research, but the format for internal citation and the Works Cited section remains the same.

Edith Wharton's "The Eyes": The Inescapable Recognition

Carol Sheridan
ENG 1102
March 15, 1987

(Students should check
with their instructors
about where *this*
information should
appear.)

lead-in

    Edith Wharton's ''The Eyes'' is, in many ways, not a typical

ghost story. It contains no stormy nights in ancient castles,

no bloody figures, no dungeons. In fact, there is no ghostly

body at all, only a pair of eyes. Yet the story creates a sense

of terror for what it reveals about human evil. R. W. B. Lewis

citing a direct quote
from a critic

calls it one of Wharton's finest short stories, '' a subtle

study in human egotism at its most extreme and self-deceiv-

ing'' (288). Through the narrator's own account of the phantom

thesis

eyes, we realize that one can hide his evil actions from

himself——but only for a time.

plot summary

    The structure of ''The Eyes'' is somewhat complicated. As

the story begins, the first narrator describes an evening's

conversation at the home of Culwin, an older, wealthy man

noted for his fine dinners and cultured conversation. The

seven guests amuse one another by telling ghost stories around

the fire, but Culwin contributes nothing. As the time grows

later, five guests depart, leaving only the first narrator, an

old acquaintance of Culwin, and Phil Frenham, Culwin's latest
young friend, and Culwin himself. When Frenham challenges
Culwin to tell his own ghost story, Culwin becomes the central
narrator of the central tale.

plot summary

Years earlier, as Culwin tells it, he had been haunted, on
two very different occasions, by a pair of hideous eyes
glaring at him from the darkness. On the first occasion, the
eyes had appeared when Culwin had decided to ''do the right
thing'' and marry his adoring cousin Alice Nowell, a woman he
pitied but did not love. When he broke the engagement, the
eyes disappeared. Three years later, the eyes appeared again,
when Culwin encouraged and supported a charming young man,
Gilbert Noyes, who had dreams of becoming a writer. Rather
than lose Noyes's companionship, Culwin deceived Noyes into
believing he had literary talent. Immediately, the terrible
eyes returned to haunt Culwin's nights, and they did not leave
until, months later, Culwin cruelly cast Noyes aside. Until
the night he recounts this story, Culwin has no idea why the
eyes came to him. But suddenly, as he watches his new young
friend Frenham react to the tale in horror, Culwin realizes
the evil eyes are his own.

protagonist

Why should such a horror come to Culwin? The answer lies in
the hidden evil of his nature. On the surface, Culwin is a
good-natured, cultivated man, well-educated and well-man-
nered. He is noted for his cultivation of young, talented men,
for his encouragement of their talents. True, he has never
been very involved in the emotional conflicts others face,

instead he is ''a humorous detached observer of the immense muddled show of life'' (41), but then he has never been actively evil, either. At least this is what Culwin's friends, and he himself, believe of his nature.

The hidden side of Culwin is only subtly revealed. The ''light, spacious and orderly'' nature of his environment (42) is also ''somewhat cold and drafty'' (41), and the coldness of Culwin's house comes from the coldness of his heart. He has no deep feelings; as a student of the human race, he has concluded that ''all men were superfluous, and women only necessary because someone had to do the cooking'' (41). Even Culwin's one habitual human association, his recruiting of talented young men for his social circle, is a kind of ''experimentation'' (42). To a writer like Edith Wharton, who, as E. K. Brown says, believed deeply that one must welcome intense experience and must openly express his de-sires (19), this lack of feeling is truly wicked. And equally sinister is the way Culwin's good intentions become somehow twisted into bad ones, as in his experiences with Alice Nowell and Gilbert Noyes. But this hidden evil is only revealed in Culwin's encounters with the eyes.

We must consider Culwin's actions immediately before each appearance of the eyes, and his subsequent reactions, to understand him. Just before the first appearance of the eyes, Culwin feels a ''glow of self-righteousness'' (46) after proposing marriage to the innocent and worshipful Alice. Although he feels no love for her at all, he congratulates

---

Margin annotations:

citing a quote from the story

antagonist

citing quotes from the story

citing a quote from the story

citing a critic, paraphrased

first key scene

citing quote from story

himself for saving her from a life of mediocrity. As Blake Nevius notes, ''It is at the moments when his [Culwin's] unconsciously selfish motives are at widest variance with his actions that the eyes appear to accuse him'' (98). That night, the eyes, old, sunken, redlined and hideous, appear. The most

unpleasant part of them is their look of ''vicious security.''

To Culwin, they are the eyes of a person ''who had done a lot of harm in his life, but had always kept just inside the danger lines . . . not the eyes of a coward but of someone much too clever to take risks'' (48). Culwin does not make the connection between his casual manipulation of Alice's feelings, his egotism in believing he can make her feel happiness without risking any feeling himself, and the look in the eyes. He cannot see himself yet.

In the second appearance of the eyes, Culwin again deceives himself. He convinces himself that he is encouraging Gilbert Noyes's ambition out of kindness, not selfishness. In reality, he wants to keep the adoring young man in his power. Even

when the eyes become those of ''vampires with a taste for young flesh'' and seem ''to gloat over the taste of a good conscience'' (56), Culwin cannot see them as a reflection of

his own sins. He does not recognize what Cynthia Griffin Wolff calls the ''sinister, parasitic relationship'' Culwin develops with his followers (102).

In the reaction of his latest follower, Phil Frenham, to Culwin's story, Culwin finally sees himself. In this climactic scene, after Frenham hears of Noyes's disintegration and despair, Frenham buries his face in his hands. Frenham sees his own future in Noyes's past; he sees what Culwin will do to him. Culwin will use him and then cast him aside when he becomes boring. When Culwin, misunderstanding Frenham's reaction, asks, ''<u>Have</u> you seen the eyes?'' Culwin sees himself in a mirror on the wall. As Frenham raises his head, Culwin ''and the image in the glass confronted each other with a glare of slowly gathering hate'' (61). Culwin cannot hide from himself any longer.

Culwin's realization is intensified by Wharton's technical skills. Wharton uses the ghostly eyes, of course, as a symbol of Culwin's inner evil. And she reinforces this horror by other, repeated images of eyes. As a young man, Culwin appeared to be ''a charming little man with nice eyes,'' but in Culwin's old age even his friend describes ''the red blink of (his) eyes in a face like mottled bark'' (41). The contrast between the eyes of innocent people, about to be destroyed by Culwin, and the ghostly eyes, is stressed. When the eyes first frighten Culwin, he tries to remember Alice's eyes ''as wholesome as fresh water'' (49) to drive the spirits away. When he has deceived Noyes, he is remembering the young man's ''blissful eyes'' (55) as the evil ones return.

Other images of Culwin foreshadow the revelation of his sins. His love of gourmet dinners is connected to his need for adoring and talented followers. One friend even, humorously, compares him to an ogre, saying Culwin liked his followers ''juicy'' (42). In another description, as he begins his tale,

---

Margin notes:

citing quote from story

techniques

citing quotes from the story

techniques

citing quotes from the story

Culwin ''cowered gnomelike among his cushions,'' and he shot his head out of a mist of cigar smoke ''with a queer tortoise-like motion he sometimes had'' (43). These are early hints that Culwin is not quite human.

conclusion

Through the apparition of the eyes, Culwin is forced to face his lack of humanity. This revelation is not accompanied by bolts of lightning; it does not take place in a haunted castle, but it is nevertheless frightening. For it is truly horrible to consider the evil a person can do in the name of kindness.

Works Cited

Brown, E. K. ''Edith Wharton,'' <u>Etudes Anglaises</u> 2 (1938): 16—36.

Lewis, R. W. B. <u>Edith Wharton: A Biography</u>. New York: Harper, 1975.

Nevius, Blake. <u>Edith Wharton: A Study of Her Fiction</u>. Berkeley: Univ. of California Press, 1961.

Wharton, Edith. <u>The Ghost Stories of Edith Wharton</u>. New York: Popular Library, 1973.

Wolff, Cynthia Griffin. <u>A Feast of Words: The Triumph of Edith Wharton</u>. New York: Oxford Univ. Press, 1977.

Note:

Give the pages of an article.

Do not give the pages for books.

Alphabetize entries by author's name. If there is no author (usually for articles), alphabetize by the title of the article.

Double-space within and between each entry.

Every line *except* the first line of each entry is indented five spaces from the left-hand margin.

OTHER SUBJECTS TO WRITE ABOUT

So far, you have seen the basics—analyzing and writing about short stories, plays and poems, writing the critical research paper. There are other ways to write about these kinds of literature, and there are other kinds of literature to write about. This section will explore some options, some other ways to write and things to write about. Just keep in mind that whatever form of literature you write about, and whatever form your writing takes, good writing demands a careful reading of literature, and an essay grounded in the specifics of that literary work.

WRITING ABOUT THE NOVEL

You can write about a novel using the same structure you used to write about a short story. Both short stories and novels express themes, and both depict a conflict between a protagonist and antagonist. Both kinds of fiction employ such literary techniques as symbols, images, irony, and foreshadowing. So the basis for critical analysis of a novel can be

   I Introduction
     Lead-in
     Thesis statement (a one-sentence statement of theme)
  II Short plot summary
 III Analysis of protagonist(s)
  IV Analysis of antagonist(s)
   V Tracing of conflict through key scenes
  VI Identification of climax and solution

VII Discussion of literary techniques
VIII Conclusion—restating theme

Differences from the Story Analysis

There are a few significant differences that will distinguish the essay on a novel from one on a short story. All the differences stem from the fact that a novel is longer than a short story.

1 Since the novel is longer, its plot may be far more complex than that of a short story. It may even have one main plot, and several subplots. It may have several interlocking main plots. In either case, it will have more than one protagonist and antagonist.

2 Analyzing the novel and determining one theme can be difficult. You will have many more possible themes to choose from, and *you must focus on one—* if you are to focus your essay.

3 Similarly, the plot will be involved. In the short story analysis, the plot summary and the tracing of conflicts sections of your essay may cover the same events, with a different emphasis in the two sections. In the novel analysis, your plot summary may skim the important events of the entire novel, but your section tracing and interpreting conflict may be limited to considering a few key events central to the one theme you have selected to discuss. The conflicts section may gloss over (or even ignore) parts of the plot summary not too significant to your statement of theme.

4 To sum up, if you are asked to write a critical analysis of all aspects of a novel (theme, characters, conflicts, techniques), be sure to limit your focus to a single theme so that your topic is manageable. Concentrate on interpretation, not on plot summary.

Other Ways to Analyze a Novel

Another option in writing literary analysis of a novel is to narrow your focus even further. You may write a well-developed paper on any one element of the novel:

1 Analysis of the protagonist
2 Analysis of the antagonist
3 Tracing the conflict of the novel
4 Analyzing, in depth, one central scene of the novel
5 Analyzing the literary techniques of the novel
6 Careful analysis of one significant technique used in the novel.

If you choose one of the options, be sure to support your points with many specific examples and direct quotes from the novel. And remember to show the relevance of whatever element (character, conflict, technique) you are discussing by connecting that element to the novel's theme.

WRITING ABOUT FILM

Because you may think of film as a form of entertainment and nothing more, or as a mysterious blending of technical magic and art that is "way above your head," you may be lost when asked to write about a film. Granted, film entertains, but so do plays and short stories. And granted, the techniques and artistry that combine to produce good films can be intimidating to the new-comer. But you can easily write about film if you regard it as a form of literature.

Like other kinds of literature, many films depict a conflict between charac-ters, a conflict which reaches a climax and is resolved. Like other kinds of literature, films make points; they express themes. Therefore you can approach the analysis of film as you do the analysis of a short story or a novel. You can use the same basic structure you have used for the short story or novel.

The Basic Outline for Analyzing Film

> **I** Introduction
> Lead-in
> Thesis (a one-sentence statement of the film's theme)
> **II** Short plot summary
> **III** Analysis of protagonist
> **IV** Analysis of antagonist
> **V** Tracing of conflict through key scenes
> **VI** Identification of climax and solution
> **VII** Analysis of techniques
> **VIII** Conclusion—restating theme

Naturally, there are some significant differences between writing about a short story and writing about a film. A film has no "author," but it does have a(n)

1 Director who determines much of the film's technique, who is illuminating the film's meaning as he or she presented each scene
2 Author of the screenplay, who wrote the script for the film.

The names of the director and screenwriter are important; watch for them as you view the credits of the film.

It may be impossible to determine "who did what" to create the film. Did the screenwriter decide to add that special detail to a scene, did the director and the film editor transform the impact of a scene by editing it a certain way? While you cannot be expected to know the answers to such questions, you may need to do a little preliminary research into the film you are writing about. If you know the year the film was first released, you can read contemporary reviews of the film. There are also many excellent books and journals that discuss the art of the film, the history of films, specific films, and the works of various directors, screenwriters, etc. If you read a little about a film before you view it, you can enhance your own viewing of the film. *The more you know what to look for, the more you will see.*

Viewing a Film Critically

If you are going to write about a specific film, you cannot watch it the way you would a Saturday matinee, casually and carelessly.

You must watch it *attentively*, with a notebook in hand. You may think it is impossible to take notes in the dark, but you'll be surprised how quickly you can get used to it! Note the director, screenwriter, the characters' names (as well as the names of the actors who portray them). Note the key scenes, the details of the setting, snatches of significant dialogue (perhaps lines or phrases that are repeated in different parts of the film), the techniques used.

If at all possible, view the film twice. Try to see beyond the plot to the literary patterns developing, the structure of the conflict, the expressions of theme.

Film Techniques

Films, like all types of literature, rely on certain literary techniques to express and enhance meaning. Like novels and short stories, films utilize irony, foreshadowing, symbolism, images, and imagery. Like plays, films rely heavily on dialogue to convey meaning. Like poems, films can condense meaning into a single image, a startling connection.

But film is a special form, and it has its own characteristic techniques. While it would take several intensive courses in film to make a person fairly proficient in recognizing film technique, there are some basic film devices you can acquaint yourself with. Such knowledge will help you derive deeper meaning from, and a deeper understanding of, film. As you view a film, ask yourself such questions as

How is music being used in this film?

Is there background music throughout, or is music used only in key scenes?
Is the music intrusive or does it seem to blend into the film effectively?
Is music used to underscore emotion or to heighten suspense? Is the music used to inject emotion which would be better expressed by effective dialogue and/or effective visual techniques?

What kinds of unusual camera angles are used?

The normal camera angle puts the viewer at eye level.
Does the film use a high or low level? For what purpose?

What kinds of photographic shots are used—and when?

A panoramic shot is a wide, expansive view; a scene is a closer, more limited view; a close-up narrows the view to an actor or actors.

Is a dissolve used? This is a shot that gradually disappears as another image takes its place.

Is a fade-in used? Here a shot darkens to black (fade-out) or lightens to a new picture (fade-in).

Does the film use fast or slow motion?

Does the film use a freeze-frame? This is a stop in the motion.

Does the camera ever pan? Here the camera is held in one place but is moved vertically or horizontally.

Is a mask used? A mask blacks out part of the screen.

Is there any of montage? A montage is a series of quick images or shots, often used to move the story forward. For example, in older movies, a montage of the pages of a calendar fly off the wall, indicating the days flying by.

Is there any use of soft focus? This is a kind of blurred quality.

Is the film (or any part of it) shot in a specific color tint?

How does the story move forward?

Are the events in chronological order? Is there any use of a voice-over (a narrator)? Are there significant or startling cuts (transitions from one visual image to another)?

If you notice *any* film technique, ask yourself *why* it is used. What does it add to the film? Just as you would relate any other literary technique, consider how film techniques enhance the film's themes. This linking of technique to theme will help you unify your analysis of a film, so that all the specifics of your essay connect to the meaning of the film as a whole.

Other Ways to Analyze Film

Another way to analyze a film is to focus on one aspect—the film's protagonist and/or antagonist, conflict, or techniques. You can discuss one aspect in depth. Your essay will be unified if you can link the aspect you are discussing to a dominant theme of the film.

Essentials of a Film Analysis

As in a critical analysis of any form of literature, the test of your essay will be its use of specifics—details, examples, included in your interpretation. A long plot summary, disguised as analysis, will not do. A careful interpretation, supported by many references to the details of the film, will do very well. Such an interpretation demands an attentive viewing, with careful note taking, as the basis of a good analysis.

WRITING ABOUT TWO WORKS: A COMPARISON

At some time, you may be asked to write an essay that discusses two works— short stories, plays, or poems. You may have to consider two works by the same author, or two works by different authors. What you will, most likely, need to focus on is the similarities in the works so that your paper is not just two analyses of two separate works. However, your essay can also take some notice of differences.

It's not that difficult to identify similarities; as with most writing, the easiest way to begin is with *lists*. To familiarize yourself with the process, take a look at Edith Wharton's short story ''The Eyes'' and John Cheever's short story ''The Swimmer,'' and consider how you could write an essay about them.

You can start with two lists—one for differences, and one for similarities. That way, much of what you notice can be put somewhere.

Differences: ''The Eyes'' and ''The Swimmer''

''The Eyes'' was published in 1910.
''The Swimmer'' was published in 1964.
''The Eyes'' is a ghost story.
''The Swimmer'' is about life in suburbia and isn't supernatural.
''The Eyes'' covers the events of one night but flashes back to incidents of many years.
''The Swimmer'' seems to cover one afternoon.
The style of ''The Eyes'' makes it harder to read than ''The Swimmer.''
The main character of ''The Eyes'' is single and rich and doesn't work for a living.
The main character of ''The Swimmer'' has to work and has a family.

Similarities: ''The Eyes'' and ''The Swimmer''

Men are the main characters of both stories.
Both men don't seem to know their inner selves too well.
Both stories have somewhat weird endings.
Both men are pretty selfish.
Both men hurt other people.
Both men get hints that something is wrong in their lives.
Both men stay pretty much the same throughout the stories.
Both men learn awful things at the end of the stories.

After you have lists, look at them carefully. Look closely at the ''similarities'' list. Does it lead you anywhere? The list on ''The Eyes'' and ''The Swimmer'' seems to be leading toward some point about the main characters. Are they alike in personality? In what happens to them? In why it happens? Maybe you can come up with a *thesis* by looking at these *similar* characters.

They don't know themselves well.
They ignore hints about something being wrong.
They hurt others.
They learn some awful things.

Now try to come up with a thesis, for example:

In both ''The Eyes'' and ''The Swimmer,'' you can observe the dangers of self-deception as the protagonists' blindness to their own flaws leads to destruction and misery.

Now, with a thesis, you can begin a rough outline of your essay. This outline can focus on the similarities between the stories: you can use the differences in the lead-in and in the detail of the individual paragraphs. If your assignment is to start with two works with an obvious similarity (of character or setting or theme) and to highlight differences, then you will, of course, structure your essay around differences. But in most cases, an essay on two works is structured around similarities, and you are not expected to give an equal amount of attention to differences.

You can organize your essay one of two ways: *subject-by-subject* or *point-by-point*. Later in this section, you will see an example of an essay using the subject-by-subject structure, and an essay organizing the same material in a point-by-point structure.

When you write in a subject-by-subject structure, you begin with a thesis that covers both the works you are analyzing, but then you devote one half of the body of your paper to only *one* work (the first subject), and the second half of the body of your paper to the *other* work (the second subject). You conclude by discussing the two works together again.

This is an easy structure, but it has a couple of drawbacks. When you get to the second work you are discussing, you must remember to discuss the same aspects of it that you discussed about the first work. That is, if you discussed foreshadowing in the first work, you need to discuss foreshadowing in the second work. And you need to *remind* your reader that what you are saying about the second work *points up its similarities* to the first work. Without these reminders, your paper will split itself into two essays on two works. The reminders, whether they are repeated key words, or phrases, or sentences, or even entire paragraphs, are *transitions*, ways of linking the two subjects. Transitions should be smooth and should be used frequently.

When you write in a point-by-point structure, you also begin with a thesis about both works, but, instead of then shifting to discussing one work in its entirety and then the other, you keep shifting between the two works. That is, if you notice that foreshadowing is similar in both works (your first point), you will do a section on foreshadowing as it appears in your first work *and* in your second. Your next point may be that both works use similar symbols, so, after you make that point, you will discuss the symbols in one work, and then in the other. And so on, to your next point. In this kind of structure, you still need transitions, but they are needed most frequently as you shift back and forth in discussing the two works.

Which structure is better? That's up to you, and depends on which one you feel creates a clearer presentation of your ideas. Which structure is easier? That's up to you, and depends on what works most smoothly for you.

But whether you organize your essay in a subject-by-subject or point-by-point structure, *be sure to conclude your comparison/contrast by tying the works together in some significant way*. Write at least one paragraph that brings the works back together, and say something besides the fact that the works are similar in this, this, and this way. You will write a better conclusion if you ask yourself, "How do these similarities reveal a common concern? Or a common message? Or a common theme?" In other words, what's the *point* of your comparison?

People make comparisons every day. They tell their friends that restaurant A and restaurant B have nearly the same menu, the same decor, and similar prices. But the comparison usually has some point: restaurant A is a deliberate copy of B, or restaurant A will take customers away from B. Evidence, even in casual conversation, leads somewhere. So should your written comparison/contrast.

The tie-together in the conclusion is particularly important if the similarities you have noted are about parts of the works—parts like specific characters or literary techniques. In such cases, you can widen the significance of these similarities by relating them to *theme*. And even if your essay is already focused on similarities of theme, be sure to come back to a general tie-together of the themes of both works in your conclusion.

Note: Citations. When you quote from more than one literary work, as you will in a comparison/contrast essay, your instructor may want you to cite the pages of each work. Be sure to check whether your instructor wants such citation.

In the following pages, you will see two comparison/contrast essays on "The Eyes" and "The Swimmer." The first uses the subject-by-subject structure.

As you read it, concentrate on how this structure works. To help you concentrate, *underline the thesis* of the essay and the *topic sentence of each paragraph*. Also *underline* all the *words, phrases, and sentences* that are used as *transitions*. There is also one entire paragraph that is used as a *transition paragraph*. Underline that paragraph also. Note how the concluding paragraph ties the two stories together.

Sample Essay on Edith Wharton's "The Eyes" and John Cheever's "The Swimmer": A Comparison Using the Subject-by-Subject Structure

Edith Wharton's ''The Eyes'' and John Cheever's ''The Swim-

mer'' hardly seem to have much in common. They were published

more than fifty years apart, and one is a ghost story while the

other is a story about a Sunday in American suburbia. Yet,

despite superficial differences, the stories share a common

concern, expressed in the conflicts of the two protagonists,
Wharton's Andrew Culwin, and Cheever's Neddy Merill. In depicting men who are blind to their own flaws, and in tracing
the effects of this blindness, Wharton and Cheever focus on a
similar theme. In both ''The Eyes'' and ''The Swimmer,'' we
observe the dangers of self-deception, as the protagonists'
refusal to see their own flaws leads to destruction and
misery.

On the surface, Wharton's story does not appear to be about
a man with inner failings. Instead, Andrew Culwin appears to
be a man who is rightly complacent about his values and
attitudes. A well-educated, wealthy man, Culwin has not led a
life of wild dissipation, but instead ''had always been
possessed of a leisure which he had nursed and protected''; he
has devoted his time to ''the cultivation of a fine intelligence and a few judiciously chosen habits'' (41). His
relationships with others seem to show compassion and consideration. He says he proposes to his poor cousin Alice, for
example, out of a desire to make her happy; his reward is ''a
glow of self-righteousness'' (46). He encourages the dreams
of Gilbert Noyes, an aspiring writer without much talent,
because, he says, ''the human plant generally needs warmth to
flower'' (53), and again his declared intentions are kind and
warm.

But Culwin, despite his professed good intentions, is essentially a selfish man. His decision to marry Alice is a
condescending act; he feels so superior to Alice that his

proposal is, to him, a kind of gift. And he is drawn to her
because she makes him feel superior. When he meets Alice,
Culwin is dreaming of writing a great masterpiece, but he
cannot do it. Alice is his adoring assistant; to Culwin she is
''a nice girl'' who is ''just what I needed to restore my
faith . . . principally in myself'' (45). Similarly, Culwin
encourages Gilbert Noyes' fantasies of literary success because Gilbert, who worships Culwin, is so charming a
companion. Deceiving Gilbert, Culwin deceives himself as to
his motives.

Culwin may be blind to his own selfishness, but the reader
soon perceives the problem and its effects. Although Wharton
gives no description of Alice's suffering when Culwin suddenly rejects her, the earlier descriptions of her
sensitivity and trust hint at what pain she must feel at
Culwin's rejection. As for Gilbert Noyes, Culwin callously
describes the stages of his decline: repeated rejection of his
manuscripts, ''despair'' (58), and finally, ''he became nothing. . . . He vegetated in an office. . . . I was told he drank''
(59). Though Culwin tries to deny his complicity in these
damaged lives, the reader sees the real Culwin in the mirror
of the ghostly eyes, ''eyes which had grown hideous gradually,
which had built up their baseness coralwise, bit by bit''
(55), and which express the ''vicious security'' (48) of a man
who cannot feel but instead manipulates others. In the eyes
that haunt Culwin, we soon see Culwin's true nature.

''The Eyes'' is a very different kind of horror story, then, because Wharton uses the supernatural element to express a very realistic evil. The spectral eyes are only symbols of a very human failing, of Culwin's egotism as it grows slowly, corrupting him and wounding others. The eyes appear whenever Culwin is most selfish and most blind to his selfishness. They first visit him after his ''good deed'' of proposing to Alice; when he begins to manipulate Gilbert Noyes, they visit frequently. And at the end of the story, when Culwin has captured another young protege, the eyes again appear. But this time it is a victim who sees them——in Culwin's face. Then Culwin himself is forced to recognize them, in a mirror, and also in Frenham's refusal to look in Culwin's face. For Culwin, self-confrontation comes very late, but he is not spared the horror of facing himself. It is a sight more frightening than a traditional ghost in a haunted castle.

In another tale of self-confrontation, ''The Swimmer,'' John Cheever does not use the supernatural element. But he, like Wharton, traces the conflict of a man who is blind to his own failings and whose blindness destroys him and hurts others. Again, the story is about a man who evades his inner flaws and is haunted by a hidden self.

Like Andrew Culwin, Cheever's protagonist Neddy Merill initially thinks he is a man who has made a success of himself. When Neddy decides to devote a lazy afternoon to a long swim (across his neighbors' pools to his home), he feels like a winner. That morning, he had slid down his bannister and jogged to breakfast with vitality and energy. Cheever says Neddy ''might have been compared to a summer's day'' and Neddy conveys an impression of ''youth, sport, and clement weather'' (265). He appears to be a man who has achieved material success—a house in wealthy Bullet Park, a social life with affluent people—and personal happiness, for his wife Lucinda is sharing his Sunday, and they have four beautiful daughters.

But Neddy shares Culwin's self-centered personality. Like Culwin, he regards himself as a superior being; he has repeatedly rejected the invitations of the Biswangers, and yet he thinks he is doing them a favor when he crashes their party and invades their pool, feeling only ''indifference'' and ''charity'' (272). When he visits his ex-mistress, Shirley Adams, Neddy's memories of the affair reveal his cruelty. ''It had been . . . a lighthearted affair, although she had wept when he broke it off. . . . Would she, God forbid, weep again?'' (273). He seems to feel no compunction about dropping in on a woman he hurt, only distaste for the scene she might make. His attitude toward Shirley Adams is much like Culwin's toward ''poor'' Alice, condescension and arrogance. And Neddy reveals no hint of guilt about his unfaithfulness to his wife, for the affair pleased him; such love is ''the pain killer, the brightly colored pill that would put the spring back into his step'' (273). Infidelity makes him feel good about himself, just as Alice made Culwin feel good, and self is all that matters.

While Neddy may be oblivious to the fact of his blind egotism, the reader is not. Just as Culwin's selfishness spreads a layer of misery around him, Neddy's inner failings spread

pain. Hints that all is not right in Neddy's world fill
Cheever's story. When Mrs. Halloran says, ''We've been <u>terri-
bly</u> sorry to hear about all your misfortunes, Neddy'' (271),
Neddy doesn't understand, but the reader senses some evil is
to come. Similarly, when Neddy overhears Grace Biswanger
talking about a family that ''went for broke overnight''
(273), Neddy does not recognize the family as his, but the
connection is clear. In Shirley Adams' refusal to give Neddy
''another cent'' (273), the reader, but not Neddy, catches another reference to concealed pain.

And while Cheever does not employ the supernatural to underscore Neddy's conflict, he does, like Wharton, resort to a
nonrealistic element. He condenses the events of years into
one afternoon to track Neddy's slow descent into emptiness.
How can what began as a summer afternoon, for example, suddenly become autumn? Why does Neddy smell autumn flowers at
the end of a summer day? Why, that same evening, should he see
''Andromeda, Cepheus, and Cassiopeia'' (274) in the sky instead of summer constellations? Obviously, time is not used
realistically in this account, because Neddy has used the
passing of days, months, and years to <u>hide</u> from the reality of
himself. Even his blindness gives way to a moment of insight
halfway through his swim, when he asks himself, ''Was his memory failing or had he so disciplined it in the represssion of
unpleasant facts that he had damaged his sense of truth?''
(269). Time, like truth, has slipped from Neddy's grasp. He
can't seem to comprehend either anymore, and Cheever makes

this confusion clear in his concentration of events into one dramatic day. Like Culwin, Neddy finally sees himself long after others have seen through him. Confronting his decrepit, empty house, Neddy sees the emptiness of his life.

Self-confrontation is a long time coming for Neddy Merill and Andrew Culwin. For most of their lives, both protagonists seem unaware that their worst enemy is themselves. By concealing their flaws from themselves, their unacknowledged egotism festers and spreads, destroying them and damaging those around them. For both Wharton and Cheever, the extent of the hidden evil is effectively demonstrated in a nonrealistic way. For Wharton, the horror of egotism is made more terrible than the apparitions of a traditional ghost story. For Cheever, the evil of self-deception is demonstrated by blending a series of wasted days into one terrible afternoon. The differences of setting, of dates of publication, of technique of the two stories are balanced by a common focus. Both authors warn us that those who evade their interior ghosts will, eventually, have to face them.

Works Cited

Cheever, John. ''The Swimmer.'' The Stories of John Cheever. New York: Alfred A. Knopf, 1964. 264—274.

Wharton, Edith. ''The Eyes.'' The Ghost Stories of Edith Wharton. New York: Popular Library, 1973. 39—62.

The following essay organizes the *same material* you have just read in a point-by-point structure. Read it, and concentrate on the organization. To help you see the structure, underline the *thesis*, the *topic sentence* of each paragraph, and every *word*, *phrase*, or *sentence* of *transition*. Be aware that, with this structure, one paragraph may have *two key, or topic, sentences*. One topic sentence will cover the point to be made in its own paragraph and in the next paragraph; it will be a sentence about both works. The second topic sentence will explain how that point applies to one of the works. In the next paragraph, the topic sentence will show how the point applies to the second work. Also notice the tie-together in the concluding paragraph.

Sample Essay on Edith Wharton's "The Eyes" and John Cheever's "The Swimmer"; A Comparison/Contrast Using the Point-by-Point Structure

Edith Wharton's ''The Eyes'' and John Cheever's ''The Swimmer'' hardly seem to have much in common. They were published more than fifty years apart, and one is a ghost story, while the other is a story about a Sunday in suburbia. Yet, despite superficial differences, the stories share a common concern, expressed in the conflicts of the two protagonists, Wharton's Andrew Culwin and Cheever's Neddy Merill. In depicting men who are blind to their own flaws, and in tracing the effects of their blindness, Wharton and Cheever focus on a similar theme. In both ''The Eyes'' and ''The Swimmer,'' we observe the dangers of self-deception as the protagonists' refusal to see their own flaws leads to destruction and misery.

Both Wharton and Cheever introduce their conflicts by describing men who feel pretty good about themselves. On the surface, ''The Eyes'' does not appear to be about a man with inner failings. Instead, Andrew Culwin appears to be a man who is rightly complacent about his values and attitudes. A well-educated, wealthy man, Culwin has not lead a life of wild dissipation, but instead ''had always been possessed of a leisure which he had nursed and protected''; he has devoted his time to ''the cultivation of a fine intelligence and a few judiciously chosen habits'' (41). His relationships with others seem to show compassion and consideration. He says he proposes to his poor cousin Alice, for example, out of a desire to make her happy; his reward is ''a glow of self-righteousness'' (46). He encourages the dreams of Gilbert Noyes, an aspiring writer without much talent, because, Culwin says, ''the human plant generally needs warmth to flower'' (53), and again his declared intentions are kind and warm.

Like Andrew Culwin, Cheever's protagonist Neddy Merill initially thinks he is a man who has made a success of himself. When Neddy decides to devote a lazy afternoon to a long swim (across his neighbors' pools to his home), he feels like a winner. That morning, he had slid down his bannister and jogged to breakfast with vitality and energy. Cheever says Neddy ''might have been compared to a summer's day,'' and Neddy conveys an impression of ''youth, sport, and clement weather'' (265). He appears to be a man who has achieved material success—a house in wealthy Bullet Park, a social life with affluent people—and personal happiness, for his wife Lucinda is sharing his Sunday, and they have four beautiful daughters.

But neither Neddy nor Culwin are as good as they appear to be, for both are essentially self-centered. Despite his professed good intentions, Culwin is a selfish man. His decision to marry Alice is a condescending act; he feels so superior to Alice that his proposal is, to him, a kind of gift. And he is drawn to her because she makes him feel superior. When he meets Alice, Culwin is dreaming of writing a great masterpiece, but he cannot do it. Alice is his adoring assistant; to Culwin she is ''a nice girl'' who is ''just what I needed to

restore my faith . . . principally in myself'' (45). Similarly, Culwin encourages Gilbert Noyes' fantasies of literary
success because Gilbert, who worships Culwin, is so charming a
companion. Deceiving Gilbert, Culwin deceives himself as to
his motives.

Neddy Merill shares Culwin's self-centered personality.
Like Culwin, he regards himself as a superior being; he has
repeatedly rejected the invitations of the Biswangers, and
yet he thinks he is doing them a favor when he crashes their
party and invades their pool, feeling only ''indifference''
and ''charity'' (272). When he visits his ex-mistress,
Shirley Adams, Neddy's memories of the affair reveal his cruelty. ''It had been . . . a lighthearted affair, although she
had wept when he broke it off. . . . Would she, God forbid, weep
again?'' (273). He seems to feel no compunction about dropping
in on a woman he hurt, only distaste for the scene she might
make. His attitude toward Shirley Adams is much like Culwin's
toward ''poor'' Alice, condescension and arrogance. And Neddy
reveals no hint of guilt about his unfaithfulness to his wife,
for the affair pleased him; such love is ''the pain killer,
the brightly colored pill that would put the spring back into
his step'' (273). Infidelity makes him feel good about himself, just as Alice made Culwin feel, and self is all that
matters.

Neddy and Culwin may be unaware of their core of egotism,
but the reader is not. In Culwin's case, the reader soon identifies both the flaw and its effects. Although Wharton gives
no description of Alice's suffering when Culwin suddenly

rejects her, the earlier descriptions of her sensitivity and trust hint at what pain she must feel at Culwin's rejection. As for Gilbert Noyes, Culwin callously describes the stages of his decline: repeated rejection of his manuscripts, ''despair'' (58), and, finally, ''he became nothing. . . . He vegetated in an office. . . . I was told he drank'' (59). Though Culwin tries to deny his complicity in these damaged lives, the reader sees the real Culwin in the mirror of the ghostly eyes, ''eyes which had grown hideous gradually, which had built up their baseness coralwise, bit by bit'' (55), and which express the ''vicious security'' (48) of a man who cannot feel but instead manipulates others. In the eyes that haunt Culwin, we soon see Culwin's true nature.

We also see the egotism that Neddy Merill cannot see, and we see its effects. Just as Culwin's selfishness spreads a layer of misery around him, Neddy's inner failings spread pain. Hints that all is not right in Neddy's world fill Cheever's story. When Mrs. Halloran says, ''We've been terribly sorry to hear about all your misfortunes, Neddy'' (271), Neddy doesn't understand, but the reader senses some evil is to come. Similarly, when Neddy overhears Grace Biswanger talking about a family that ''went for broke overnight'' (273), Neddy does not recognize the family as his, but the connection is clear. In Shirley Adams' refusal to give Neddy ''another cent'' (273), the reader, but perhaps not Neddy, catches another reference to concealed pain.

Neddy, like Culwin, is blind, and the blindness and eventual enlightenment of both characters are underscored by a nonrealistic element in the stories. ''The Eyes'' is an unusual kind of horror story because Wharton uses a supernatural element to express a very realistic evil. The spectral eyes are only symbols of a very human failing, of Culwin's egotism as it grows slowly, corrupting him and wounding others. The eyes appear whenever Culwin is most selfish and most blind to his selfishness. They first visit him after his ''good deed'' of proposing to Alice; when he begins to manipulate Gilbert Noyes, they visit frequently. At the end of the story, when Culwin has captured another young protege, the eyes again appear. But this time it is a victim who sees them, in Culwin's face. Then Culwin himself is forced to recognize them, in a mirror, and also in Frenham's refusal to look in Culwin's face. For Culwin, self-confrontation comes very late, but he is not spared the horror of himself. It is a sight more frightening than a traditional ghost in a haunted castle.

While John Cheever does not employ the supernatural to underscore Neddy's conflict, he does, like Wharton, resort to a nonrealistic element. He condenses the events of years into one afternoon to track Neddy's slow descent into emptiness. How can what began as a summer afternoon, for example, suddenly become autumn? Why does Neddy smell autumn flowers at the end of a summer day? Why, that same night, should he see ''Andromeda, Cepheus, and Cassiopeia'' (274) in the sky instead of summer constellations? Obviously, time is not used realistically in this account, because Neddy has used the passing of days, months and years to hide from the reality of himself. Even his blindness gives way to a moment of insight halfway through his swim, when he asks himself, ''Was his memory failing or had he so disciplined it in the repression of

unpleasant facts that he had damaged his sense of truth?''
(269). Time, like truth, has slipped from Neddy's grasp. He
can't seem to comprehend either any more, and Cheever makes
this confusion clear in his concentration of events into one
dramatic day. Like Culwin, Neddy finally sees himself long
after others have seen through him. Confronting his decrepit,
empty house, Neddy sees the emptiness of his life.

Self-confrontation is a long time coming for Neddy Merill
and Andrew Culwin. For most of their lives, both protagonists
seem unaware that their worst enemy is themselves. By concealing their flaws from themselves, their unacknowledged egotism
festers and spreads, destroying them and damaging those
around them. For both Wharton and Cheever, the extent of the
hidden evil is effectively demonstrated in a nonrealistic
way. For Wharton, the horror of egotism is made more terrible
than the apparitions of a traditional ghost story. For
Cheever, the evil of self-destruction is demonstrated by
blending a series of wasted days into one terrible afternoon.
The differences of setting, of dates of publication, of technique of the two stories are balanced by a common focus. Both
authors warn us that those who evade their interior ghosts
will, eventually, have to face them.

Works Cited

Cheever, John. ''The Swimmer.'' The Stories of John Cheever.
   New York: Alfred A. Knopf, 1964. 264—174.

Wharton, Edith. ''The Eyes.'' The Ghost Stories of Edith
   Wharton. New York: Popular Library, 1973. 39—62.

READINGS IN LITERATURE

A Good Man Is Hard to Find

Flannery O'Connor

The grandmother didn't want to go to Florida. She wanted to visit some of her connections in east Tennessee and she was seizing every chance to change Bailey's mind. Bailey was the son she lived with, her only boy. He was sitting on the edge of his chair at the table, bent over the orange sports section of the *Journal.* "Now look here, Bailey," she said, "see here, read this," and she stood with one hand on her thin hip and the other rattling the newspaper at his bald head. "Here this fellow that calls himself The Misfit is aloose from the Federal Pen and headed toward Florida and you read here what it says he did to these people. Just you read it. I wouldn't take my children in any direction with a criminal like that aloose in it. I couldn't answer to my conscience if I did."

Bailey didn't look up from his reading so she wheeled around then and faced the children's mother; a young mother in slacks, whose face was as broad and innocent as a cabbage and was tied around with a green headkerchief that had two points on the top like rabbit's ears. She was sitting on the sofa, feeding the baby his apricots out of a jar. "The children have been to Florida before," the old lady said. "You all ought to take them somewhere else for a change so they would see different parts of the world and be broad. They never have been to east Tennessee."

The children's mother didn't seem to hear her, but the eight-year-old boy, John Wesley, a stocky child with glasses, said, "If you don't want to go to Florida, why dontcha stay at home?" He and the little girl, June Star, were reading the funny papers on the floor.

"She wouldn't stay at home to be queen for a day," June Star said without raising her yellow head.

"Yes, and what would you do if this fellow, The Misfit, caught you?" the grandmother asked.

"I'd smack his face," John Wesley said.

"She wouldn't stay at home for a million bucks," June Star said. "Afraid she'd miss something. She has to go everywhere we go."

"All right, Miss," the grandmother said. "Just remember that the next time you want me to curl your hair."

June Star said her hair was naturally curly.

The next morning the grandmother was the first one in the car, ready to go. She had her big black valise that looked like the head of a hippopotamus in one corner, and underneath it she was hiding a basket with Pitty Sing, the cat, in it. She didn't intend for the cat to be left alone in the house for three days because he would miss her too much and she was afraid he might brush against one of the gas burners and accidentally asphyxiate himself. Her son, Bailey, didn't like to arrive at a motel with a cat.

She sat in the middle of the back seat with John Wesley and June Star on either side of her. Bailey and the children's mother and the baby sat in the front and they left Atlanta at eight forty-five with the mileage on the car at 55890. The grandmother wrote this down because she thought it would be interesting to say how many miles they had been when they got back. It took them twenty minutes to reach the outskirts of the city.

The old lady settled herself comfortably, removing her white cotton gloves and putting them up with her purse on the shelf in front of the back window. The children's mother still had on slacks and still had her head tied up in a green kerchief, but the grandmother had on a navy blue straw sailor hat with a bunch of white violets on the brim and a navy blue dress with a small white dot in the print. Her collar and cuffs were white organdy trimmed with lace and at her neckline she had pinned a purple spray of cloth violets containing a sachet. In case of an accident, anyone seeing her dead on the highway would know at once that she was a lady.

She said she thought it was going to be a good day for driving, neither too hot nor too cold, and she cautioned Bailey that the speed limit was fifty-five miles an hour and that the patrolmen hid themselves behind bill-boards and small clumps of trees and sped out after you before you had a chance to slow down. She pointed out interesting details of the scenery: Stone Mountain, the blue granite that in some places came up to both sides of the highway; the brilliant red clay banks slightly streaked with purple; and the various crops that made rows of green lack-work on the ground. The trees were full of silver-white sunlights and the meanest of them sparkled. The children were reading comic magazines and their mother had gone back to sleep.

"Let's go through Georgia fast so we won't have to look at it much." John Wesley said.

"If I were a little boy," said the grandmother, "I wouldn't talk about my native state that way. Tennessee has the mountains and Georgia has the hills."

"Tennessee is just a hillybilly dumping ground," John Wesley said, "and Georgia is a lousy state too."

"You said it," June Star said.

"In my time," said the grandmother, folding her thin veined fingers, "children were more respectful of their native states and their parents and everything else. People did right then. Oh look at the cute little pickaninny!" she said and pointed to a Negro child standing in the door of a shack. "Wouldn't that make a picture, now?" she asked and they all turned and looked at the little Negro out of the back window. He waved.

"He didn't have any britches on," June Star said.

"He probably didn't have any," the grandmother explained. "Little niggers in the country don't have things like we do. If I could paint, I'd paint that picture," she said.

The children exchanged comic books.

The grandmother offered to hold the baby and the children's mother passed him over the front seat to her. She set him on her knee and bounced him and told him about the things they were passing. She rolled her eyes and screwed up her mouth and stuck her leathery thin face into his smooth bland one. Occasionally he gave her a faraway smile. They passed a large cotton field with five or six graves fenced in the middle of it, like a small island. "Look at the graveyard!" the grandmother said, pointing it out. "That was the old family burying ground. That belonged to the plantation."

"Where's the plantation?" John Wesley asked.

"Gone With the Wind," said the grandmother. "Ha. Ha."

When the children finished all the comic books they had brought, they opened the lunch and ate it. The grandmother ate a peanut butter sandwich and an olive and would not let the children throw the box and the paper napkins out the window. When there was nothing else to do they played a game by choosing a cloud and making the other two guess what shape it suggested. John Wesley took one the shape of a cow and June Star guessed a cow and John Wesley said, no, an automobile, and June Star said he didn't play fair, and they began to slap each other over the grandmother.

The grandmother said she would tell them a story if they would keep quiet. When she told a story, she rolled her eyes and waved her head and was very dramatic. She said once when she was a maiden lady she had been courted by a Mr. Edgar Atkins Teagarden from Jasper, Georgia. She said he was a very good-looking man and a gentleman and that he brought her a watermelon every Saturday afternoon with his initials cut in it, E. A. T. Well, one Saturday, she said, Mr. Teagarden brought the watermelon and there was nobody at home and he left it on the front porch and returned in his buggy to Jasper, but she never got the watermelon, she said, because a nigger boy ate it when he saw the initials, E. A. T.! This story tickled John Wesley's funny bone and he giggled and giggled but June Star didn't think it was any good. She said she wouldn't marry a man that just brought her a watermelon on Saturday. The grandmother said she would have done well to marry Mr. Teagarden because he was a gentleman and had bought Coca-Cola stock when it first came out and that he had died only a few years ago, a very wealthy man.

They stopped at The Tower for barbecued sandwiches. The Tower was a part-stucco and part-wood filling station and dance hall set in a clearing outside of Timothy. A fat man named Red Sammy Butts ran it and there were signs stuck here and there on the building and for miles up and down the highway saying, TRY RED SAMMY'S FAMOUS BARBECUE. NONE LIKE FAMOUS RED SAMMY'S! RED SAM! THE FAT BOY WITH THE HAPPY LAUGH, A VETERAN! RED SAMMY'S YOUR MAN!

Red Sammy was lying on the bare ground outside The Tower with his head under a truck while a gray monkey about a foot high, chained to a small chinaberry tree, chattered nearby. The monkey sprang back into the tree and got on the highest limb as soon as he saw the children jump out of the car and run toward him.

Inside, the Tower was a long dark room with a counter at one end and tables at the other and dancing space in the middle. They all sat down at a broad table next to the nickelodeon and Red Sam's wife, a tall burnt-brown woman with hair and eyes lighter than her skin, came and took their order. The children's mother put a dime in the machine and played "The Tennessee Waltz," and the grandmother said that tune always made her want to dance. She asked Bailey if he would like to dance but he only glared at her. He didn't have a naturally sunny disposition like she did and trips made him nervous. The grandmother's brown eyes were very bright. She swayed her head from side to side and pretended she was dancing in her chair. June Star said play something she could tap to so the children's mother put in another dime and played a fast number and June Star stepped out onto the dance floor and did her tap routine.

"Ain't she cute?" Red Sam's wife said, leaning over the counter. "Would you like to come be my little girl?"

"No, I certainly wouldn't," June Star said. "I wouldn't live in a broken-down place like this for a million bucks!" and she ran back to the table.

"Ain't she cute?" the woman repeated, stretching her mouth politely.

"Aren't you ashamed?" hissed the grandmother.

Red Sam came in and told his wife to quit lounging on the counter and hurry up with these people's order. His khaki trousers reached just to his hip bones and his stomach hung over them like a sack of meal swaying under his shirt. He came over and sat down at a table nearby and let out a combination sigh and yodel. "You can't win," he said. "You can't win," and he wiped his sweating red face off with a gray handkerchief. "These days you don't know who to trust," he said. "Ain't that the truth?"

"People are certainly not nice like they used to be," said the grandmother.

"Two fellers come in here last week," Red Sammy said, "driving a Chrysler. It was an old beat-up car but it was a good one and these boys looked all right to me. Said they worked at the mill and you know I let them fellers charge the gas they bought? Now why did I do that?"

"Because you're a good man!" the grandmother said at once.

"Yes'm, I suppose so," Red Sam said as if he were struck with this answer.

His wife brought the orders, carrying the five plates all at once without a tray, two in each hand and one balanced on her arm. "It isn't a soul in this green world of God's that you can trust," she said. "And I don't count nobody out of that, not nobody," she repeated, looking at Red Sammy.

"Did you read about that criminal, The Misfit, that's escaped?" asked the grandmother.

"I wouldn't be a bit surprised if he didn't attack this place right here," said the woman. "If he hears about it being here, I wouldn't be none surprised to see him. If he hears it's two cent in the cash register, I wouldn't be a tall surprised if he. . . ."

"That'll do," Red Sam said. "Go bring these people their Co'-Colas," and the woman went off to get the rest of the order.

"A good man is hard to find," Red Sammy said. "Everything is getting terrible. I remember the day you could go off and leave your screen door unlatched. Not no more."

He and the grandmother discussed better times. The old lady said that in her opinion Europe was entirely to blame for the way things were now. She said the way Europe acted you would think we were made of money and Red Sam said it was no use talking about it, she was exactly right. The children ran outside into the white sunlight and looked at the monkey in the lacy chinaberry tree. He was busy catching fleas on himself and biting each one carefully between his teeth as if it were a delicacy.

They drove off again into the hot afternoon. The grandmother took cat naps and woke up every few minutes with her own snoring. Outside of Toombsboro she woke up and recalled an old plantation that she had visited in this neighborhood once when she was a young lady. She said the house had six white columns across the front and that there was an avenue of oaks leading up to it and two little wooden trellis arbors on either side in front where you sat down with your suitor after a stroll in the garden. She recalled exactly which road to turn off to get to it. She knew that Bailey would not be willing to lose any time looking at an old house, but the more she talked about it, the more she wanted to see it once again and find out if the little twin arbors were still standing. "There was a secret panel in this house," she said craftily, not telling the truth but wishing that she were, "and the story went that all the family silver was hidden in it when Sherman came through but it was never found. . . ."

"Hey!" John Wesley said. "Let's go see it! We'll find it! We'll poke all the wood work and find it! Who lives there? Where do you turn off at? Hey Pop, can't we turn off there?"

"We never have seen a house with a secret panel!" June Star shrieked. "Let's go to the house with the secret panel! Hey, Pop, can't we go see the house with the secret panel!"

"It's not far from here, I know," the grandmother said. "It wouldn't take over twenty minutes."

Bailey was looking straight ahead. His jaw was as rigid as a horseshoe. "No," he said.

The children began to yell and scream that they wanted to see the house with the secret panel. John Wesley kicked the back of the front seat and June Star hung over her mother's shoulder and whined desperately into her ear that they never had any fun even on their vacation, that they could never do what THEY wanted to do. The baby began to scream and John Wesley kicked the back of the seat so hard that his father could feel the blows in his kidney.

"All right!" he shouted and drew the car to a stop at the side of the road. "Will you all shut up? Will you all just shut up for one second? If you don't shut up, we won't go anywhere."

"It would be very educational for them," the grandmother murmured.

"All right," Bailey said, "but get this. This is the only time we're going to stop for anything like this. This is the one and only time."

"The dirt road that you have to turn down is about a mile back," the grandmother directed. "I marked it when we passed."

"A dirt road," Bailey groaned.

After they had turned around and were headed toward the dirt road, the grandmother recalled other points about the house, the beautiful glass over the front doorway and the candle lamp in the hall. John Wesley said that the secret panel was probably in the fireplace.

"You can't go inside this house," Bailey said. "You don't know who lives there."

"While you all talk to the people in front, I'll run around behind and get in a window," John Wesley suggested.

"We'll all stay in the car," his mother said.

They turned onto the dirt road and the car raced roughly along in a swirl of pink dust. The grandmother recalled the times when there were no paved roads and thirty miles was a day's journey. The dirt road was hilly and there were sudden washes in it and sharp curves on dangerous embankments. All at once they would be on a hill, looking down over the blue tops of trees for miles around, then the next minute, they would be in a red depression with the dust-coated trees looking down on them.

"This place had better turn up in a minute, "Bailey said. "or I'm going to turn around."

The road looked as if no one had traveled on it in months.

"It's not much farther," the grandmother said and just as she said it, a horrible thought came to her. The thought was so embarrassing that she turned red in the face and her eyes dilated and her feet jumped up, upsetting her valise in the corner. The instant the valise moved, the newspaper top she had over the basket under it rose with a snarl and Pitty Sing, the cat, sprang onto Bailey's shoulder.

The children were thrown to the floor and their mother, clutching the baby, was thrown out the door onto the ground; the old lady was thrown into the front seat. The car turned over once and landed right-side-up in a gulch on the side of the road. Bailey remained in the driver's seat with the cat—gray-striped with a broad white face and an orange nose—clinging to his neck like a caterpillar.

As soon as the children saw they could move their arms and legs, they scrambled out of the car, shouting, "We've had an ACCIDENT!" The grandmother was curled up under the dashboard, hoping she was injured so that

Bailey's wrath would not come down on her all at once. The horrible thought she had had before the accident was that the house she had remembered so vividly was not in Georgia but in Tennessee.

Bailey removed the cat from his neck with both hands an flung it out the window against the side of a pine tree. Then he got out of the car and started looking for the children's mother. She was sitting against the side of the red gutted ditch, holding the screaming baby, but she only had a cut down her face and a broken shoulder. "We've had an ACCIDENT" the children screamed in a frenzy of delight.

"But nobody's killed," June Star said with disappointment as the grandmother limped out of the car, her hat still pinned to her head but the broken front brim standing up at a jaunty angle and the violet spray hanging off the side. They all sat down in the ditch, except the children, to recover from the shock. They were all shaking.

"Maybe a car will come along," said the children's mother hoarsely.

"I believe I have injured an organ," said the grandmother, pressing her side, but no one answered her. Bailey's teeth were clattering. He had on a yellow sport shirt with bright blue parrots designed in it and his face was as yellow as the shirt. The grandmother decided that she would not mention that the house was in Tennessee.

The road was about ten feet above and they could see only the tops of the trees on the other side of it. Behind the ditch they were sitting in there were more woods, tall and dark and deep. In a few minutes they saw a car some distance away on top of a hill, coming slowly as if the occupants were watching them. The grandmother stood up and waved both arms dramatically to attract their attention. The car continued to come on slowly, disappeared around a bend and appeared again, moving even slower, on top of the hill they had gone over. It was a big black battered hearselike automobile. There were three men in it.

It came to a stop just over them and for some minutes, the driver looked down with a steady expressionless gaze to where they were sitting, and didn't speak. Then he turned his head and muttered something to the other two and they got out. One was a fat boy in black trousers and a red sweat shirt with a silver stallion embossed on the front of it. He moved around on the right side of them and stood staring, his mouth partly open in a kind of loose grin. The other had on khaki pants and a blue striped coat and a gray hat pulled down very low, hiding most of his face. He came around slowly on the left side. Neither spoke.

The driver got out of the car and stood by the side of it, looking down at them. He was an older man than the other two. His hair was just beginning to gray and he wore silver-rimmed spectacles that gave him scholarly look. He had a long creased face and didn't have on any shirt or undershirt. He had on blue jeans that were too tight for him and was holding a black hat and a gun. The two boys also had guns.

"We've had an ACCIDENT!" the children screamed.

The grandmother had the peculiar feeling that the bespectacled man was someone she knew. His face was as familiar to her as if she had known him all her life but she could not recall who he was. He moved away from the car and began to come down the embankment, placing his feet carefully so that he wouldn't slip. He had on tan and white shoes and no socks, and his ankles were red and thin. "Good afternoon," he said. "I see you all had you a little spill."

"We turned over twice!" said the grandmother.

"Oncet," he corrected. "We see it happen. Try their car and see will it run, Hiram," he said quietly to the boy with the gray hat.

"What you got that gun for?" John Wesley asked. "Whatcha gonna do with that gun?"

"Lady," the man said to the children's mother, "would you mind calling them children to sit down by you? Children make me nervous. I want all you all to sit down right together there where you're at."

"What are you telling us what to do for?" June Star asked.

Behind them the line of woods gaped like a dark open mouth. "Come here," said their mother.

"Look here now," Bailey began suddenly, "we're in a predicament! We're in. . . ."

The grandmother shrieked. She scrambled to her feet and stood staring. "You're The Misfit!" she said. "I recognized you at once!"

"Yes'm," the man said, smiling slightly as if he were pleased in spite of himself to be known, "but it would have been better for all of you, lady, if you hadn't of reckernized me."

Bailey turned his head sharply and said something to his mother that shocked even the children. The old lady began to cry and The Misfit reddened.

"Lady," he said, "don't you get upset. Sometimes a man says things he don't mean. I don't reckon he meant to talk to you thataway."

"You wouldn't shoot a lady, would you?" the grandmother said and removed a clean handkerchief from her cuff and began to slap at her eyes with it.

The Misfit pointed the toe of his shoe into the ground and made a little hole and then covered it up again. "I would hate to have to," he said.

"Listen," the grandmother almost screamed, "I know you're a good man. You don't look a bit like you have common blood. I know you must come from nice people!"

"Yes mam," he said, "finest people in the world." When he smiled he showed a row of strong white teeth. "God never made a finer woman than my mother and my daddy's heart was pure gold," he said. The boy with the red sweat shirt had come around behind them and was standing with his gun at his hip. The Misfit squatted down on the ground. "Watch them children, Bobby Lee," he said. "You know they make me nervous." He looked at the six of them huddled together in front of him and he seemed to be embarrassed as if he couldn't think of anything to say. "Ain't a cloud in the sky," he remarked, looking up at it. "Don't see no sun but don't see no cloud neither."

"Yes, it's a beautiful day," said the grandmother. "Listen," she said, "you shouldn't call yourself The Misfit because I know you're a good man at heart. I can just look at you and tell."

"Hush!" Bailey yelled. "Hush! Everybody shut up and let me handle this!"

He was squatting in the position of a runner about to sprint forward but he didn't move.

"I pre-chate that, lady," The Misfit said and drew a little circle in the ground with the butt of his gun.

"It'll take a half a hour to fix this here car," Hiram called, looking over the raised hood of it.

"Well, first you and Bobby Lee get him and that little boy to step over yonder with you," The Misfit said, pointing to Bailey and John Wesley. "The boys want to ask you something," he said to Bailey. "Would you mind stepping back in them woods there with them?"

"Listen," Bailey began, "we're in a terrible predicament! Nobody realizes what this is," and his voice cracked. His eyes were as blue and intense as the parrots in his shirt and he remained perfectly still.

The grandmother reached up to adjust her hat brim as if she were going to the woods with him but it came off in her hand. She stood staring at it and after a second she let it fall on the ground. Hiram pulled Bailey up by the arm as if he were assisting an old man. John Wesley caught hold of his father's hand and Bobby Lee followed. They went off toward the woods and just as they reached the dark edge, Bailey turned and supporting himself against a gray naked pine trunk, he shouted, "I'll be back in a minute, Mamma, wait on me!"

"Come back this instant!" his mother shrilled but they all disappeared into the woods.

"Bailey Boy!" the grandmother called in a tragic voice but she found she was looking at The Misfit squatting on the ground in front of her. "I just know you're a good man," she said desperately. "You're not a bit common!"

"Nome, I ain't a good man," The Misfit said after a second as if he had considered her statement carefully, "but I ain't the worst in the world neither. My daddy said I was a different breed of dog from my brothers and sisters. 'You know,' Daddy said, 'it's some that can live their whole life out without asking about it and it's others has to know why it is, and this boy is one of the latters. He's going to be into everything!'" He put on his black hat and looked up suddenly and then away deep into the woods as if he were embarrassed again. "I'm sorry. I don't have on a shirt before you ladies," he said, hunching his shoulders slightly. "We buried our clothes that we had on when we escaped and we're just making do until we can get better. We borrowed these from some folks we met," he explained.

"That's perfectly all right," the grandmother said. "Maybe Bailey has an extra shirt in his suitcase."

"I'll look and see terrectly," The Misfit said.

"Where are they taking him?" the children's mother screamed.

"Daddy was a card himself," The Misfit said. "You couldn't put anything over on him. He never got in trouble with the Authorities though. Just had the knack of handling them."

"You could be honest too if you'd only try," said the grandmother. "Think how wonderful it would be to settle down and live a comfortable life and not have to think about somebody chasing you all the time."

The Misfit kept scratching in the ground with the butt of his gun as if he were thinking about it. "Yes'm, somebody is always after you," he murmured.

The grandmother noticed how thin his shoulder blades were just behind his hat because she was standing up looking down on him. "Do you ever pray?" she asked.

He shook his head. All she saw was the black hat wiggle between his shoulder blades. "Nome," he said.

There was a pistol shot from the woods, followed closely by another. Then silence. The old lady's head jerked around. She could hear the wind move through the tree tops like a long satisfied insuck of breath. "Bailey Boy!" she called.

"I was a gospel singer for a while," The Misfit said. "I been most everything. Been in the arm service, both land and sea, at home and abroad, been twict married, been an undertaker, been with the railroads, plowed Mother Earth, been in a tornado, seen a man burnt alive oncet," and he looked up at the children's mother and the little girl who were sitting close together, their faces white and their eyes glass: "I even seen a woman flogged," he said.

"Pray, pray," the grandmother began, "pray, pray. . . ."

"I never was a bad boy that I remember of," The Misfit said in an almost dreamy voice, "but somewheres along the line I done something wrong and got sent to the penitentiary. I was buried alive," and he looked up and held her attention to him by a steady stare.

"That's when you should have started to pray," she said. "What did you do to get sent to the penitentiary that first time?"

"Turn to the right, it was a wall," The Misfit said, looking up again at the cloudless sky. "Turn to the left, it was a wall. Look up it was a ceiling, look down it was a floor. I forget what I done, lady. I set there and set there, trying to remember what it was I done and I ain't recalled it to this day. Oncet in a while, I would think it was coming to me, but it never come."

"Maybe they put you in by mistake," the old lady said vaguely.

"Nome," he said. "It wasn't no mistake. They had the papers on me."

"You must have stolen something," she said.

The Misfit sneered slightly. "Nobody had nothing I wanted," he said. "It was a head-doctor at the penitentiary said what I had done was kill my daddy but I known that for a lie. My daddy died in nineteen ought nineteen of the epidemic flu and I never had a thing to do with it. He was buried in the Mount Hopewell Baptist churchyard and you can go there and see for yourself."

"If you would pray," the old lady said, "Jesus would help you."

"That's right," The Misfit said.

"Well then, why don't you pray?" she asked trembling with delight suddenly.

"I don't want no hep," he said. "I'm doing all right by myself."

Bobby Lee and Hiram came ambling back from the woods. Bobby Lee was dragging a yellow shirt with bright blue parrots in it.

"Throw me that shirt, Bobby Lee," The Misfit said. The shirt came flying at him and landed on his shoulder and he put it on. The grandmother couldn't name what the shirt reminded her of. "No, lady," The Misfit said while he was buttoning it up, "I found out the crime don't matter. You can do one thing or you can do another, kill a man or take a tire off his car, because sooner or later you're going to forget what it was you done and just be punished for it."

The children's mother had begun to make heaving noises as if she couldn't get her breath. "Lady," he asked, "would you and that little girl like to step off yonder with Bobby Lee and Hiram and join your husband?"

"Yes, thank you," the mother said faintly. Her left arm dangled helplessly and she was holding the baby, who had gone to sleep, in the other. "Hep that lady up, Hiram," The Misfit said as she struggled to climb out of the ditch, "and Bobby Lee, you hold onto that little girl's hand."

"I don't want to hold hands with him," June Star said. "He reminds me of a pig."

The fat boy blushed and laughed and caught her by the arm and pulled her off into the woods after Hiram and her mother.

Alone with The Misfit, the grandmother found that she had lost her voice. There was not a cloud in the sky nor any sun. There was nothing around her but woods. She wanted to tell him that he must pray. She opened and closed her mouth several times before anything came out. Finally she found herself saying, "Jesus, Jesus," meaning, Jesus will help you, but the way she was saying it, it sounded as if she might be cursing.

"Yes'm," The Misfit said as if he agreed. "Jesus thrown everything off balance. It was the same case with Him as with me except He hadn't committed any crime and they could prove I had committed one because they had the papers on me. Of course," he said, "they never shown me my papers. That's why I sign myself now. I said long ago, you get you a signature and sign everything you do and keep a copy of it. Then you'll know what you done and you can hold up the crime to the punishment and see do they match and in the end you'll have something to prove you ain't been treated right. I call myself The Misfit," he said, "because I can't make what all I done wrong fit what all I gone through in punishment."

There was a piercing scream from the woods, followed closely by a pistol report. "Does it seem right to you, lady, that one is punished a heap and another ain't punished at all?"

"Jesus!" the old lady cried. "You've got good blood! I know you wouldn't shoot a lady! I know you come from nice people! Pray! Jesus, you ought not to shoot a lady. I'll give you all the money I've got!"

"Lady," The Misfit said, looking beyond her far into the woods, "there never was a body that give the undertaker a tip."

There were two more pistol reports and the grandmother raised her head like a parched old turkey hen crying for water and called, "Bailey Boy, Baily Boy!" as if her heart would break.

"Jesus was the only One that ever raised the dead," The Misfit continued, "and He shouldn't have done it. He thrown everything off balance. If He did what He said, then it's nothing for you to do but throw away everything and follow Him, and if He didn't then it's nothing for you to do but enjoy the few minutes you got left the best way you can—by killing somebody or burning down his house or doing some other meanness to him. No pleasure but meanness,'' he said and his voice had become almost a snarl.

"Maybe He didn't raise the dead,'' the old lady mumbled, not knowing what she was saying and feeling so dizzy that she sank down in the ditch with her legs twisted under her.

"I wasn't there so I can't say He didn't,'' The Misfit said. "I wisht I had of been there,'' he said, hitting the ground with his fist. "It ain't right I wasn't there because if I had of been there I would of known. Listen lady,'' he said in a high voice, "if I had of been there I would of known and I wouldn't be like I am now.'' His voice seemed about to crack and the grandmother's head cleared for an instant. She saw the man's face twisted close to her own as if he were going to cry and she murmured, "Why, you're one of my babies. You're one of my own children!'' She reached out and touched him on the shoulder. The Misfit sprang back as if a snake had bitten him and shot her three times through the chest. Then he put his gun down on the ground and took off his glasses and began to clean them.

Hiram and Bobby Lee returned from the woods and stood over the ditch, looking down at the grandmother who half sat and half lay in a puddle of blood with her legs crossed under her like a child's and her face smiling up at the cloudless sky.

Without his glasses, The Misfit's eyes were red-rimmed and pale and defenseless-looking. "Take her off and throw her where you thrown the others,'' he said, picking up the cat that was rubbing itself against his leg.

"She was a talker, wasn't she?'' Bobby Lee said, sliding down the ditch with a yodel.

"She would of been a good woman,'' The Misfit said, "if it had been somebody there to shoot her every minute of her life.''

"Some fun!'' Bobby Lee said.

"Shut up, Bobby Lee,'' The Misfit said. "It's no real pleasure in life.''

Death in the Woods

Sherwood Anderson

I

She was an old woman and lived on a farm near the town in which I lived. All country and small-town people have seen such old women, but no one knows much about them. Such an old woman comes into town driving an old worn-out horse or she comes afoot carrying a basket. She may own a few hens and have eggs to sell. She brings them in a basket and takes them to a grocer. There she trades them in. She gets some salt pork and some beans. Then she gets a pound or two of sugar and some flour.

Afterwards she goes to the butcher's and asks for some dog-meat. She may spend ten or fifteen cents, but when she does she asks for something. Formerly the butchers gave liver to anyone who wanted to carry it away. In our family we were always having it. Once one of my brothers got a whole cow's liver at the slaughterhouse near the fair grounds in our town. We had it until we were sick of it. It never cost a cent. I have hated the thought of it ever since.

The old farm woman got some liver and a soup-bone. She never visited with anyone, and as soon as she got what she wanted she lit out for home. It made quite a load for such an old body. No one gave her a lift. People drive right down a road and never notice an old woman like that.

There was such an old woman who used to come into town past our house one summer and fall when I was a young boy and was sick with what was called inflammatory rheumatism. She went home later carrying a heavy pack on her back. Two or three large gaunt-looking dogs followed at her heels.

The old woman was nothing special. She was one of the nameless ones that hardly anyone knows, but she got into my thoughts. I have just suddenly now, after all these years, remembered her and what happened. It is a story. Her name was Grimes, and she lived with her husband and son in a small unpainted house on the bank of a small creek four miles from town.

The husband and son were a tough lot. Although the son was but twenty-one, he had already served a term in jail. It was whispered about that the woman's husband stole horses and ran them off to some other county. Now and then, when a horse turned up missing, the man had also disappeared. No one ever caught him. Once, when I was loafing at Tom Whitehead's livery-barn, the man came there and sat on the bench in front. Two or three other men were there, but no one spoke to him. He sat for a few minutes and then got up and went away. When he was leaving he turned around and stared at the men. There was a look of defiance in his eyes. "Well, I have tried to be friendly. You don't want to talk to me. It has been so wherever I have gone in this town. If, some day, one of your fine horses turns up missing, well, then what?" He did not say anything actually. "I'd like to bust one of you on the jaw," was about what his eyes said. I remember how the look in his eyes made me shiver.

The old man belonged to a family that had had money once. His name was Jake Grimes, had owned a sawmill when the country was new, and had made money. Then he got to drinking and running after women. When he died there wasn't much left.

Jake blew in the rest. Pretty soon there wasn't any more lumber to cut and his land was nearly all gone.

He got his wife off a German farmer, for whom he went to work one June day in the wheat harvest. She was a young thing then and scared to death. You see, the farmer was up to something with the girl—she was, I think, a bound girl and his wife had her suspicions. She took it out on the girl when the man wasn't around. Then, when the wife had to go off to town for supplies, the farmer got after her. She told young Jake that nothing really ever happened, but he didn't know whether to believe it or not.

He got her pretty easy himself, the first time he was out with her. He wouldn't have married her if the German farmer hadn't tried to tell him where to get off. He got her to go riding with him in his buggy one night when he was threshing on the place, and then he came for her the next Sunday night.

She managed to get out of the house without her employer's seeing, but when she was getting into the buggy he showed up. It was almost dark, and he just popped up suddenly at the horse's head. He grabbed the horse by the bridle and Jake got out his buggy-whip.

They had it out all right! The German was a tough one. Maybe he didn't care whether his wife knew or not. Jake hit him over the face and shoulders with the buggy-whip, but the horse got to acting up and he had to get out.

Then the two men went for it. The girl didn't see it. The horse started to run away and went nearly a mile down the road before the girl got him stopped. Then she managed to tie him to a tree beside the road. (I wonder how I know all this. It must have stuck in my mind from small-town tales when I was a boy.) Jake found her there after he got through with the German. She was huddled up in the buggy seat, crying, scared to death. She told Jake a lot of stuff, how the German had tried to get her, how he chased her once into the barn, how another time, when they happened to be alone in the house together, he tore her dress open clear down the front. The German, she said, might have got her that time if he hadn't heard his old woman drive in at the gate. She had been off to town for supplies. Well, she would be putting the horse in the barn. The German managed to sneak off to the fields without his wife seeing. He told the girl he would kill her if she told. What could she do? She told a lie about ripping her dress in the barn when she was feeding the stock. I remember now that she was a bound girl and did not know where her father and mother were. Maybe she did not have any father. You know what I mean.

Such bound children were often enough cruelly treated. They were children who had no parents, slaves really. There were very few orphan homes then. They were legally bound into some home. It was a matter of pure luck how it came out.

II

She married Jake and had a son and daughter, but the daughter died.

Then she settled down to feed stock That was her job. At the German's place she had cooked the food for the German and his wife. The wife was a strong woman with big hips and worked most of the time in the fields with her husband. She fed them and fed the cows in the barn, fed the pigs, the horses and the chickens. Every moment of every day, as a young girl, was spent feeding something.

Then she married Jake Grimes and he had to be fed. She was a slight thing, and when she had been married for three or four years, and after the two children were born, her slender shoulders became stooped.

Jake always had a lot of big dogs around the house, that stood near the unused sawmill near the creek. He was always trading horses when he wasn't stealing something and had a lot of poor bony ones about. Also he kept three or four pigs and a cow. They were all pastured in the few acres left of the Grimes place and Jake did little enough work.

He went into debt for a threshing outfit and ran it for several years, but it did not pay. People did not trust him. They were afraid he would steal the grain at night. He had to go a long way off to get work and it cost too much to get there. In the winter he hunted and cut a little firewood, to be sold in some nearby town. When the son grew up he was just like the father. They got drunk together. If there wasn't anything to eat in the house when they came home the old man gave his old woman a cut over the head. She had a few chickens of her own and had to kill one of them in a hurry. When they were all killed she wouldn't have any eggs to sell when she went to town, and then what would she do?

She had to scheme all her life about getting things fed, getting the pigs fed so they would grow fat and could be butchered in the fall. When they were butchered her husband took most of the meat off to town and sold it. If he did not do it first the boy did. They fought sometimes and when they fought the old woman stood aside trembling.

She had got the habit of silence anyway—that was fixed. Sometimes, when she began to look old—she wasn't forty yet—and when the husband and son were both off, trading horses or drinking or hunting or stealing, she went around the house and the barnyard muttering to herself.

How was she going to get everything fed?—that was her problem. The dogs had to be fed. There wasn't enough hay in the barn for the horses and the cow. If she didn't feed the chickens how could they lay eggs? Without eggs to sell how could she get things in town, things she had to have to keep the life of the farm going? Thank heaven, she did not have to feed her husband—in a certain way. That hadn't lasted long after their marriage and after the babies came. Where he went on his long trips she did not know. Sometimes he was gone from home for weeks, and after the boy grew up they went off together.

They left everything at home for her to manage and she had no money. She knew no one. No one ever talked to her in town. When it was winter she had to gether sticks of wood for her fire, had to try to keep the stock fed with very little grain.

The stock in the barn cried to her hungrily, the dogs followed her about. In the winter the hens laid few enough eggs. They huddled in the corners of the barn and she kept watching them. If a hen lays an egg in the barn in the winter and you do not find it, it freezes and breaks.

One day in winter the old woman went off to town with a few eggs and the dogs followed her. She did not get started until nearly three o'clock and the snow was heavy. She hadn't been feeling very well for several days and so she went muttering along, scantily clad, her shoulders stooped. She had an old grain bag in which she carried her eggs, tucked away down in the bottom. There weren't many of them, but in winter the price of eggs is up. She would get a little meat in exchange for the eggs, some salt pork, a little sugar, and some coffee perhaps. It might be the butcher would give her a piece of liver.

When she had got to town and was trading in her eggs the dogs lay by the door outside. She did pretty well, got the things she needed, more than she had hoped. Then she went to the butcher and he gave her some liver and some dog-meat.

It was the first time anyone had spoken to her in a friendly way for a long time. The butcher was alone in his shop when she came in and was annoyed by the thought of such a sick-looking old woman out on such a day. It was bitter cold and the snow, that had let up during the afternoon, was falling again. The butcher said something about her husband and her son, swore at them, and the old woman stared at him, a look of mild surprise in her eyes as he talked. He said that if either the husband or the son were going to get any of the liver or the heavy bones with scraps of meat hanging to them that he had put into the grain bag, he'd see him starve first.

Starve, eh? Well, things had to be fed. Men had to be fed, and the horses that weren't any good but maybe could be traded off, and the poor thin cow that hadn't given any milk for three months.

Horses, cows, pigs, dogs, men.

III

The old woman had to get back before darkness came if she could. The dogs followed at her heels, sniffing at the heavy grain bag she had fastened on her back. When she got to the edge of town she stopped by a fence and tied the bag on her back with a piece of rope she had carried in her dress-pocket for just that purpose. That was an easier way to carry it. Her arms ached. It was hard when she had to crawl over fences and once she fell over and landed in the snow. The dogs went frisking about. She had to struggle to get to her feet again, but she made it. The point of climbing over the fences was that there was a short cut over a hill and through a woods. She might have gone around by the road, but it was a mile farther that way. She was afraid she couldn't make it. And then, besides, the stock had to be fed. There was a little hay left and a little corn. Perhaps her husband and son would bring some home when they came. They had driven off in the only buggy the Grimes family had, a rickety thing, a rickety horse hitched to the buggy, two other rickety horses led by halters. They were going to trade horses, get a little money if they could. They might come home drunk. It would be well to have something in the house when they came back.

The son had an affair on with a woman at the county seat, fifteen miles away. She was a rough enough woman, a tough one. Once, in the summer, the son had brought her to the house. Both she and the son had been drinking. Jake Grimes was away and the son and his woman ordered the old woman about like a servant. She didn't mind much; she was used to it. Whatever happened she never said anything. That was her way of getting along. She had managed that way when she was a young girl at the German's and ever since she had married Jake. That time her son brought his woman to the house they stayed all night, sleeping together just as though they were married. It hadn't shocked the old woman, not much. She had got past being shocked early in life.

With the pack on her back she went painfully along across an open field, wading in the deep snow, and got into the woods.

There was a path, but it was hard to follow. Just beyond the top of the hill, where the woods was thickest, there was a small clearing. Had someone once thought of building a house there? The clearing was as large as a building lot in town, large enough for a house and a garden. The path ran along the side of the clearing, and when she got there the old woman sat down to rest at the foot of a tree.

It was a foolish thing to do. When she got herself placed, the pack against the tree's trunk, it was nice, but what about getting up again? She worried about that for a moment and then quietly closed her eyes.

She must have slept for a time. When you are about so cold you can't get any colder. The afternoon grew a little warmer and the snow came thicker than ever. Then after a time the weather cleared. The moon even came out.

There were four Grimes dogs that had followed Mrs. Grimes into town, all tall gaunt fellows. Such men as Jake Grimes and his son always keep just such dogs. They kick and abuse them, but they stay. The Grimes dogs, in order to keep from starving, had to do a lot of foraging for themselves, and they had been at it while the old woman slept with her back to the tree at the side of the clearing. They had been chasing rabbits in the woods and in adjoining fields and in their ranging had picked up three other farm dogs.

After a time all the dogs came back to the clearing. They were excited about something. Such nights, cold and clear and with a moon, do things to dogs. It may be that some old instinct, come down from the time when they were wolves and ranged the woods in packs on winter nights, comes back into them.

The dogs in the clearing, before the old woman, had caught two or three rabbits and their immediate hunger had been satisfied. They began to play, running in circles in the clearing. Round and round they ran, each dog's nose at the tail of the next dog. In the clearing, under the snow-laden trees and under the wintry moon they made a strange picture, running thus silently, in a circle their running had beaten in the soft snow. The dogs made no sound. They ran around and around in the circle.

It may have been that the old woman saw them doing that before she died. She may have awakened once or twice and looked at the strange sight with dim old eyes.

She wouldn't be very cold now, just drowsy. Life hangs on a long time. Perhaps the old woman was out of her head. She may have dreamed of her girlhood, at the German's, and before that, when she was a child and before her mother lit out and left her.

Her dreams couldn't have been very pleasant. Not many pleasant things had happened to her. Now and then one of the Grimes dogs left the running circle and came to stand before her. The dog thrust his face close to her face. His red tongue was hanging out.

The running of the dogs may have been a kind of death ceremony. It may have been that the primitive instinct of the wolf, having been aroused in the dogs by the night and the running, made them somehow afraid.

"Now we are no longer wolves. We are dogs, the servants of men. Keep alive, man! When man dies we become wolves again."

When one of the dogs came to where the old woman sat with her back against the tree and thrust his nose close to her face he seemed satisfied and went back to run with the pack. All the Grimes dogs did it at some time during the evening, before she died. I knew all about it afterward, when I grew to be a man, because once in a woods in Illinois, on another winter night, I saw a pack of dogs act just like that. The dogs were waiting for me to die as they had waited for the old woman that night when I was a child, but when it happened to me I was a young man and had no intention whatever of dying.

The old woman died softly and quietly. When she was dead and when one of the Grimes dogs had come to her and had found her dead all the dogs stopped running.

They gathered about her.

Well, she was dead now. She had fed the Grimes dogs when she was alive, what about now?

There was the pack on her back, the grain bag containing the piece of salt pork, the liver the butcher had given her, the dog-meat, the soup bones. The butcher in town, having been suddenly overcome with a feeling of pity, had loaded her grain bag heavily. It had been a big haul for the old woman.

It was a big haul for the dogs now.

IV

One of the Grimes dogs sprang suddenly out from among the others and began worrying the pack on the old woman's back. Had the dogs really been wolves that one would have been the leader of the pack. What he did, all the others did.

All of them sank their teeth into the grain bag the old woman had fastened with ropes to her back.

They dragged the old woman's body out into the open clearing. The worn-out dress was quickly torn from her shoulders. When she was found, a day or two later, the dress had been torn from her body clear to the hips, but the dogs had not touched her body. They had got the meat out of the grain bag, that was all. Her body was frozen still when it was found, and the shoulders were so narrow and the body so slight that in death it looked like the body of some charming young girl.

Such things happened in towns of the Middle West, on farms near town, when I was a boy. A hunter out after rabbits found the old woman's body and did not touch it. Something, the beaten round path in the little snow-covered clearing, the silence of the place, the place where the dogs had worried the body trying to pull the grain bag away or tear it open—something startled the man and he hurried off to town.

I was in Main Street with one of my brothers who was town newsboy and who was taking the afternoon papers to the stores. It was almost night.

The hunter came into a grocery and told his story. Then he went to a hardware shop and into a drugstore. Men began to gather on the sidewalks. Then they started out along the road to the place in the woods.

My brother should have gone on about his business of distributing papers but he didn't. Everyone was going to the woods. The undertaker went and the town marshal. Several men got on a dray and rode out to where the path left the road and went into the woods, but the horses weren't very sharply shod and slid about on the slippery roads. They made no better time than those of us who walked.

The town marshal was a large man whose leg had been injured in the Civil War. He carried a heavy cane and limped rapidly along the road. My brother and I followed at his heels, and as we went other men and boys joined the crowd.

It had grown dark by the time we got to where the old woman had left the road but the moon had come out. The marshal was thinking there might have been a murder. He kept asking the hunter questions. The hunter went along with his gun across his shoulders, a dog following at his heels. It isn't often a rabbit hunter has a chance to be so conspicuous. He was taking full advantage of it, leading the procession with the town marshal. "I didn't see any wounds. She was a beautiful young girl. Her face was buried in the snow. No, I didn't know her." As a matter of fact, the hunter had not looked closely at the body. He had been frightened. She might have been murdered and someone might spring out from behind a tree and murder him. In a woods, in the late afternoon, when the trees are all bare and there is white snow on the ground, when all is silent, something creepy steals over the mind and body. If something strange or uncanny has happened in the neighborhood all you think about is getting away from there as fast as you can.

The crowd of men and boys had got to where the old woman had crossed the field and went, following the marshal and the hunter, up the slight incline and into the woods.

My brother and I were silent. He had his bundle of papers in a bag slung across his shoulder. When he got back to town he would have to go on distributing his papers before he went home to supper. If I went along, as he had no doubt already determined I should, we would both be late. Either mother or our older sister would have to warm our supper.

Well, we would have something to tell. A boy did not get such a chance very often. It was lucky we just happened to go into the grocery when the hunter came in. The hunter was a country fellow. Neither of us had ever seen him before.

Now the crowd of men and boys had got to the clearing. Darkness comes quickly on such winter nights, but the full moon made everything clear. My brother and I stood near the tree, beneath which the old woman had died.

She did not look old, lying there in that light, frozen and still. One of the men turned her over in the snow and I saw everything. My body trembled with some strange mystical feeling and so did my brother's. It might have been the cold.

Neither of us had ever seen a woman's body before. It may have been the snow, clinging to the frozen flesh, that made it look so white and lovely, so like marble. No woman had come with the party from town; but one of the men, he was the town blacksmith, took off his overcoat and spread it over her. Then he gathered her into his arms and started off to town, all the others following silently. At that time no one knew who she was.

V

I had seen everything, had seen the oval in the snow, like a miniature race track, where the dogs had run, had seen how the men were mystified, had seen the white bare young-looking shoulders, had heard the whispered comments of the men.

The men were simply mystified. They took the body to the undertaker's, and when the blacksmith, the hunter, the marshal and several others had got inside they closed the door. If father had been there perhaps he could have got in, but we boys couldn't.

I went with my brother to distribute the rest of his papers and when we got home it was my brother who told the story.

I kept silent and went to bed early. It may have been I was not satisfied with the way he told it.

Later, in the town, I must have heard other fragments of the old woman's story. She was recognized the next day and there was an investigation.

The husband and son were found somewhere and brought to town and there was an attempt to connect them with the woman's death, but it did not work. They had perfect enough alibis.

However, the town was against them. They had to get out. Where they went I never heard.

I remember only the picture there in the forest, the men standing about, the naked girlish-looking figure, face down in the snow, the tracks made by the running dogs and the clear cold winter sky above. White fragments of clouds were drifting across the sky. They went racing across the little open space among the trees.

The scene in the forest had become for me, without my knowing it, the foundation for the real story I am now trying to tell. The fragments, you see, had to be picked up slowly, long afterwards.

Things happened. When I was a young man I worked on the farm of a German. The hired-girl was afraid of her employer. The farmer's wife hated her.

I saw things at that place. Once later, I had a half-uncanny, mystical adventure with dogs in an Illinois forest on a clear, moonlit winter night. When I was a schoolboy, and on a summer day, I went with a boy friend out along a creek some miles from town and came to the house where the old woman had lived. No one had lived in the house since her death. The doors were broken from the hinges; the window lights were all broken. As the boy and I stood in the road outside, two dogs, just roving farm dogs no doubt, came running around the corner of the house. The dogs were tall, gaunt fellows and came down to the fence and glared through at us, standing in the road.

The whole thing, the story of the old woman's death, was to me as I grew older like music heard from far off. The notes had to be picked up slowly one at a time. Something had to be understood.

The woman who died was one destined to feed animal life. Anyway, that is all she ever did. She was feeding animal life before she was born, as a child, as a young woman working on the farm of the German, after she married, when she grew old and when she died. She fed animal life in cows, in chickens, in pigs, in horses, in dogs, in men. Her daughter had died in childhood and with her one son she had no articulate relations. On the night when she died she was hurrying homeward, bearing on her body food for animal life.

She died in the clearing in the woods and even after her death continued feeding animal life.

You see it is likely that, when my brother told the story, that night when we got home and my mother and sister sat listening, I did not think he got the point. He was too young and so was I. A thing so complete has its own beauty.

I shall not try to emphasize the point. I am only explaining why I was dissatisfied then and have been ever since. I speak of that only that you may understand why I have been impelled to try to tell the simple story over again.

The Swimmer

John Cheever

It was one of those midsummer Sundays when everyone sits around saying: "I *drank* too much last night." You might have heard it whispered by the parishioners leaving church, heard it from the lips of the priest himself, struggling with his cassock in the *vestiarium*, heard it from the golf links and the tennis courts, heard it from the wild-life preserve where the leader of the Audubon group was suffering from a terrible hangover. "I *drank* too much," said Donald Westerhazy. "We all *drank* too much," said Lucinda Merill. "It must have been the wine," said Helen Westerhazy. "I *drank* too much of that claret."

This was at the edge of the Westerhazys' pool. The pool, fed by an artesian well with a high iron content, was a pale shade of green. It was a fine day. In the west there was a massive stand of cumulus cloud so like a city seen from a distance—from the bow of an approaching ship—that it might have had a name. Lisbon. Hackensack. The sun was hot. Neddy Merill sat by the green water, one hand in it, one around a glass of gin. He was a slender man—he seemed to have the especial slenderness of youth—and while he was far from young he had slid down his banister that morning and given the bronze back-side of Aphrodite on the hall table a smack, as he jogged toward the smell of coffee in his dining room. He might have been compared to a summer's day, particularly the last hours of one, and while he lacked a tennis racket or a sail bag the impression was definitely one of youth, sport, and clement weather. He had been swimming, and now he was breathing deeply, stertorously as if he could gulp into his lungs the components of that moment, the heat of the sun, the intenseness of his pleasure. It all seemed to flow into his chest. His own house stood in Bullet Park, eight miles to the south, where his four beautiful daughters would have had their lunch and might be playing tennis. Then it occurred to him that by taking a dogleg to the southwest he could reach his home by water.

His life was not confining and the delight he took in his observation could not be explained by its suggestion of escape. He seemed to see, with a cartographer's eye, that string of swimming pools, that quasi-subterranean stream that curved across the country. He had made a discovery, a contribution to modern geography; he would name the stream Lucinda after his wife. He was not a practical joker nor was he a fool but he was determinedly original and had a vague and modest idea of himself as a legendary figure. The day was beautiful and it seemed to him that a long swim might enlarge and celebrate its beauty.

He took off a sweater that was hung over his shoulders and dove in. He had an inexplicable contempt for men who did not hurl themselves into pools. He swam a choppy crawl, breathing either with every stroke or every fourth stroke and counting somewhere well in the back of his mind the one- two one-two of a flutter kick. It was not a serviceable stroke for long distances but the domestication of swimming had saddled the sport with some customs and in his part of the world a crawl was customary. To be embraced and sustained by the light green water was less a pleasure, it seemed, than the resumption of a natural condition, and he would have liked to swim without trunks, but this was not possible, considering his project. He hoisted himself up on the far curb—he never used the ladder—and started across the lawn. When Lucinda asked where he was going he said he was going to swim home.

The only maps and charts he had to go by were remembered or imaginary but these were clear enough. First there were the Grahams, the Hammers, the Lears, the Howlands, and the Crosscups. He would cross Ditmar Street to the Bunkers and come, after a short portage, to the Levys, the Welchers; and the public pool in Lancaster. Then there were the Hallorans, the Sachses, the Biswangers, Shirley Adams, the Gilmartins, and the Clydes. The day was lovely, and that he lived in a world so generously supplied with water seemed like a clemency, a beneficence. His heart was high and he ran across the grass. Making his way home by an uncommon route gave him the feeling that he was a pilgrim, an explorer, a man with a destiny, and he knew that he would find friends all along the way; friends would line the banks of the Lucinda River.

He went through a hedge that separated the Westerhazys' land from the Grahams', walked under some flowering apple trees, passed the shed that housed their pump and filter, and came out at the Grahams' pool. "Why Neddy," Mrs. Graham said, "what a marvelous surprise. I've been trying to get you on the phone all morning. Here let me get you a drink." He saw then, like any explorer, that the hospitable customs and traditions of the natives would have to be handled with diplomacy if he was ever going to reach his destination. He did not want to mystify or seem rude to the Grahams nor did he have the time to linger there. He swam the length of their pool and joined them in the sun and was rescued, a few minutes later, by the arrival of two car-loads of friends from Connecticut. During the uproarious reunions he was able to slip away. He went down by the front of the Grahams' house, stepped over a thorny hedge, and crossed a vacant lot to the Hammers'. Mrs. Hammer, looking up from her roses, saw him swim by although she wasn't quite sure who it was. The Lears heard him splashing past the open windows of their living room. The Howlands and the Crosscups were away. After leaving the Howlands' he crossed Ditmar Street and started for the Bunkers', where he could hear, even at that distance, the noise of a party.

The water refracted the sound of voices and laughter and seemed to suspend it in midair. The Bunkers' pool was on a rise and he climbed some stairs to a terrace where twenty-five or thirty men and women were drinking. The only person in the water was Rusty Towers, who floated there on a rubber raft. Oh how bonny and lush were the banks of the Lucinda River! Prosperous men and women gathered by the sapphire-colored waters while caterer's men in white coats passed them cold gin. Overhead a red de Haviland trainer was circling around and around and around in the sky with something like the glee of a child in a swing. Ned felt a passing affection for the scene, a tenderness for the gathering, as if it was something he might touch. In the distance he heard thunder. As soon as Enid Bunker saw him she began to scream: "Oh look who's here! What a marvelous surprise! When Lucinda said that you couldn't come I thought I'd *die*." She made her way to him through the crowd, and when they had finished kissing she led him to the bar, a progress that was slowed by the fact that he stopped to kiss eight or ten other women and shake the hands of as many men. A smiling bartender he had seen at a hundred parties gave him a gin and tonic and he stood by the bar for a moment, anxious not to get stuck in any conversation that would delay his voyage. When he seemed about to be surrounded he dove in and swam close to the side to avoid colliding with Rusty's raft. At the far end of the pool he bypassed the Tomlinsons with a broad smile and jogged up the garden path. The gravel cut his feet but this was the only unpleasantness. The party was confined to the pool, and as he went toward the house he heard the brilliant, watery sound of voices fade, heard the noise of a radio from the Bunkers' kitchen, where someone was listening to a ballgame. Sunday afternoon. He made his way through the parked cars and down the grassy border of their driveway to Alewives' Lane. He did not want to be seen on the road in his bathing trunks but there was no traffic and he made the short distance to the Levys' driveway, marked with a private property sign and a green tube for the *New York Times*. All the doors and windows of the big house were open but there were no signs of life; not even a dog barked. He went around the side of the house to the pool and saw that the Levys had only recently left. Glasses and bottles and dishes of nuts were on a table at the deep end, where there was a bathhouse or gazebo, hung with Japanese lanterns. After swimming the pool he got himself a glass and poured a drink. It was his fourth or fifth drink and he had swum nearly half the length of the Lucinda River. He felt tired, clean, and pleased at that moment to be alone; pleased with everything.

It would storm. The stand of cumulus cloud—that city—had risen and darkened, and while he sat there he heard the percussiveness of thunder again. The de Haviland trainer was still circling overhead and it seemed to Ned that he could almost hear the pilot laugh with pleasure in the afternoon; but when there was another peal of thunder he took off for home. A train whistle blew and he wondered what time it had gotten to be. Four! Five? He thought of the provincial station at that hour, where a waiter, his tuxedo concealed by a raincoat, a dwarf with some flowers wrapped in newspaper, and a woman who had been crying would be waiting for the local. It was suddenly growing dark; it was that moment when the pin-headed birds seem to organize their song into some acute and knowledgeable recognition of the storm's approach. Then there was a fine noise of rushing water from the crown of an oak at his back, as if a spigot there had been turned. Then the noise of fountains came from the crowns of all the tall trees. Why did he love storms, what was the meaning of his excitement when the door sprang open and the rain wind fled rudely up the stairs, why had the simple task of shutting the windows of an old house seemed fitting and urgent, why did the first watery notes of a storm wind have for him the unmistakable sound of good news, cheer, glad tidings? Then there was an explosion, a smell of cordite, and rain lashed the Japanese lanterns that Mrs. Levy had bought in Kyoto the year before last, or was it the year before that?

He stayed in the Levys' gazebo until the storm had passed. The rain had cooled the air and he shivered. The force of the wind had stripped a maple of its red and yellow leaves and scattered them over the grass and the water. Since it was midsummer the tree must be blighted, and yet he felt a peculiar sadness at this sign of autumn. He braced his shoulders, emptied his glass, and started for the Welchers' pool. This meant crossing the Lindleys' riding ring and he was surprised to find it over-grown with grass and all the jumps dismantled. He wondered if the Lindleys had sold their horses or gone away for the summer and put them out to board. He seemed to remember having heard something about the Lindleys and their horses but the memory was unclear. On he went, barefoot through the wet grass, to the Welchers', where he found their pool was dry.

This breach in his chain of water disappointed him absurdly, and he felt like some explorer who seeks a torrential headwater and finds a dead stream. He was disappointed and mystified. It was common enough to go away for the summer but no one ever drained his pool. The Welchers had definitely gone away. The pool furniture was folded, stacked, and covered with a tarpaulin. The bathhouse was locked. All the windows of the house were shut, and when he went around to the driveway in front he saw a for-sale sign nailed to a tree. When had he last heard from the Welchers—when, that is, had he and Lucinda last regretted an invitation to dine with them. It seemed only a week or so ago. Was his memory failing or had he so disciplined it in the repression of unpleasant facts that he had damaged his sense of the truth? Then in the distance he heard the sound of a tennis game. This cheered him, cleared away all his apprehensions and let him regard the overcast sky and the cold air with indifference. This was the day that Neddy Merill swam across the county. That was the day! He started off then for his most difficult portage.

Had you gone for a Sunday afternoon ride that day you might have seen him, close to naked, standing on the shoulders of route 424, waiting for a chance to cross. You might have wondered if he was the victim of foul play, had his car broken down, or was he merely a fool. Standing barefoot in the deposits of the highway—beer cans, rags, and blowout patches—exposed to all kinds of ridicule, he seemed pitiful. He had known when he started that this was a part of his journey—it had been on his maps—but confronted with the lines of traffic, worming through the summery light, he found himself unprepared. He was laughed at, jeered at, a beer can was thrown at him, and he had no dignity or humor to bring to the situation. He could have gone back, back to the Westerhazys', where Lucinda would still be sitting in the sun. He had signed nothing, vowed nothing, pledged nothing not even to himself. Why, believing as he did, that all human obduracy was susceptible to common sense, was he unable to turn back? Why was he determined to complete his journey even if it meant putting his life in danger? At what point had this prank, this joke, this piece of horseplay become serious? He could not go back, he could not even recall with any clearness the green water at the Westerhazys', the sense of inhaling the day's components, the friendly and relaxed voices saying that they had *drunk* too much. In the space of an hour, more or less, he had covered a distance that made his return impossible.

An old man, tooling down the highway at fifteen miles an hour, let him get to the middle of the road, where there was a grass divider. Here he was exposed to the ridicule of the northbound traffic, but after ten or fifteen minutes he was able to cross. From here he had only a short walk to the Recreation Center at the edge of the Village of Lancaster, where there were some handball courts and a public pool.

The effect of the water on voices, the illusion of brilliance and suspense, was the same here as it had been at the Bunkers' but the sounds here were louder, harsher, and more shrill, and as soon as he entered the crowded enclosure he was confronted with regimentation. "ALL SWIMMERS MUST TAKE A SHOWER BEFORE USING THE POOL. ALL SWIMMERS MUST USE THE FOOTBATH. ALL SWIMMERS MUST WEAR THEIR IDENTIFICATION DISKS." He took a shower, washed his feet in a cloudy and bitter solution and made his way to the edge of the water. It stank of chlorine and looked to him like a sink. A pair of lifeguards in a pair of towers blew police whistles at what seemed to be regular intervals and abused the swimmers through a public address system. Neddy remembered the sapphire water at the Bunkers' with longing and thought that he might contaminate himself—damage his own prosperousness and charm—by swimming in this murk, but he reminded himself that he was an explorer, a pilgrim, and that this was merely a stagnant bend in the Lucinda River. He dove, scowling with distaste, into the chlorine and had to swim with his head above water to avoid collisions, but even so he was bumped into, splashed and jostled. When he got to the shallow end both lifeguards were shouting at him; "Hey, you, you without the identification disk, get outa the water." He did, but they had no way of pursuing him and he went through the reek of suntan oil and chlorine out through the hurricane fence and passed the handball courts. By crossing the road he entered the wooded part of the Halloran estate. The woods were not cleared and the footing was treacherous and difficult until he reached the lawn and the clipped beech hedge that encircled their pool.

The Hallorans were friends, an elderly couple of enormous wealth who seemed to bask in the suspicion that they might be Communists. They were zealous reformers but they were not Communists, and yet when they were accused, as they sometimes were, of subversion, it seemed to gratify and excite them. Their beech hedge was yellow and he guessed this had been blighted like the Levys' maple. He called hullo, hullo, to warn the Hallorans of his approach, to palliate his invasion of their privacy. The Hallorans, for reasons that had never been explained to him, did not wear bathing suits. No explanations were in order, really. Their nakedness was a detail in their uncompromising zeal for reform and he stepped politely out of his trunks before he went through the opening in the hedge.

Mrs. Halloran, a stout woman with white hair and a serene face, was reading the *Times*. Mr. Halloran was taking beech leaves out of the water with a scoop. They seemed not surprised or displeased to see him. Their pool was perhaps the oldest in the county, a fieldstone rectangle, fed by a brook. It had no filter or pump and its waters were the opaque gold of the stream.

"I'm swimming across the county," Ned said.

"Why, I didn't know one could," exclaimed Mrs. Halloran.

"Well, I've made it from the Westerhazys'," Ned said. "That must be about four miles."

He left his trunks at the deep end, walked to the shallow end, and swam this stretch. As he was pulling himself out of the water he heard Mrs. Halloran say: "We've been *terribly* sorry to hear about all your misfortunes, Neddy."

"My misfortunes?" Ned asked. "I don't know what you mean."

"Why, we heard that you'd sold the house and that your poor children . . ."

"I don't recall having sold the house," Ned said, "and the girls are at home."

"Yes," Mrs. Halloran sighed. "Yes . . ." Her voice filled the air with an unseasonable melancholy and Ned spoke briskly. "Thank you for the swim."

"Well, have a nice trip," said Mrs. Halloran.

Beyond the hedge he pulled on his trunks and fastened them. They were loose and he wondered if, during the space of an afternoon, he could have lost some weight. He was cold and he was tired and the naked Hallorans and their dark water had depressed him. The swim was too much for his strength but how could he have guessed this, sliding down the banister that morning and sitting in the Westerhazys' sun? His arms were lame. His legs felt rubbery and ached at the joints. The worst of it was the cold in his bones and the feeling that he might never be warm again. Leaves were falling down around him and he smelled woodsmoke on the wind. Who would be burning wood at this time of year?

He needed a drink. Whiskey would warm him, pick him up, carry him through the last of his journey, refresh his feeling that it was original and valorous to swim the county. Channel swimmers took brandy. He needed a stimulant. He crossed the lawn in front of the Hallorans' house and went down a little path to where they had built a house for their only daughter Helen and her husband Eric Sachs. The Sachses' pool was small and he found Helen and her husband there.

"Oh, *Neddy*," Helen said. "Did you lunch at Mother's?"

"Not *really*," Ned said. "I *did* stop to see your parents." This seemed to be explanation enough. "I'm terribly sorry to break in on you like this but I've taken a chill and I wonder if you'd give me a drink."

"Why, I'd *love* to," Helen said, "but there hasn't been anything in this house to drink since Eric's operation. That was three years ago."

Was he losing his memory, had his gift for concealing painful facts let him forget that he had sold his house, that his children were in trouble, and that his friend had been ill? His eyes slipped from Eric's face to his abdomen, where he saw three pale, sutured scars, two of them at least a foot long. Gone was his navel, and what, Neddy thought, would the roving hand, bed-checking one's gifts at 3 A.M. make of a belly with no navel, no link to birth, this breach in the succession?

"I'm sure you can get a drink at the Biswangers'," Helen said. "They're having an enormous do. You can hear it from here. Listen!"

She raised her head and from across the road, the lawns, the gardens, the woods, the fields, he heard again the brilliant noise of voices over water. "Well, I'll get wet," he said, still feeling that he had no freedom of choice about his means of travel. He dove into the Sachses' cold water and, gasping, close to drowning, made his way from one end of the pool to the other. "Lucinda and I want *terribly* to see you," he said over his shoulder, his face set toward the Biswangers'. "We're sorry it's been so long and we'll call you *very* soon."

He crossed some fields to the Biswangers' and the sounds of revelry there. They would be honored to give him a drink, they would be happy to give him a drink, they would in fact be lucky to give him a drink. The Biswangers invited him and Lucinda for dinner four times a year, six weeks in advance. They were always rebuffed and yet they continued to send out their invitations, unwilling to comprehend the rigid and undemocratic realities of their society. They were the sort of people who discussed the price of things at cocktails, exchanged market tips during dinner, and after dinner told dirty stories to mixed company. They did not belong to Neddy's set—they were not even on Lucinda's Christmas card list. He went toward their pool with feelings of indifference, charity, and some unease, since it seemed to be getting dark and these were the longest days of the year. The party when he joined it was noisy and large. Grace Biswanger was the kind of hostess who asked the optometrist, the veterinarian, the real estate dealer and the dentist. No one was swimming and the twilight, reflected on the water of the pool, had a wintry gleam. There was a bar and he started for this. When Grace Biswanger saw him she came toward him, not affectionately as he had every right to expect, but bellicosely.

"Why, this party has everything," she said loudly, "including a gate crasher."

She could not deal him a social blow—there was no question about this and he did not flinch. "As a gate crasher," he asked politely, "do I rate a drink?"

"Suit yourself," she said. "You don't seem to pay much attention to invitations."

She turned her back on him and joined some guests, and he went to the bar and ordered a whiskey. The bartender served him but he served him rudely. His was a world in which the caterer's men kept the social score, and to be rebuffed by a part-time barkeep meant that he had suffered some loss of social esteem. Or perhaps the man was new and uninformed. Then he heard Grace at his back say: "They went for broke overnight—nothing but income—and he showed up drunk one Sunday and asked us to loan him five thousand dollars. . . ." She was always talking about money. It was worse than eating your peas off a knife. He dove into the pool, swam its length and went away.

The next pool on his list, the last but two, belonged to his old mistress, Shirley Adams. If he had suffered any injuries at the Biswangers' they would be cured here. Love—sexual roughhouse in fact—was the supreme elixir, the painkiller, the brightly colored pill that would put the spring back into his step, the joy of life in his heart. They had had an affair last week, last month, last year. He couldn't remember. It was he who had broken it off, his was the upper hand, and he stepped through the gate of the wall that surrounded her pool with nothing so considered as self-confidence. It seemed in a way to be his pool as the lover, particularly the illicit lover, enjoys the possessions of his mistress with an authority unknown to holy matrimony. She was there, her hair the color of brass, but her figure, at the edge of the lighted, cerulean water, excited in him no profound memories. It had been, he thought, a lighthearted affair, although she had wept when he broke it off. She seemed confused to see him and he wondered if she was still wounded. Would she, God forbid, weep again?

"What do you want?" she asked.

"I'm swimming across the county."

"Good Christ. Will you ever grow up?"

"What's the matter?"

"If you've come here for money," she said, "I won't give you another cent."

"You could give me a drink."

"I could but I won't. I'm not alone."

"Well, I'm on my way."

He dove in and swam the pool, but when he tried to haul himself up onto the curb he found that the strength in his arms and his shoulders had gone, and he paddled to the ladder and climbed out. Looking over his shoulder he saw, in the lighted bathhouse, a young man. Going out onto the dark lawn he smelled chrysanthemums or marigolds—some stubborn autumnal fragrance—on the night air, strong as gas. Looking overhead he saw that the stars had come out, but why should he seem to see Andromeda, Cepheus, and Cassiopeia? What had become of the constellations of midsummer? He began to cry.

It was probably the first time in his adult life that he had ever cried, certainly the first time in his life that he had ever felt so miserable, cold, tired, and bewildered. He could not understand the rudeness of the caterer's barkeep or the rudeness of a mistress who had come to him on her knees and showered his trousers with tears. He had swum too long, and his nose and his throat were sore from the water. What he needed then was a drink, some company, and some clean dry clothes, and while he could have cut directly across the road to his home he went on to the Gilmartins' pool. Here, for the first time in his life, he did not dive but went down the steps into the icy water and swam a hobbled side stroke that he might have learned as a youth. He staggered with fatigue on his way to the Clydes' and paddled the length of their pool, stopping again and again with his hand on the curb to rest. He climbed up the ladder and wondered if he had the strength to get home. He had done what he wanted, he had swum the county, but he was so stupefied with exhaustion that his triumph seemed vague. Stooped, holding onto the gateposts for support, he turned up the driveway of his own house.

The place was dark. Was it so late that they had all gone to bed? Had Lucinda stayed at the Westerhazys' for supper? Had the girls joined her there or gone someplace else? Hadn't they agreed, as they usually did on Sunday, to regret all their invitations and stay at home? He tried the garage doors to see what cars were in but the doors were locked and rust came off the handles onto his hands. Going toward the house, he saw that the force of the thunderstorm had knocked one of the rain gutters loose. It hung down over the front door like an umbrella rib, but it could be fixed in the morning. The house was locked, and he thought that the stupid cook or the stupid maid must have locked the place up until he remembered that it had been some time since they had employed a maid or a cook. He shouted, pounded on the door, tried to force it with his shoulder, and then, looking in at the windows, saw that the place was empty.

A Worn Path

Eudora Welty

It was December—a bright frozen day in the early morning. Far out in the country there was an old Negro woman with her head tied in a red rag, coming along a path through the pinewoods. Her name was Phoenix Jackson. She was very old and small and she walked slowly in the dark pine shadows, moving a little from side to side in her steps, with the balanced heaviness and lightness of a pendulum in a grandfather clock. She carried a thin, small cane made from an umbrella, and with this she kept tapping the frozen earth in front of her. This made a grave and persistent noise in the still air, that seemed meditative like the chirping of a solitary little bird.

She wore a dark striped dress reaching down to her shoe tops, and an equally long apron of bleached sugar sacks, with a full pocket: all neat and tidy, but every time she took a step she might have fallen over her shoe-laces, which dragged from her unlaced shoes. She looked straight ahead. Her eyes were blue with age. Her skin had a pattern all its own of numberless branching wrinkles and as though a whole little tree stood in the middle of her forehead, but a golden color ran underneath, and the two knobs of her cheeks were illuminated by a yellow burning under the dark. Under the red rag her hair came down on her neck in the frailest of ringlets, still black, and with an odor like copper.

Now and then there was a quivering in the thicket. Old Phoenix said, "Out of my way, all you foxes, owls, beetles, jack rabbits, coins, and wild animals! . . . Keep out from under these feet, little bob-whites. . . . Keep the big wild hogs out of my path. Don't let none of those come running my direction. I got a long way." Under her small black-freckled hand her cane, limber as a buggy whip, would switch at the brush as if to rouse up any hiding things.

On she went. The woods were deep and still. The sun made the pine needles almost too bright to look at, up where the wind rocked. The cones dropped as light as feathers. Down in the hollow was the mourning dove—it was not too late for him.

The path ran up a hill. "Seem like there is chains about my feet, time I get this far," she said, in the voice of argument old people keep to use with themselves. "Something always take a hold of me on this hill—pleads I should stay."

After she got to the top she turned and gave a full, severe look behind her where she had come. "Up through pines," she said at length. "Now down through oaks."

Her eyes opened their widest, and she started down gently. But before she got to the bottom of the hill a bush caught her dress.

Her fingers were busy and intent, but her skirts were full and long, so that before she could pull them free in one place they were caught in another. It was not possible to allow the dress to tear. "I in the thorny bush," she said.

"Thorns, you doing your appointed work. Never want to let folks pass—no sir. Old eyes thought you was a pretty little *green* bush."

Finally, trembling all over, she stood free, and after a moment dared to stoop for her cane.

"Sun so high!" she cried, leaning back and looking, while the thick tears went over her eyes. "The time getting all gone here."

At the foot of this hill was a place where a log was laid across the creek.

"Now comes the trial," said Phoenix.

Putting her right foot out, she mounted the log and shut her eyes. Lifting her skirt, levelling her cane fiercely before her, like a festival figure in some parade, she began to march across. Then she opened her eyes and she was safe on the other side.

"I wasn't as old as I thought," she said.

But she sat down to rest. She spread her skirts on the bank around her and folded her hands over her knees. Up above her was a tree in a pearly cloud of mistletoe. She did not dare to close her eyes, and when a little boy brought her a little plate with a slice of marble-cake on it she spoke to him. "That would be acceptable," she said. But when she went to take it there was just her own hand in the air.

So she left that tree, and had to go through a barbed-wire fence. There she had to creep and crawl, spreading her knees and stretching her fingers like a baby trying to climb the steps. But she talked loudly to herself: she could not let her dress be torn now, so late in the day, and she could not pay for having her arm or her leg sawed off if she got caught fast where she was.

At last she was safe through the fence and risen up out in the clearing. Big dead trees, like black men with one arm, were standing in the purple stalks of the withered cotton field. There sat a buzzard.

"Who you watching?"

In the furrow she made her way along.

"Glad this not the season for bulls," she said, looking sideways, "and the good Lord made his snakes to curl up and sleep in the winter. A pleasure I don't see no two-headed snake coming around that tree, where it come once. It took a while to get by him, back in the summer."

She passed through the old cotton and went into a field of dead corn. It whispered and shook and was taller than her head. "Through the maze now," she said, for there was no path.

Then there was something tall, black, and skinny there, moving before her.

At first she took it for a man. It could have been a man dancing in the field. But she stood still and listened, and it did not make a sound. It was as silent as a ghost.

"Ghost," she said sharply, "who be you the ghost of? For I have heard of nary death close by."

But there was no answer—only the ragged dancing in the wind.

She shut her eyes, reached out her hand, and touched a sleeve. She found a coat and inside that an emptiness, cold as ice.

"You scarecrow," she said. Her face lighted. "I ought to be shut up for good," she said with laughter. "My senses is gone. I too old. I the oldest people I ever know. Dance, old scarecrow," she said, "while I dancing with you."

She kicked her foot over the furrow, and with mouth drawn down, shook her head once or twice in a little strutting way. Some husks blew down and whirled in streamers about her skirts.

Then she went on, parting her way from side to side with the cane, through the whispering field, At last she came to the end, to a wagon track where the silver grass blew between the red ruts. The quail were walking around like pullets, seeming all dainty and unseen.

"Walk pretty," she said. "This the easy place. This the easy going."

She followed the track, swaying through the quiet bare fields, through the little strings of trees silver in their dead leaves, past cabins silver from weather, with the doors and windows boarded shut, all like old women under a spell sitting there. "I walking in their sleep," she said, nodding her head vigorously.

In a ravine she went where a spring was silently flowing through a hollow log. Old Phoenix bent and drank. "Sweet-gum makes the water sweet," she said, and drank more. "Nobody know who made this well, for it was here when I was born."

The track crossed a swampy part where the moss hung as white as lace from every limb. "Sleep on, alligators, and blow you bubbles." Then the track went into the road.

Deep, deep the road went down between the high green-colored banks. Overhead the live-oaks met, and it was as dark as a cave.

A black dog with a lolling tongue came up out of the weeds by the ditch. She was meditating, and not ready, and when he came at her she only hit him a little with her cane. Over she went in the ditch, like a little puff of milk-weed.

Down there, her senses drifted away. A dream visited her, and she reached her hand up, but nothing reached down and gave her a pull. So she lay there and presently went to talking. "Old woman," she said to herself, "that black dog come up out of the weeds to stall you off, and now there he sitting on his fine tail, smiling at you."

A white man finally came along and found her—a hunter, a young man, with his dog on a chain.

"Well, Granny!" he laughed. "What are you doing there?"

"Lying on my back like a June-bug waiting to be turned over, mister," she said, reaching up her hand.

He lifted her up, gave her a swing in the air, and set her down. "Anything broken, Granny?"

"No sir, them old dead weeds is springy enough," said Phoenix, when she had got her breath. "I thank you for your trouble."

"Where do you live, Granny?" he asked, while the two dogs were growling at each other.

"Away back yonder, sir, behind the ridge. You can't even see it from here."

"On your way home?"

"No, sir, I going to town."

"Why, that's too far! That's as far as I walk when I come out myself, and I get something for my trouble." He patted the stuffed bag he carried, and there hung down a little closed claw. It was one of the bob-whites, with its beak hooked bitterly to show it was dead. "Now you go on home, Granny!"

"I bound to go to town, mister," said Phoenix. "The time come around."

He gave another laugh, filling the whole landscape. "I know you old colored people! Wouldn't miss going to town to see Santa Claus!"

But something held Old Phoenix very still. The deep lines in her face went into a fierce and different radiation. Without warning, she had seen with her own eyes a flashing nickel fall out of the man's pocket onto the ground.

"How old are you, Granny?" he was saying.

"There is no telling, mister," she said, "no telling."

Then she gave a little cry and clapped her hands and said, "Git on away from here, dog! Look! Look at that dog!" She laughed as if in admiration. "He ain't scared of nobody. He a big black dog." She whispered, "Sic him!"

"Watch me get rid of that cur," said the man. "Sic him, Pete! Sic him!"

Phoenix heard the dogs fighting, and heard the man running and throwing sticks. She even heard a gunshot. But she was slowly bending forward by that time, further and further forward, the lids stretched down over her eyes, as if she were doing this in her sleep. Her chin was lowered almost to her knees. The yellow palm of her hand came out from the fold of her apron. Her fingers slid down and along the ground under the piece of money with the grace and care they would have in lifting an egg from under a sitting hen. Then she slowly straightened up, she stood erect, and the nickel was in her apron pocket. A bird flew by. Her lips moved. "God watching me the whole time. I come to stealing."

The man came back, and his own dog panted about them. "Well, I scared him off that time," he said, and then he laughed and lifted his gun and pointed it at Phoenix.

She stood straight and faced him.

"Doesn't the gun scare you?" he said, still pointing it.

"No, sir, I seen plenty go off closer by, in my day, and for less than what I done," she said, holding utterly still.

He smiled, and shouldered the gun. "Well, Granny," he said, "you must be a hundred years old, and scared of nothing. I'd give you a dime if I had any money with me. But you take my advice and stay home, and nothing will happen to you."

"I bound to go on my way, mister," said Phoenix. She inclined her head in the red rag. Then they went in different directions, but she could hear the gun shooting again and again over the hill.

She walked on. The shadows hung from the oak trees to the road like curtains. Then she smelled wood-smoke, and smelled the river, and she saw a steeple and the cabins on their steep steps. Dozens of little black children whirled around her. There ahead was Natchez shining. Bells were ringing. She walked on.

In the paved city it was Christmas time. There were red and green electric lights strung and crisscrossed everywhere, and all turned on in the daytime. Old Phoenix would have been lost if she had not distrusted her eyesight and depended on her feet to know where to take her.

She paused quietly on the sidewalk where people were passing by. A lady came along in the crowd, carrying an armful of red-, green-, and silver-wrapped presents; she gave off perfume like the red roses in hot summer, and Phoenix stopped her.

"Please, missy, will you lace up my shoe?" She held up her foot.

"What do you want, Grandma?"

"See my shoe," said Phoenix. "Do all right for out in the country, but wouldn't look right to go in a big building."

"Stand still then, Grandma," said the lady. She put her packages down on the sidewalk beside her and laced and tied both shoes tightly.

"Can't lace 'em with a cane," said Phoenix. "Thank you, missy. I doesn't mind asking a nice lady to tie up my shoe, when I gets out on the street."

Moving slowly and from side to side, she went into the big building and into a tower of steps, where she walked up and around and around until her feet knew to stop.

She entered a door, and there she saw nailed up on the wall the document that had been stamped with the gold seal and framed in the gold frame, which matched the dream that was hung up in her head.

"Here I be," she said. There was a fixed and ceremonial stiffness over her body.

"A charity case, I suppose," said an attendant who sat at the desk before her.

But Phoenix only looked above her head. There was sweat on her face, the wrinkles in her skin shone like a bright net.

"Speak up, Grandma," the woman said. "What's your name? We must have your history, you know. Have you been here before? What seems to be the trouble with you?"

Old Phoenix only gave a twitch to her face as if a fly were bothering her.

"Are you deaf?" cried the attendant.

But then the nurse came in.

"Oh, that's just old Aunt Phoenix," she said. "She doesn't come for herself—she has a little grandson. She makes these trips just as regular as clockwork. She lives away back off the Old Natchez Trace." She bent down. "Well, Aunt Phoenix, why don't you just take a seat? We won't keep you standing after your long trip." She pointed.

The old woman sat down, bolt upright in the chair.

"Now, how is the boy?" asked the nurse.

Old Phoenix did not speak.

"I said, how is the boy?"

But Phoenix only waited and stared straight ahead, her face very solemn and withdrawn into rigidity.

"Is his throat any better?" asked the nurse. "Aunt Phoenix, don't you hear me? Is your grandson's throat any better since the last time you came for the medicine?"

With her hands on her knees, the old woman waited, silent, erect and motionless, just as if she were in armour.

"You mustn't take up our time this way, Aunt Phoenix," the nurse said. "Tell us quickly about your grandson, and get it over. He isn't dead, is he?"

At last there came a flicker and then a flame of comprehension across her face, and she spoke.

"My grandson. It was my memory had left me. There I sat and forgot why I made my long trip."

"Forgot?" The nurse frowned. "After you came so far?"

Then Phoenix was like an old woman begging a dignified forgiveness for waking up frightened in the night. "I never did go to school. I was too old at the Surrender," she said in a soft voice. "I'm an old woman without an education. It was my memory fail me. My little grandson, he is just the same, and I forgot it in the coming."

"Throat never heals, does it?" said the nurse, speaking in a loud, sure voice to Old Phoenix. By now she had a card with something written on it, a little list. "Yes. Swallowed lye. When was it—January—two-three years ago—"

Phoenix spoke unasked now. "No, missy, he not dead, he just the same. Every little while his throat begin to close up again, and he not able to swallow. He not get his breath. He not able to help himself. So the time come around, and I go on another trip for the soothing medicine."

"All right. The doctor said as long as you came to get it, you could have it," said the nurse. "But it's an obstinate case."

"My little grandson, he sit up there in the house all wrapped up, waiting by himself," Phoenix went on. "We is the only two left in the world. He suffer and it don't seem to put him back at all. He got a sweet look. He going to last. He wear a little patch quilt and peep out holding his mouth open like a little bird. I remembers so plain now. I not going to forget him again, no, the whole enduring time. I could tell him from all the others in creation."

"All right." The nurse was trying to hush her now. She brought her a bottle of medicine. "Charity," she said, making a check mark in a book.

Old Phoenix held the bottle close to her eyes and then carefully put it into her pocket.

"I thank you," she said.

"It's Christmas time, Grandma," said the attendant. "Could I give you a few pennies out of my purse?"

"Five pennies is a nickel," said Phoenix stiffly.

"Here's a nickel," said the attendant.

Phoenix rose carefully and held out her hand. She received the nickel and then fished the other nickel out of her pocket and laid it beside the new one.

She stared at her palm closely, with her head on one side.

Then she gave a tap with her cane on the floor.

"This is what come to me to do," she said. "I going to the store and buy my child a little windmill they sells, made out of paper. He going to find it hard to believe there such a thing in the world. I'll march myself back where he waiting, holding it straight up in this hand."

She lifted her free hand, gave a little nod, turned around, and walked out of the doctor's office. Then her slow step began on the stairs, going down.

The Eyes

Edith Wharton

We had been put in the mood for ghosts, that evening, after an excellent dinner at our old friend Culwin's, by a tale of Fred Murchard's—the narrative of a strange personal visitation.

Seen through the haze of our cigars, and by the drowsy gleam of a coal fire, Culwin's library, with its oak walls and dark old bindings, made a good setting for such evocations; and ghostly experiences at first hand being, after Murchard's opening, the only kind acceptable to us, we proceeded to take stock of our group and tax each member for a contribution. There were eight of us, and seven contrived, in a manner more or less adequate, to fulfill the condition imposed. It surprised us all to find that we could muster such a show of supernatural impressions, for none of us, excepting Murchard himself and young Phil Frenham—whose story was the slightest of the lot—had the habit of sending our souls into the invisible. So that, on the whole, we had every reason to be proud of our seven "exhibits," and none of us would have dreamed of expecting an eighth from our host.

Our old friend, Mr. Andrew Culwin, who had sat back in his armchair, listening and blinking through the smoke circles with the cheerful tolerance of a wise old idol, was not the kind of man likely to be favored with such contacts, though he had imagination enough to enjoy, without envying, the superior privileges of his guests. By age and by education he belonged to the stout Positivist tradition, and his habit of thought had been formed in the days of the epic struggle between physics and metaphysics. But he had been, then and always, essentially a spectator, a humorous detached observer of the immense muddled variety show of life, slipping out of his seat now and then for a brief dip into the convivialities at the back of the house, but never, as far as one knew, showing the least desire to jump on the stage and do a "turn."

Among his contemporaries there lingered a vague tradition of his having, at a remote period, and in a romantic clime, been wounded in a duel; but this legend no more tallied with what we younger men knew of his character than my mother's assertion that he had once been "a charming little man with nice eyes" corresponded to any possible reconstitution of his physiognomy.

"He never can have looked like anything but a bundle of sticks," Murchard had once said of him. "Or a phosphorescent log, rather," someone else amended; and we recognized the happiness of this description of his small squat trunk, with the red blink of the eyes in a face like mottled bark. He had always been possessed of a leisure which he had nursed and protected, instead of squandering it in vain activities. His carefully guarded hours had been devoted to the cultivation of a fine intelligence and a few judiciously chosen habits; and none of the disturbances common to human experience seemed to have crossed his sky. Nevertheless, his dispassionate survey of the universe had not raised his opinion of that costly experiment, and his study of the human race seemed to have resulted in the conclusion that all men were superfluous, and women necessary only because someone had to do the cooking. On the importance of this point his convictions were absolute, and gastronomy was the only science which he revered as a dogma. It must be owned that his little dinners were a strong argument in favor of this view, besides being a reason— though not the main one—for the fidelity of his friends.

Mentally he exercised a hospitality less seductive but no less stimulating. His mind was like a forum, or some open meeting place for the exchange of ideas: somewhat cold and drafty, but light, spacious and orderly—a kind of academic grove from which all the leaves have fallen. In this privileged area a dozen of us were wont to stretch our muscles and expand our lungs; and, as if to prolong as much as possible the tradition of what we felt to be a vanishing institution, one or two neophytes were now and then added to our band.

Young Phil Frenham was the last, and the most interesting, of these recruits, and a good example of Murchard's somewhat morbid assertion that our old friend "liked 'em juicy." It was indeed a fact that Culwin, for all his dryness, specially tasted the lyric qualities in youth. As he was far too good an Epicurean to nip the flowers of soul which he gathered for his garden, his friendship was not a disintegrating influence: on the contrary, it forced the young idea to robuster bloom. And in Phil Frenham he had a good subject for experimentation. The boy was really intelligent, and the soundness of his nature was like the pure paste under a fine glaze. Culwin had fished him out of a fog of family dullness, and pulled him up to a peak in Darien; and the adventure hadn't hurt him a bit. Indeed, the skill with which Culwin had contrived to stimulate his curiosities without robbing them of their bloom of awe seemed to me a sufficient answer to Murchard's ogreish metaphor. There was nothing hectic in Frenham's efforescence, and his old friend had not laid even a finger tip on the sacred stupidities. One wanted no better proof of that than the fact that Frenham still reverenced them in Culwin.

"There's a side of him you fellows don't see. *I* believe that story about the duel!" he declared; and it was of the very essence of this belief that it should impel him—just as our little party was dispersing—to turn back to our host with the joking demand: "And now you've got to tell us about *your* ghost!"

The outer door had closed on Murchard and the others; only Frenham and I remained; and the devoted servant who presided over Culwin's destinies, having brought a fresh supply of soda water, had been laconically ordered to bed.

Culwin's sociability was a night-blooming flower, and we knew that he expected the nucleus of his group to tighten around him after midnight. But Frenham's appeal seemed to disconcert him comically, and he rose from the chair in which he had just reseated himself after his farewells in the hall.

"*My* ghost? Do you suppose I'm fool enough to go to the expense of keeping one of my own, when there are so many charming ones in my friends' closets? Take another cigar," he said, revolving toward me with a laugh.

Frenham laughed too, pulling up his slender height before the chimney piece as he turned to face his short bristling friend.

"Oh," he said, "you'd never be content to share if you met one you really liked."

Culwin had dropped back into his armchair, his shock head embedded in the hollow of worn leather, his little eyes glimmering over a fresh cigar.

"Liked—*liked*? Good Lord!" he growled.

"Ah, you *have*, then!" Frenham pounced on him in the same instant, with a side glance of victory at me; but Culwin cowered gnomelike among his cushions, dissembling himself in a protective cloud of smoke.

"What's the use of denying it? You've seen everything, so of course you've seen a ghost!" his young friend persisted, talking intrepidly into the cloud. "Or, if you haven't seen one, it's only because you've seen two!"

The form of the challenge seemed to strike our host. He shot his head out of the mist with a queer tortoise-like motion he sometimes had, and blinked approvingly at Frenham.

"That's it," he flung at us on a shrill jerk of laughter; "it's only because I've seen two!"

The words were so unexpected that they dropped down and down into a deep silence, while we continued to stare at each other over Culwin's head, and Culwin stared at his ghosts. At length Frenham, without speaking, threw himself into the chair on the other side of the hearth, and leaned forward with his listening smile. . . .

II

"Oh, of course they're not show ghosts—a collector wouldn't think anything of them. . . . Don't let me raise your hopes . . . their one merit is their numerical strength: the exceptional fact of their being *two*. But, as against this, I'm bound to admit that at any moment I could probably have exorcised them both by asking my doctor for a prescription, or my oculist for a pair of spectacles. Only, as I never could make up my mind whether to go to the doctor or the oculist—whether I was afflicted by an optical or a digestive delusion—I left them to pursue their interesting double life, though at times they made mine exceedingly uncomfortable. . . .

"Yes—uncomfortable; and you know how I hate to be uncomfortable! But it was part of my stupid pride, when the thing began, not to admit that I could be disturbed by the trifling matter of seeing two.

"And then I'd no reason, really, to suppose I was ill. As far as I knew I was simply bored—horribly bored. But it was part of my boredom—I remember—that I was feeling so uncommonly well, and didn't know how on earth to work off my surplus energy. I had come back from a long journey—down in South America and Mexico—and had settled down for the winter near New York with an old aunt who had known Washington Irving and corresponded with N. P. Willis. She lived, not far from Irvington, in a damp Gothic villa overhung by Norway spruces and looking exactly like a memorial emblem done in hair. Her personal appearance was in keeping with this image, and her own hair—of which there was little left—might have been sacrificed to the manufacture of the emblem.

"I had just reached the end of an agitated year, with considerable arrears to make up in money and emotion, and theoretically it seemed as though my aunt's mild hospitality would be as beneficial to my nerves as to my purse. But the deuce of it was that as soon as I felt myself safe and sheltered my energy began to revive; and how was I to work it off inside of a memorial emblem? I had, at that time, the illusion that sustained intellectual effort could engage a man's whole activity; and I decided to write a great book—I forget about what. My aunt, impressed by my plan, gave up to me her Gothic library, filled with classics bound in black cloth and daguerreotypes of faded celebrities; and I sat down at my desk to win myself a place among their number. And to facilitate my task she lent me a cousin to copy my manuscript.

"The cousin was a nice girl, and I had an idea that a nice girl was just what I needed to restore my faith in human nature, and principally in myself. She was neither beautiful nor intelligent—poor Alice Nowell!—but it interested me to see any woman content to be so uninteresting, and I wanted to find out the secret of her content. In doing this I handled it rather rashly, and put it out of joint—oh, just for a moment! There's no fatuity in telling you this, for the poor girl had never seen anyone but cousins. . . .

"Well, I was sorry for what I'd done, of course, and confoundedly bothered as to how I should put it straight. She was staying in the house, and one evening, after my aunt had gone to bed, she came down to the library to fetch a book she'd mislaid, like any artless heroine, on the shelves behind us. She was pink-nosed and flustered, and it suddenly occurred to me that her hair, though it was fairly thick and pretty, would look exactly like my aunt's when she grew older. I was glad I had noticed this, for it made it easier for me to decide to do what was right; and when I had found the book she hadn't lost I told her I was leaving for Europe that week.

"Europe was terribly far off in those days, and Alice knew at once what I meant. She didn't take it in the least as I'd expected—it would have been easier if she had. She held her book very tight, and turned away a moment to wind up the lamp on my desk—it had a ground-glass shade with vine leaves, and glass drops around the edge, I remember. Then she came back, held out her hand, and said: 'Good-bye.' And as she said it she looked straight at me and kissed me. I had never felt anything as fresh and shy and brave as her kiss. It was worse than any reproach, and it made me ashamed to deserve a reproach from her. I said to myself: 'I'll marry her, and when my aunt dies she'll leave us this house, and I'll sit here at the desk and go on with my book; and Alice will sit over there with her embroidery and look at me as she's looking now. And life will go on like that for any number of years.' The prospect frightened me a little, but at the time it didn't frighten me as much as doing anything to hurt her; and ten minutes later she had my seal ring on her finger, and my promise that when I went abroad she should go with me.

"You'll wonder why I'm enlarging on this incident. It's because the evening on which it took place was the very evening on which I first saw the queer sight I've spoken of. Being at that time an ardent believer in a necessary sequence between cause and effect, I naturally tried to trace some kind of link between what had just happened to me in my aunt's library, and what was to happen a few hours later on the same night; and so the coincidence between the two events always remained in my mind.

"I went up to bed with rather a heavy heart, for I was bowed under the weight of the first good action I had ever consciously committed; and young as I was, I saw the gravity of my situation. Don't imagine from this that I had hitherto been an instrument of destruction. I had been merely a harmless young man, who had followed his bent and declined all collaboration with Providence. Now I had suddenly undertaken to promote the moral order of the world, and I felt a good deal like the trustful spectator who has given his gold watch to the conjurer, and doesn't know in what shape he'll get it back when the trick is over. . . . Still, a glow of self-righteousness tempered my fears, and I said to myself as I undressed that when I'd got used to being good it probably wouldn't make me as nervous as it did at the start. And by the time I was in bed, and had blown out my candle, I felt that I really *was* getting used to it, and that, as far as I'd got, it was not unlike sinking down into one of my aunt's very softest wool mattresses.

"I closed my eyes on this image, and when I opened them it must have been a good deal later, for my room had grown cold, and intensely still. I was waked by the queer feeling we all know—the feeling that there was something in the room that hadn't been there when I fell asleep. I sat up and strained my eyes into the darkness. The room was pitch black, and at first I saw nothing; but gradually a vague glimmer at the foot of the bed turned into two eyes staring back at me. I couldn't distinguish the features attached to them, but as I looked the eyes grew more and more distinct: they gave out a light of their own.

"The sensation of being thus gazed at was far from pleasant, and you might suppose that my first impulse would have been to jump out of bed and hurl myself on the invisible figure attached to the eyes. But it wasn't—my impulse was simply to lie still. . . . I can't say whether this was due to an immediate sense of the uncanny nature of the apparition—to the certainty that if I did jump out of bed I should hurl myself on nothing—or merely to the benumbing effect of the eyes themselves. They were the very worst eyes I've ever seen: a man's eyes—but what a man! My first thought was that he must be frightfully old. The orbits were sunk, and the thick red-lined lids hung over the eyeballs like blinds of which the cords are broken. One lid drooped a little lower than the other, with the effect of a crooked leer; and between these folds of flesh, with their scant bristle of lashes, the eyes themselves, small glassy disks with an agate-like rim, looked like sea pebbles in the grip of a starfish.

"But the age of the eyes was not the most unpleasant thing about them. What turned me sick was their expression of vicious security. I don't know how else to describe the fact that they seemed to belong to a man who had done a lot of harm in his life, but had always kept just inside the danger lines. They were not the eyes of a coward, but of someone much too clever to take risks; and my gorge rose at their look of base astuteness. Yet even that wasn't the worst; for as we continued to scan each other I saw in them a tinge of derision, and felt myself to be its object.

"At that I was seized by an impulse of rage that jerked me to my feet and pitched me straight at the unseen figure. But of course there wasn't any figure there, and my fists struck at emptiness. Ashamed and cold, I groped about for a match and lit the candles. The room looked just as usual—as I had known it would; and I crawled back to bed, and blew out the lights.

"As soon as the room was dark again the eyes reappeared; and I now applied myself to explaining them on scientific principles. At first I thought the illusion might have been caused by the glow of the last embers in the chimney; but the fireplace was on the other side of my bed, and so placed that the fire could not be reflected in my toilet glass, which was the only mirror in the room. Then it struck me that I might have been tricked by the reflection of the embers in some polished bit of wood or metal; and though I couldn't discover any object of the sort in my line of vision, I got up again, groped my way to the hearth, and covered what was left of the fire. But as soon as I was back in bed the eyes were back at its foot.

"They were an hallucination, then: that was plain. But the fact that they were not due to any external dupery didn't make them a bit pleasanter. For if they were a projection of my inner consciousness, what the deuce was the matter with that organ? I had gone deeply enough into the mystery of morbid pathological states to picture the conditions under which an exploring mind might lay itself open to such a midnight admonition; but I couldn't fit it to my present case. I had never felt more normal, mentally and physically; and the only unusual fact in my situation—that of having assured the happiness of an amiable girl—did not seem of a kind to summon unclean spirits about my pillow. But there were the eyes still looking at me.

"I shut mine, and tried to evoke a vision of Alice Nowell's. They were not remarkable eyes, but they were as wholesome as fresh water, and if she had

had more imagination—or longer lashes—their expression might have been interesting. As it was, they did not prove very efficacious, and in a few moments I perceived that they had mysteriously changed into the eyes at the foot of the bed. It exasperated me more to feel these glaring at me through my shut lids than to see them, and I opened my eyes again and looked straight into their hateful stare. . . .

"And so it went on all night. I can't tell you what that night was like, nor how long it lasted. Have you ever lain in bed, hopelessly wide awake, and tried to keep your eyes shut, knowing that if you opened 'em you'd see something you dreaded and loathed? It sounds easy, but it's devilishly hard. Those eyes hung there and drew me. I had the *vertige de l'abîme,* and their red lids were the edge of my abyss. . . . I had known nervous hours before: hours when I'd felt the wind of danger on my neck; but never this kind of strain. It wasn't that the eyes were awful; they hadn't the majesty of the powers of darkness. But they had—how shall I say?—a physical effect that was the equivalent of a bad smell: their look left a smear like a snail's. And I didn't see what business they had with me, anyhow—and I stared and stared, trying to find out.

"I don't know what effect they were trying to produce; but the effect they *did* produce was that of making me pack my portmanteau and bolt to town early the next morning. I left a note for my aunt, explaining that I was ill and had gone to see my doctor; and as a matter of fact I did feel uncommonly ill—the night seemed to have pumped all the blood out of me. But when I reached town I didn't go to the doctor's. I went to a friend's rooms, and threw myself on a bed, and slept for ten heavenly hours. When I woke it was the middle of the night, and I turned cold at the thought of what might be waiting for me. I sat up, shaking, and stared into the darkness; but there wasn't a break in its blessed surface, and when I saw that the eyes were not there I dropped back into another long sleep.

"I had left no word for Alice when I fled, because I meant to go back the next morning. But the next morning I was too exhausted to stir. As the day went on the exhaustion increased, instead of wearing off like the fatigue left by an ordinary night of insomnia: the effect of the eyes seemed to be cumulative, and the thought of seeing them again grew intolerable. For two days I fought my dread; and on the third evening I pulled myself together and decided to go back the next morning. I felt a good deal happier as soon as I'd decided, for I knew that my abrupt disappearance, and the strangeness of my not writing, must have been very distressing to poor Alice. I went to bed with an easy mind, and fell asleep at once; but in the middle of the night I woke, and there were the eyes. . . .

"Well, I simply couldn't face them; and instead of going back to my aunt's I bundled a few things into a trunk and jumped aboard the first steamer for England. I was so dead tired when I got on board that I crawled straight into my berth, and slept most of the way over; and I can't tell you the bliss it was to wake from those long dreamless stretches and look fearlessly into the dark, *knowing* that I shouldn't see the eyes. . . .

"I stayed abroad for a year, and then I stayed for another; and during that time I never had a glimpse of them. That was enough reason for prolonging my stay if I'd been on a desert island. Another was, of course, that I had perfectly come to see, on the voyage over, the complete impossibility of my marrying Alice Nowell. The fact that I had been so slow in making this discovery annoyed me, and made me want to avoid explanations. The bliss of escaping at one stroke from the eyes, and from this other embarrassment, gave my freedom an extraordinary zest; and the longer I savored it the better I liked its taste.

"The eyes had burned such a hole in my consciousness that for a long time I went on puzzling over the nature of the apparition, and wondering if it would ever come back. But as time passed I lost this dread, and retained only the precision of the image. Then that faded in its turn.

"The second year found me settled in Rome, where I was planning, I believe, to write another great book—a definitive work on Etruscan influences in Italian art. At any rate, I'd found some pretext of the kind for taking a sunny apartment in the Piazza di Spagna and dabbling about in the Forum; and there, one morning, a charming youth came to me. As he stood there in the warm light, slender and smooth and hyacinthine, he might have stepped from a ruined altar—one to Antinous, say; but he'd come instead from New York, with a letter from (of all people) Alice Nowell. The letter—the first I'd had from her since our break—was simply a line introducing her young cousin, Gilbert Noyes, and appealing to me to befriend him. It appeared, poor lad, that he 'had talent,' and 'wanted to write'; and, an obdurate family having insisted that his calligraphy should take the form of double entry, Alice had intervened to win him six months' respite, during which he was to travel abroad on a meager pittance, and somehow prove his ability to increase it by his pen. The quaint conditions of the test struck me first: it seemed about as conclusive as a medieval 'ordeal.' Then I was touched by her having sent him to me. I had always wanted to do her some service, to justify myself in my own eyes rather than hers; and here was a beautiful occasion.

"I imagine it's safe to lay down the general principle that predestined geniuses don't, as a rule, appear before one in the spring sunshine of the Forum looking like one of its banished gods. At any rate, poor Noyes wasn't a predestined genius. But he *was* beautiful to see, and charming as a comrade. It was only when he began to talk literature that my heart failed me. I knew all the symptoms so well—the things he had 'in him,' and the things outside him that impinged! There's the real test, after all. It was always—punctually, inevitably, with the inexorableness of mechanical law—it was *always* the wrong thing that struck him. I grew to find a certain fascination in deciding in advance exactly which wrong thing he'd select; and I acquired an astonishing skill at the game. . . .

"The worst of it was that his *bêtise* wasn't of the too obvious sort. Ladies who met him at picnics thought him intellectual; and even at dinners he passed for clever. I, who had him under the microscope, fancied now and then that he might develop some kind of a slim talent, something that he could make 'do' and be happy on; and wasn't that, after all, what I was concerned with? He was so charming—he continued to be so charming—that he called forth all my charity in support of this argument; and for the first few months I really believed there was a chance for him. . . .

"Those months were delightful. Noyes was constantly with me, and the more I saw of him the better I liked him. His stupidity was a natural grace—it was as beautiful, really, as his eyelashes. And he was so gay, so affectionate, and so happy with me, that telling him the truth would have been about as pleasant as slitting the throat of some gentle animal. At first I used to wonder what had put into that radiant head the detestable delusion that it held a brain. Then I began to see that it was simply protective mimicry—an instinctive ruse to get away from family life and an office desk. Not that Gilbert didn't—dear lad!—believe in himself. There wasn't a trace of hypocrisy in him. He was sure that his 'call' was irresistible, while to me it was the saving grace of his situation that it *wasn't,* and that a little money, a little leisure, a little pleasure would have turned him into an inoffensive idler. Unluckily, however, there was no hope of money, and with the alternative of the office desk before him he couldn't postpone his attempt at literature. The stuff he turned out was deplorable, and I see now that I knew it from the first. Still, the absurdity of deciding a man's whole future on a first trial seemed to justify me in withholding my verdict, and perhaps even in encouraging him a little, on the ground that the human plant generally needs warmth to flower.

"At any rate, I proceeded on that principle, and carried it to the point of getting his term of probation extended. When I left Rome he went with me, and we idled away a delicious summer between Capri and Venice. I said to myself: 'If he has anything in him, it will come out now,' and it *did*. He was never more enchanting and enchanted. There were moments of our pilgrimage when beauty born of murmuring sound seemed actually to pass into his face—but only to issue forth in a flood of the palest ink. . . .

"Well, the time came to turn off the tap; and I knew there was no hand but mine to do it. We were back in Rome, and I had taken him to stay with me, not wanting him to be alone in his *pension* when he had to face the necessity of renouncing his ambition. I hadn't, of course, relied solely on my own judgment in deciding to advise him to drop literature. I had sent his stuff to various people—editors and critics—and they had always sent it back with the same chilling lack of comment. Really there was nothing on earth to say.

"I confess I never felt more shabby than I did on the day when I decided to have it out with Gilbert. It was well enough to tell myself that it was my duty to knock the poor boy's hopes into splinters—but I'd like to know what act of gratuitous cruelty hasn't been justified on that plea? I've always shrunk from usurping the functions of Providence, and when I have to exercise them I decidedly prefer that it shouldn't be on an errand of destruction. Besides, in the last issue, who was I to decide, even after a year's trial, if poor Gilbert had it in him or not?

"The more I looked at the part I'd resolved to play, the less I liked it; and I liked it still less when Gilbert sat opposite me, with his head thrown back in the lamplight, just as Phil's is now. . . . I'd been going over his last manuscript, and he knew it, and he knew that his future hung on my verdict—we'd tacitly agreed to that. The manuscript lay between us, on my table—a novel, his first novel, if you please!—and he reached over and laid his hand on it, and looked up at me with all his life in the look.

"I stood up and cleared my throat, trying to keep my eyes away from his face and on the manuscript.

" 'The fact is, my dear Gilbert,' I began—

"I saw him turn pale, but he was up and facing me in an instant.

" 'Oh, look here, don't take on so, my dear fellow! I'm not so awfully cut up as all that!' His hands were on my shoulders, and he was laughing down on me from his full height, with a kind of mortally stricken gaiety that drove the knife into my side.

"He was too beautifully brave for me to keep up any humbug about my duty. And it came over me suddenly how I should hurt others in hurting him: myself first, since sending him home meant losing him; but more particularly poor Alice Nowell, to whom I had so longed to prove my good faith and my desire to serve her. It really seemed like failing her twice to fail Gilbert.

"But my intuition was like one of those lightning flashes that encircle the whole horizon, and in the same instant I saw what I might be letting myself in for if I didn't tell the truth. I said to myself: 'I shall have him for life'—and I'd never yet seen anyone, man or woman, whom I was quite sure of wanting on those terms. Well, this impulse of egotism decided me. I was ashamed of it, and to get away from it I took a leap that landed me straight in Gilbert's arms.

" 'The thing's all right, and you're all wrong!' I shouted up at him; and as he hugged me, and I laughed and shook in his clutch, I had for a minute the sense of self-complacency that is supposed to attend the footsteps of the just. Hang it all, making people happy *has* its charms.

"Gilbert, of course, was for celebrating his emancipation in some spectacular manner; but I sent him away alone to explode his emotions, and went to bed to sleep off mine. As I undressed I began to wonder what their aftertaste would be—so many of the finest don't keep! Still, I wasn't sorry, and I meant to empty the bottle, even if it *did* turn a trifle flat.

"After I got into bed I lay for a long time smiling at the memory of his eyes—his blissful eyes. . . . Then I fell asleep, and when I woke the room was deathly cold, and I sat up with a jerk—and there were *the other eyes*. . . .

"It was three years since I'd seen them, but I'd thought of them so often that I fancied they could never take me unawares again. Now, with their red sneer on me, I knew that I had never really believed they would come back, and that I was as defenceless as ever against them. . . . As before, it was the insane irrelevance of their coming that made it so horrible. What the deuce were they after, to leap out at me at such a time? I had lived more or less carelessly in the years since I'd seen them, though my worst indiscretions were not dark enough to invite the searchings of their infernal glare; but at this particular moment I was really in what might have been called a state of grace; and I can't tell you how the fact added to their horror. . . .

"But it's not enough to say they were as bad as before: they were worse. Worse by just so much as I'd learned of life in the interval; by all the damnable implications my wider experience read into them. I saw now what I hadn't seen before: that they were eyes which had grown hideous gradually, which had built up their baseness coralwise, bit by bit, out of a series of small turpitudes slowly accumulated through the industrious years. Yes—it came to me that what made them so bad was that they'd grown bad so slowly. . . .

"There they hung in the darkness, their swollen lids dropped across the little watery bulbs rolling loose in the orbits, and the puff of flesh making a muddy shadow underneath—and as their stare moved with my movements, there came over me a sense of their tacit complicity, of a deep hidden understanding between us that was worse than the first shock of their strangeness. Not that I understood them; but that they made it so clear that someday I should. . . . Yes, that was the worst part of it, decidedly; and it was the feeling that became stronger each time they came back. . . .

"For they got into the damnable habit of coming back. They reminded me of vampires with a taste for young flesh, they seemed so to gloat over the taste of a good conscience. Every night for a month they came to claim their morsel of mine: since I'd made Gilbert happy they simply wouldn't loosen their fangs. The coincidence almost made me hate him, poor lad, fortuitous as I felt it to be. I puzzled over it a good deal, but couldn't find any hint of an explanation except in the chance of his association with Alice Nowell. But then the eyes had let up on me the moment I had abandoned her, so they could hardly be the emissaries of a woman scorned, even if one could have pictured poor Alice charging such spirits to avenge her. That set me thinking, and I began to wonder if they would let up on me if I abandoned Gilbert. The temptation was insidious, and I had to stiffen myself against it; but really, dear boy! he was too charming to be sacrificed to such demons. And so, after all, I never found out what they wanted. . . ."

III

The fire crumbled, sending up a flash which threw into relief the narrator's gnarled face under its grey-black stubble. Pressed into the hollow of the chair back, it stood out an instant like an intaglio of yellowish red-veined stone, with spots of enamel for the eyes; then the fire sank and it became once more a dim Rembrandtish blur.

Phil Frenham, sitting in a low chair on the opposite side of the hearth, one long arm propped on the table behind him, one hand supporting his thrown-back head, and his eyes fixed on his old friend's face, had not moved since the tale began. He continued to maintain his silent immobility after Culwin had ceased to speak, and it was I who, with a vague sense of disappointment at the sudden drop of the story, finally asked: "But how long did you keep on seeing them?"

Culwin, so sunk into his chair that he seemed like a heap of his own empty clothes, stirred a little as if in surprise at my question. He appeared to have half-forgotten what he had been telling us.

"How long? Oh, off and on all that winter. It was infernal. I never got used to them. I grew really ill."

Frenham shifted his attitude, and as he did so his elbow struck against a small mirror in a bronze frame standing on the table behind him. He turned and changed its angle slightly; then he resumed his former attitude, his dark head thrown back on his lifted palm, his eyes intent on Culwin's face. Something in his silent gaze embarrassed me, and as if to divert attention from it I pressed on with another question:

"And you never tried sacrificing Noyes?"

"Oh, no. The fact is I didn't have to. He did it for me, poor boy!"

"Did it for you? How do you mean?"

"He wore me out—wore everybody out. He kept on pouring out his lamentable twaddle, and hawking it up and down the place till he became a thing of terror. I tried to wean him from writing—oh, ever so gently, you understand, by throwing him with agreeable people, giving him a chance to make himself felt, to come to a sense of what he *really* had to give. I'd foreseen this solution from the beginning—felt sure that, once the first ardor of authorship was quenched, he'd drop into his place as a charming parasitic thing, the kind of chronic Cherubino for whom, in old societies, there's always a seat at table, and a shelter behind the ladies' skirts. I saw him take his place as 'the poet': the poet who doesn't write. One knows the type in every drawing room. Living in that way doesn't cost much—I'd worked it all out in my mind, and felt sure that, with a little help, he could manage it for the next few years; and meanwhile he'd be sure to marry. I saw him married to a widow, rather older, with a good cook and a well-run house. And I actually had my eye on the widow. . . . Meanwhile I did everything to help the transition—lent him money to ease his conscience, introduced him to pretty women to make him forget his vows. But nothing would do him: he had but one idea in his beautiful obstinate head. He wanted the laurel and not the rose, and he kept on repeating Gautier's axiom, and battering and filing at his limp prose till he'd spread it out over Lord knows how many hundred pages. Now and then he would send a barrelful to a publisher, and of course it would always come back.

"At first it didn't matter—he thought he was 'misunderstood.' He took the attitudes of genius, and whenever an opus came home he wrote another to keep it company. Then he had a reaction of despair, and accused me of deceiving him, and Lord knows what. I got angry at that, and told him it was he who had deceived himself. He'd come to me determined to write, and I'd done my best to help him. That was the extent of my offence, and I'd done it for his cousin's sake, not his.

"That seemed to strike home, and he didn't answer for a minute. Then he said: 'My time's up and my money's up. What do you think I'd better do?'

" 'I think you'd better not be an ass,' I said.

" 'What do you mean by being an ass?' he asked.

"I took a letter from my desk and held it out to him.

" 'I mean refusing this offer of Mrs. Ellinger's: to be her secretary at a salary of five thousand dollars. There may be a lot more in it than that.'

"He flung out his hand with a violence that struck the letter from mine. 'Oh, I know well enough what's in it!' he said, red to the roots of his hair.

" 'And what's the answer if you know?' I asked.

"He made none at the minute, but turned away slowly to the door. There, with his hand on the threshold, he stopped to say, almost under his breath: 'Then you really think my stuff's no good?'

"I was tired and exasperated, and I laughed. I don't defend my laugh—it was in wretched taste. But I must plead in extenuation that the boy was a fool, and that I'd done my best for him—I really had.

"He went out of the room, shutting the door quietly after him. That afternoon I left for Frascati, where I'd promised to spend the Sunday with some friends. I was glad to escape from Gilbert, and by the same token, as I learned that night, I had also escaped from the eyes. I dropped into the same lethargic sleep that had come to me before when I left off seeing them; and when I woke the next morning in my peaceful room above the ilexes, I felt the utter weariness and deep relief that always followed on that sleep. I put in two blessed nights at Frascati, and when I got back to my rooms in Rome I found that Gilbert had gone. . . . Oh, nothing tragic had happened—the episode never rose to *that*. He'd simply packed his manuscripts and left for America—for his family and the Wall Street desk. He left a decent enough note to tell me of his decision, and behaved altogether, in the circumstances, as little like a fool as it's possible for a fool to behave. . . ."

IV

Culwin paused again, and Frenham still sat motionless, the dusky contour of his young head reflected in the mirror at his back.

"And what became of Noyes afterward?" I finally asked, still disquieted by a sense of incompleteness, by the need of some connecting thread between the parallel lines of the tale.

Culwin twitched his shoulders. "Oh, nothing became of him—because he became nothing. There could be no question of 'becoming' about it. He vegetated in an office, I believe, and finally got a clerkship in a consulate, and married drearily in China. I saw him once in Hong Kong, years afterward. He was fat and hadn't shaved. I was told he drank. He didn't recognize me."

"And the eyes?" I asked, after another pause which Frenham's continued silence made oppressive.

Culwin, stroking his chin, blinked at me meditatively through the shadows. "I never saw them after my last talk with Gilbert. Put two and two together if you can. For my part, I haven't found the link."

He rose, his hands in his pockets, and walked stiffly over to the table on which reviving drinks had been set out.

"You must be parched after this dry tale. Here, help yourself, my dear fellow. Here, Phil—" He turned back to the hearth.

Frenham made no response to his host's hospitable summons. He still sat in his low chair without moving, but as Culwin advanced toward him, their eyes met in a long look; after which the young man, turning suddenly, flung his arms across the table behind him, and dropped his face upon them.

Culwin, at the unexpected gesture, stopped short, a flush on his face.

"Phil—what the deuce? Why, have the eyes scared *you*? My dear boy—my dear fellow—I never had such a tribute to my literary ability, never!"

He broke into a chuckle at the thought, and halted on the hearth-rug, his hands still in his pockets, gazing down at the youth's bowed head. Then, as Frenham still made no answer, he moved a step or two nearer.

"Cheer up, my dear Phil! It's years since I've seen them—apparently I've done nothing lately bad enough to call them out of chaos. Unless my present evocation of them has made *you* see them; which would be their worst stroke yet!"

His bantering appeal quivered off into an uneasy laugh, and he moved still nearer, bending over Frenham, and laying his gouty hands on the lad's shoulders.

"Phil, my dear boy, really—what's the matter? Why don't you answer? *Have* you seen the eyes?"

Frenham's face was still hidden, and from where I stood behind Culwin I saw the latter, as if under the rebuff of this unaccountable attitude, draw back slowly from his friend. As he did so, the light of the lamp on the table fell full on his congested face, and I caught its reflection in the mirror behind Frenham's head.

Culwin saw the reflection also. He paused, his face level with the mirror, as if scarcely recognizing the countenance in it as his own. But as he looked his expression gradually changed, and for an appreciable space of time he and the image in the glass confronted each other with a glare of slowly gathering hate. Then Culwin let go of Frenham's shoulders, and drew back a step. . . .

Frenham, his face still hidden, did not stir.

PLAYS

Antigone

Sophocles

CHARACTERS IN THE PLAY

CREON, *King of Thebes, brother of* JOCASTA, *the mother and wife of* OEDIPUS

EURYDICE, *Queen of Thebes, wife of* CREON

HAEMON, *son of* CREON

ANTIGONE
ISMENE } *daughters of* OEDIPUS *and* JOCASTA

TIRESIAS, *a prophet*

GUARD

MESSENGER

CHORUS *of Theban Elders*

ATTENDANTS

SCENE: *Courtyard of the royal palace at Thebes. Daybreak.*

Enter ANTIGONE *and* ISMENE

ANTIGONE:
　　Dear sister! Dear Ismene! How many evils
　　Our father, Oedipus, bequeathed to us!
　　And is there one of them—do you know of one
　　That Zeus has not showered down upon our heads?
　　I have seen pain, dishonor, shame, and ruin,
　　I have seen them all, in what we have endured.
　　And now comes this new edict by the King
　　Proclaimed throughout the city. Have you heard?
　　Do you not know, even yet, our friends are threatened?
　　They are to meet the fate of enemies.　　　　　　10
ISMENE:
　　Our friends, Antigone? No, I have heard
　　Nothing about them either good or bad.

I have no news except that we two sisters
Lost our two brothers when they killed each other.
I know that the Argive army fled last night,
But what that means, or whether it makes my life
Harder or easier, I cannot tell.

ANTIGONE:

This I was sure of. So I brought you here
Beyond the palace gates to talk alone.

ISMENE:

What is the matter? I know you are deeply troubled.   20

ANTIGONE:

Yes, for our brothers' fate. Creon has given
An honored burial to one, to the other
Only unburied shame. Eteocles
Is laid in the earth with all the rites observed
That give him his due honor with the dead.
But the decree concerning Polyneices
Published through Thebes is that his wretched body
Shall lie unmourned, unwept, unsepulchered.
Sweet will he seem to the vultures when they find him,
A welcome feast that they are eager for.   30
This is the edict the good Creon uttered
For your observance and for mine—yes, mine.
He is coming here himself to make it plain
To those who have not heard. Nor does he think it
Of little consequence, because whoever
Does not obey is doomed to death by stoning.
Now you can show you are worthy of your birth,
Or bring disgrace upon a noble house.

ISMENE:

What can I do, Antigone? As things are,
What can I do that would be of any help?   40

ANTIGONE:

You can decide if you will share my task.

ISMENE:

What do you mean? What are you planning to do?

ANTIGONE:

I intend to give him burial. Will you help?

ISMENE:

To give him burial! Against the law?

ANTIGONE:

He is our brother. I will do my duty,
Yours too, perhaps. I never will be false.

ISMENE:

Creon forbids it! You are too rash, too headstrong.

ANTIGONE:

He has no right to keep me from my own.

ISMENE:

Antigone! Think! Think how our father perished
In scorn and hatred when his sins, that he   50
Himself discovered, drove him to strike blind
His eyes by his own hand. Think how his mother,
His wife—both names were hers—ended her life
Shamefully hanging in a twisted noose.
Think of that dreadful day when our two brothers,
Our wretched brothers, fought and fell together,
Each slayer and each slain. And now we too,
Left all alone, think how in turn we perish,
If, in defiance of the law, we brave
The power of the commandment of a king.   60
O think Antigone! We who are women
Should not contend with men; we who are weak
Are ruled by the stronger, so that we must obey
In this and in matters that are yet more bitter.
And so I pray the dead to pardon me
If I obey our rulers, since I must.
To be too bold in what we do is madness.

ANTIGONE:

I will not urge you. And I would not thank you
For any help that you might care to give me,
Do what you please, but I will bury him,   70
And if I die for that, I shall be happy.
Loved, I shall rest beside the one I loved.
My crime is innocence, for I owe the dead
Longer allegiance than I owe the living.
With the dead I lie forever. Live, if you choose,
Dishonoring the laws the gods have hallowed.

ISMENE:

No, I dishonor nothing. But to challenge
Authority—I have not strength enough.

ANTIGONE:

Then make that your excuse. I will go heap
The earth above the brother that I love.   80

ISMENE:

O Sister, Sister! How I fear for you!

ANTIGONE:

No, not for me. Set your own life in order.

ISMENE:

Well then, at least, tell no one of your plan.
Keep it close hidden, as I too will keep it.

ANTIGONE:
  Oh! Publish it! Proclaim it to the world!
  Then I will hate you less than for your silence.
ISMENE:
  Your heart is hot for deeds that chill the blood.
ANTIGONE:
  I know that I give pleasure where I should.
ISMENE:
  Yes, if you can, but you will try in vain.
ANTIGONE:
  When my strength fails, then I shall try no longer.   90
ISMENE:
  A hopeless task should never be attempted.
ANTIGONE:
  Your words have won their just reward: my hatred
  And the long-lasting hatred of the dead.
  But leave me and the folly that is mine
  To undergo the worst that can befall me.
  I shall not suffer an ignoble death.
ISMENE:
  Go then, Antigone, if you must go.
  And yet remember, though your act is foolish,
  That those who love you do so with all their hearts.

                    Exeunt ANTIGONE *and* ISMENE. *Enter* CHORUS

CHORUS:
  Sunbeam, eye of the golden day, on Thebes the seven-gated,   100
    On Dircé's streams you have dawned at last, O fairest of light.
  Dawned on our foes, who had come enflamed by the quarrel of
                    Polyneices,
      Shone on their glittering arms, made swifter their headlong flight.
      From Argos they came with their white shields flashing,
        Their helmets, crested with horsehair, agleam:
      An army that flew like a snow-white eagle
        Across our borders with shrilling scream.

  Above our roofs it soared, at our gates with greedy jaws it was gaping;
    But before their spears tasted our blood, and before our circle of
                    towers
  Felt the flame of their torches, they turned to flight. The foes of the
                    Theban dragon   110
      Found the surge and clamor of battle too fierce for their feebler
                    powers.
        For Zeus, who abhors a proud tongue's boasting,
          Seeing their river of armor flow

Clashing and golden, struck with his lightning
To silence the shout of our foremost foe.

He crashed to the earth with his torch, who had scaled the top of our
ramparts,
Raging in frenzy against us, breathing tempestuous hate,
Raging and threatening in vain. And mighty Ares, our ally,
Dealing havoc around him, apportioned to other foemen their fate.
For at seven portals, their seven leaders,   120
Down to the earth their bronze arms threw
In tribute to Zeus, the lord of the battle;
Save the fated brothers, the wretched two,
Who went to their common doom together,
Each wielding a spear that the other slew.

Now glorious Victory smiles upon jubilant Thebes rich in chariots.
Let us give free rein to our joy, forgetting our late-felt war;
Let us visit in night-long chorus the temples of all the immortals,
With Bacchus, who shakes the land in the dances, going before.
But behold! The son of Monoeceus approaches,   130
Creon, the new-crowned King of the land,
Made King by new fortunes the gods have allotted.
What step has he pondered? What has he planned
To lay before us, his council of elders,
Who have gathered together at his command?

ENTER CREON

CREON:
Elders of Thebes, our city has been tossed
By a tempestuous ocean, but the gods
Have steadied it once more and made it safe.
You, out of all the citizens, I have summoned,
Because I knew that you once reverenced   140
The sovereignty of Laius, and that later,
When Oedipus was King and when he perished,
Your steadfast loyalty upheld his children.
And now his sons have fallen, each one stained
By his brother's blood, killed by his brother's hand,
So that the sovereignty devolves on me,
Since I by birth am nearest to the dead.
Certainly no man can be fully known,
Known in his soul, his will, his intellect,
Until he is tested and has proved himself   150
In statesmanship. Because a city's ruler,
Instead of following the wisest counsel,
May through some fear keep silent. Such a man

I think contemptible. And one whose friend
Has stronger claims upon him than his country,
Him I consider worthless. As for me,
I swear by Zeus, forever all-beholding,
That I would not keep silence, if I saw
Ruin instead of safety drawing near us;
Nor would I think an enemy of the state   160
Could be my friend. For I remember this:
Our country bears us all securely onward,
And only while it sails a steady course
Is friendship possible. Such are the laws
By which I guard the greatness of the city.
And kindred to them is the proclamation
That I have made to all the citizens
Concerning the two sons of Oedipus:
Eteocles, who has fallen in our defence,
Bravest of warriors, shall be entombed   170
With every honor, every offering given
That may accompany the noble dead
Down to their rest. But as for Polyneices,
He came from exile eager to consume
The city of his fathers with his fire
And all the temples of his fathers' gods,
Eager to drink deep of his kindred's blood,
Eager to drag us off to slavery.
To this man, therefore, nothing shall be given.
None shall lament him, none shall do him honor.   180
He shall be left without a grave, his corpse
Devoured by birds and dogs, a loathsome sight.
Such is my will. For never shall the wicked
Be given more approval than the just,
If I have power to stop it. But whoever
Feels in his heart affection for his city
Shall be rewarded both in life and death.
CHORUS:
Creon, son of Menoeceus, it has pleased you
So to pass judgment on our friend and foe,
And you may give commands to all of us,   190
The living and the dead. Your will is law.
CREON:
Then see that this command is carried out.
CHORUS:
Sir, lay that burden on some younger man.
CREON:
Sentries have been assigned to guard the body.

CHORUS:

Then what additional duty would you give us?

CREON:

Never to countenance the disobedient.

CHORUS:

Who is so stupid as to long for death?

CREON:

Death is indeed the punishment. Yet men
Have often been destroyed by hope of gain.

Enter GUARD

GUARD:

My Lord, I cannot say that I have hurried,   200
Or that my running has made me lose my breath.
I often stopped to think, and turned to go back.
I stood there talking to myself: 'You fool,'
I said, 'Why do you go to certain death?'
And then: 'You idiot, are you still delaying?
If someone else tells Creon, you will suffer.'
I changed my mind this way, getting here slowly,
Making a short road long. but still, at last,
I did decide to come. And though my story
Is nothing much to tell, yet I will tell it.   210
One thing I know. I must endure my fate,
But nothing more than that can happen to me.

CREON:

What is the matter? What is troubling you?

GUARD:

Please let me tell you first about myself.
I did not do it. I did not see who did.
It is not right for me to be punished for it.

CREON:

You take good care not to expose yourself.
Your news must certainly be something strange.

GUARD:

Yes, it is strange—dreadful. I cannot speak.

CREON:

Oh, tell it, will you? Tell it and go away!   220

GUARD:

Well, it is this. Someone has buried the body,
Just now, and gone—has sprinkled it with dust
And given it other honors it should have.

CREON:

What are you saying? Who has dared to do it?

GUARD:

    I cannot tell. Nothing was to be seen:
    No mark of pickaxe, no spot where a spade
    Had turned the earth. The ground was hard and dry,
    Unbroken—not a trace of any wheels—
    No sign to show who did it. When the sentry
    On the first watch discovered it and told us,   230
    We were struck dumb with fright. For he was hidden
    Not by a tomb but a light coat of dust,
    As if a pious hand had scattered it.
    There were no tracks of any animal,
    A dog or wild beast that had come to tear him.
    We all began to quarrel, and since no one
    Was there to stop us, nearly came to blows.
    Everyone was accused, and everyone
    Denied his guilt. We could discover nothing.
    We were quite willing to handle red-hot iron,   240
    To walk through fire, to swear by all the gods
    That we were innocent of the deed itself,
    And innocent of taking any part
    In planning it or doing it. At last
    One of us spoke. We trembled and hung our heads,
    For he was right; we could not argue with him,
    Yet his advice was bound to cause us trouble.
    He told us all this had to be reported,
    Not kept a secret. We all agreed to that.
    We drew lots for it, and I had no luck.   250
    I won the prize and was condemned to come.
    So here I stand, unwilling, because I know
    The bringer of bad news is never welcome.

CHORUS:

    Sir, as he spoke, I have been wondering.
    Can this be, possibly, the work of gods?

CREON:

    Be silent! Before you madden me! You are old.
    Would you be senseless also? What you say
    Is unendurable. You say the gods
    Cared for this corpse. Then was it for reward,
    Mighty to match his mighty services,   260
    That the gods covered him? He who came to burn
    Their pillared temples and their votive offerings,
    Ravage their land, and trample down the state.
    Or is it your opinion that the gods
    Honor the wicked? Inconceivable!

However, from the first, some citizens
Who found it difficult to endure this edict,
Muttered against me, shaking their heads in secret,
Instead of bowing down beneath the yoke,
Obedient and contented with my rule.   270
These are the men who are responsible,
For I am certain they have bribed the guards
To bury him. Nothing is worse than money.
Moneys lays waste to cities, banishes
Men from their homes, indoctrinates the heart,
Perverting honesty to works of shame,
Showing men how to practice villainy,
Subduing them to every godless deed.
But all those men who got their pay for this
Need have no doubt their turn to pay will come.   280
(*to the* GUARD) Now, you. As I still honor Zeus the King,
I tell you, and I swear it solemnly,
Either you find the man who did this thing,
The very man, and bring him here to me,
Or you will not just die. Before you die,
You will be tortured until you have explained
This outrage, so that later when you steal
You will know better where to look for money
And not expect to find it everywhere.
Ill-gotten wealth brings ruin and not safety.   290

GUARD:
Sir, may I speak? Or shall I merely go?
CREON:
You can say nothing that is not offensive.
GUARD:
Do I offend your hearing or your heart?
CREON:
Is it your business to define the spot?
GUARD:
The criminal hurts your heart, and I your ears.
CREON:
Still talking? Why, you must have been born talking!
GUARD:
Perhaps. But I am not the guilty man.
CREON:
You are. And what is more you sold yourself.
GUARD:
You have judged me, sir, and have misjudged me, too.
CREON:
Be clever about judging if you care to.   300

But you will say that treachery leads to sorrow.
Unless you find the man and show him to me.

Exit CREON

GUARD:
Finding him is the best thing that could happen.
Fate will decide. But however that may be,
You never are going to see me here again.
I have escaped! I could not have hoped for that.
I owe the gods my thanks for guarding me.

Exit GUARD

CHORUS:
Many the marvelous things; but none that can be
   More of a marvel than man! This being that braves
With the south wind of winter the whitened streaks of the sea,   310
   Threading his way through the troughs of engulfing waves.
And the earth most ancient, the eldest of all the gods.
   Earth, undecaying, unwearied, he wears away with his toil;
Forward and back with his plowshare, year after year, he plods,
   With his horses turning the soil.

Man in devising excels. The birds of the air,
   That light-minded race, he entangles fast in his toils.
Wild creatures he catches, casting about them his snare,
   And the salt-sea brood he nets in his woven coils.
The tireless bull he has tamed, and the beast whose lair   320
   Is hidden deep in the wilds, who roams in the wooded hills.
He has fitted a yoke that the neck of the shaggy-maned horse
          will bear;
   He is master of all through his skills.

He has taught himself speech, and wind-like thought, and the lore
   Of ruling a town. He has fled the arrows of rain,
The searching arrows of frost he need fear no more,
   That under a starry sky are endured with pain.
Provision for all he has made—unprovided for naught,
   Save death itself, that in days to come will take shape.
From obscure and deep-seated disease he has subtly wrought   330
A way of escape.

Resourceful and skilled, with an inconceivable art,
   He follows his course to a good or an evil end.
When he holds the canons of justice high in his heart
   And has sworn to the gods the laws of the land to defend,
Proud stands his city; without a city is he
   Who with ugliness, rashness, or evil dishonors the day.

Let me shun his thoughts. Let him share no hearthstone with me,
    Who acts in this way!

CHORUS:

    Look there! Look there! What portent can this be? 340
    Antigone! I know her, it is she!
    Daughter of Oedipus a prisoner brought?
    You defied Creon? You in folly caught?

Enter GUARD *with* ANTIGONE

GUARD:

    She did it. Here she is. We caught this girl
    As she was burying him. Where is the King?

CHORUS:

    Leaving the palace there, just as we need him.

Enter CREON

CREON:

    Why do you need my presence? What has happened?

GUARD:

    My Lord, no one should take a solemn oath
    Not to do something, for his second thoughts
    Make him a liar. I vowed not to hurry back. 350
    I had been battered by your storm of threats.
    But when a joy comes that exceeds our hopes,
    No other happiness can equal it.
    So I have broken my vow. I have returned,
    Bringing this girl along. She was discovered
    Busy with all the rites of burial.
    There was no casting lots, no, not this time!
    Such luck as this was mine and no one else's.
    Now sir, take her yourself, examine her,
    Convict her, do what you like. But as for me, 360
    I have the right to a complete acquittal.

CREON:

    This is the girl you caught? How? Where was she?

GUARD:

    Burying the dead man, just as I have told you.

CREON:

    Do you mean that? Or have you lost your mind?

GUARD:

    Your order was that he should not be buried.
    I saw her bury him. Is that all clear?

CREON:

    How was she seen? You caught her in the act?

GUARD:

    This was what happened. When we had gotten back,

With your threats following us, we swept away
The dust that covered him. We left him bare,   370
A rotting corpse. And then we sat to windward,
Up on the hillside, to avoid the stench.
All of us were alert, and kept awake
Threatening each other. No one could get careless.
So the time passed, until the blazing sun
Stood at the zenith, and the heat was burning.
Then suddenly the wind came in a blast,
Lifting a cloud of dust up from the earth,
Troubling the sky and choking the whole plain,
Stripping off all the foliage of the woods,   380
Filling the breadth of heaven. We closed our eyes
And bore the affliction that the gods had sent us.
When it had finally stopped, we saw this girl.
She wailed aloud with a sharp, bitter cry,
The cry a bird gives seeing its empty nest
Robbed of its brood. And she too, when she saw
The naked body, was loud in her lament
And cursed the men who had uncovered him.
Quickly she sprinkled him with dust, and then
Listing a pitcher, poured out three libations   390
To do him honor. When we ran and caught her,
She was unterrified. When we accused her
Both of her earlier and her present act,
She made no effort to deny the charges.
I am part glad, part sorry. It is good
To find that you yourself have gotten clear,
But to bring trouble on your friends is hard.
However, nothing counts except my safety.

CREON (*to* ANTIGONE):
Go   You there. You, looking at the ground. Tell me.
Do you admit this or deny it? Which?   400

ANTIGONE:
Yes, I admit it. I do not deny it.

CREON (*to* GUARD):
Go. You are free. The charge is dropped.

Exit GUARD

Now you,
Answer this question. Make your answer brief.
You knew there was a law forbidding this?

ANTIGONE:
Of course I knew it. Why not? It was public.

CREON:
And you have dared to disobey the law?

ANTIGONE:

Yes. For this law was not proclaimed by Zeus,
Or by the gods who rule the world below.
I do not think your edicts have such power
That they can override the laws of heaven,   410
Unwritten and unfailing, laws whose life
Belongs not to today or yesterday
But to time everlasting; and no man
Knows the first moment that they had their being.
If I transgressed these laws because I feared
The arrogance of man, how to the gods
Could I make satisfaction? Well I know,
Being a mortal, that I have to die,
Even without your proclamations. Yet
If I must die before my time is come,   420
That is a blessing. Because to one who lives,
As I live, in the midst of sorrows, death
Is of necessity desirable.
For me, to face death is a trifling pain
That does not trouble me. But to have left
The body of my brother, my own brother,
Lying unburied would be bitter grief.
And if these acts of mine seem foolish to you,
Perhaps a fool accuses me of folly.

CHORUS:

The violent daughter of a violent father.   430
She cannot bend before a storm of evils.

CREON (*to* ANTIGONE):

Stubborn? Self-willed? People like that, I tell you,
Are the first to come to grief. The hardest iron,
Baked in the fire, most quickly flies to pieces.
An unruly horse is taught obedience
By a touch of the curb. How can you be so proud?
You, a mere slave? (*to* CHORUS) She was well schooled already
In insolence, when she defied the law.
And now look at her! Boasting, insolent,
Exulting in what she did. And if she triumphs
And goes unpunished, I am no man—she is.   440
If she were more than niece, if she were closer
Than anyone who worships at my altar,
She would not even then escape her doom,
A dreadful death. Nor would her sister. Yes,
Her sister had a share in burying him.
(*to* ATTENDANT) Go bring her here. I have just seen her, raving,
Beside herself. Even before they act,

Traitors who plot their treason in the dark
Betray themselves like that. Detestable!
(*to* ANTIGONE) But hateful also is an evil-doer
Who, caught red-handed, glorifies the crime.

ANTIGONE:

Now you have caught me, will you do more than kill me?

CREON:

No, only that. With that I am satisfied.

ANTIGONE:

Then why do you delay? You have said nothing
I do not hate. I pray you never will.
And you hate what I say. Yet how could I
Have won more splendid honor than by giving
Due burial to my brother? All men here
Would grant me their approval, if their lips
Were not sealed up in fear. But you, a king,
Blessed by good fortune in much else besides,
Can speak and act with perfect liberty.

CREON:

All of these Thebans disagree with you.

ANTIGONE:

No. They agree, but they control their tongues.

CREON:

You feel no shame in acting without their help?

ANTIGONE:

I feel no shame in honoring a brother.

CREON:

Another brother died who fought against him.

ANTIGONE:

Two brothers. The two sons of the same parents.

CREON:

Honor to one is outrage to the other.

ANTIGONE:

Eteocles will not feel himself dishonored.

CREON:

What! When his rites are offered to a traitor?

ANTIGONE:

It was his brother, not his slave, who died.

CREON:

One who attacked the land that he defended.

ANTIGONE:

The gods still wish those rites to be performed.

CREON:

Are the just pleased with the unjust as their equals?

ANTIGONE:

That may be virtuous in the world below.

CREON:

No. Even there a foe is never a friend.

ANTIGONE:

I am not made for hatred but for love.

CREON:

Then go down to the dead. If you must love,
Love them. While I yet live, no woman rules me.   **480**

CHORUS:

Look there. Ismene, weeping as sisters weep.
The shadow of a cloud of grief lies deep
On her face, darkly flushed; and in her pain
Her tears are falling like a flood of rain.

CREON:

You viper! Lying hidden in my house,
Sucking my blood in secret, while I reared,
Unknowingly, two subverters of my throne.
Do you confess that you have taken part
In this man's burial, or deny it? Speak.

ISMENE:

If she will recognize my right to say so,   **490**
I shared the action and I share the blame.

ANTIGONE:

No. That would not be just. I never let you
Take any part in what you disapproved of.

ISMENE:

In your calamity, I am not ashamed
To stand beside you, beaten by this tempest.

ANTIGONE:

The dead are witnesses of what I did,
To love in words alone is not enough.

ISMENE:

Do not reject me, Sister! Let me die
Beside you, and do honor to the dead.

ANTIGONE:

No. You will neither share my death nor claim   **500**
What I have done. My death will be sufficient.

ISMENE:

What happiness can I have when you are gone?

ANTIGONE:

Ask Creon that. He is the one you value.

ISMENE:

Do you gain anything by taunting me?

ANTIGONE:

Ah, no! By taunting you, I hurt myself.

ISMENE:
   How can I help you? Tell me what I can do.
ANTIGONE:
   Protect yourself. I do not grudge your safety.
ISMENE:
   Antigone! Shall I not share your fate?
ANTIGONE:
   We both have made our choices: life, and death.
ISMENE:
   At least I tried to stop you. I protested.   510
ANTIGONE:
   Some have approved your way; and others, mine.
ISMENE:
   Yet now I share your guilt. I too am ruined.
ANTIGONE:
   Take courage. Live your life. But I long since
   Gave myself up to death to help the dead.
CREON:
   One of them has just lost her senses now.
   The other has been foolish all her life.
ISMENE:
   We cannot always use our reason clearly.
   Suffering confuses us and clouds our minds.
CREON:
   It clouds your mind. You join in her wrong-doing.
ISMENE:
   How is life possible without my sister?   520
CREON:
   Your sister? You have no sister. She is dead.
ISMENE:
   Then you will kill the wife your son has chosen?
CREON:
   Yes. There are other fields that he can plow.
ISMENE:
   He will not find such an enduring love.
CREON:
   A wicked woman for my son? No, never!
ANTIGONE:
   O Haemon, Haemon! How your father wrongs you!
CREON:
   You and your marriage! Let me hear no more!
CHORUS:
   You are unyielding? You will take her from him?
CREON:
   Death will act for me. Death will stop the marriage.

CHORUS:

  It seems, then, you have sentenced her to death.   **530**

CREON:

  Yes. And my sentence you yourselves accepted.

  Take them inside. From now on, they are women,

  And have no liberty. For even the bold

  Seek an escape when they see death approaching.

                      Exeunt ANTIGONE, ISMENE, *and* ATTENDANTS

CHORUS:

    Blesséd the life that has no evil known,

For the gods, striking, strike down a whole race—

    Doomed parent and doomed child both overthrown.

As when the fierce breath of the winds of Thrace

    Across the darkness of the sea has blown

A rushing surge; black sand from deep below   **540**

    Comes boiling up; wind-beaten headlands moan,

Fronting the full shock of the billow's blow.

    The race of Oedipus, from days of old,

To long dead sorrows add new sorrows' weight.

    Some god has sent them sufferings manifold.

None may release another, for their fate

    Through generations loosens not its hold.

Now is their last root cut, their last light fled,

    Because of frenzy's curse, words overbold,

And dust, the gods' due, on the bloodstained dead.   **550**

    O Zeus, what human sin restricts thy might?

Thou art unsnared by all-ensnaring sleep

    Or tireless mouths. Unaging thou dost keep

Thy court in splendor of Olympian light.

    And as this law was true when time began,

Tomorrow and forever it shall be:

    Naught beyond measure in the life of man

        From fate goes free.

    For hope, wide-ranging, that brings good to some,

To many is a false lure of desire   **560**

    Light-minded, giddy; and until the fire

Scorches their feet, they know now what will come.

    Wise is the famous adage: that to one

Whom the gods madden, evil, soon or late,

    Seems good; then can he but a moment shun

        The stroke of fate.

    But Haemon comes, of your two sons the last.

Is his heart heavy for the sentence passed

Upon Antigone, his promised bride,
And for his hope of marriage now denied? 570

Enter HAEMON

CREON:
　　We soon shall know better than seers could tell us.
　　My son, Antigone is condemned to death.
　　Nothing can change my sentence. Have you learned
　　Her fate and come here in a storm of anger,
　　Or do you love me and support my acts?

HAEMON:
　　Father, I am your son. Your greater knowledge
　　Will trace the pathway that I mean to follow.
　　My marriage cannot be of more importance
　　Than to be guided always by your wisdom.

CREON:
　　Yes, Haemon, this should be the law you live by! 580
　　In all things to obey your father's will.
　　Men pray for children round them in their homes
　　Only to see them dutiful and quick
　　With hatred to requite their father's foe,
　　With honor to repay their father's friend.
　　But what is there to say of one whose children
　　Prove to be valueless? That he has fathered
　　Grief for himself and laughter for his foes.
　　Then, Haemon, do not, at the lure of pleasure,
　　Unseat your reason for a woman's sake. 590
　　This comfort soon grows cold in your embrace:
　　A wicked wife to share your bed and home.
　　Is there a deeper wound than to find worthless
　　The one you love? Turn from this girl with loathing,
　　As from an enemy, and let her go
　　To get a husband in the world below.
　　For I have found her openly rebellious,
　　Her only out of all the city. Therefore,
　　I will not break the oath that I have sworn.
　　I will have her killed. Vainly she will invoke 600
　　The bond of kindred blood the gods make sacred.
　　If I permit disloyalty to breed
　　In my own house, I nurture it in strangers.
　　He who is righteous with his kin is righteous
　　In the state also. Therefore, I cannot pardon
　　One who does violence to the laws or thinks
　　To dictate to his rulers; for whoever
　　May be the man appointed by the city,
　　That man must be obeyed in everything,

Little or great, just or unjust. And surely 610
He who was thus obedient would be found
As good a ruler as he was a subject;
And in a storm of spears he would stand fast
With loyal courage at his comrade's side.
But disobedience is the worst of evils.
For it is this that ruins cities; this
Makes our homes desolate; armies of allies
Through this break up in rout. But most men find
Their happiness and safety in obedience.
Therefore we must support the law, and never 620
Be beaten by a woman. It is better
To fall by a man's hand, if we must fall,
Than to be known as weaker than a girl.

CHORUS:

We may in our old age have lost our judgment,
And yet to us you seem to have spoken wisely.

HAEMON:

The gods have given men the gift of reason,
Greatest of all things that we call our own.
I have no skill, nor do I wish to have it,
To show where you have spoken wrongly. Yet
Some other's thought, beside your own, might prove 630
To be of value. Therefore it is my duty,
My natural duty as your son, to notice,
On your behalf, all that men say, or do,
Or find to blame. For your frown frightens them,
So that the citizen dares not say a word
That would offend you. I can hear, however,
Murmurs in darkness and laments for her.
They say: 'No woman ever less deserved
Her doom, no woman ever was to die
So shamefully for deeds so glorious. 640
For when her brother fell in bloody battle,
She would not let his body lie unburied
To be devoured by carrion dogs or birds.
Does such a woman not deserve reward,
Reward of golden honor?' This I hear,
A rumor spread in secrecy and darkness.
Father, I prize nothing in life so highly
As your well-being. How can children have
A nobler honor than their father's fame
Or father than his son's? Then do not think 650
Your mood must never alter; do not feel
Your word, and yours alone, must be correct.

For if a man believes that he is right
And only he, that no one equals him
In what he says or thinks, he will be found
Empty when searched and tested. Because a man
Even if he be wise, feels no disgrace
In learning many things, in taking care
Not to be over-rigid. You have seen
Trees on the margin of a stream in winter: 660
And those resisting perish root and branch.
So, too, the mariner who never slackens
His taut sheet overturns his craft and spends
Keel uppermost the last part of his voyage.
Let your resentment die. Let yourself change.
For I believe—if I, a younger man,
May have a sound opinion—it is best
That men by nature should be wise in all things.
But most men find they cannot reach that goal; 670
And when this happens, it is also good
To learn to listen to wise counselors.

CHORUS:

Sir, when his words are timely, you should heed them.
And Haemon, you should profit by his words.
Each one of you has spoken reasonably.

CREON:

Are men as old as I am to be taught
How to behave by men as young as he?

HAEMON:

Not to do wrong. If I am young, ignore
My youth. Consider only what I do.

CREON:

Have you done well in honoring the rebellious? 680

HAEMON:

Those who do wrong should not command respect.

CREON:

Then that disease has not infected her?

HAEMON:

All of our city with one voice denies it.

CREON:

Does Thebes give orders for the way I rule?

HAEMON:

How young you are! How young in saying that!

CREON:

Am I to govern by another's judgment?

HAEMON:

A city that is one man's is no city.

CREON:

A city is the king's. That much is sure.

HAEMON:

You would rule well in a deserted country.

CREON:

This boy defends a woman, it appears. 690

HAEMON:

If you are one, I am concerned for you.

CREON:

To quarrel with your father does not shame you?

HAEMON:

Not when I see you failing to do justice.

CREON:

Am I unjust when I respect my crown?

HAEMON:

Respect it! When you trample down religion?

CREON:

Infamous! Giving first place to a woman!

HAEMON:

But never to anything that would disgrace me.

CREON:

Each word you utter is a plea for her.

HAEMON:

For you, too, and for me, and for the gods.

CREON:

You shall not marry her this side of death. 700

HAEMON:

Then if she dies, she does not die alone.

CREON:

What! Has it come to this? You threaten me?

HAEMON:

No. But I tell you your decree is useless.

CREON:

You will repent this. You! Teaching me wisdom!

HAEMON:

I will not call you mad. You are my father.

CREON:

You woman's slave! Your talk will not persuade me.

HAEMON:

Then what you want is to make all the speeches.

CREON:

So. Now by all the gods in heaven above us,
One thing is certain: you are going to pay
For taunting and insulting me. (*to* ATTENDANTS) Bring out 710
That hated object. Let her die this moment,

Here, at her bridegroom's feet, before his eyes.

HAEMON:

No, you are wrong. Not at my feet. And never
Will you see eyes upon my face again.
Rage, rave, with anyone who can bear to listen.

Exit HAEMON

CHORUS:

Sir, he is gone; his anger gives him speed.
Young men are bitter in their agony.

CREON:

Let him imagine more than man can do,
Or let him do more. Never shall he save
These two girls; they are going to their doom.   720

CHORUS:

Do you intend to put them both to death?

CREON:

That was well said. No, not the innocent.

CHORUS:

And the other? In what way is she to die?

CREON:

Along a desolate pathway I will lead her,
And shut her, living, in a rocky vault
With no more food than will appease the gods,
So that the city may not be defiled.
Hades, who is the only god she worships,
May hear her prayers, and rescue her from death.
Otherwise she will learn at last, though late,   730
That to revere the dead is useless toil.

Exit CREON

CHORUS:

None may withstand you, O love unconquered,
  Seizing the wealth of man as your prey,
In the cheek of a maiden keeping your vigil,
  Till night has faded again to day.
You roam the wilds to men's farthest dwellings,
  You haunt the boundless face of the sea.
No god may escape you, no short-lived mortal
  From the madness that love inflicts may flee.

You twist our minds until ruin follows.   740
  The just to unrighteous ways you turn.
You have goaded kinsman to strive with kinsman
  Till the fires of bitter hatred burn.
In the eyes of a bride you shine triumphant;

Beside the eternal laws your throne
Eternal stands, for great Aphrodite,
 Resistless, works her will on her own.

But now I too am moved. I cannot keep
 Within the bounds of loyalty. I weep
When I behold Antigone, the bride,   750
 Nearing the room where all at last abide.

           Enter ANTIGONE, *guarded*

ANTIGONE:
 See me, my countrymen! See with what pain
I tread the path I shall not tread again,
Looking my last upon the light of day
 That shines for me no more.
Hades, who gives his sleep to all, me, living, leads away
 To Acheron's dark shore.
Not mine the hymeneal chant, not mine the bridal song,
 For I, a bride, to Acheron belong.

CHORUS:
 Glorious, therefore, and with praise you tread   760
The pathway to the deep gulf of the dead.
You have not felt the force of fate's decrees,
Struck down by violence, wasted by disease;
But of your own free will you choose to go,
Alone of mortals, to the world below.

ANTIGONE:
 I know how sad a death she suffered, she
Who was our guest here, Phrygian Niobe.
Stone spread upon her, close as ivy grows,
  And locked her in its chains.
Now on her wasted form, men say, fall ceaselessly the
    snows,   770
  Fall ceaselessly the rains;
While from her grieving eyes drop tears, tears that
    her bosom steep.
 And like hers, my fate lulls me now to sleep.

CHORUS:
 She was a goddess of the gods' great race;
Mortals are we and mortal lineage trace.
But for a woman the renown is great
In life and death to share a godlike fate.

ANTIGONE:
 By our fathers' gods, I am mocked! I am mocked! Ah! why,
 You men of wealth, do you taunt me before I die?   780
O sacred grove of the city! O waters that flow

From the spring of Dircé! Be witness; to you I cry.
What manner of woman I am you know
And by what laws, unloved, unlamented, I go
    To my rocky prison, to my unnatural tomb.
        Alas, how ill-bestead!
    No fellowship have I; no others can share my doom,
Neither mortals nor corpses, neither the quick nor the dead.

CHORUS:
    You have rushed forward with audacious feet
And dashed yourself against the law's high seat.   790
That was a grievous fall, my child, and yet
In this ordeal you pay your father's debt.

ANTIGONE:
    You have touched on the heaviest grief that my heart
           can hold:
Grief for my father, sorrow that never grows old
For our famous house and its doom that the fates have spun.
    My mother's bed! Ah! How can its horrors be told?
My mother who yielded her love to one
Who was at once my father and her son.
    Born of such parents, with them henceforth I abide,
        Wretched, accursed, unwed.   800
    And you, Polyneices, you found an ill-fated bride,
And I, the living, am ruined by you, the dead.

CHORUS:
    A pious action may of praise be sure,
But he who rules a land cannot endure
An act of disobedience to his rule.
Your own self-will you have not learned to school.

ANTIGONE:
    Unwept, unfriended, without marriage song,
Forth on my road I miserable am led;
    I may not linger. Not for long
Shall I, most wretched, see the holy sun.   810
My fate no friend bewails, not one;
    For me no tear is shed.

                    Enter CREON

CREON:
Do you not know that singing and lamentation
Would rise incessantly as death approached,
If they could be of service? Lead her away!
Obey my orders. Shut her in her grave
And leave her there, alone. Then she can take
Her choice of living in that home, or dying.

I am not stained by the guilt of this girl's blood,
But she shall see the light of day no longer.   820
ANTIGONE:
O tomb! O cavern! Everlasting prison!
O bridal-chamber! To you I make my way
To join my kindred, all those who have died
And have been greeted by Persephone.
The last and far most miserable of all,
I seek them now, before I have lived my life.
Yet high are the hopes I cherish that my coming
Will be most welcome to my father; welcome,
Mother, to you; and welcome to you, Brother.
For when you died I ministered to you all,   830
With my own hands washed you and dressed your bodies,
And poured libations at your graves. And now,
Because I have given to you, too, Polyneices,
Such honors as I could, I am brought to this.
And yet all wise men will approve my act.
Not for my children, had I been a mother,
Not for a husband, for his moldering body,
Would I have set myself against the city
As I have done. And the law sanctions me.
Losing a husband, I might find another.   840
I could have other children. But my parents
Are hidden from me in the underworld,
So that no brother's life can bud and bloom
Ever again. And therefore, Polyneices,
I paid you special honor. And for this
Creon has held me guilty of evil-doing,
And leads me captive for my too great boldness.
No bridal bed is mine, no bridal song,
No share in the joys of marriage, and no share
In nursing children and in tending them.   850
But thus afflicted, destitute of friends,
Living, I go down to the vaults of death.
What is the law of heaven that I have broken?
Why should I any longer look to the gods,
Ill-fated as I am? Whose aid should I invoke,
When I for piety am called impious?
If this pleases the gods, then I shall learn
That sin brought death upon me. But if the sin
Lies in my judges, I could wish for them
No harsher fate than they have decreed for me.   860
CHORUS:
Still the storm rages; still the same gusts blow,

Troubling her spirit with their savage breath.
CREON:
    Yes. And her guards will pay for being slow.
ANTIGONE:
    Ah! With those words I have drawn close to death.
CREON:
    You cannot hope that you will now be freed
    From the fulfillment of the doom decreed.
ANTIGONE:
    O Thebes, O land of my fathers, O city!
O gods who begot and guarded my house from of old!
    They seize me, they snatch me away!
    Now, now! They show no pity.   870
    They give no second's delay.
You elders, you leaders of Thebes, behold me, behold!
    The last of the house of your kings, the last.
    See what I suffer. See the doom
    That is come upon me, and see from whom,
Because to the laws of heaven I held fast.

                              Exeunt ANTIGONE *and* GUARDS

CHORUS:
    This likewise Danaë endured:
The light of heaven she changed for a home brass-bound,
    In a tomb-like chamber close immured.
And yet, O my child, her race was with honor crowned,   880
    And she guarded the seed of Zeus gold-showered.
But naught from the terrible power of fate is free
    Neither war, nor city walls high-towered,
Nor wealth, nor black ships beaten by the sea.

    He too bowed down beneath his doom,
The son of Dryas, swift-angered Edonian king,
    Shut fast in a rocky prison's gloom.
How he roused the god with his mad tongue's mocking sting,
    As his frenzy faded, he came to know;
For he sought to make the god-filled maenads mute,   890
    To quench the Bacchic torches' glow,
And angered the Muses, lovers of the flute.

By the double sea and the dark rocks steely blue
    The beach of Bosporus lies and the savage shore
Of Thracian Salmydessus. There the bride
    Of Phineus, whose fierce heart no mercy knew,
Dealt his two sons a blow that for vengeance cried;
    Ares beheld her hand, all stained with gore,

Grasping the pointed shuttle that pierced through
  Their eyes that saw no more. 900

In misery pining, their lot they lamented aloud,
  Sons of a mother whose fortune in marriage was ill.
From the ancient line of Erechtheus her blood she traced;
  Nurtured in caves far-distant and nursed in cloud,
Daughter of Boreas, daughter of gods, she raced
  Swift as a steed on the slope of the soaring hill.
And yet, O child, O child, she also bowed
  To the long-lived fates' harsh will.

Enter TIRESIAS *and* BOY

TIRESIAS:
  Elders of Thebes, we have come to you with one
  Finding for both the pathway that we followed, 910
  For in this fashion must the blind be guided.
CREON:
  What tidings, old Tiresias, are you bringing?
TIRESIAS:
  I will inform you, I the seer. Give heed.
CREON:
  To ignore your counsel has not been my custom.
TIRESIAS:
  Therefore you kept Thebes on a steady course.
CREON:
  I can bear witness to the help you gave.
TIRESIAS:
  Mark this. You stand upon the brink of ruin.
CREON:
  What terrible words are those? What do you mean?
TIRESIAS:
  My meaning is made manifest by my art
  And my art's omens. As I took my station 920
  Upon my ancient seat of augury,
  Where round me birds of every sort come flocking,
  I could no longer understand their language.
  It was drowned out in a strange, savage clamor,
  Shrill, evil, frenzied, inarticulate.
  The whirr of wings told me their murderous talons
  Tore at each other. Filled with dread, I then
  Made trial of burnt sacrifice. The altar
  Was fully kindled, but no clear, bright flame
  Leaped from the offering; only fatty moisture 930
  Oozed from the flesh and trickled on the embers,
  Smoking and sputtering. The bladder burst,

And scattered in the air. The folds of fat
Wrapping the thigh-bones melted and left them bare.
Such was the failure of the sacrifice,
That did not yield the sign that I was seeking.
I learned these things from this boy's observation;
He is my guide as I am guide to others.
Your edict brings this suffering to the city,
For every hearth of ours has been defiled   940
And every altar. There the birds and dogs
Have brought their carrion, torn from the corpse
Of ill-starred Polyneices. Hence, the gods
Refuse our prayers, refuse our sacrifice,
Refuse the flame of our burnt-offerings.
No birds cry clearly and auspiciously,
For they are glutted with a slain man's blood.
Therefore, my son, consider what has happened.
All men are liable to grievous error;   950
But he who, having erred, does not remain
Inflexible, but rather makes amends
For ill, is not unwise or unrewarded.
Stubborn self-will incurs the charge of folly.
Give to the fallen the honors he deserves
And do not stab him. Are you being brave
When you inflict new death upon the dead?
Your good I think of; for your good I speak,
And a wise counselor is sweet to hear
When the advice he offers proves of value.

CREON:

Old man, all of you shoot your arrows at me   960
Like archers at a target. You have used
Even the art of prophecy in your plotting.
Long have the tribe of prophets traded in me,
Like a ship's cargo. Drive whatever bargain
May please you, buy, sell, heap up for yourself
Silver of Sardis, gold of India. Yet
I tell you this: that man shall not be buried,
Not though the eagles of Zeus himself should bear
The carrion morsels to their master's throne.
Not even from the dread of such pollution   970
Will I permit his burial, since I know
There is no mortal can defile the gods.
But even the wisest men disastrously
May fall, Tiresias, when for money's sake
They utter shameful words with specious wisdom.

TIRESIAS:

Ah! Do men understand, or even consider—

CREON:

Consider what? Doubtless some platitude!

TIRESIAS:

How precious beyond any wealth is prudence.

CREON:

How full of evil is the lack of prudence.

TIRESIAS:

Yet you are sick, sick with that same disease.   980

CREON:

I will not in reply revile a prophet.

TIRESIAS:

You do. You say my prophecy is false.

CREON:

Well, all the race of seers are mercenary.

TIRESIAS:

And love of base wealth marks the breed of tyrants.

CREON:

Are you aware that you address your King?

TIRESIAS:

I made you King by helping you save Thebes.

CREON:

Wise in your art and vicious in your acts.

TIRESIAS:

Do not enrage me. I should keep my secret.

CREON:

Reveal it. Speak. But do not look for profit.

TIRESIAS:

You too will find no profit in my words.   990

CREON:

How can you earn your pay? I will not change.

TIRESIAS:

Then know this. Yes, be very sure of it.
Only a few more times will you behold
The swift course of the chariot of the sun
Before you give as payment for the dead
Your own dead flesh and blood. For you have thrust
A living soul to darkness, in a tomb
Imprisoned without pity. And a corpse,
Belonging to the gods below you keep
Unpurified, unburied, unrevered.   1000
The dead are no concern either of yours
Or of the gods above, yet you offend them.
So the avengers, the destroyers, Furies
Of Hades and the gods, lurking in ambush,

Wait to inflict your sins upon your head.
Do you still think my tongue is lined with silver?
A time will come, and will not linger coming,
That will awaken in your house the wailing
Of men and women. Hatred shakes the cities,
Hatred of you. Their sons are mangled corpses,   1010
Hallowed with funeral rites by dogs or beasts
Or birds who bear the all-polluting stench
To every city having hearth or altar.
You goaded me, and therefore like an archer
I shoot my angry arrows at your heart,
Sure arrows; you shall not escape their sting.
Boy, lead me home. Let him expend his rage
On younger men, and let him learn to speak
With a more temperate tongue, and school his heart
To feelings finer than his present mood.   1020

Exeunt TIRESIAS *and* BOY

CHORUS:
Sir, he is gone, with fearful prophecies.
And from the time that these dark hairs have whitened,
I have known this: never has he foretold
Anything that proved false concerning Thebes.
CREON:
I also know it well, and it dismays me,
To yield is bitter. But to resist, and bring
A curse upon my pride is no less bitter.
CHORUS:
Son of Menoeceus, listen. You must listen.
CREON:
What should I do? Tell me, I will obey.
CHORUS:
Go. Free the girl. Release her from the cavern,   1030
And build a tomb for the man you would not bury.
CREON:
So that is your advice—that I should yield?
CHORUS:
Sir, you should not delay. The gods are swift
In cutting short man's folly with their curse.
CREON:
How hard it is to change! Yet I obey.
I will give up what I had set my heart on.
No one can stand against the blows of fate.
CHORUS:
Go. Go yourself. These things are not for others.

CREON:
   I will go this moment. Guards there! All of you!
   Take up your axes. Quick! Quick! Over there,   1040
   I imprisoned her myself, and I myself
   Will set her free. And yet my mind misgives me.
   Never to break the ancient law is best.

                                             Exit CREON

CHORUS:
        Thou art known by many a name.
     O Bacchus! To thee we call.
     Cadmean Semele's glory and pride,
Begotten of Zeus, whose terrible lightnings flame,
        Whose thunders appall.
Bacchus, thou dost for us all in thy love provide.
     Over Icaria thou dost reign,   1050
     And where the worshippers journey slow
     To the rites of Eleusis, where mountains shield
The multitudes crossing Demeter's welcoming plain.
Thou makest this mother-city of maenads thine own,
     A city beside the rippling flow
Of the gentle river, beside the murderous field
     Where the teeth of the dragon were sown.

        In the torches' wind-blown flare
     Thou art seen, in their flicker and smoke.
     Where the two-fold peaks of Parnassus gleam.   1060
Corycian nymphs, as they move through the ruddy glare,
        Thee, Bacchus, invoke.
They move in their dance beside the Castalian stream.
     O Bacchus, guardian divine!
     down from the slopes of Nysa's hills
     Where a mantle of ivy covers the ground,
From headlands rich with the purple grape and the vine,
Thou comest to us, thou comest. O be not long!
     Thy triumph the echoing city fills.
The streets are loud with thy praises; the highways
              resound,   1070
     Resound with immortal song.

Thou honorest highly our Theban city,
     Thou, and thy mother by lightning slain.
Our people sicken. O Bacchus have pity!
     Across the strait with its moaning wave,
Down from Parnassus, come thou again!
     Come with thy healing feet, and save!

O thou who leadest the stars in chorus,
    Jubilant stars with their breath of fire,
Offspring of Zeus, appear before us!   1080
    Lord of the tumult of night, appear!
With the frenzied dance of thy maenad choir,
    Bacchus, thou giver of good, draw near!

Enter MESSENGER

MESSENGER:
    You of the house of Cadmus and Amphíon,
    No man's estate can ever be established
    Firmly enough to warrant praise or blame.
    Fortune, from day to day, exalts the lucky
    And humbles the unlucky. No one knows
    Whether his present lot can long endure.
    For Creon once was blest, as I count blessings;   1090
    He had saved this land of Cadmus from its foes;
    He was the sovereign and ruled alone,
    The noble father of a royal house.
    And now, all has been lost. Because a man
    Who has forfeited his joy is not alive,
    He is a living corpse. Heap, if you will,
    Your house with riches; live in regal pomp.
    Yet if your life is unhappy, all these things
    Are worth not even the shadow of a vapor
    Put in the balance against joy alone.   1100
CHORUS:
    What new disaster has the King's house suffered?
MESSENGER:
    Death. And the guilt of death lies on the living.
CHORUS:
    The guilt of death! Who has been killed? Who killed him?
MESSENGER:
    Haemon is killed, and by no stranger's hand.
CHORUS:
    He killed himself? Or did his father kill him?
MESSENGER:
    He killed himself, enraged by his murderous father.
CHORUS:
    Tiresias! Now your prophecy if fulfilled.
MESSENGER:
    Consider, therefore, what remains to do.
CHORUS:
    There is the Queen, wretched Eurydice.
    Perhaps mere chance has brought her from the palace;   1110

Perhaps she has learned the news about her son.

Enter EURYDICE

EURYDICE:
Thebans, I heard you talking here together
When I was on my way to greet the goddess,
Pallas Athene, and to pray to her.
Just as I loosed the fastening of the door,
The words that told of my calamity
Struck heavily upon my ear. In terror
I fell back fainting in my women's arms.
But now, repeat your story. I shall hear it
As one who is not ignorant of grief.   1120

MESSENGER:
My Lady, I will bear witness to what I saw,
And will omit no syllable of the truth.
Why should I comfort you with words that later
Would prove deceitful? Truth is always best.
Across the plain I guided my Lord Creon
To where unpitied Polyneices lay,
A corpse mangled by dogs. Then we besought
Hecate, goddess of the roads, and Pluto
To moderate their wrath, and to show mercy.
We washed the dead with ceremonial water.   1130
Gathering the scattered fragments that remained,
With fresh-cut boughs we burned them. We heaped up
A mound of native earth above his ashes.
Then we approached the cavern of Death's bride,
The rock-floored marriage-chamber. While as yet
We were far distant, someone heard the sound
Of loud lament in that unhallowed place,
And came to tell our master. As the King
Drew near, there floated through the air a voice,
Faint, indistinct, that uttered a bitter cry.   1140
The King burst out in anguish: 'Can it be
That I, in my misery, have become a prophet?
Will this be the saddest road I ever trod?
My son's voice greets me. Quickly, slaves! Go quickly!
When you have reached the sepulcher, get through
The opening where the stones are wrenched away,
Get to the mouth of the burial chamber. Look,
See if I know his voice—Haemon's, my son's—
Or if I am deluded by the gods.'
We followed our despairing master's bidding   1150
And in the farthest recess of the tomb

We found Antigone, hanging, with her veil
Noosed round her neck. And with her we found Haemon,
His arms flung round her waist, grieving aloud
For his bride lost in death, his ruined marriage,
His father's deeds. But when his father saw him,
Creon cried piteously and going in,
Called to him brokenly: 'My son, my son,
What have you done? What are you thinking of?
What dreadful thing has driven you out of your mind?   1160
Son, come away. I beg you. I beseech you.'
But Haemon glared at him with furious eyes
Instead of answering, spat in his face,
And drew his sword. His father turned to fly
So that he missed his aim. Immediately,
In bitter self-reproach, the wretched boy
Leaned hard against his sword, and drove it deep
Into his side. Then while his life yet lingered,
With failing strength he drew Antigone close;
And as he lay there gasping heavily,   1170
Over her white cheek his blood ebbed away.
The dead lie clasped together. He is wedded,
Not in this world but in the house of Death.
He has borne witness that of all the evils
Afflicting man, the worst is lack of wisdom.

Exit EURYDICE

CHORUS:
What does that mean? Who can interpret it?
The Queen has gone without a single word.
MESSENGER:
It startles me. And yet I hope it means
That hearing these dreadful things about her son,
She will not let herself show grief in public   1180
But will lament in private with her women.
Schooled in discretion, she will do no wrong.
CHORUS:
How can we tell? Surely too great a silence
Is no less ominous than too loud lament.
MESSENGER:
Then I will enter. Perhaps she is concealing
Some secret purpose in her passionate heart.
I will find out, for you are right in saying
Too great a silence may be ominous.

Exit MESSENGER. *Enter* CREON *with* ATTENDANTS,
carrying the body of HAEMON *on a bier*

CHORUS:
>Thebans, look there! The King himself draws near,
>Bearing a load whose tale is all too clear. 1190
>This is a work—if we dare speak our thought—
>That not another's but his own hands wrought.

CREON:
>O, how may my sin be told?
>The stubborn, death-fraught sin of a darkened brain!
>Behold us here, behold
>Father and son, the slayer and the slain!
>Pain, only pain
>Has come of my design.
>Fate struck too soon; too soon your spirit fled.
>My son, my young son, you are lying dead 1200
>Not for your folly, but for mine, for mine.

CHORUS:
>Sir, you have come to learn the right too late.

CREON:
>My lesson has been bitter and complete.
>Some god has struck me down with crushing weight,
>Filling my heart with cruelty and hate,
>Trampling my happiness beneath his feet.
>Grief, bitter grief, is man's fate.

Enter MESSENGER

MESSENGER (*indicating* HAEMON):
>Your load is heavy, Sir, but there is more.
>That is the burden you are bearing now.
>Soon you must bear new woe within your house. 1210

CREON:
>And what worse misery can follow this?

MESSENGER:
>Your wife is dead, a mother like her son.
>Poor woman, by her own hand she has died.

CREON:
>By her own hand she died.
>Death, spare me! Can you never have your fill?
>Never be satisfied?
>Herald of evil, messenger of ill,
>Your harsh words kill,
>They smite me now anew.
>My wife is dead—You tell me my wife is dead. 1220
>Death after death is heaped upon my head.
>Speak to me, boy. Is what you tell me true?

MESSENGER:
>It is no longer hidden. Sir, look there.

(The body of EURYDICE *is disclosed through the palace doors)*

CREON:

Another horror that makes blind mine eyes!
What further agony has fate in store?
My dead son's body in my arms I bore,
    And now beside him his dead mother lies.
        I can endure no more.

MESSENGER:

There at the altar with a keen-edged knife
She stabbed herself; and as her eyes were darkened,   1230
She wailed the death of Megareus, her son,
Who earlier had met a noble fate;
She wailed for Haemon; then, with her last breath,
You, as the slayer of your sons, she cursed.

CREON:

I am shaken with terror, with terror past belief.
Is there none here to end my anguish? None?
    No sword to pierce me? Broken with my grief,
So steeped in agony that we are one.

MESSENGER:

Sir, as she died, she burdened you with guilt,
Charging you with the death of both your sons.   1240

CREON:

And by what act of violence did she die?

MESSENGER:

Hearing the shrill lament for Haemon's fate,
Deep in her heart she drove the bright blade home.

CREON (*to* HAEMON):

I am your slayer, I alone.
I am guilty, only I.
    I, and none other, must atone.
    Lead me away. The truth I own.
    Nothing is left, except to die.

CHORUS:

If anything can be good, those words are good.
For when calamity has come upon us,   1250
The thing that is the briefest is the best.

CREON:

Draw near me, death! O longed for death, draw near!
Most welcome destiny, make no delay.
    Tell me my last hour, my last breath, is here.
I have no wish to see another day.

CHORUS:

Such things are yet to come. We are concerned

With doing what must needs be done today.
The future rests in other hands than ours.
CREON:
That is my whole desire That is my prayer.
CHORUS:
No. Do not pray. Men must accept their doom.   1260
CREON:
    My life's work there before me lies.
My folly slew my wife, my son.
    I know not where to turn mine eyes.
All my misdeeds before me rise.
    Lead me away, brought low, undone.

                                              Exit CREON

CHORUS:
    The crown of happiness is to be wise.
    Honor the gods, and the gods' edicts prize.
    They strike down boastful men and men grown bold.
    Wisdom we learn at last, when we are old.

Tartuffe or the Imposter

Molière *(Translated by John Wood)*

CHARACTERS IN THE PLAY

MADAME PERNELLE, *mother of Orgon*

ORGON

ELMIRE, *his wife*

DAMIS, *his son*

MARIANE, *his daughter, in love with Valère*

VALÈRE, *in love with Mariane*

CLÉANTE, *brother-in-law of Orgon*

TARTUFFE, *a hypocrite*

DORINE, *maid to Mariane*

MR LOYAL, *a tipstaff*

FLIPOTE, *maid to Madame Pernelle*

AN OFFICER

THE SCENE *is* ORGON's *house in Paris.*

ACT I

[*Enter* MADAME PERNELLE and FLIPOTE, ELMIRE, MARIANE,
CLÈANTE, DAMIS, DORINE.]

MADAME PERNELLE: Come, Flipote, come along. Let me be getting away from
them.

ELMIRE: You walk so fast one can hardly keep up with you.

MADAME PERNELLE: Never mind, my dear, never mind! Don't come any
further. I can do without all this politeness.

ELMIRE: We are only paying you the respect that is due to you. Why must you
be in such a hurry to go, mother?

MADAME PERNELLE: Because I can't bear to see the goings-on in this house
and because there's no consideration shown to me at all. I have had a very
unedifying visit indeed! All my advice goes for nothing here. There's no
respect paid to anything. Everybody airs his opinions—the place is a veritable Bedlam!

DORINE: If . . .

MADAME PERNELLE: For a servant you have a good deal too much to say for
yourself, my girl. You don't know your place. You give your opinion on
everything.

DAMIS: But . . .

MADAME PERNELLE: You, my lad, are just a plain fool. I'm your grandmother
and I'm telling you so! I warned your father a hundred times over that you
showed all the signs of turning out badly and bringing him nothing but
trouble.

MARIANE: I think . . .

MADAME PERNELLE: Oh Lord, yes! You are his little sister, and you put on
your demure looks as if butter wouldn't melt in your mouth—but it's just as
they say, 'Still waters run deep.' I hate to think of what you do on the sly.

ELMIRE: But mother . . .

MADAME PERNELLE: My dear, if you'll allow me to say so you go about these
things in the wrong way entirely. You ought to set them an example. Their
own mother did very much better. You are extravagant. It distresses me to
see the way you go about dressed like a duchess. A woman who's concerned
only with pleasing her husband has no need for so much finery, my dear.

CLÈANTE: Oh come, after all madam . . .

MADAME PERNELLE: As for you, sir, I have the greatest esteem, affection, and
respect for you as the brother of Elmire but if I were in her husband's place I
should entreat you never to set foot in the house. You keep on advocating a
way of life which no respectable people should follow. If I speak a little
bluntly—well, that's my way. I don't mince matters. I say what I think.

DAMIS: Your Mr Tartuffe is undoubtedly a very lucky man . . .

MADAME PERNELLE: He's a *good* man and people would do well to listen to him. It enrages me to hear him criticized by a dolt such as you.

DAMIS: What! Am I to allow a sanctimonious bigot to come and usurp tyran-
nical authority here in the very house? Are we to have no pleasure at all
unless his lordship deigns to approve?

DORINE: If we took notice of him we should never be able to do anything
without committing a sin. He forbids everything—pious busybody that he is!

MADAME PERNELLE: And whatever he forbids deserves to be forbidden. He
means to lead you along the road to Salvation. My son ought to make you all
love him.

DAMIS: No, grandmother, neither my father nor anyone else could make me
have any liking for him. It would be hypocrisy for me to say anything else.
His behaviour infuriates me at every turn. I can only see one end to it. It'll
come to a row between this scoundrel and me. It's bound to.

DORINE: It really is a scandalous thing to see a mere nobody assuming a
position of authority in the house, a beggar without shoes to his feet when he
first came, all the clothes he had to his back not worth sixpence, and getting
so far above himself as to interfere with everything and behave as if he were
the master.

MADAME PERNELLE: Mercy on us! It would be a lot better if the whole place
were under his pious instruction.

DORINE: You imagine he's a saint but believe me, he's nothing but a hypocrite!

MADAME PERNELLE: Listen to her talking!

DORINE: I wouldn't trust myself with him without good security or his man
Laurence either.

MADAME PERNELLE: I don't know what the servant is really like, but the
master's a good man, that I *will* warrant. The only reason you dislike him
and are so set against him is that he tells you all the truth about yourselves:
it's sin that rouses his wrath. Everything he does is done in the cause of the
Lord.

DORINE: Hm! Then why is it—particularly just recently—that he can't bear to
have anyone coming about the place? What is there sinful in calling on
someone in an ordinary straightforward way that he should make such a
hullabaloo about it? Shall I tell you what I think—between ourselves—[*she
indicates* ELMIRE] I believe he's jealous on account of the mistress. Upon my
word I do!

MADAME PERNELLE: Hold your tongue and mind what you are saying! He's
not the only one who takes exception to visitors. All these people coming
here and causing a disturbance, carriages for ever standing at the door, and
swarms of noisy footmen and lackeys make a bad impression on the whole
neighbourhood. I'm willing to believe that there's no harm in it really, but it
sets people talking and that's not a good thing.

CLÈANTE: And do you propose, madam, to stop people talking? It would be a
poor affair if we had to give up our best friends for fear of the silly things that
people might say about us and even if we did, do you think you could shut
everybody's mouth? There's no defence against malicious tongues, so let's

pay no heed to their tittle-tattle; let us try to live virtuously and leave the gossips to say what they will.

DORINE: It's our neighbour, Daphne, and that little husband of hers who have been speaking ill of us, isn't it? Folk whose own behaviour is most ridiculous are always to the fore in slandering others. They never miss a chance of seizing on the last glimmering suspicion of an affair, or gleefully spreading the news and twisting things the way they want folk to believe. They think they can justify their own goings-on by painting other people's behaviour in the same colours as their own and so hope to give an air of innocence to their intrigues or throw on other people some share of the criticism their own actions only too well deserve.

MADAME PERNELLE: All this talk is beside the point. Everybody knows that Orante's life is an example to everybody. She's a God-fearing woman and I hear she strongly condemns the company that comes here.

DORINE: She's a wonderful example—a really good woman! It's quite true that she leads a strict sort of life but it's age that has made her turn pious. We all know that she's virtuous only because she has no alternative. So long as she was able to attract men's attentions she enjoyed herself to the full, but now that she finds her eyes losing their lustre she resolves to renounce the world which is slipping away from her and conceal the fading of her charms beneath an elaborate pretence of high principles. That's what coquettes come to in the end. It's hard for them to see their admirers desert them. Left alone and unhappy, the only course left to them is to turn virtuous. Their righteous severity condemns everything and forgives nothing. They rail against other people's way of life—not in the interests of righteousness but from envy—because they can't bear that anyone else should enjoy the pleasures which age had left them no power to enjoy.

MADAME PERNELLE: [*to* ELMIRE] These, daughter, are the sort of idle stories they serve up to please you. I have to hold my tongue when I'm at your house for Mistress Chatterbox here holds forth all day long. Nevertheless I will have my turn. What I say is that it was the wisest thing my son ever did to take into his house this holy man whom the Lord sent just when he was needed, to reclaim your minds from error. For the good of your souls you should hearken to him for he reproves nothing but what is deserving of reproof. This giddy round of balls, assemblies, and routs is all a device of the Evil One. In such places one never hears a word of godliness, nothing but idle chatter, singing, and nonsensical rigamaroles: often enough the neighbours come in for their share and slander and gossip go the rounds. Even sensible heads are turned in the turmoil of that sort of gathering, a thousand idle tongues get busy about nothing and, as a learned doctor said the other day, it becomes a veritable tower of Babylon where everybody babbles never-endingly—but to come to the point I was making. [*pointing to* CLÈANTE] What! The gentleman is sniggering already is he? Go find a laughing-stock elsewhere and don't—[*to* ELMIRE] Daughter, good-bye. I'll say no more, but I'd have you know I have even less opinion of this household than I had. It will be a long time before I set foot in here again. [*giving* FLIPOTE *a slap*] Hey you! What are you dreaming and gaping at? God bless my soul! I'll warm your ears for you. Come slut. Let's be off.

[*Exeunt all but* CLÈANTE *and* DORINE.]

CLÉANTE: I won't go out in case she starts on me again. How the old woman . . .

DORINE: It's a pity she can't hear you talking like that! She'd tell you what she thinks about you, and whether she's of an age that you can call her 'old woman' or not!

CLÉANTE: Didn't she get worked up against us—and all about nothing! How she dotes on her Tartuffe!

DORINE: Oh! It's nothing compared with her son. If you'd seen him you'd agree he was much worse. During the late disturbances he gained the reputation of being a reliable man and showed courage in the King's service, but since he took a fancy to Tartuffe he seems to have taken leave of his senses. He addresses him as brother and holds him a hundred times dearer than wife or mother, daughter or son. The man's the sole confidant of all his secrets and his trusted adviser in everything. He caresses and cossets him and he couldn't show more tenderness to a mistress. He insists on his taking the place of honour at table, and delights in seeing him devour enough for half a dozen. He has to have all the tit-bits and if he happens to belch it's 'Lord, preserve you!'[1] In short, he's crazy about him. He's his all in all, his hero: he admires everything he does, quotes him at every turn, his every trivial action is wonderful and every word he utters an oracle. As for Tartuffe, he knows his weakness and means to make use of it. He has a hundred ways of deceiving him, gets money out of him constantly by means of canting humbug, and assumes the right to take us to task. Even his lout of a servant has taken to instructing us, comes and harangues us with wild fanatical eyes, and throws away our ribbons, patches, and paint. The other day the dog tore up with his own hands a handkerchief he found in the *Flowers of Sanctity*. He said it was a dreadful thing to sully sacred things with the devil's trappings.

[*Re-enter* ELMIRE *and* MARIANE.]

ELMIRE: You are lucky to have missed the harangue she delivered at the gate. But I caught sight of my husband and as he didn't see me I'll go and wait for him upstairs.

CLÉANTE: I'll await him here to save time. I only want to say good morning.

[*Exeunt* ELMIRE *and* MARIANE.]

DAMIS: Have a word with him about my sister's marriage. I suspect that Tartuffe is opposing it and that it's he who is driving my father to these evasions. You know how closely concerned I am. Valère and my sister are in love and I, as you know, am no less in love with his sister, and if . . .

---

[1] *Molière's note:* It is a servant speaking.

DORINE: Here he comes.

[*Enter* ORGON.]

ORGON: Ah, good morning, brother.

CLÉANTE: I was just going. I'm glad to see you back again. There isn't much life in the countryside just now.

ORGON: Dorine—[*to* CLÉANTE] a moment brother, please—excuse me if I ask the news of the family first and set my mind at rest. [*to* DORINE] Has everything gone well the few days I've been away? What have you been doing? How is everyone?

DORINE: The day before yesterday the mistress was feverish all day. She had a dreadful headache.

ORGON: And Tartuffe?

DORINE: Tartuffe? He's very well: hale and hearty; in the pink.

ORGON: Poor fellow!

DORINE: In the evening she felt faint and couldn't touch anything, her headache was so bad.

ORGON: And Tartuffe?

DORINE: He supped with her She ate nothing but he very devoutly devoured a couple of partridges and half a hashed leg of mutton.

ORGON: Poor fellow!

DORINE: She never closed her eyes all through the night. She was too feverish to sleep and we had to sit up with her until morning.

ORGON: And Tartuffe?

DORINE: Feeling pleasantly drowsy, he went straight to his room, jumped into a nice warm bed, and slept like a top until morning.

ORGON: Poor fellow!

DORINE: Eventually she yielded to our persuasions, allowed herself to be bled, and soon felt much relieved.

ORGON: And Tartuffe?

DORINE: He dutifully kept up his spirits, and took three or four good swigs of wine at breakfast to fortify himself against the worst that might happen and to make up for the blood the mistress had lost.

ORGON: Poor fellow!

DORINE: They are both well again now so I'll go ahead and tell the mistress how glad you are to hear that she's better.

[*Exit*]

CLÉANTE: She's laughing at you openly, brother, and, though I don't want to anger you, I must admit that she's right. Did anyone ever hear of such absurd behaviour? Can the man really have gained such influence over you as to make you forget everything else, so that after having rescued him from poverty you should be ready to . . .

ORGON: Enough brother! You don't know the man you are talking about.

CLÉANTE: I grant you I don't know him, but then, to see what sort of fellow he is, one need only . . .

ORGON: Brother, you would be charmed with him if you knew him. You would be delighted beyond measure . . . he's a man who . . . who . . . ah! a man . . . in short, a man! Whoever follows his precepts enjoys a profound peace of mind and looks upon the world as so much ordure. Yes, under his influence I'm becoming another man. He's teaching me how to forgo affection and free myself from all human ties. I could see brother, children, mother, wife, all perish without caring that much!

CLÉANTE: Very humane sentiments, I must say, brother!

ORGON: Ah! Had you seen how I first met him you would have come to feel for him as I do. Every day he used to come to church and modestly fall on his knees just beside me. He would draw the eyes of the whole congregation by the fervour with which he poured forth his prayers, sighing, groaning, kissing the ground in transports of humility. When I went out he would step in front of me to offer me the Holy water at the door. Having learned from his servant—a man who follows his example in every way—who he was and how needy his condition, I offered him alms, but he would always modestly return a part. 'Too much,' he'd say, 'too much by half. I'm not worthy of your pity.' When I wouldn't have it back he'd go and bestow it on the poor before my very eyes. At length Heaven inspired me to give him shelter in my house, since when all things seem to prosper here. He keeps a reproving eye upon everything and, mindful of my honour, his concern for my interests extends even to my wife. He warns me of those who make eyes at her and is ten times more jealous for her than I am myself. You wouldn't believe the lengths to which his piety extends: the most trivial failing on his own part he accounts a sin: the slightest thing may suffice to shock his conscience—so much so that the other day he was full of self-reproach for having caught a flea while at his prayers and killed it with too much vindictiveness.

CLÉANTE: Gad! You are crazy, brother, that's what I think—or are you trying to pull my leg with a tale like this? What do you intend all this foolery . . .

ORGON: Brother, what you are saying savours of atheism. You *are* somewhat tainted with it at heart. As I have warned you a dozen times you'll bring some serious trouble upon yourself.

CLÉANTE: That's the way your sort of people usually talk. You would have everyone as purblind as yourselves. If one sees things clearly one's an atheist: whoever doesn't bow the knee to pious flummery is lacking in faith and respect for sacred things. No, no! Your threats don't frighten me! I know what I'm talking about and Heaven sees what's in my heart. We are not all duped by humbugs. Devotion, like courage, may be counterfeit. Just as, when honour puts men to the test, the truly brave and not those who make the biggest noise, so the truly pious, whose example we should ever follow, are not those who make the greatest show. What! Would you make no distinction between hypocrisy and true religion? Would you class both together, describe them in the same terms, respect the mask as you would the face itself, treat artifice and sincerity alike, confound appearance and reality, accept the shadow for the substance, base coin for true? Men, in the main, are strangely made. They can never strike the happy mean: the bounds of reason seem too narrow for them: they must needs overact whatever part they play and often ruin the noblest things because they will go to extremes and push them too far. This, brother, is all by the way—

ORGON: Yes, yes, there's no doubt you are a most reverend doctor. You have a monopoly of knowledge, you are unique in wisdom and enlightenment, Sir Oracle, the Cato of our age. In comparison the rest of us are fools—

CLÉANTE: No brother. I'm no reverend doctor; I've no monopoly of knowledge. I merely claim to be able to discriminate between false and true. Just as I know no kind of man more estimable than those who are genuinely religious, nothing in the whole world nobler or finer than the holy fervour of true piety, so I know nothing more odious than those whited sepulchres of specious zeal, those charlatans, those professional zealots, who with sacrilegious and deceitful posturings abuse and mock to their heart's content everything which men hold most sacred and holy; men who put self-interest first, who trade and traffic in devotion, seek to acquire credit and dignities by turning up their eyes in transports of simulated zeal. I mean the people who tread with such extraordinary ardour the godly road to fortune, burning with devotion but seeking material advantage, preaching daily the virtues of solitude and retirement while following the life of courts, shaping their zeal to their vices, quick, revengeful, faithless, scheming, who when they wish to destroy, hide their vindictive pride under the cloak of religion. They are the most dangerous in that they turn against us in their bitter rage the very weapons which men revere and use the passion for which they are respected to destroy us with a consecrated blade. One sees all too much of falsehood such as this. Yet the truly devout are easy to recognize. Our own age offers us many a glorious example, brother. Look at Ariston, Periander, Oronte, Alcidamus, Polydore, Clitander! Their claims no one can deny; theirs is no braggart virtue, no intolerable ostentation of piety; their religion is gentle and humane; they don't censure our actions: they would consider such strictures arrogant: leaving pride of eloquence to others they rebuke our conduct by their own: they don't assume from appearances that others are in fault: they are always ready to think well of people. No 'cabales' for them, no intrigues! their whole concern is to live virtuously: they show no anger against sinners: they reserve their hate for sin itself: nor do they take upon themselves the interests of Heaven with a zeal beyond anything that Heaven itself displays. These are my sort of men: this is how one should conduct oneself: this is the example one should follow! Your man, however, is of another kind. You vaunt his zeal in all good faith but I think you are deceived by false appearances.

ORGON: My dear brother-in-law, have you finished?

CLÉANTE: Yes.

ORGON: [going] I'm much obliged to you.

CLÉANTE: One word, brother, please. Let us leave this topic. You remember that you promised Valère your daughter's hand?

ORGON: Yes.

CLÉANTE: And you named a day for the happy event.

ORGON: True.

CLÉANTE: Why then defer the ceremony?

ORGON: I don't know.

CLÉANTE: Have you something else in mind?

ORGON: Maybe.

CLÉANTE: Do you intend to break your word?

ORGON: I never said so.

CLÉANTE: There is nothing, I believe, to prevent your keeping your promise.

ORGON: That's as may be.

CLÉANTE: Why such circumspection in giving an answer? Valère has asked me to come and see you.

ORGON: God be praised!

CLÉANTE: What am I to tell him?

ORGON: Whatever you please.

CLÉANTE: But I need to know your intentions. What do you mean to do?

ORGON: The will of Heaven.

CLÉANTE: But, speaking seriously, Valère has your promise—are you standing to it or not?

ORGON: Good-bye. [*Exit.*]

CLÉANTE: I fear he is going to be disappointed in his love. I must warn him of the way things are going.

ACT II

[ORGON, MARIANE]

ORGON: Mariane.

MARIANE: Yes, father.

ORGON: Come here. I want a word with you in private.

MARIANE: What are you looking for? [*He is looking into a closet.*]

ORGON: I'm looking to see that there's no one to overhear us. This little place is just right for eavesdropping. Now, we are all right. I've always known that you have an obedient disposition, Mariane, and you've always been very dear to me.

MARIANE: I am very grateful for your fatherly affection.

ORGON: I'm pleased to hear you say so, my girl—and if you want to deserve it you should be at pains to do what I want.

MARIANE: That is my most earnest wish.

ORGON: Very well. What have you to say about our guest, Tartuffe?

MARIANE: What have I to say?

ORGON: Yes, you! Mind how you answer.

MARIANE: Oh dear! I'll say anything you like about him.

[*Enter* DORINE, *unobserved; she takes up her position behind* ORGON.]

ORGON: That's very sensible. Then let me hear you say, my dear, that he is a
   wonderful man, that you love him, and you'd be glad to have me choose him
   for your husband. Eh?

[MARIANE *starts in surprise.*]

MARIANE: Eh?

ORGON: What's the matter?

MARIANE: *What* did you say?

ORGON: What?

MARIANE: I must have misheard you.

ORGON: How d'ye mean?

MARIANE: Who is it, father, I'm to say I love and be glad to have you choose as
   my husband?

ORGON: Tartuffe!

MARIANE: But, father, I assure you I don't feel like that at all. Why make me
   tell such an untruth?

ORGON: But I mean it to be the truth and it's sufficient for you that it's what I
   have decided.

MARIANE: What, father! You really want me to . . .

ORGON: My intention, my girl, is that you should marry Tartuffe and make him
   one of the family. He shall be your husband. I have made up my mind about
   that and it's for me to decide . . . [*seeing* DORINE] What are *you* doing here?
   You must be mighty curious, my lass, to come eavesdropping like that.

DORINE: I don't really know master how the rumour arose—whether it's
   guesswork or coincidence, but when I heard about this marriage I treated it
   as a joke.

ORGON: Why? Is it unbelievable?

DORINE: So much so that I *won't* believe it though you tell me yourself.

ORGON: I know how to make you believe it.

DORINE: Yes, yes, but you are telling us it as a joke.

ORGON: I'm telling you what's going to happen and before long too!

DORINE: Oh, rubbish!

ORGON: [*to* MARIANE] It's no joking matter I tell you!

DORINE: No! Don't you believe your Papa! He's teasing!

ORGON: I'm telling you . . .

DORINE It's no good. We shan't believe you.

ORGON: If I once get annoyed.

DORINE: All right! We believe you then and so much the worse for you. Why!
   How can you, master! You with all the appearance of a sensible man—and a
   venerable beard like you have—how can you be so silly as to . . .

ORGON: Listen! You have got into the habit of taking liberties lately. I tell you,
   my girl, I don't like it at all!

DORINE: Do let us discuss it without getting cross, master, please. You really
   must have made it all up for a joke. Your daughter isn't at all the right person

to marry a bigot and he ought to have other things to think about. Anyhow, what use is such an alliance to you? With all the money you have why go and choose a beggar for a son-in-law?

ORGON: Be quiet! If he's poor that's all the more reason for respecting him. Understand that! His is an honourable poverty. That's beyond question. It should raise him above material consequence for he's allowed himself to be deprived of his means by his indifference to temporal matters and his unswerving attachment to the things which are eternal. My help may be able to afford him the means to escape from embarrassment and enter into his own possessions again—lands which are quite well known in his part of the country. Moreover, whatever his present condition may appear to be, he's certainly a gentleman.

DORINE: Yes. That's what *he* says, but that kind of boasting doesn't go well with his piety. A man who chooses the saintly life shouldn't crack up his birth and family so much. The humble ways of piety don't go well with such-like ambitions. Why take pride in that sort of thing? But there, you'd rather not discuss that. Let's leave the queston of his family and talk about the man himself! Could you really bear to hand over your daughter to a fellow like that? Shouldn't you consider what's due to her and what the consequences of such a marriage might be! Let me tell you that when a girl isn't allowed her own choice in marriage her virtue's in jeopardy: her resolve to live as a good woman depends on the qualities of the husband she's given. Those whose wives are unfaithful have often made them what they are. There are some husbands it's not easy to remain faithful to and whoever gives a girl a husband she detests is responsible to Heaven for the sins she commits. Just think then what perils this scheme of yours may involve you in!

ORGON: [*to* MARIANE] Well, I declare, I have to take lessons from her as to how to do my own business!

DORINE: You couldn't do better than follow my advice.

ORGON: Let's waste no more time on such nonsense, my girl. I'm your father and I know what's good for you. I had promised you to Valère, but apart from the fact that he's said to be a bit of a gambler I suspect him of being a free thinker. I don't see him at church much.

DORINE: I suppose you'd have him run there at the very moment you get there yourself like some folk who only go there to be noticed.

ORGON: I'm not asking for your opinion. [*to* MARIANE] Moreover Tartuffe stands well with Heaven and that surpasses all earthly riches. This marriage will give you everything you could wish for, a perpetual source of pleasure and delight. You'll live together loving and faithful just like two babes—like a pair of turtle doves. No differences will ever arise between you and you'll be able to do just what you like with him.

DORIN: Will she? She won't do anything with him but make him a cuckold, believe me!

ORGON: Sh! What a way to talk!

DORINE: I tell you he has all the looks of one—he's born to it, master, and all your daughter's virtue couldn't prevent it.

ORGON: Stop interrupting me! Just hold your tongue and don't be for ever putting your nose in where you have no business.

DORINE: I'm only telling you for your own good, master.

[*Every time he turns to speak to his daughter she interrupts.*]

ORGON: You don't need to trouble. Just be quiet!

DORINE: If it wasn't that I'm fond of you . . .

ORGON: I don't *want* you to be fond of me.

DORINE: Yes, but I'm *determined* to be fond of you—whether *you* like it or not.

ORGON: Tcha!

DORINE: I'm concerned for your good name, and I won't have you making yourself the butt of everyone's gibes.

ORGON: Will you never be quiet?

DORINE: I could never forgive myself if I let you make such an alliance.

ORGON: Will you be quiet, you reptile, with your impudent . . .

DORINE: Ah! Fancy a godly man like you getting angry!

ORGON: Yes! This ridiculous nonsense is more than my temper can stand. I insist on your holding your tongue.

DORINE: Right, but I shan't *think* any the less because I don't say anything.

ORGON: Think if you like but take care you don't talk or . . . that's enough. (*turning to* MARIANE] I've weighed everything carefully as a wise man should . . .

DORINE: It's maddening not to be able to speak. [*She stops as he turns his head.*]

ORGON: Without his being exactly a beauty Tartuffe's looks are . . .

DORINE: Yes! A lovely mug hasn't he?

ORGON: Such . . . that even if his other advantages don't appeal to you . . .

[ORGON *turns and faces* DORINE, *looking at her with arms folded.*]

DORINE: She *would* be well off wouldn't she? If *I* were in her place no man would marry me against my will—not with impunity. I would show him, ay, and soon after the ceremony too, that a woman has always ways and means of getting her own back.

ORGON: So what I say hasn't any effect on you at all?

DORINE: What are you grumbling about? I'm not talking to you.

ORGON: Then what *are* you doing?

DORINE: I'm talking to myself.

ORGON: Very well. [*aside*] I shall have to give her a back-hander for her impudence yet. [*He stands ready to box her ears.* DORINE *every time he looks at her stands rigid and without speaking.*] You can't do otherwise, my girl, than approve what I have in mind for you . . . and believe that the husband . . . I have chosen for you . . . [*to* DORINE] Why aren't you talking to yourself now?

DORINE: I've nothing to say to myself.

ORGON: Not a word even?

DORINE: Not a word thank you!

ORGON: But I was waiting for you . . .

DORINE: I'm not so silly as that!

ORGON: Well now, my girl, you must show how obedient you are and fall in with my choice.

DORINE: [*running away*] I'd scorn to take such a husband! [*He takes a slap at her and misses.*]

ORGON: She's a thorough pest is that girl of yours! If I live with her any longer I shall do something I shall be sorry for. I'm in no state to go on now. I'm so incensed at her impudence I shall have to go outside to recover myself.

[*Exit* ORGON.]

DORINE: Have you lost your tongue? Do I have to do all the talking for you? Fancy letting him put a ridiculous proposal like that to you and never saying a word in reply!

MARIANE: What would you have me do in face of the absolute power of my father?

DORINE: Whatever is needed to ward off the danger.

MARIANE: But what?

DORINE: Tell him one can't love at another's bidding; that you'll marry to suit yourself, not him; that *you* are the person concerned and therefore it's *you* the husband has to please not him; and that, if he has such a fancy for his precious Tartuffe, he can marry him himself and there's nothing to stop him.

MARIANE: I confess that a father's authority is such that I have never had the temerity to say anything.

DORINE: Well, let us get down to business. Valère has made proposals for you. I ask you, *do* you love him or don't you?

MARIANE: You do my love great injustice, Dorine. How can you ask such a question? Haven't I opened my heart to you many and many a time? Don't you know how much I love him?

DORINE: How do I know that you meant what you said or that the young man really appeals to you?

MARIANE: You do me grievous wrong to doubt it, Dorine. I've shown my true feelings all too clearly.

DORINE: So you *do* love him, then?

MARIANE: Indeed I do.

DORINE: And, so far as you know, he loves you too?

MARIANE: I believe so.

DORINE: And you both want to be married?

MARIANE: Assuredly!

DORINE: Then what do you mean to do about this other proposal?

MARIANE: To die by my own hand if they force me to submit to it.

DORINE: Splendid! That's something I never thought of! You only need die and you are finished with your troubles. There's no doubt that's a wonderful remedy. That sort of talk infuriates me!

MARIANE: Oh dear, you are tiresome, Dorine. You have no sympathy at all for other people's troubles.

DORINE: I've no sympathy with folk who talk nonsense and are as faint-hearted as you are when it comes to the point.

MARIANE: But what do you expect me to do? If I'm timid . . .

DORINE: What lovers need is determination.

MARIANE: And have I wavered in my love for Valère? Surely it's for him to deal with my father.

DORINE: What! If your father's the fantastic creature he is—if he's plumb crazy over his precious Tartuffe and breaks his promise about the marriage he had decided on, is your lover to be blamed?

MARIANE: But can I reveal by flat refusal and open defiance how much I'm in love? Can I, whatever Valère's qualities may be, abandon the modesty of my sex and my filial duty? Do you want me to expose my feelings for all the world to see and . . .

DORINE: No. No. *I* don't want anything. I see that you want to marry Mr Tartuffe and, now I come to think about it, it would be wrong of me to dissuade you from such an alliance. Why should I oppose your inclinations? It's a most suitable match. Mr Tartuffe! Ha! Ha! It's not an offer to be despised, is it? Come to think of it Mr Tartuffe's a fine fellow. It's no small honour to be his better half. Everybody defers to him already. He's a man of family—where he comes from, and a fine looking fellow to boot—with his red ears and his red face. You would be sure to live happily with a husband like that.

MARIANE: Heavens!

DORINE: How delightful to be married to such a fine-looking husband!

MARIANE: Oh, please stop talking like this, and suggest some means of avoiding the marriage. It's enough. I give in. I'm ready for anything.

DORINE: No. No, a daughter must do as her father tells her even if he wants her to marry a monkey. You are very lucky. What are you complaining of? You'll be carted off to his little provincial town, and find it swarming with his relations. What fun you'll have meeting them all! You'll be taken straight into local society, visit the bailiff's wife and the councillor's lady, and they'll accord you the honour of letting you sit down with them as an equal, perhaps! In carnival time you'll be able to look forward to a ball with a grand orchestra, to wit a couple of bagpipes, and now and again Fagotin the monkey, and a marionette show. If only your husband . . .

MARIANE: Oh! I can't endure it! Why don't you help me?

DORINE: No, you must excuse me!

MARIANE: Oh, Dorine, *please* . . .

DORINE: No it must go through now—you deserve it!

MARIANE: Dear Dorine . . .

DORINE: No.

MARIANE: If my confessions of love . . .

DORINE: No. Tartuffe is your man, you shall have your fill of him.

MARIANE: You know that I've always trusted in you. Help me to . . .

DORINE: No, no! I give you my word—you shall be thoroughly Tartuffed!

MARIANE: Very well, since my miserable lot doesn't move you, leave me alone with my despair. There my heart will find relief. I have one infallible remedy for my troubles. [*She makes to go.*]

DORINE: Hey there! Come back. I won't be angry any more. I must take pity on you in spite of everything.

MARIANE: I assure you, Dorine, if they put me to this cruel torment it will be the death of me.

DORINE: Don't distress yourself. We'll find some means of preventing it. But here comes your Valère.

[*Enter* VALÈRE.]

VALÈRE: I have just heard a fine piece of news. Something I was quite unaware of!

MARIANE: What is it?

VALÈRE: That you are to marry Tartuffe.

MARIANE: That is certainly my father's intention.

VALÈRE: But your father . . .

MARIANE: He's changed his mind. He has just put the new proposal to me now.

VALÈRE: What, seriously?

MARIANE: Yes, seriously. He's determined on the match.

VALÈRE: And what is your intention?

MARIANE: I don't know.

VALÈRE: That's a fine answer! You don't know?

MARIANE: No.

VALÈRE: No?

MARIANE: What do you advise me to do?

VALÈRE: What do I advise you to do? I advise you to take him!

MARIANE: *You* advise me to do that?

VALÈRE: Yes.

MARIANE: You really mean it?

VALÈRE: Of course. It's a splendid offer—one well worth considering.

MARIANE: Very well, sir. I'll take your advice.

VALÈRE: I don't doubt you'll find little difficulty in doing so.

MARIANE: No more than you in offering it.

VALÈRE: I gave it to please you.

MARIANE: And I'll follow it—to please you.

DORINE: [*aside*] We'll see what will come of this!

VALÈRE: So this is how you love me! You were deceiving me when . . .

MARIANE: Don't let us talk of that please! You told me frankly that I should accept the husband I was offered. Well then, that's just what I intend to do— since you give me such salutary advice.

VALÈRE: Don't make what I said your excuse! You had already made up your mind. You're just seizing on a frivolous pretext to justify breaking your word.

MARIANE: That's true. You put it very well.

VALÈRE: Of course! You never really loved me at all.

MARIANE: Alas! You may think so if you like.

VALÈRE: Yes, yes. I may indeed: but I may yet forestall your design. I know on whom to bestow both my hand and my affections.

MARIANE: Oh! I don't doubt that in the least, and the love which your good qualities inspire . . .

VALÈRE: Good Lord! Let's leave my good qualities out of it. They are slight enough and your behaviour is proof of it. But I know someone who will, I hope, consent to repair my loss once she knows I am free.

MARIANE: Your loss is little enough and, no doubt, you'll easily be consoled by the change.

VALÈRE: I shall do what I can you may be sure. To find oneself jilted is a blow to one's pride. One must do one's best to forget it and if one doesn't succeed, at least one must pretend to, for to love where one's love is scorned is an unpardonable weakness.

MARIANE: A very elevated and noble sentiment, I'm sure.

VALÈRE: Of course and one that everyone must approve. Would you have me languish for you indefinitely, see you throw yourself into the arms of another and yet not bestow elsewhere the heart that you spurn?

MARIANE: On the contrary, that is just what I want. I only wish it were done already.

VALÈRE: That's what you would like?

MARIANE: Yes.

VALÈRE: You have insulted me sufficiently. You shall have your wish . . . [*makes a move to go*] and immediately!

MARIANE: Very well.

VALÈRE: [*turning back*] At least remember that it is you yourself who are driving me to this extremity.

MARIANE: Yes.

VALÈRE: And that in what I am doing, I only am following your example.

MARIANE: My example, so be it!

VALÈRE: Very well! You shall have just what you asked for.

MARIANE: So much the better!

VALÈRE: You'll never see me again.

MARIANE: Capital!

VALÈRE: [*goes but when he reaches the door he returns*] Eh?

MARIANE: What?

VALÈRE: Didn't you call?

MARIANE: Me? You are dreaming.

VALÈRE: Good. I'm going then. Good-bye!

MARIANE: Good-bye!

DORINE: I think you must be out of your senses to behave in this absurd fashion. I've let you go on squabbling to see how far you would go. Here, Mr Valère [*She takes him by the arm.* VALÈRE *pretends to resist.*]

VALÈRE: What do you want, Dorine?

DORINE: Come here!

VALÈRE: No, no. I'm too angry. Don't try to prevent me doing what she wants.

DORINE: Stop!

VALÈRE: No, no. It's all settled.

DORINE: Ah!

MARIANE: He can't bear the sight of me. He's going because I'm here. I'd better get out of his sight.

[DORINE *leaves* VALÈRE *and runs to* MARIANE.]

DORINE: The other one now! Where are you off to?

MARIANE: Let me go!

DORINE: Come back!

MARIANE: No, no, Dorine. It's no good your trying to stop me.

VALÈRE: I can see that she hates the very sight of me. Far better I should spare her the embarrassment.

DORINE: [*leaving* MARIANE *and running to* VALÈRE] You again. The devil take you before I let you go. Stop this silly nonsense and come here both of you. [*She drags them both in.*]

VALÈRE: What are you trying to do?

MARIANE: What do you want?

DORINE: To bring you together again and get you out of this mess. [*to* VALÈRE] You must be crazy to quarrel like this!

VALÈRE: Didn't you hear how she spoke to me?

DORINE: You must be out of your mind to get so annoyed.

MARIANE: But didn't you see what happened? Didn't you see how he treated me?

DORINE: [*to* VALÈRE] Sheer silliness on both sides. She wants nothing better than to be yours—I can witness. [*to* MARIANE] He loves nobody but you and desires nothing better than to be your husband—I'll stake my life on it.

MARIANE: Then why did he give me the advice he did?

VALÈRE: Why did you ask me for advice on such a question?

DORINE: You are both quite mad. Here—give me your hands, both of you. [*to* VALÈRE] Come along, you.

VALÈRE: [*giving his hand to* DORINE] What good will that do?

DORINE: [*to* MARIANE] Now yours.

MARIANE: [*giving her hand*] What's the use?

DORINE: Heavens! Be quick. Come on! You love each other better than you think.

VALÈRE: [*to* MARIANE] Come, don't do it with such an ill grace. Don't look at a fellow as if you hated him. [MARIANE *turns toward* VALÈRE *and gives a little smile.*]

DORINE: The truth is all lovers are a bit touched!

VALÈRE: Ah! But hadn't I some cause for complaint? You must admit it was cruel of you to take such pleasure in giving me such a horrible piece of news.

MARIANE: But you—aren't you the most ungrateful of men?

DORINE: Let's leave the argument to another time and think how we can prevent this dreadful marriage . . .

MARIANE: Tell us what we are to do.

DORINE: We'll try everything we can. Your father can't be serious and it's all sheer rubbish, but you had better pretend to fall in with his nonsense and give the appearance of consenting so that if it comes to the point you'll more easily be able to delay the marriage. If we can only gain time we may set everything right. You can complain of a sudden illness that will necessitate delay; another time you can have recourse to bad omens—such as having met a corpse or broken a mirror or dreamt of muddy water. Finally, the great thing is that they can't make you his wife unless you answer 'I will'. But I think, as a precaution, you had better not be found talking together. [*to* VALÈRE] Off you go and get all your friends to use their influence with her father to stand by his promise. We must ask his brother to try once again, and see if we can get the stepmother on our side. Good-bye.

VALÈRE: [*to* MARIANE] Whatever schemes we may devise you are the one I really count on.

MARIANE: [*to* VALère] I can't answer for what my father decides but I will never marry anyone but Valère.

VALÈRE: Ah, how happy you make me! Whatever they may venture to . . .

DORINE: Ah? Lovers are never tired of blathering! Be off, I tell you.

VALÈRE: [*making to go, then turning back*] Still . . .

DORINE: What a talker you are! [*pushing them both out*] You go this way and you that. Be off!

ACT III

DAMIS: May I be struck dead on the spot—call me the most miserable blackguard alive if I let either fear or favour prevent me—if I don't think out some master stroke!

DORINE: For goodness sake, don't get so excited! Your father has only just mentioned it. People don't do everything they intend to. There's a deal of difference between talking about a thing and doing it.

DAMIS: I must put a stop to the dog's machinations! I'll have something to say to him!

DORINE: Oh, go easy! Leave your stepmother to deal with both him and your father. She has some influence with Tartuffe. He takes notice of her. I'm not sure that he isn't sweet on her. I wish to Heaven he were! That would be a lark! As a matter of fact it's on your account that she's sent for him: she intends to sound him about this marriage you are so worried about: she means to find out what he has in mind and make him see what trouble it would cause in the family if he encouraged the idea. His servant said he was at his prayers so I wasn't able to see him, but he said he'd be coming down soon. So please go away and leave me to wait for him.

DAMIS: I'll be present at the interview.

DORINE: No. They must be alone.

DAMIS: I won't say a word.

DORINE: That's what *you* think! We all know how excitable you are and that's just the way to spoil everything. Off you go.

DAMIS: No I must see it. I won't lose my temper.

DORINE: How tiresome you are. Here he comes. Do go.

[*Enter* TARTUFFE.]

TARTUFFE: [*seeing* DORINE] Laurent, put away my hair shirt and my scourge and continue to pray Heaven to send you grace. If anyone asks for me I'll be with the prisoners distributing alms.

DORINE: The impudent hypocrite!

TARTUFFE: What do you want?

DORINE: I'm to tell you . . .

TARTUFFE: For Heaven's sake! Before you speak, I pray you take this handkerchief. [*Takes handkerchief from his pocket.*]

DORINE: Whatever do you mean?

TARTUFFE: Cover your bosom. I can't bear to see it. Such pernicious sights give rise to sinful thoughts.

DORINE: You're mighty susceptible to temptation then! The flesh must make a great impression on you! I really don't know why you should get so excited. I can't say that I'm so easily roused. I could see you naked from head to foot and your whole carcass wouldn't tempt me in the least.

TARTUFFE: Pray, speak a little more modestly or I shall have to leave the room.

DORINE: No. No. *I'm* leaving *you*. All I have to say is that the mistress is coming down and would like a word with you.

TARTUFFE: Ah! Most willingly.

DORINE: [*aside*] That changes his tune. Upon my word I'm convinced there is something in what I said.

TARTUFFE: Will she be long?

DORINE: I think I hear her now. Yes, here she comes. I'll leave you together.

[*Exit* DORINE. *Enter* ELMIRE.]

TARTUFFE: May the bounty of Heaven ever bestow on you health of body and of mind, and extend you blessings commensurate with the prayers of the most humble of its devotees!

ELMIRE: I'm very grateful for these pious wishes. Let us sit down. We shall be more comfortable.

TARTUFFE: Do you feel better of your indisposition?

ELMIRE: Very much. The feverishness soon left me.

TARTUFFE: My prayers have too little merit to have obtained this favour from on high; yet all the petitions I have addressed to Heaven have been concerned with your recovery.

ELMIRE: You are too solicitous on my behalf.

TARTUFFE: One cannot be too solicitous for your precious health. I would have sacrificed my own life for the sake of yours.

ELMIRE: That is carrying Christian charity rather far but I'm truly grateful for your kindness.

TARTUFFE: I do far less for you than you deserve.

ELMIRE: I wanted to speak to you in private on a certain matter. I'm pleased that no one can overhear us.

TARTUFFE: I too am delighted. I need hardly say how pleased I am to find myself alone with you. It's an opportunity which I have besought Heaven to accord me—vainly until this moment.

ELMIRE: What I want is that you should speak frankly and conceal nothing from me.

TARTUFFE: And my sole desire is that you should accord me the singular favour of allowing me to express all that is in my heart and assure you that anything I have said against those who were paying homage to your charms was not spoken in malice against you but rather that the intensity of my pious zeal and pure . . .

ELMIRE: I take it in that sense and believe that it arises from your concern for my salvation.

TARTUFFE: That is indeed so, madam, and such is the fervour of my . . . [*Squeezing her fingers.*]

ELMIRE: Oh! You're hurting me . . .

TARTUFFE: It comes from excess of devotion. I never intended to hurt you. [*Putting his hand upon her knee*] I would rather . . .

ELMIRE: What is your hand doing there?

TARTUFFE: I'm feeling your dress. How soft the material is!

ELMIRE: Please don't. I'm dreadfully ticklish.
[*She pushes back her chair.* TARTUFFE *brings his closer.*]

TARTUFFE: What marvellous lace! They do wonderful work nowadays. Things are so much better made than they used to be.

ELMIRE: Very true, but let us return to our business. They say my husband intends to break his promise to Valère and give his daughter to you. Tell me, is it true?

TARTUFFE: He did mention something about it, but to tell the truth, madam, that isn't the happiness I aspire to. All my hopes of felicity lie in another direction.

ELMIRE: That's because you have no interest in temporal things.

TARTUFFE: My breast does not enclose a heart of flint!

ELMIRE: I'm sure your thoughts are all turned Heavenward. Your desires are not concerned with anything here below.

TARTUFFE: A passion for the beauties which are eternal does not preclude a temporal love. Our senses can and do respond to those more perfect works of Heaven's creation, whose charms are exemplified in beings such as you and embodied in rarest measure in yourself. Heaven has lavished upon you a beauty that dazzles the eyes and moves the hearts of men. I never look upon your flawless perfections without adoring in you the great Author of all nature and feeling my heart filled with ardent love for that fair form in which He has portrayed Himself. At first I feared lest this secret passion which consumes me might be some subtle snare of the accursed one. I even resolved to avoid your sight, believing you to be an obstacle to my salvation; but at length I came to realize, O fairest among women, that there need be nothing culpable in my passion and that I could reconcile it with virtue. Since then I have surrendered to it heart and soul. It is, I admit, no small presumption on my part to address to you this offer of my love, but I rely upon your generosity and in no wise upon my own unworthy self: my hopes, my happiness, my peace are in your keeping: on you my bliss or future misery depends: my future hangs on your decree: make me for ever happy if such be your will, wretched if you would have it so.

ELMIRE: A very gallant declaration but a little surprising I must confess! It seems to me you ought to steel yourself more firmly against temptation and consider more deeply what you are about. A pious man like you, a holy man whom everyone . . .

TARTUFFE: Ah! But I'm not less a man for being devout! Confronted by your celestial beauty one can but let love have its way and make no demur. I realize that such a declaration coming from me may well seem strange but, after all, madam, I'm not an angel. If you condemn this declaration of mine you must lay the blame on your own enchanting loveliness. From the first moment that I beheld its more than mortal splendours you have ruled supreme in my affection. Those glances, goddess-like and gracious beyond all description, broke down my stubborn heart's resistance, surmounted every obstacle, prayers, fasting, tears, and turned all my thoughts to love of you. My eyes, my sighs, have told you a thousand times what I am now seeking to express in words. If you should turn a kindly eye upon the tribulations of your unworthy slave, if in your generosity you should choose to afford me consolation and deign to notice my insignificance, then I would offer you for ever, O miracle of loveliness, a devotion beyond compare. Moreover, your honour runs no risk with me; at my hands you need fear no danger of disgrace; these courtly gallants that women are so fond of noise their deeds abroad, they are for ever bragging of their conquests, never receiving a favour but they must divulge it, profaning with blabbing tongues (which folk still put their trust in) the altar to which they bring their offerings. But men of our sort burn with discreeter fires; our secrets are for ever sure; our concern for our own reputation is a safeguard for those we love, and to those who trust us we offer love without scandal, satisfaction without fear.

ELMIRE: I have listened to what you say and your eloquence has made your meaning sufficiently clear, but are you not afraid that I might take it into my head to tell my husband of this charming declaration of yours and that such a disclosure might impair his friendly feelings for you?

TARTUFFE: I know you are too kind, that you will pardon my temerity, condone as human frailty the transports of a passion which offends you, and, when you consult your glass, reflect that I'm not blind and that a man is but flesh and blood.

ELMIRE: Others might perhaps take a different course but I prefer to show discretion. I shall say nothing to my husband, but in return I must ask one thing of you—that you give your support openly and sincerely to the marriage of Valère and Mariane, renounce the exercise of that improper influence by which you have sought to promote your own hopes at the expense of another and . . .

DAMIS: [*coming out of the closet where he has been hidden*] No, no! This must be made known! I was in there and heard everything. Heaven's mercy has brought me here to confound the arrogance of a villain who intends me harm: it has offered me the opportunity to be revenged upon his insolence and hypocrisy, to undeceive my father, and lay bare the soul of this scoundrel who talks to you of love!

ELMIRE: No, Damis, it is sufficient that he should mend his ways and endeavour to deserve the pardon I have promised him. I have given my word so don't make me break it. I'm not one to make a fuss: a wife makes light of follies such as these and never troubles her husband with them.

DAMIS: You may have your reasons for doing this but I have mine for doing otherwise. Your wish to spare him is absurd. He has already triumphed sufficiently over my just resentment with his insolence and humbug and made enough trouble among us. The scoundrel has ruled my father long enough and thwarted my love as well as Valère's. My father must be shown what a perfidious wretch he is and Providence now offers a simple means of doing it. I'm answerable to Heaven for this opportunity and it's too favourable to be neglected. Not to make use of it would be to deserve to lose it.

ELMIRE: Damis . . .

DAMIS: No. Pardon me—I must trust to my own judgement. I'm overjoyed. Nothing you say can dissuade me from the pleasure of revenge. I'll finish the business without more ado, and [*seeing* ORGON] here comes the instrument of my satisfaction.

[*Enter* ORGON.]

DAMIS: We have interesting news for you father. Something has just occurred which will astonish you. You are well repaid for your kindness! The gentleman sets a very high value on the consideration you have shown for him! He has just been demonstrating his passionate concern for you and he stops at nothing less than dishonouring your bed. I have just overheard him making a disgraceful declaration of his guilty passion for your wife. She in kind-heartedness and over-anxiety to be discreet was all for keeping it secret but I can't condone such shameless behaviour. I consider it would be a gross injustice to you to keep it from you.

ELMIRE: Well, I still think a wife shouldn't disturb her husband's peace of mind by repeating such silly nonsense to him; one's honour is in no wise involved. It's sufficient that we women should know how to defend ourselves. That's what I think and if you had taken notice of me you would not have said anything at all. [*Exit.*]

ORGON: Oh Heavens! Can what they say be true?

TARTUFFE: Yes, brother, I am a guilty wretch, a miserable sinner steeped in iniquity, the greatest villain that ever existed; not a moment of my life but is sullied with some foul deed: it's a succession of wickedness and corruption. I see now that Heaven is taking this opportunity of chastising me for my sins. Whatever crime I may be charged with, far be it from me to take pride in denying it! Believe what they tell you. Set no bounds to your resentment! Hound me like a felon from your doors! Whatever shame is heaped upon me I shall have deserved much more.

ORGON: [*to his son*] Ah! Miscreant! How dare you seek to tarnish his unspotted virtue with this false accusation?

DAMIS: What! Can a pretence of meekness from this hypocrite make you deny . . .

ORGON: Silence! You accursed plague!

TARTUFFE: Ah, let him speak. You do wrong to accuse him. You would do better to believe what he tells you. Why should you take such a favourable view of me? After all, do you know what I am capable of? Why should you trust appearances? Do you think well of me because of what I seem to be? No, no, you are letting yourself be deceived by outward show. I am, alas, no better than they think; everyone takes me for a good man but the truth is I'm good for nothing. [*speaking to* DAMIS] Yes, my son, speak freely, call me deceitful, infamous, abandoned, thief, murderer, load me with names yet more detestable, I'll not deny them. I've deserved them all, and on my knees I'll suffer the ignominy, in expiation of my shameful life.

ORGON: [*to* TARTUFFE] Brother, this is too much. [*to his son*] Doesn't your heart relent, you dog!

DAMIS: What! Can what he says so far prevail with you that . . .

ORGON: [*raising up* TARTUFFE] Silence you scoundrel! [*to* TARTUFFE] Rise brother—I beg you. [*to his son*] You scoundrel!

DAMIS: He may—

ORGON: Silence!

DAMIS: This is beyond bearing! What! I'm to . . .

ORGON: Say another word and I'll break every bone in your body!

TARTUFFE: In God's name, brother, calm yourself. I would rather suffer any punishment than he should receive the slightest scratch on my account.

ORGON: [*to his son*] Ungrateful wretch!

TARTUFFE: Leave him in peace! If need be, I'll ask your pardon for him on my knees . . .

ORGON: [*to* TARTUFFE] Alas! What are you thinking of? [*to his son*] See how good he is to you, you dog!

DAMIS: Then . . .

ORGON: Enough!

DAMIS: What! Can't I . . .

ORGON: Enough, I say! I know too well why you attack him. You hate him. Every one of you, wife, children, servants, all are in full cry against him. You use every impudent means to drive this devout and holy person from my house: but the more you strive to banish him the more determined I am not to let him go. I'll hasten his marriage with my daughter and confound the pride of the whole family.

DAMIS: You mean to make her accept his hand?

ORGON: Yes, you scoundrel, and this very evening to spite you all. Ah! I defy the lot of you. I'll have you know that I'm the master and I'll be obeyed. Come, retract your accusation instantly, you wretch! Down on your knees and beg forgiveness!

DAMIS: Who? Me? Of a villain whose impostures . . .

ORGON: So you refuse, you scoundrel, do you? And abuse him too! A stick! Give me a stick! [*to* TARTUFFE] Don't try to restrain me! [*to his son*] Out of my house this instant and never darken my doors again!

DAMIS: Yes, I'll go but . . .

ORGON: Out! Leave the house! Be off! I disinherit you, you dog! And take my curse into the bargain.

[*Exit* DAMIS.]

ORGON: What a way to insult a holy man!

TARTUFFE: May Heaven forgive him the sorrow that he causes me! Ah, if you only knew how much it grieves me to see them try to blacken me in my brother's esteem—

ORGON: Alas!

TARTUFFE: The mere thought of such ingratitude is unbearable to me . . . it horrifies me . . . it wrings my heart so that I cannot speak . . . it will be the death of me.

ORGON: [*weeping, runs to the door through which he drove forth his son*] Scoundrel! I'm sorry I kept my hands off you and didn't fell you on the spot! [*to* TARTUFFE] Compose yourself brother. Don't give way to your feelings.

TARTUFFE: Let us put an end to these painful dissensions. When I see what troubles I cause here I feel that I must leave you, brother.

ORGON: What! Are you mad?

TARTUFFE: They hate me. I see now they are trying to make you doubt my sincerity.

ORGON: What does it matter? Do you think I listen to them?

TARTUFFE: But they'll not fail to try again. These same reports you have rejected now you may believe another time.

ORGON: No, brother, never!

TARTUFFE: Ah, brother, a wife can easily influence her husband's mind.

ORGON: No. No!

TARTUFFE: Let me go and by going hence remove all occasion for them to attack me.

ORGON: No. No. You shall stay. My very life depends upon it.

TARTUFFE: Well then if it be so, I must sacrifice myself. But if you would only . . .

ORGON: Yes?

TARTUFFE: Let it be so. We'll speak of it no more but I know now what I must do. Reputation is a brittle thing: friendship requires that I should forestall every whisper, every shadow of suspicion. I must forswear the company of your wife and you will never see . . .

ORGON: No! You *shall* see her in spite of them all. Nothing gives me greater joy than to annoy them. You shall appear with her constantly and—to show my defiance, I'll make you my sole heir. I'll make a gift to you in due form of all my goods here and now. My true, dear, friend whom I now take as my son-in-law, you are dearer to me than son or wife or kin. Will you not accept what I am offering you?

TARTUFFE: Heaven's will be done in all things.

ORGON: Poor fellow! Let us go and draft the document at once. And let the whole envious pack of them burst with their own vexation at the news!

ACT IV

[CLÉANTE, TARTUFFE]

CLÉANTE: Yes, everyone is talking about it and, believe me, the sensation the news has made has done your reputation no good. This is an opportune time to tell you briefly and bluntly what I think about it. I won't go into details of the reports that are going about; setting them on one side and taking the matter at its worst, let us suppose that Damis did behave badly and that you were accused unjustly. Wouldn't it be the Christian thing to pardon the offence and forgo your revenge? Can you allow a son to be turned out of his father's house because of your quarrel with him? I tell you again—and I'm speaking frankly—that everybody thinks it shocking—people of all sorts, high and low alike. If you'll take notice of me you'll come to terms and not push things to extremes. Sacrifice your resentment as a Christian should and reconcile the son to his father again.

TARTUFFE: Alas! For my own part, I would willingly do so. I harbour no resentment against him, sir. I forgive him everything. I don't blame him at all. I would do anything I could for him and gladly, but the interests of Heaven forbid it. If he comes back here, then I must go. After such unheard-of behaviour any further relations between us would create a scandal. God knows what people might think of it! They would impute it to purely material considerations on my part and say that, knowing I was guilty, I feigned a charitable concern for my accuser; that in my heart of hearts I was afraid of him, and sought an arrangement with him to keep his mouth shut.

CLÉANTE: That's just putting me off with specious excuses. Your arguments are all too far fetched. Why should you take upon yourself the interests of religion? Can't God punish the guilty without assistance from us? Leave

Him to look after his own vengeance. Remember rather that He ordains that we should forgive those who offend against us. When you are following orders from on high why worry about human judgements? What! Lose the glory of doing a good deed for trivial considerations of what people may think! No. No. Let us just obey Heaven's commands and not bother our heads about anything else.

TARTUFFE: I have already said I forgive him. That's doing what Heaven commands, but Heaven doesn't command me to live with him after the scandal and the insults put on me today.

CLÉANTE: And does it command you to lend an ear to his father's fantastic caprices? Or to accept the gift of possessions to which you have no rightful claim?

TARTUFFE: People who know me will not suspect me of self-interest. Worldly wealth makes little appeal to me. Its tawdry glitter doesn't dazzle me. If I resolve to accept the gift the father insists on offering me it's only because I fear that such possessions may fall into unworthy hands or pass to people who will use them for evil purposes and not employ them as I intend to do, to the glory of God and the good of my neighbour.

CLÉANTE: My good sir, put aside these delicate scruples! They'll get you into trouble with the rightful heir. Let him enjoy his possessions at his own peril without worrying your head about it, consider how much better it would be that he should make ill use of them than that you should find yourself accused of defrauding him! I'm only surprised that you could permit such a proposal without embarrassment. Does any of the maxims of true piety enjoin one to plunder a lawful heir? If Heaven has really inspired you with an insurmountable inability to live in the same house as Damis, wouldn't it be better that you should prudently withdraw rather than let a son be hounded from his father's house on your account in the fact of all right and reason? Believe me, that would be showing some sense of decency and . . .

TARTUFFE: It is now half past three, sir. Certain pious obligations require my presence upstairs without delay. Excuse my leaving you so soon.

[*Exit* TARTUFFE.]

CLÉANTE: Ah!

[*Enter* ELMIRE, MARIANE, DORINE.]

DORINE: Please join with us in trying to help her, Sir. She's in dreadful distress. The betrothal her father has arranged for this evening has reduced her to despair. Here he comes. I beseech you, give us your help. Let us try by hook or crook to frustrate this wretched scheme which is worrying us all.

ORGON: Ah! I'm pleased to find you all here. [*to* MARIANE] I have something in this document to please you. You know what it is.

MARIANE: [*on her knees*] Father, in the name of Heaven which is witness to my unhappiness, and by everything that can move your heart, forgo your rights as a father and absolve me from the dire necessity of obeying you in this matter. Don't drive me, by harsh insistence on your rights, to complain to

Heaven of being your daughter; don't condemn to misery the life you have bestowed upon me. If, contrary to the one dear hope I cherished, you now forbid me to give myself to the man I love, save me at least—on my knees I implore you—from the torment of belonging to a man I abhor! Don't drive me to some act of desperation by pushing your authority to the extreme.

ORGON: [*moved*] Steel your heart, man, now! No human weakness!

MARIANE: Your affection for him doesn't trouble me: show it to the full; give him your wealth and, if that's not enough, let him have mine. I consent with all my heart and freely give it to you, but at least don't include me with it. Rather let me spend such sad days as may remain to me within the austere walls of a convent.

ORGON: Oh yes! Of course, girls are all for going into convents as soon as their fathers' wishes conflict with their wanton designs! Get up! The harder you find it to accept him the better for your soul! Marry and mortify the flesh but don't plague me any more with your bawling and crying!

DORINE: But what . . .

ORGON: You be quiet! Mind your own business. I absolutely forbid you to say a single word.

CLÉANTE: If I might be allowed to offer you a word of advice . . .

ORGON: Brother, your advice is always excellent, most cogent, and I value it extremely, but I hope you will allow me to manage without it!

ELMIRE: [*to her husband*] I am at a loss to know what to say after what we have seen; I can only marvel at your blindness. You must be bewitched by the man—infatuated—to deny the truth of what we told you today.

ORGON: With all due deference to you I judge things as I see them. I know your indulgence for that worthless son of mine. You were afraid to admit that he had played a trick on this unfortunate man. But you took it too calmly for me to believe you. Had the accusation been true you would have been in a very different state of mind.

ELMIRE: Why should a woman have to behave as if her honour is imperilled by a mere declaration of love? Is there no answering but with blazing eyes and furious tongue? For my part I just laugh at such advances. I don't like all this fuss at all. I would rather we protected our good name by less violent means. I have no use for virtuous harridans who defend their honour with tooth and claw and scratch a man's eyes out at the slightest word. Heaven preserve me from that sort of rectitude! No woman need be a dragon of vindictiveness. A snub coolly and discreetly given is, I think, sufficiently effective in rebuffing advances.

ORGON: All the same, I know where I stand and I'm not going to be put off.

ELMIRE: I wonder more and more at this strange infatuation, but what would you say if I were actually to show you that we are telling you the truth.

ORGON: Show me?

ELMIRE: Yes.

ORGON: Rubbish!

ELMIRE: Supposing I could contrive a means of letting you see with your own eyes.

ORGON: The very idea!

ELMIRE: What a man you are! Do at least give an answer. I'm not asking you to take my word for it. Supposing that I arranged for you to see and hear everything from some point of vantage, what would you say then about this Godly man of yours?

ORGON: I should say nothing—because it just can't be done.

ELMIRE: This delusion has lasted too long. I have had enough of being accused of deceiving you. It's necessary now for my own satisfaction that I make you a witness to the truth of everything I have said and without more ado.

ORGON: Very well. I'll take you at your word. We'll see what you can do. Let me see how you make good your promise.

ELMIRE: [*to* DORINE] Ask him to come here.

DORINE: He's cunning. He may be difficult to catch.

ELMIRE: No. People are easily taken in by what they love and vanity predisposes them to deception. Have him come down. [*to* CLÉANTE *and* MARIANE] You two must retire.

[*Exeunt.*]

ELMIRE: Help me to bring the table up. Now get under it.

ORGON: What!

ELMIRE: It's essential that you should be completely hidden.

ORGON: But why under the table?

ELMIRE: Oh, for Heaven's sake leave it to me! I know what I'm doing. You shall see in due course. Get under there and, mind now, take care that he doesn't see or hear you.

ORGON: You are asking a good deal of me, I must say, but I suppose I must see it through now.

ELMIRE: I don't think you'll have any cause to complain but I'm going to play a rather unusual role. Don't be shocked. [ORGON *is under the table.*] I must be allowed to say whatever I like—it will be to convince you as I promised. Since you reduce me to it, I intend to coax this hypocrite to drop his mask, to flatter his impudent desires and encourage his audacity. I shall lead him on merely for the purpose of opening your eyes and exposing him completely. I can stop as soon as you say you give in: things will only go so far as you wish them to go: it will be for you to call a halt to his insensate passion just as soon as you think he has gone far enough: you can spare your poor wife by exposing her to no more than is necessary to disabuse you. It's your affair, and it will be for you to decide . . . but here he comes. Keep in and take care not to be seen.

[*Enter* TARTUFFE.]

TARTUFFE: I was informed that you wished to speak to me here.

ELMIRE: Yes, I have a secret to tell you—but shut the door before I begin and have a good look round in case we should be overheard. We don't want another business like this morning's. I was never so surprised in my life. Damis made me terribly frightened on your account. You must have seen what efforts I made to check him and quieten him down. The truth is I was so taken aback that it never entered my head to deny his accusations, but there—thank Heaven it all turned out for the best! We are much more secure now in consequence. Your reputation saved us. My husband is incapable of thinking ill of you. He insists on our being together to show his contempt for idle rumour. So now I can be in here with you without fear of reproach and can reveal to you that I'm perhaps only too ready to welcome your love.

TARTUFFE: I find it difficult to follow your meaning, madam. Only a while ago you spoke very differently.

ELMIRE: How little you know the heart of woman if such a rebuff has offended you! How little you understand what we mean to convey when we defend ourselves so feebly! At such moments our modesty and the tender sentiments you arouse in us are still in conflict. However compelling the arguments of passion may be we are still too diffident to confess it: we shrink from an immediate avowal but our manner sufficiently reveals that in our heart of hearts we surrender: though our lips must in honour deny our true feelings, such refusals in fact promise everything. I realize that I am making a very frank admission: it shows little regard for womanly modesty but since I *am* speaking—should I have been so anxious to restrain Damis, should I have listened so indulgently, do you think, to your declaration of love, should I have taken it as I did if I had not welcomed it? Moreover, when I sought to make you renounce the marriage which had just been announced what was that intended to convey to you, if not that I took an interest in you and regretted the conclusion of a marriage which would force me to share an affection I wanted entirely to myself?

TARTUFFE: Ah, Madam, it is indeed delightful to hear such words from the lips of one I love! The honey of your words sets coursing through my whole being sensations more delicious than I have ever known before. My supreme concern is to find favour in your eyes. My hopes of bliss lie in your love. Yet you must forgive me if my heart still dares to entertain some doubt of its own felicity. Suppose what you are saying proved to be no more than a virtuous strategem to induce me to abandon this impending marriage. If I may be allowed to put the matter frankly, I'll never trust these promises until I have been vouchsafed some small foretaste of the favours for which I yearn—that alone will reassure me and give me absolute confidence in your intentions towards me.

ELMIRE: [*coughing to attract her husband's attention*] Why must you go so fast? Would you have me reveal at once all that I feel for you? I have overstepped the bounds of modesty in confessing my feelings and yet it isn't enough for you! Can there be no satisfying you without going to ultimate lengths?

TARTUFFE: The less one deserves the less one dares to hope, and words are poor assurances of love. One cannot but mistrust a prospect of felicity: one must enjoy it before one can believe in it. Knowing how little I deserve your favours I doubt the outcome of my own temerity. I'll believe nothing until you give me proofs tangible enough to satisfy my passion.

ELMIRE: Heavens! What an importunate lover you are! I just don't know where I am. You quite overwhelm me—is there no denying you? Is there no evading your demands? Won't you even allow me a breathing space? How can you be so insistent, so peremptory, so merciless? How can you take such advantage of one's fondness for you?

TARTUFFE: But if you look upon my advances with a favourable eye, why refuse me convincing proof?

ELMIRE: How can I consent to what you ask without offending Him whose name is ever on your lips?

TARTUFFE: If fear of Heaven is the only obstacle to my passion that is a barrier I can easily remove. That need not restrain you.

ELMIRE: But they threaten us with the wrath of Heaven.

TARTUFFE: I can dissipate these foolish fears for you. I know the way to remove such scruples. It is true that certain forms of indulgence[2] are forbidden but there are ways and means of coming to terms with Heaven, of easing the restraints of conscience according to the exigencies of the case, of redressing the evil of the action by the purity of the intention. I can instruct you in these secrets, Madam. Only allow yourself to be led by me. Satisfy my desires and have not the slightest fear. I will answer for everything and take the sin upon myself. You have a bad cough, Madam.

ELMIRE: Yes! I'm in great distress.

TARTUFFE: Would you care for a little of this liquorice?

ELMIRE: It's a most obstinate cold. I fear that all the liquorice in the world won't help me now.

TARTUFFE: It is certainly very trying.

ELMIRE: More so than I can say.

TARTUFFE: As I was saying then, your scruples can easily be removed. You are assured of absolute secrecy with me and the harm of any action lies only in its being known. The public scandal is what constitutes the offence: sins sinned in secret are no sins at all.

ELMIRE: [*after coughing again*] Very well then, I see that I must make up my mind to yield and consent to accord you everything you wish. It's no use hoping that anything less will satisfy or convey conviction. It's hard indeed to go to such lengths: it's very much against my will that I do so but since, it seems, I *have* to do it, since I'm not believed in spite of all I've said, since proofs still more convincing are required—I must resign myself to doing what's required of me. But if in consenting I offend, so much the worse for him who forces me to such extremity. The fault can surely not be accounted mine.

TARTUFFE: Yes, Madam, upon me be it and . . .

ELMIRE: Just open the door a moment and make sure that my husband isn't in the gallery.

TARTUFFE: Why worry about him? Between ourselves—he's a fellow one can

---

[2] *Molière's footnote:* "It is a scoundrel speaking"

lead by the nose. He glories in our association. I've got him to the stage where though he saw everything with his own eyes he wouldn't believe it.

ELMIRE: All the same, do go out a moment, please, and have a good look round.

ORGON: [*coming out from under the table*] Yes! I must admit it! The man's an abominable scoundrel! I can't get over it! I'm in a daze.

ELMIRE: But why come out so soon? You can't mean what you say! Get under the table again! It's not time yet. Wait till the very end and make quite sure. Don't trust to mere conjecture.

ORGON: No! No! Hell itself never produced anything more wicked.

ELMIRE: Good Heavens! You mustn't believe as easily as that. Wait until you are utterly convinced before you give in. Don't be too hasty! You might be mistaken! [*She puts her husband behind her.*]

[*Re-enter* TARTUFFE.]

TARTUFFE: Everything favours me, Madam. I've looked in all the rooms. There's no one there and now my rapture . . .

ORGON: [*stopping him*] Steady! You are letting your amorous desires run away with you. You shouldn't get so excited! Ah ha, my godly friend, you would deceive me, would you? How you give way to temptation! You meant to marry my daughter and yet you coveted my wife! For a long time I couldn't believe that it was really true and thought to hear you change your tune: but the proof has gone far enough. I'm convinced, and, for my part, I ask nothing further.

ELMIRE: [*to* TARTUFFE] It was very disagreeable to me to do it. I was driven to treat you like this.

TARTUFFE: [*to* ORGON] What! You believe . . .

ORGON: Come, let's have no more of it, please. Get out of the house without more ado.

TARTUFFE: My intention . . .

ORGON: That sort of talk won't do now. You must leave the house forthwith.

TARTUFFE: You are the one who must leave the house—you who talk as if you were master. This house is mine and I'll have you realize it. What's more, I'll show you how vainly you resort to these devices for picking a quarrel with me. You little know what you are doing when you insult me. I have the means to confound and punish your imposture, avenge the affront to Heaven, and make those who talk of making me leave the house regret it.

[*Exit* TARTUFFE.]

ELMIRE: What is he talking about? What does he mean?

ORGON: Alas! I don't know what to do. This is no laughing matter.

ELMIRE: Why? What . . .

ORGON: What he said makes me realize my mistake. My deed of gift begins to worry me.

ELMIRE: Your deed of gift . . . ?

ORGON: Yes, there's no going back upon it now, but there's something else that worries me.

ELMIRE: What is it?

ORGON: I'll tell you everything but I must go at once and see whether a certain casket is still upstairs.

ACT V

[ORGON, CLÉANTE]

CLÉANTE: Where are you off to?

ORGON: Alas! How do I know?

CLÉANTE: The first thing is to consider what's to be done.

ORGON: It's the casket that's worrying me. I'm more concerned about that than anything else.

CLÉANTE: Is there some important secret about the casket?

ORGON: Argas, my lamented friend, left it with me for safe keeping. He put it into my hands himself in the greatest secrecy. He selected me for this when he fled the country. It contains documents on which, he told me, his life and property depended.

CLÉANTE: Then why did you trust them to someone else?

ORGON: Because of a scruple of conscience. I went straight to this scoundrel and took him into my confidence. He persuaded me that it was better to let him have the casket for safe keeping so that in case of inquiry I could deny that I had it, and yet safeguard my conscience so far as giving false testimony was concerned.

CLÉANTE: You're in a difficult position it seems to me. Both the deed of gift and your action in confiding the casket to him were, if I may say so, very ill considered; he's in a position to lead you a pretty dance! What's more it was most imprudent to provoke him when he has such a hold upon you. You ought to have been more conciliatory in dealing with him.

ORGON: What! A fellow who could hide such double dealing, such wickedness, under the outward semblance of ardent piety, a man whom I took into my house as a penniless beggar . . . No, that's finished with: I'll have no more to do with godly men. I'll hold them in utter abhorrence in future. I'll consider nothing too bad for them!

CLÉANTE: There you go again! No moderation in anything! You are incapable of being temperate and sensible; you seem to have no idea of behaving reasonably. You must always be rushing from one extreme to the other. You see your mistake now; you've learned that you were taken in by an assumed piety; but what's the good of correcting one error by an even greater one, and failing to make a distinction between a scoundrelly good for nothing and genuinely good men? Because an audacious rogue has deceived you by a pretentious assumption of virtue and piety must you go and think everybody is like him and that there are no truly devout people nowadays? Leave such foolish inferences to the unbelievers; distinguish between virtue and the outward appearance of it, don't be so hasty in bestowing your esteem, and keep a sense of proportion. Be on your guard if you can against paying deference to imposture but say nothing against true devotion, and if you must run to extremes, better err on the same side as you did before.

[*Enter* DAMIS.]

DAMIS: Is it true, father, that this soundrel is threatening you, that he's insensible to every benefit, and that in his wicked and outrageous pride he is turning your own generosity against you?

ORGON: It is, my son, and a dreadful grief it is to me too.

DAMIS: Leave it to me! I'll crop his ears for him. No half-measures with a rascal like that! I'll undertake to rid you of him without delay. I'll settle the business! I'll deal with him.

CLÉANTE: That's typical young man's talk. Moderate your feelings for goodness sake! We live in an age and under a government where it goes ill with those who resort to violence.

[*Enter* MADAME PERNELLE.]

MADAME PERNELLE: What's all this? What are these strange goings-on I have been hearing about?

ORGON: Ay! Strange indeed and I've seen them with my own eyes too. This is the reward I get for my pains. In sheer kindness of heart I relieve a man in his misery, receive him into my house, treat him like a brother, load him with kindness, give him my daughter, everything I possess, and what does the infamous scoundrel do but foully endeavour to seduce my wife! Not content with that he has the audacity to turn my own benevolence against me and threatens to ruin me with the weapons my own unwise generosity has put into his hand, deprive me of my possessions, and reduce me to the beggary from which I rescued him.

DORINE: Poor fellow!

MADAME PERNELLE: My son, I just can't believe that he has been guilty of such wickedness.

ORGON: How d'ye mean?

MADAME PERNELLE: People are always envious of the righteous.

ORGON: Whatever are you talking about, mother?

MADAME PERNELLE: I mean that there are queer goings-on in this house and I know very well how much they hate him.

ORGON: What has their hatred to do with what I'm telling you?

MADAME PERNELLE: I told you a hundred times when you were a little boy.
'Virtue, on earth, is persecuted ever
The envious die, but envy never.'

ORGON: But what has this to do with what has happened?

MADAME PERNELLE: They'll have made up a hundred idle tales about him.

ORGON: I've already told you that I *saw it all myself.*

MADAME PERNELLE: There are no limits to the malice of slanderous tongues.

ORGON: You'll make me swear, mother, I've told you I saw his wickedness with my own eyes.

MADAME PERNELLE: Malicious tongues spread their poison abroad and nothing here below is proof against them.

ORGON: This is ridiculous talk. I *saw* him, I tell you, *saw him* with my own eyes! When I say I saw him I mean I really did see it! Must I go on saying it? How many times am I to tell you? Must I bawl it at the top of my voice?

MADAME PERNELLE: Good Heavens, appearances can often be deceptive. One shouldn't judge by what one sees.

ORGON: You'll drive me mad!

MADAME PERNELLE: It's human nature to think evil of people. Goodness is often misinterpreted.

ORGON: Am I to interpret it as kindly solicitude when I see him trying to kiss my wife?

MADAME PERNELLE: One ought never to make accusations without just cause. You should have waited until you were quite certain of his intentions.

ORGON: What the devil! How was I to be more certain? I should have waited, should I, until he . . . You'll drive me to say something I shouldn't.

MADAME PERNELLE: No, no! He's far too good a man. I just can't imagine he meant to do what you are saying he did.

ORGON: Look here! If you weren't my mother—I don't know what I wouldn't say to you—I'm so angry.

DORINE: Serves you right, master; it's the way of the world. *You* refused to believe once and now she won't believe you.

CLÉANTE: We are wasting time with this nonsense which we ought to be using for making plans. We can't afford to go to sleep in face of the scoundrel's threats.

DAMIS: Why! Do you think he'll really have the audacity to carry them out?

ELMIRE: I can't think he would have a case. His ingratitude is too glaring.

CLÉANTE: I shouldn't rely on that. He'll find means to justify whatever he does to you. Intrigue has landed people in difficulties on less evidence than this before now. I repeat what I said before: when he was in so strong a position as he is, you should never have provoked him so far.

ORGON: True. But what could I do? The audacity of the villain was such that I wasn't master of my feelings.

CLÉANTE: I only wish we could patch up some sort of reconciliation.

ELMIRE: Had I known what a strong position he was in I would never have been a party to making such a fuss . . .

ORGON: [*to* DORINE] What does *this* fellow want? Go at once and see. I'm in a fine state for anyone to come to see me.

[*Enter* MR LOYAL.]

MR LOYAL: Good afternoon, dear sister. Pray let me speak with the master.

DORINE: He has company. I don't suppose he can see anyone just now.

MR LOYAL: I'm not for being troublesome. I don't think he'll find *my* visit unsatisfactory. He'll be pleased with what I've come about.

DORINE: Your name?

MR LOYAL: Just tell him that I'm here on behalf of Mr Tartuffe and for his own good.

DORINE: [*to* ORGON] It's a man who's come on behalf of Mr Tartuffe. He's very civil about it. He says that his business is something that you will be pleased to hear.

CLÉANTE: [*to* ORGON] We must see who the man is and what he wants.

ORGON: Perhaps he's come to reconcile us. How should I behave to him?

CLÉANTE: Don't show your resentment. If he's for coming to an agreement you must listen to him.

MR LOYAL: How d'ye do, sir. May Heaven bless you and confound all who seek to do you harm.

ORGON: [*aside to* CLÉANTE] This civil beginning confirms my impression. It means a reconciliation.

MR LOYAL: I have always been very devoted to your family. I was once in your father's service.

ORGON: I'm sorry not to recognize you. You must forgive me but I don't know your name.

MR LOYAL: Loyal's the name. Norman by birth and bailiff to the court; and let them envy me that want to. I can rightly claim to have discharged my duty with credit this forty year now, Heaven be praised, and now I've come, sir, to serve this writ upon you, excusing the liberty.

ORGON: What! You've come to . . .

MR LOYAL: Now take it quiet, sir. It's only a writ, an order to quit the house at once, you and yours, bag and baggage, and make way for others, without delay and without fail as herein provided.

ORGON: What, me! Leave the house?

MR LOYAL: That's it, sir, if you don't mind. This house is now, as you be duly aware, good Mr Tartuffe's and no argument about it. He's lord and master of your possessions from now on by virtue of the deed that I be the bearer of. It's in the due form and there's no disputing it.

DAMIS: What marvellous impudence!

MR LOYAL: [*to* DAMIS] I want nothing to do with you, sir. It's this gentleman I'm dealing with. He's reasonable and good to deal with and he knows too well what a good man's duty is to want to interfere with the course of justice.

ORGON: But . . .

MR LOYAL: Yes sir. I know you'd never resist authority, not on any consideration. You'll allow me to carry out my orders as a gentleman should.

DAMIS: You may as easily find yourself getting a hiding for all your black gown, Mr Bailiff.

MR LOYAL: Ask your son to hold his tongue, sir, or retire. I should be very sorry to have to report you.

DORINE: He should be *Dis*loyal, not Loyal, by the look of him.

MR LOYAL: I have a soft spot for godly men, sir, and I only took service of this writ in consideration for you sir, and just to be helpful and to stop the job falling to anybody who mightn't have the same feeling for you that I have and wouldn't have gone about things so considerate-like.

ORGON: And what could be worse than ordering a man out of his own house?

MR LOYAL: We are giving you time. I'll give a stay of execution till tomorrow. I'll just come and pass the night here with a dozen or so of my men without fuss or scandal. I must ask for the keys as a matter of form, of course, before you go to bed. I'll take pains not to disturb your rest and I'll see that there's nothing that isn't as it should be. But tomorrow morning you'll have to look slippy and clear everything out of here down to the last article. My men will help you. I've picked a handy lot so that they can get everything out for you. Nobody could treat you fairer than that and, seeing as I'm showing you every consideration, I ask the same from you, sir—that is, that you won't do nothing to hinder me in discharge of my duty.

ORGON: [aside] I'd willingly give the last hundred louis I possess for the pleasure of landing him a punch on his ugly snout!

CLÉANTE: [whispers to ORGON] Steady. Don't do anything foolish.

DAMIS: I can hardly restrain myself before such unheard-of insolence. I'm itching to be at him.

DORINE: That broad back of yours could do with a good dusting, Mr Loyal.

MR LOYAL: I could get you into trouble for talking like that, my lass. The law applies to women as well, you know.

CLÉANTE: [to LOYAL] That's enough, sir. We'll leave it at that. Give us the document and go.

MR LOYAL: Good day then. The Lord be with you all.

[Exit MR LOYAL.]

ORGON: Ay, and the Devil take you and him who sent you! Well mother, you see now whether I was right or not. On the other point you can judge from the writ. Do you realize now what a rascal he is?

MADAME PERNELLE: I don't know whether I'm on my head or my heels.

DORINE: You have no cause for complaint and no right to blame him. It all fits in with his pious intentions; it's all part of his love for his neighbour. He knows how possessions corrupt a man and it's pure charity on his part to rob you of everything that might stand in the way of your salvation.

ORGON: Be quiet! I'm always having to remind you!

CLÉANTE: Let us go and take counsel on what course to follow.

ELMIRE: Go and expose the ungrateful scoundrel! This last act of his must invalidate the deed of gift. His treachery must appear too obvious to permit him the success we fear.

[Enter VALÈRE]

VALÈRE: I'm very sorry to bring you bad news, sir, but I'm obliged to do so because you are in most urgent danger. A very close friend who knows the interest I have reason to take in your welfare has violated the secrecy due to affairs of state and sent me intelligence, in confidence. The purport of it is that you must fly immediately. The scoundrel, who has so long imposed upon you, denounced you to the King an hour ago and, among various charges made against you, put into his hands a casket which belonged to a disaffected person whose secrets he contends you have kept in breach of your duty as a subject. I know no particulars of the offence with which you are charged but a warrant has been issued for your arrest and to ensure effective service of it Tartuffe himself is commanded to accompany the person who is to apprehend you.

CLÉANTE: And so he strengthens his hand! That's how he means to make himself master of your possessions.

ORGON: I must admit, the man really is a brute!

VALÈRE: The slightest delay may be fatal to you. I have my carriage at the door to take you away, and a thousand guineas which I have brought for you. We must lose no time: this is a shattering blow—there's no avoiding it except by flight. I offer you my services to conduct you to some place of safety. I'll stay with you until you are out of danger.

ORGON: Alas! How can I repay your kindness? But I must leave my thanks to another time. May Heaven allow me some day to return this service! Farewell! Take care all of you . . .

CLÉANTE: Go at once, brother. We'll see that everything necessary is done.

[*Enter* TARTUFFE *and an* OFFICER.]

TARTUFFE: Gently, sir, gently, don't run so fast. You don't need to go very far to find a lodging. You are a prisoner in the King's name.

ORGON: Villain! To keep this trick to the last! This is the blow whereby you finish me, the master stroke of all your perfidy!

TARTUFFE: Your insults are powerless to move me. I am schooled to suffer everything in the cause of Heaven.

CLÉANTE: Remarkable meekness indeed!

DAMIS: How impudently the dog makes mockery of Heaven.

TARTUFFE: Not all your rage can move me. I have no thought for anything but to fulfil my duty.

MARIANE: What credit can you hope to reap from this? How can you regard such employment as honourable?

TARTUFFE: Any employment must needs be honourable which proceeds from that authority which sent me hither.

ORGON: And do you not remember, ungrateful wretch, that it was my charitable hand which rescued you from indigence?

TARTUFFE: Yes, I am mindful of the assistance I received from you, but my first duty is to the interests of my King and that sacred obligation is so strong as to extinguish in me all gratitude to you. To that allegiance I would sacrifice friends, wife, kinsmen, and myself with them.

ELMIRE: Impostor!

DORINE: How cunningly he cloaks his villainies with the mantle of all that we most revere!

CLÉANTE: If this consuming zeal of which you boast is as great as you say, why didn't it come to light until he had caught you making love to his wife? Why didn't it occur to you to denounce him until your attempt to dishonour him had forced him to turn you out? If I mention the gift it isn't to deter you from doing your duty but, nevertheless, if you want to treat him as a criminal now, why did you consent to accept anything from him before?

TARTUFFE: Pray deliver me from this futile clamour, sir! Proceed to the execution of your orders.

OFFICER: Yes. I have indeed waited too long already and you do well to recall me to my duty. In fulfilment of my instructions I command you to accompany me forthwith to the prison in which you are to be lodged.

TARTUFFE: What? Me, sir?

OFFICER: Yes, you.

TARTUFFE: But why to prison?

OFFICER: I am not accountable to you. [*to* ORGON] Calm your fears, sir. We live under the rule of a prince inimical to fraud, a monarch who can read men's hearts, whom no impostor's art deceives. The keen discernment of that lofty mind at all times sees things in their true perspective; nothing can disturb the firm constancy of his judgement nor lead him into error. On men of worth he confers immortal glory but his favour is not shown indiscriminately: his love for good men and true does not preclude a proper detestation of those who are false. This man could never deceive him—he has evaded more subtle snares than his. From the outset he discerned to the full the baseness of the villain's heart and in coming to accuse you he betrayed himself and by a stroke of supreme justice revealed himself as a notorious scoundrel of whose activities under another name His Majesty was already informed. The long history of his dark crimes would fill volumes. In short, the King, filled with detestation for his base ingratitude and wickedness to you, added this to his other crimes and only put me under his orders to see to what lengths his impudence would go and to oblige him to give you full satisfaction. All documents he says he has of yours I am to take from him in your presence and restore them to you and His Majesty annuls by act of sovereign prerogative the deed of gift of your possessions that you made to him. Moreover, he pardons you that clandestine offence in which the flight of your friend involved you: this clemency he bestows upon you in recognition of your former loyal service and to let you see that he can reward a good action when least expected, that he is never insensible to true merit and chooses rather to remember good than ill.

DORINE: Heaven be praised!

MADAME PERNELLE: Now I can breathe again.

ELMIRE: A happy end to all our troubles!

MARIANE: Who could have foretold this?

ORGON: [*to* TARTUFFE] So you see, you villain, you . . .

CLÉANTE: Ah! Brother forbear. Do not stoop to such indignity. Leave the unhappy creature to his fate. Add nothing to the remorse which must now overwhelm him. Rather hope that he may henceforward return to the paths of virtue, reform his life, learn to detest his vices, and so earn some mitigation of the justice of the King. Meanwhile, for your own part, you must go on your knees and render appropriate thanks for the benevolence His Majesty has shown to you.

ORGON: Yes, that's well said. Let us go and offer him our humble thanks for all his generosity to us. Then, that first duty done, we have another to perform—to crown the happiness of Valère, a lover who has proved both generous and sincere.

THE VISIT

Friedrich Duerrenmatt (*Adapted by Maurice Valency*)

CHARACTERS

(*In order of appearance*)

HOFBAUER (FIRST MAN)

HELMESBERGER (SECOND MAN)

WECHSLER (THIRD MAN)

VOGEL (FOURTH MAN)

PAINTER

STATION MASTER

BURGOMASTER

TEACHER

PASTOR

ANTON SCHILL

CLAIRE ZACHANASSIAN

CONDUCTOR

PEDRO CABRAL

BOBBY

POLICEMAN

FIRST GRANDCHILD

SECOND GRANDCHILD

MIKE

MAX

FIRST BLIND MAN

SECOND BLIND MAN

ATHLETE

FRAU BURGOMASTER

FRAU SCHILL

DAUGHTER

SON

DOCTOR NÜSSLIN

FRAU BLOCK (FIRST WOMAN)

TRUCK DRIVER

REPORTER

TOWNSMAN

The action of the play takes place in and around the little town of Güllen, somewhere in Europe.

There are three acts.

Act One

A railway-crossing bell starts ringing. Then is heard the distant sound of a locomotive whistle. The curtain rises.

The scene represents, in the simplest possible manner, a little town some-where in Central Europe. The time is the present. The town is shabby and ruined, as if the plague had passed there. Its name, Güllen, is inscribed on the shabby signboard which adorns the façade of the railway station. This edifice is summarily indicated by a length of rusty iron paling, a platform parallel to the proscenium, beyond which one imagines the rails to be, and a baggage truck standing by a wall on which a torn timetable, marked "Fahrplan," is affixed by three nails. In the station wall is a door with a sign: "Eintritt Verboten."[1] This leads to the STATION MASTER'S *office.*

Left of the station is a little house of gray stucco, formerly whitewashed. It has a tile roof, badly in need of repair. Some shreds of travel posters still adhere to the windowless walls. A shingle hanging over the entrance, left, reads: "Männer."[2] On the other side of the shingle reads: "Damen."[3] Along

---

[1] No Entrance.
[2] Men.
[3] Ladies.

the wall of the little house there is a wooden bench, backless, on which four men are lounging cheerlessly, shabbily dressed, with cracked shoes. A fifth man is busied with paintpot and brush. He is kneeling on the ground, painting a strip of canvas with the words: "Welcome, Clara."

The warning signal rings uninterruptedly. The sound of the approaching train comes closer and closer. The STATION MASTER *issues from his office, advances to the center of the platform and salutes.*

The train is heard thundering past in a direction parallel to the footlights, and is lost in the distance. The men on the bench follow its passing with a slow movement of their heads, from left to right.

FIRST MAN: The "Emperor." Hamburg-Naples.

SECOND MAN: Then comes the "Diplomat."

THIRD MAN: Then the "Banker."

FOURTH MAN: And at eleven twenty-seven the "Flying Dutchman." Venice-Stockholm.

FIRST MAN: Our only pleasure—watching trains.

> (*The station bell rings again. The* STATION MASTER *comes out of his office and salutes another train. The men follow its course, right to left*)

FOURTH MAN: Once upon a time the "Emperor" and the "Flying Dutchman" used to stop here in Güllen. So did the "Diplomat," the "Banker," and the "Silver Comet."

SECOND MAN: Now it's only the local from Kaffigen and the twelve-forty from Kalberstadt.

THIRD MAN: The fact is, we're ruined.

FIRST MAN: What with the Wagonworks shut down . . .

SECOND MAN: The Foundry finished . . .

FOURTH MAN: The Golden Eagle Pencil Factory all washed up . . .

FIRST MAN: It's life on the dole.

SECOND MAN: Did you say life?

THIRD MAN: We're rotting.

FIRST MAN: Starving.

SECOND MAN: Crumbling.

FOURTH MAN: The whole damn town.

> (*The station bell rings*)

THIRD MAN: Once we were a center of industry.

PAINTER: A cradle of culture.

FOURTH MAN: One of the best little towns in the country.

FIRST MAN: In the world.

SECOND MAN: Here Goethe slept.

FOURTH MAN: Brahms composed a quartet.

THIRD MAN: Here Berthold Schwarz invented gunpowder.

PAINTER: And I once got first prize at the Dresden Exhibition of Contemporary Art. What am I doing now? Painting signs.

(The station bell rings. The STATION MASTER *comes out. He throws away a cigarette butt. The men scramble for it)*

FIRST MAN: Well, anyway, Madame Zachanassian will help us.

FOURTH MAN: If she comes . . .

THIRD MAN: If she comes.

SECOND MAN: Last week she was in France. She gave them a hospital.

FIRST MAN: In Rome she founded a free public nursery.

THIRD MAN: In Leuthenau, a bird sanctuary.

PAINTER: They say she got Picasso to design her car.

FIRST MAN: Where does she get all that money?

SECOND MAN: An oil company, a shipping line, three banks and five railways—

FOURTH MAN: And the biggest string of geisha houses in Japan.

(From the direction of the town come the BURGOMASTER, *the* PASTOR, *the* TEACHER *and* ANTON SCHILL. *The* BURGOMASTER, *the* TEACHER *and* SCHILL *are men in their fifties. The* PASTOR *is ten years younger. All four are dressed shabbily and are sad-looking. The* BURGOMASTER *looks official.* SCHILL *is tall and handsome, but graying and worn; nevertheless a man of considerable charm and presence. He walks directly to the little house and disappears into it)*

PAINTER: Any news, Burgomaster? Is she coming?

ALL: Yes, is she coming?

BURGOMASTER: She's coming. The telegram has been confirmed. Our distinguished guest will arrive on the twelve-forty from Kalberstadt. Everyone must be ready.

TEACHER: The mixed choir is ready. So is the children's chorus.

BURGOMASTER: And the church bell, Pastor?

PASTOR: The church bell will ring. As soon as the new bell ropes are fitted. The man is working on them now.

BURGOMASTER: The town band will be drawn up in the market place and the Athletic Association will form a human pyramid in her honor—the top man will hold the wreath with her initials. Then lunch at the Golden Apostle. I shall say a few words.

TEACHER: Of course.

BURGOMASTER: I had thought of illuminating the town hall and the cathedral, but we can't afford the lamps.

PAINTER: Burgomaster—what do you think of this?

(He shows the banner)

BURGOMASTER: *(Calls)* Schill! Schill!

TEACHER: Schill!

*(*SCHILL *comes out of the little house)*

SCHILL: Yes, right away. Right away.

BURGOMASTER: This is more in your line. What do you think of this?

SCHILL: *(Looks at the sign)* No, no, no. That certainly won't do, Burgomaster.

It's much too intimate. It shouldn't read: "Welcome, Clara." It should read: "Welcome, Madame . . ."

TEACHER: Zachanassian.

BURGOMASTER: Zachanassian.

SCHILL: Zachanassian.

PAINTER: But she's Clara to us.

FIRST MAN: Clara Wäscher.

SECOND MAN: Born here.

THIRD MAN: Her father was a carpenter. He built this.

(All turn and stare at the little house)

SCHILL: All the same . . .

PAINTER: If I . . .

BURGOMASTER: No, no, no. He's right. You'll have to change it.

PAINTER: Oh, well, I'll tell you what I'll do. I'll leave this and I'll put "Welcome, Madame Zachanassian" on the other side. Then if things go well, we can always turn it around.

BURGOMASTER: Good idea. (*To* SCHILL) Yes?

SCHILL: Well, anyway, it's safer. Everything depends on the first impression.
  (*The train bell is heard. Two clangs. The* PAINTER *turns the banner over and goes to work*)

FIRST MAN: Hear that? The "Flying Dutchman" has just passed through Leuthenau.

FOURTH MAN: Eleven twenty.

BURGOMASTER: Gentlemen, you know that the millionairess is our only hope.

PASTOR: Under God.

BURGOMASTER: Under God. Naturally. Schill, we depend entirely on you.

SCHILL: Yes, I know. You keep telling me.

BURGOMASTER: After all, you're the only one who really knew her.

SCHILL: Yes, I knew her.

PASTOR: You were really quite close to one another, I hear, in those days.

SCHILL: Close? Yes, we were close, there's no denying it. We were in love. I was young—good-looking, so they said—and Clara—you know, I can still see her in the great barn coming toward me—like a light out of the darkness. And in the Konradsweil Forest she'd come running to meet me—barefooted—her beautiful red hair streaming behind her. Like a witch. I was in love with her, all right. But you know how it is when you're twenty.

PASTOR: What happened?

SCHILL: (*Shrugs*) Life came between us.

BURGOMASTER: You must give me some points about her for my speech.

(He takes out his notebook)

SCHILL: I think I can help you there.

TEACHER: Well, I've gone through the school records. And the young lady's marks were, I'm afraid to say, absolutely dreadful. Even in deportment. The only subject in which she was even remotely passable was natural history.

BURGOMASTER: Good in natural history. That's fine. Give me a pencil.

(He makes a note)

SCHILL: She was an outdoor girl. Wild. Once, I remember, they arrested a tramp, and she threw stones at the policeman. She hated injustice passionately.

BURGOMASTER: Strong sense of justice. Excellent.

SCHILL: And generous . . .

ALL: Generous?

SCHILL: Generous to a fault. Whatever little she had, she shared—so good-hearted. I remember once she stole a bag of potatoes to give to a poor widow.

BURGOMASTER: (*Writing in notebook*) Wonderful generosity—

TEACHER: Generosity.

BURGOMASTER: That, gentlemen, is something I must not fail to make a point of.

SCHILL: And such a sense of humor. I remember once when the oldest man in town fell and broke his leg, she said, "Oh, dear, now they'll have to shoot him."

BURGOMASTER: Well, I've got enough. The rest, my friend, is up to you.

(*He puts the notebook away*)

SCHILL: Yes, I know, but it's not so easy. After all, to part a woman like that from her millions—

BURGOMASTER: Exactly. Millions. We have to think in big terms here.

TEACHER: If she's thinking of buying us off with a nursery school—

ALL: Nursery school!

PASTOR: Don't accept.

TEACHER: Hold out.

SCHILL: I'm not so sure that I can do it. You know, she may have forgotten me completely.

BURGOMASTER: (*He exchanges a look with the* TEACHER *and the* PASTOR) Schill, for many years you have been our most popular citizen. The most respected and the best loved.

SCHILL: Why, thank you . . .

BURGOMASTER: And therefore I must tell you—last week I sounded out the political opposition, and they agreed. In the spring you will be elected to succeed me as Burgomaster. By unanimous vote.

(*The others clap their hands in approval*)

SCHILL: But, my dear Burgomaster—!

BURGOMASTER: It's true.

TEACHER: I'm a witness. I was at the meeting.

SCHILL: This is—naturally, I'm terribly flattered—It's a completely unexpected honor.

BURGOMASTER: You deserve it.

SCHILL: Burgomaster! Well, well—! (*Briskly*) Gentlemen, to business. The first chance I get, of course, I shall discuss our miserable position with Clara.

TEACHER: But tactfully, tactfully—

SCHILL: What do you take me for? We must feel our way. Everything must be correct. Psychologically correct. For example, here at the railway station, a single blunder, one false note, could be disastrous.

BURGOMASTER: He's absolutely right. The first impression colors all the rest. Madame Zachanassian sets foot on her native soil for the first time in many years. She sees our love and she sees our misery. She remembers her youth, her friends. The tears well up into her eyes. Her childhood companions throng about her. I will naturally not present myself like this, but in my black coat with my top hat. Next to me, my wife. Before me, my two grandchildren all in white, with roses. My God, if it only comes off as I see it! If only it comes off. (*The station bell begins ringing*) Oh, my god! Quick! We must get dressed.

FIRST MAN: It's not her train. It's only the "Flying Dutchman."

PASTOR: (*Calmly*) We have still two hours before she arrives.

SCHILL: For God's sake, don't let's lose our heads. We still have a full two hours.

BURGOMASTER: Who's losing their heads? (*To* FIRST *and* SECOND MAN) When her train comes, you two, Helmesberger and Vogel, will hold up the banner with "Welcome Madame Zachanassian." The rest will applaud.

THIRD MAN: Bravo!

(He applauds)

BURGOMASTER: But, please, one thing—no wild cheering like last year with the government relief committee. It made no impression at all and we still haven't received any loan. What we need is a feeling of genuine sincerity. That's how we greet with full hearts our beloved sister who has been away from us so long. Be sincerely moved, my friends, that's the secret; be sincere. Remember you're not dealing with a child. Next a few brief words from me. Then the church bell will start pealing—

PASTOR: If he can fix the ropes in time.

(The station bell rings)

BURGOMASTER: —Then the mixed choir moves in. And then—

TEACHER: We'll form a line down here.

BURGOMASTER: Then the rest of us will form in two lines leading from the station—

(He is interrupted by the thunder of the approaching train. The men crane their heads to see it pass. The STATION MASTER *advances to the platform and salutes. There is a sudden shriek of air brakes. The train screams to a stop. The four men jump up in consternation)*

PAINTER: But the "Flying Dutchman" never stops!

FIRST MAN: It's stopping.

SECOND MAN: In Güllen!

THIRD MAN: In the poorest—

FIRST MAN: The dreariest—

SECOND MAN: The lousiest—

FOURTH MAN: The most God-forsaken hole between Venice and Stockholm.

STATION MASTER: It cannot stop!

(*The train noises stop. There is only the panting of the engine*)

PAINTER: It's stopped!

(*The* STATION MASTER *runs out*)

OFFSTAGE VOICES: What's happened? Is there an accident?

(*A hubbub of offstage voices, as if the passengers on the invisible train were alighting*)

CLAIRE: (*Offstage*) Is this Güllen?

CONDUCTOR: (*Offstage*) Here, here, what's going on?

CLAIRE: (*Offstage*) Who the hell are you?

CONDUCTOR: (*Offstage*) But you pulled the emergency cord, madame!

CLAIRE: (*Offstage*) I always pull the emergency cord.

STATION MASTER: (*Offstage*) I must ask you what's going on here.

CLAIRE: (*Offstage*) And who the hell are you?

STATION MASTER: (*Offstage*) I'm the Station Master, madame, and I must ask you—

CLAIRE: (*Enters*) No!

(*From the right* CLAIRE ZACHANASSIAN *appears. She is an extraordinary woman. She is in her fifties, red-haired, remarkably dressed, with a face as impassive as that of an ancient idol, beautiful still, and with a singular grace of movement and manner. She is simple and unaffected, yet she has the haughtiness of a world power. The entire effect is striking to the point of the unbelievable. Behind her comes her fiancé,* PEDRO CABRAL, *tall, young, very handsome, and completely equipped for fishing, with creel and net, and with a rod case in his hand. An excited* CONDUCTOR *follows*)

CONDUCTOR: But, madame, I must insist! You have stopped "The Flying Dutchman." I must have an explanation.

CLAIRE: Nonsense. Pedro.

PEDRO: Yes, my love?

CLAIRE: This is Güllen. Nothing has changed. I recognize it all. There's the forest of Konradsweil. There's a brook in it full of trout, where you can fish. And there's the roof of the great barn. Ha! God! What a miserable blot on the map.

(*She crosses the stage and goes off with* PEDRO)

SCHILL: My God! Clara!

TEACHER: Claire Zachanassian!

ALL: Claire Zachanassian!

BURGOMASTER: And the town band? The town band! Where is it?

TEACHER: The mixed choir! The mixed choir!

PASTOR: The church bell! The church bell!

BURGOMASTER: (*To the* FIRST MAN) Quick! My dress coat. My top hat. My grandchildren. Run! Run! (FIRST MAN *runs off. The* BURGOMASTER *shouts after him*) And don't forget my wife!

(General panic. The THIRD MAN *and* FOURTH MAN *hold up the banner, on which only part of the name has been painted: "Wel-come Mad—"* CLAIRE *and* PEDRO *re-enter, right)*

CONDUCTOR: *(Mastering himself with an effort)* Madame. The train is waiting. The entire international railway schedule has been disrupted. I await your explanation.

CLAIRE: You're a very foolish man. I wish to visit this town. Did you expect me to jump off a moving train?

CONDUCTOR: *(Stupefied)* You stopped the "Flying Dutchman" because you wished to visit the town?

CLAIRE: Naturally.

CONDUCTOR: *(Inarticulate)* Madame!

STATION MASTER: Madame, if you wished to visit the town, the twelve forty from Kalberstadt was entirely at your service. Arrival in Güllen, one seventeen.

CLAIRE: The local that stops at Loken, Beisenbach, and Leuthenau? Do you expect me to waste three-quarters of an hour chugging dismally through this wilderness?

CONDUCTOR: Madame, you shall pay for this!

CLAIRE: Bobby, give him a thousand marks.

*(*BOBBY*, her butler, a man in his seventies, wearing dark glasses, opens his wallet. The townspeople gasp)*

CONDUCTOR: *(Taking the money in amazement)* But, madame!

CLAIRE: And three thousand for the Railway Widows' Relief Fund.

CONDUCTOR: *(With the money in his hands)* But we have no such fund, madame.

CLAIRE: Now you have.

(The BURGOMASTER *pushes his way forward)*

BURGOMASTER: *(He whispers to the* CONDUCTOR *and* TEACHER*)* The lady is Madame Claire Zachanassian!

CONDUCTOR: Claire Zachanassian? Oh, my God! But that's naturally quite different. Needless to say, we would have stopped the train if we'd had the slightest idea. *(He hands the money back to* BOBBY*)* Here, please, I couldn't dream of it. Four thousand. My God!

CLAIRE: Keep it. Don't fuss.

CONDUCTOR: Would you like the train to wait, madame, while you visit the town? The administration will be delighted. The cathedral porch. The town hall—

CLAIRE: You may take the train away. I don't need it any more.

STATION MASTER: All aboard!

(He puts his whistle to his lips. PEDRO *stops him)*

PEDRO: But the press, my angel. They don't know anything about this. They're still in the dining car.

CLAIRE: Let them stay there. I don't want the press in Güllen at the moment. Later they will come by themselves. (To STATION MASTER) And now what are you waiting for?

STATION MASTER: All aboard!

> (*The* STATION MASTER *blows a long blast on his whistle. The train leaves. Meanwhile, the* FIRST MAN *has brought the* BURGOMASTER's *dress coat and top hat. The* BURGOMASTER *puts on the coat, then advances slowly and solemnly*)

CONDUCTOR: I trust madame will not speak of this to the administration. It was a pure misunderstanding.

> (*He salutes and runs for the train as it starts moving*)

BURGOMASTER: (*Bows*) Gracious lady, as Burgomaster of the town of Güllen, I have the honor—

> (*The rest of the speech is lost in the roar of the departing train. He continues speaking and gesturing, and at last bows amid applause as the train noises end*)

CLAIRE: Thank you, Mr. Burgomaster.

> (*She glances at the beaming faces, and lastly at* SCHILL, *whom she does not recognize. She turns upstage*)

SCHILL: Clara!

CLAIRE: (*Turns and stares*) Anton?

SCHILL: Yes. It's good that you've come back.

CLAIRE: Yes. I've waited for this moment. All my life. Ever since I left Güllen.

SCHILL: (*A little embarrassed*) That is very kind of you to say, Clara.

CLAIRE: And have you thought about me?

SCHILL: Naturally. Always. You know that.

CLAIRE: Those were happy times we spent together.

SCHILL: Unforgettable.

> (*He smiles reassuringly at the* BURGOMASTER)

CLAIRE: Call me by the name you used to call me.

SCHILL: (*Whispers*) My kitten.

CLAIRE: What?

SCHILL: (*Louder*) My kitten.

CLAIRE: And what else?

SCHILL: Little witch.

CLAIRE: I used to call you my black panther. You're gray now, and soft.

SCHILL: But you are still the same, little witch.

CLAIRE: I am the same? (*She laughs*) Oh, no, my black panther, I am not at all the same.

SCHILL: (*Gallantly*) In my eyes you are. I see no difference.

CLAIRE: Would you like to meet my fiancé? Pedro Cabral. He owns an enormous plantation in Brazil.

SCHILL: A pleasure.

CLAIRE: We're to be married soon.

SCHILL: Congratulations.

CLAIRE: He will be my eighth husband. (PEDRO *stands by himself downstage, right*) Pedro, come here and show your face. Come along, darling—come here! Don't sulk. Say hello.

PEDRO: Hello.

CLAIRE: A man of few words! Isn't he charming? A diplomat. He's interested only in fishing. Isn't he handsome, in his Latin way? You'd swear he was a Brazilian. But he's not—he's a Greek. His father was a White Russian. We were betrothed by a Bulgarian priest. We plan to be married in a few days here in the cathedral.

BURGOMASTER: Here in the cathedral? What an honor for us!

CLAIRE: No. it was my dream, when I was seventeen, to be married in Güllen cathedral. The dreams of youth are sacred, don't you think so, Anton?

SCHILL: Yes, of course.

CLAIRE: Yes, of course. I think so, too. Now I would like to look at the town. (*The mixed choir arrives, breathless, wearing ordinary clothes with green sashes*) What's all this? Go away. (*She laughs*) Ha! Ha! Ha!

TEACHER: Dear lady—(*He steps forward, having put on a sash also*) Dear lady, as Rector of the high school and a devotee of that noble muse, Music, I take pleasure in presenting the Güllen mixed choir.

CLAIRE: How do you do?

TEACHER: Who will sing for you an ancient folk song of the region, with specially amended words—if you will deign to listen.

CLAIRE: Very well. Fire away.

> (*The* TEACHER *blows a pitch pipe. The mixed choir begins to sing the ancient folk song with the amended words. Just then the station bell starts ringing. The song is drowned in the roar of the passing express. The* STATION MASTER *salutes. When the train has passed, there is applause*)

BURGOMASTER: The church bell! The church bell! Where's the church bell?

> (*The* PASTOR *shrugs helplessly*)

CLAIRE: Thank you, Professor. They sang beautifully. the big little blond bass—no, not that one—the one with the big Adam's apple—was most impressive. (*The* TEACHER *bows. The* POLICEMAN *pushes his way professionally through the mixed choir and comes to attention in front of* CLAIRE ZACHANASSIAN) Now, who are you?

POLICEMAN (*Clicks heels*): Police Chief Schultz. At your service.

CLAIRE (*She looks him up and down*): I have no need of you at the moment. But I think there will be work for you by and by. Tell me, do you know how to close an eye from time to time?

POLICEMAN: How else could I get along in my profession?

CLAIRE: You might practice closing both.

SCHILL (*Laughs*): What a sense of humor, eh?

BURGOMASTER (*Puts on the top hat*): Permit me to present my grandchildren, gracious lady. Hermine and Adolphine. There's only my wife still to come.

> (*He wipes the perspiration from his brow, and replaces the hat.
> The little girls present the roses with elaborate curtsies*)

CLAIRE: Thank you, my dears. Congratulations, Burgomaster. Extraordinary children.

> (*She plants the roses in* PEDRO's *arms. The* BURGOMASTER *secretly passes his tophat to the* PASTOR, *who puts it on*)

BURGOMASTER: Our pastor, madame.

(*The* PASTOR *takes off the hat and bows*)

CLAIRE: Ah. The pastor. How do you do? Do you give consolation to the dying?

PASTOR (*A bit puzzled*): That is part of my ministry, yes.

CLAIRE: And to those who are condemned to death?

PASTOR: Capital punishment has been abolished in this country, madame.

CLAIRE: I see. Well, it could be restored, I suppose.

(*The* PASTOR *hands back the hat. He shrugs his shoulders in confusion*)

SCHILL (*Laughs*): What an original sense of humor!

(*All laugh, a little blankly*)

CLAIRE: Well, I can't sit here all day—I should like to see the town.

(*The* BURGOMASTER *offers his arm*)

BURGOMASTER: May I have the honor, gracious lady?

CLAIRE: Thank you, but these legs are not what they were. This one was broken in five places.

SCHILL (*Full of concern*): My kitten!

CLAIRE: When my airplane bumped into a mountain in Afghanistan. All the others were killed. Even the pilot. But as you see, I survived. I don't fly any more.

SCHILL: But you're as strong as ever now.

CLAIRE: Stronger.

BURGOMASTER: Never fear, gracious lady. The town doctor has a car.

CLAIRE: I never ride in motors.

BURGOMASTER: You never ride in motors?

CLAIRE: Not since my Ferrari crashed in Hong Kong.

SCHILL: But how do you travel, then, little witch? On a broom?

CLAIRE: Mike—Max! (*She claps her hands. Two huge bodyguards come in, left, carrying a sedan chair. She sits in it*) I travel this way—a bit antiquated, of course. But perfectly safe. Ha! Ha! Aren't they magnificent? Mike and Max. I bought them in America. They were in jail, condemned to the chair. I had them pardoned. Now they're condemned to my chair. I paid fifty thousand dollars apiece for them. You couldn't get them now for twice the sum. The sedan chair comes from the Louvre. I fancied it so much that the President of France gave it to me. The French are so impulsive, don't you think so, Anton? Go!

(MIKE *and* MAX *start to carry her off*)

BURGOMASTER: You wish to visit the cathedral? And the old town hall?

CLAIRE: No. The great barn. And the forest of Konradsweil. I wish to go with Anton and visit our old haunts once again.

THE PASTOR: Very touching.

CLAIRE (*To the butler*): Will you send my luggage and the coffin to the Golden Apostle?

BURGOMASTER: The coffin?

CLAIRE: Yes. I brought one with me. Go!

TEACHER: Hip-hip—

ALL: Hurrah! Hip-hip, hurrah! Hurrah!

(*They bear off in the direction of the town. The* TOWNSPEOPLE *burst into cheers. The church bell rings*)

BURGOMASTER: Ah, thank God—the bell at last.

(*The* POLICEMAN *is about to follow the others, when the two* BLIND MEN *appear. They are not young, yet they seem childish— a strange effect. Though they are of different height and features, they are dressed exactly alike, and so create the effect of being twins. They walk slowly, feeling their way. Their voices, when they speak, are curiously high and flutelike, and they have a curious trick of repetition of phrases*)

FIRST BLIND MAN: We're in—

BOTH BLIND MEN: Güllen.

FIRST MAN: We breathe—

SECOND BLIND MAN: We breathe—

BOTH BLIND MEN: We breathe the air, the air of Güllen.

POLICEMAN (*Startled*): Who are you?

FIRST BLIND MAN: We belong to the lady.

SECOND BLIND MAN: We belong to the lady. She calls us—

FIRST BLIND MAN: Kobby.

SECOND BLIND MAN: And Lobby.

POLICEMAN: Madame Zachanassian is staying at the Golden Apostle.

FIRST BLIND MAN: We're blind.

SECOND BLIND MAN: We're blind.

POLICEMAN: Blind? Come along with me, then. I'll take you there.

FIRST BLIND MAN: Thank you, Mr. Policeman.

SECOND BLIND MAN: Thanks very much.

POLICEMAN: Hey! How do you know I'm a policeman, if you're blind?

BOTH BLIND MEN: By your voice. By your voice.

FIRST BLIND MAN: All policemen sound the same.

POLICEMAN: You've had a lot to do with the police, have you, little men?

FIRST BLIND MAN: Men he calls us!

BOTH BLIND MEN: Men!

POLICEMAN: What are you then?

BOTH BLIND MEN: You'll see. You'll see.

(*The* POLICEMAN *claps his hands suddenly. The* BLIND MEN *turn sharply toward the sound. The* POLICEMAN *is convinced they are blind*)

POLICEMAN: What's your trade?

BOTH BLIND MEN: We have no trade.

SECOND BLIND MAN: We play music.

FIRST BLIND MAN: We sing.

SECOND BLIND MAN: We amuse the lady.

FIRST BLIND MAN: We look after the beast.

SECOND BLIND MAN: We feed it.

FIRST BLIND MAN: We stroke it.

SECOND BLIND MAN: We take it for walks.

POLICEMAN: What beast?

BOTH BLIND MEN: You'll see—you'll see.

SECOND BLIND MAN: We give it raw meat.

FIRST BLIND MAN: And she gives us chicken and wine.

SECOND BLIND MAN: Every day—

BOTH BLIND MEN: Every day.

POLICEMAN: Rich people have strange tastes.

BOTH BLIND MEN: Strange tastes—strange tastes.

(The POLICEMAN *puts on his helmet)*

POLICEMAN: Come along, I'll take you to the lady.

(The two BLIND MEN *turn and walk off)*

BOTH BLIND MEN: We know the way—we know the way.

(The station and the little house vanish. A sign representing the Golden Apostle descends. The scene dissolves into the interior of the inn. The Golden Apostle is seen to be in the last stages of decay. The walls are cracked and moldering, and the plaster is falling from the ancient lath. A table represents the café of the inn. The BURGOMASTER *and the* TEACHER *sit at this table, drinking a glass together. A procession of* TOWNSPEOPLE, *carrying many pieces of luggage, passes. Then comes a coffin, and, last, a large box covered with a canvas. They cross the stage from right to left)*

BURGOMASTER: Trunks. Suitcases. Boxes. *(He looks up apprehensively at the ceiling)* The floor will never bear the weight. *(As the large covered box is carried in, he peers under the canvas, then draws back)* Good God!

TEACHER: Why, what's in it?

BURGOMASTER: A live panther. *(They laugh. The* BURGOMASTER *lifts his glass solemnly)* Your health, Professor. Let's hope she puts the Foundry back on its feet.

TEACHER *(Lifts his glass)*: And the Wagonworks.

BURGOMASTER: And the Golden Eagle Pencil Factory. Once that starts moving, everything else will go. *Prosit.*

(They touch glasses and drink)

TEACHER: What does she need a panther for?

BURGOMASTER: Don't ask me. The whole thing is too much for me. The Pastor had to go home and lie down.

TEACHER *(Sets down his glass)*: If you want to know the truth, she frightens me.

BURGOMASTER *(Nods gravely)*: She's a strange one.

TEACHER: You understand, Burgomaster, a man who for twenty-two years has been correcting the Latin compositions of the students of Güllen is not unaccustomed to surprises. I have seen things to make one's hair stand on end. But when this woman suddenly appeared on the platform, a shudder tore through me. It was as though out of the clear sky all at once a fury descended upon us, beating its black wings—

(*The* POLICEMAN *comes in. He mops his face*)

POLICEMAN: Ah! Now the old place is livening up a bit!

BURGOMASTER: Ah, Schultz, come and join us.

POLICEMAN: Thank you. (*He calls*) Beer!

BURGOMASTER: Well, what's the news from the front?

POLICEMAN: I'm just back from Schiller's barn. My God! What a scene! She had us all tiptoeing around in the straw as if we were in church. Nobody dared to speak above a whisper. And the way she carried on! I was so embarrassed. I let them to go to the forest by themselves.

BURGOMASTER: Does the fiancé go with them?

POLICEMAN: With his fishing rod and his landing net. In full marching order. (*He calls again*) Beer!

BURGOMASTER: That will be her seventh husband.

TEACHER: Her eighth.

BURGOMASTER: But what does she expect to find in the Konradsweil forest?

POLICEMAN: The same thing she expected to find in the old barn, I suppose. The—the—

TEACHER: The ashes of her youthful love.

POLICEMAN: Exactly.

TEACHER: It's poetry.

POLICEMAN: Poetry.

TEACHER: Sheer poetry! It makes one think of Shakespeare, of Wagner. Of Romeo and Juliet.

(*The* SECOND MAN *comes in as a waiter. The* POLICEMAN *is served his beer*)

BURGOMASTER: Yes, you're right. (*Solemnly*) Gentlemen, I would like to propose a toast. To our great and good friend, Anton Schill, who is even now working on our behalf.

POLICEMAN: Yes! He's really working.

BURGOMASTER: Gentlemen, to the best-loved citizen of this town. My successor, Anton Schill!

(*They raise their glasses. At this point an unearthly scream is heard. It is the black panther howling offstage. The sign of the Golden Apostle rises out of sight. The lights go down. The inn vanishes. Only the wooden bench, on which the four men were lounging in the opening scene, is left on the stage, downstage right. The procession comes on upstage. The two bodyguards carry in* CLAIRE's *sedan chair. Next to it walks* SCHILL. PEDRO *walks behind, with his fishing rod. Last come the two* BLIND MEN *and the butler.* CLAIRE *alights*)

CLAIRE: Stop! Take my chair off somewhere else. I'm tired of looking at you. (*The bodyguards and the sedan chair go off*) Pedro darling, your brook is just a little further along down that path. Listen. You can hear it from here. Bobby, take him and show him where it is.

BOTH BLIND MEN: We'll show him the way—we'll show him the way.

(*They go off, left.* PEDRO *follows.* BOBBY *walks off, right*)

CLAIRE: Look, Anton. Our tree. There's the heart you carved in the bark long ago.

SCHILL: Yes. It's still there.

CLAIRE: How it has grown! The trunk is black and wrinkled. Why, its limbs are twice what they were. Some of them have died.

SCHILL: It's aged. But it's there.

CLAIRE: Like everything else. (*She crosses, examining other trees*) Oh, how tall they are. How long it is since I walked here, barefoot over the pine needles and the damp leaves! Look, Anton. A fawn.

SCHILL: Yes, a fawn. It's the season.

CLAIRE: I thought everything would be changed. But it's all just as we left it. This is the seat we sat on years ago. Under these branches you kissed me. And over there under the hawthorn, where the moss is soft and green, we would lie in each other's arms. It is all as it used to be. Only we have changed.

SCHILL: Not so much, little witch. I remember the first night we spent together, you ran away and I chased you till I was quite breathless—

CLAIRE: Yes.

SCHILL: Then I was angry and I was going home, when suddenly I heard you call and I looked up, and there you were sitting in a tree, laughing down at me.

CLAIRE: No. It was in the great barn. I was in the hayloft.

SCHILL: Were you?

CLAIRE: Yes. What else do you remember?

SCHILL: I remember the morning we went swimming by the waterfall, and afterwards we were lying together on the big rock in the sun, when suddenly we heard footsteps and we just had time to snatch up our clothes and run behind the bushes when the old pastor appeared and scolded you for not being in school.

CLAIRE: No. It was the schoolmaster who found us. It was Sunday and I was supposed to be in church.

SCHILL: Really?

CLAIRE: Yes. Tell me more.

SCHILL: I remember the time your father beat you, and you showed me the cuts on your back, and I swore I'd kill him. And the next day I dropped a tile from a roof top and split his head open.

CLAIRE: You missed him.

SCHILL: No!

CLAIRE: You hit old Mr Reiner.

SCHILL: Did I?

CLAIRE: Yes. I was seventeen. And you were not yet twenty. You were so handsome. You were the best-looking boy in town.

(*The two* BLIND MEN *begin playing mandolin music offstage, very softly*)

SCHILL: And you were the prettiest girl.

CLAIRE: We were made for each other.

SCHILL: So we were.

CLAIRE: But you married Mathilde Blumhard and her store, and I married old Zachanassian and his oil wells. He found me in a whorehouse in Hamburg. It was my hair that entangled him, the old golden beetle.

SCHILL: Clara!

CLAIRE (*She claps her hands*): Bobby! A cigar.

(BOBBY *appears with a leather case. He selects a cigar, puts it in a holder, lights it, and presents it to* CLAIRE)

SCHILL: My kitten smokes cigars!

CLAIRE: Yes. I adore them. Would you care for one?

SCHILL: Yes, please. I've never smoked one of those.

CLAIRE: It's a taste I acquired from old Zachanassian. Among other things. He was a real connoisseur.

SCHILL: We used to sit on this bench once, you and I, and smoke cigarettes. Do you remember?

CLAIRE: Yes. I remember.

SCHILL: The cigarettes I bought from Mathilde.

CLAIRE: No. She gave them to you for nothing.

SCHILL: Clara—don't be angry with me for marrying Mathilde.

CLAIRE: She had money.

SCHILL: But what a lucky thing for you that I did!

CLAIRE: Oh?

SCHILL: You were so young, so beautiful. You deserved a far better fate than to settle in this wretched town without any future.

CLAIRE: Yes?

SCHILL: If you had stayed in Güllen and married me, your life would have been wasted, like mine.

CLAIRE: Oh?

SCHILL: Look at me. A wretched shopkeeper in a bankrupt town!

CLAIRE: But you have your family.

SCHILL: My family! Never for a moment do they let me forget my failure, my poverty.

CLAIRE: Mathilde has not made you happy?

SCHILL (*Shrugs*): What does it matter?

CLAIRE: And the children?

SCHILL (*Shakes his head*): They're so completely materialistic. You know, they have no interest whatever in higher things.

CLAIRE: How sad for you.

(*A moment's pause, during which only the faint tinkling of the music is heard*)

SCHILL: Yes. You know, since you went away my life has passed by like a stupid dream. I've hardly once been out of this town. A trip to a lake years ago. It rained all the time. And once five days in Berlin. That's all.

CLAIRE: The world is much the same everywhere.

SCHILL: At least you've seen it.

CLAIRE: Yes. I've seen it.

SCHILL: You've lived in it.

CLAIRE: I've lived in it. The world and I have been on very intimate terms.

SCHILL: Now that you've come back, perhaps things will change.

CLAIRE: Naturally. I certainly won't leave my native town in this condition.

SCHILL: It will take millions to put us on our feet again.

CLAIRE: I have millions.

SCHILL: One, two, three.

CLAIRE: Why not?

SCHILL: You mean—you will help us?

CLAIRE: Yes.

(*A woodpecker is heard in the distance*)

SCHILL: I knew it—I knew it. I told them you were generous. I told them you were good. Oh, my kitten, my kitten.

(*He takes her hand. She turns her head away and listens*)

CLAIRE: Listen! A woodpecker.

SCHILL: It's all just the way it was in the days when we were young and full of courage. The sun high above the pines. White clouds, piling up on one another. And the cry of the cuckoo in the distance. And the wind rustling the leaves, like the sound of surf on a beach. Just as it was years ago. If only we could roll back time and be together always.

CLAIRE: Is that your wish?

SCHILL: Yes. You left me, but you never left my heart. (*He raises her hand to his lips*) The same soft little hand.

CLAIRE: No, not quite the same. It was crushed in the plane accident. But they mended it. They mend everything nowadays.

SCHILL: Crushed? You wouldn't know it. See, another fawn.

CLAIRE: The old wood is alive with memories.

(PEDRO *appears, right, with a fish in his hand*)

PEDRO: See what I've caught, darling. See? A pike. Over two kilos.

(*The* BLIND MEN *appear onstage*)

BOTH BLIND MEN (*Clapping their hands*): A pike! A pike! Hurrah! Hurrah!

(*As the* BLIND MEN *clap their hands,* CLAIRE *and* SCHILL *exit, and the scene dissolves. The clapping of hands is taken up on all sides. The townspeople wheel in the walls of the café. A brass band strikes up a march tune. The door of the Golden Apostle descends. The townspeople bring in tables and set them with ragged tablecloths, cracked china, and glassware. There is a table in the center, upstage, flanked by two tables perpendicular to it, right and left. The* PASTOR *and the* BURGOMASTER *come in.*)

SCHILL *enters. Other townspeople filter in, left and right. One,*
the ATHLETE, *is in gymnastic costume. The applause continues*)

BURGOMASTER: She's coming! (CLAIRE *enters upstage, center, followed by*
BOBBY) The applause is meant for you, gracious lady.

CLAIRE: The band deserves it more than I. They blow from the heart. And the
human pyramid was beautiful. You, show me your muscles. (*The* ATHLETE
kneels before her) Superb. Wonderful arms, powerful hands. Have you ever
strangled a man with them?

ATHLETE: Strangled?

CLAIRE: Yes. It's perfectly simple. A little pressure in the proper place, and
the rest goes by itself. As in politics.

(*The* BURGOMASTER's *wife comes up, simpering*)

BURGOMASTER (*Presents her*): Permit me to present my wife, Madame
Zachanassian.

CLAIRE: Annette Dummermuth. The head of our class.

BURGOMASTER (*He presents another sour-looking woman*): Frau Schill.

CLAIRE: Mathilde Blumhard. I remember the way you used to follow Anton
with your eyes, from behind the shop door. You've grown a little thin and
dry, my poor Mathilde.

SCHILL: My daughter, Ottilie.

CLAIRE: Your daughter . . .

SCHILL: My son, Karl.

CLAIRE: Your son. Two of them!

(*The town* DOCTOR *comes in, right. He is a man of fifty, strong*
and stocky, with bristly black hair, a mustache, and a saber cut
on his cheek. He is wearing an old cutaway)

DOCTOR: Well, well, my old Mercedes got me here in time after all!

BURGOMASTER: Dr. Nüsslin, the town physician. Madame Zachanassian.

DOCTOR: Deeply honored, madame.

(*He kisses her hand.* CLAIRE *studies him*)

CLAIRE: It is you who signs the death certificates?

DOCTOR: Death certificates?

CLAIRE: When someone dies.

DOCTOR: Why certainly. That is one of my duties.

CLAIRE: And when the heart dies, what do you put down? Heart failure?

SCHILL (*Laughing*): What a golden sense of humor!

DOCTOR: Bit grim, wouldn't you say?

SCHILL (*Whispers*): Not at all, not at all. She's promised us a million.

BURGOMASTER (*Turns his head*): What?

SCHILL: A million!

ALL (*Whisper*): A million!

(CLAIRE *turns toward them*)

CLAIRE: Burgomaster.

BURGOMASTER: Yes?

CLAIRE: I'm hungry. (*The girls and the waiter fill glasses and bring food. There is a general stir. All take their places at the tables*) Are you going to make a speech?

> (*The* BURGOMASTER *bows.* CLAIRE *sits next to the* BURGO-
> MASTER. *The* BURGOMASTER *rises, tapping his knife on his glass.*
> *He is radiant with good will. All applaud*)

BURGOMASTER: Gracious lady and friends. Gracious lady, it is now many years since you first left your native town of Güllen, which was founded by the Elector Hasso and which nestles in the green slope between the forest of Konradsweil and the beautiful valley of Pückenried. Much has taken place in this time, much that is evil.

TEACHER: That's true.

BURGOMASTER: The world is not what it was; it has become harsh and bitter, and we too have had our share of harshness and bitterness. But in all this time, dear lady, we have never forgotten our little Clara. (*Applause*) Many years ago you brightened the town with your pretty face as a child, and now once again you brighten it with your presence. (*Polite applause*) We haven't forgotten you, and we haven't forgotten your family. Your mother, beautiful and robust even in her old age—(*He looks for his notes on the table*)—although unfortunately taken from us in the bloom of her youth by an infirmity of the lungs. Your respected father, Siegfried Wäscher, the builder, an example of whose work next to our railway station is often visited—(SCHILL *covers his face*)—that is to say, admired—a lasting monument of local design and local workmanship. And you, gracious lady, whom we remember as a golden-haired—(*He looks at her*)—little red-headed sprite romping around our peaceful streets—on your way to school—which of us does not treasure your memory? (*He pokes nervously at his notebook*) We well remember your scholarly attainments—

TEACHER: Yes.

BURGOMASTER: Natural history . . . Extraordinary sense of justice . . . And, above all, your supreme generosity. (*Great applause*) We shall never forget how you once spent the whole of your little savings to buy a sack of potatoes for a poor starving widow who was in need of food. Gracious lady, ladies and gentlemen, today our little Clara has become the world-famous Claire Zachanassian who has founded hospitals, soup kitchens, charitable institutes, art projects, libraries, nurseries, and schools, and now that she has at last once more returned to the town of her birth, sadly fallen as it is, I say in the name of all her loving friends who have sorely missed her: Long live our Clara!

ALL: Long live our Clara!

> (*Cheers. Music. Fanfare. Applause,* CLAIRE *rises*)

CLAIRE: Mr. Burgomaster. Fellow townsmen. I am greatly moved by the nature of your welcome and the disinterested joy which you have manifested on the occasion of my visit to my native town. I was not quite the child the Burgomaster described in his gracious address . . .

BURGOMASTER: Too modest, madame.

CLAIRE: In school I was beaten—

TEACHER: Not by me.

CLAIRE: And the sack of potatoes which I presented to Widow Boll, I stole with the help of Anton Schill, not to save the old trull from starvation, but so that for once I might sleep with Anton in a real bed instead of under the trees of the forest. (*The townspeople look grave, embarrassed*) Nevertheless, I shall try to deserve your good opinion. In memory of the seventeen years I spent among you, I am prepared to hand over as a gift to the town of Güllen the sum of one billion marks. Five hundred million to the town, and five hundred million to be divided per capita among the citizens.

(There is a moment of dead silence)

BURGOMASTER: A billion marks?

CLAIRE: On one condition.

> (*Suddenly a movement of uncontrollable joy breaks out. People jump on chairs, dance about, yell excitedly. The* ATHLETE *turns handsprings in front of the speaker's table*)

SCHILL: Oh, Clara, you astonishing, incredible, magnificent woman! What a heart! What a gesture! Oh—my little witch!

(He kisses her hand)

BURGOMASTER (*Holds up his arms for order*): Quiet! Quiet, please! On one condition, the gracious lady said. Now, madame, may we know what that condition is?

CLAIRE: I will tell you. In exchange for my billion marks, I want justice.

(Silence)

BURGOMASTER: Justice, madame?

CLAIRE: I wish to buy justice.

BURGOMASTER: But justice cannot be bought, madame.

CLAIRE: Everything can be bought.

BURGOMASTER: I don't understand at all.

CLAIRE: Bobby, step forward.

> (*The butler goes to the center of the stage. He takes off his dark glasses and turns his face with a solemn air*)

BOBBY: Does anyone here present recognize me?

FRAU SCHILL: Hofer! Hofer!

ALL: Who? What's that?

TEACHER: Not Chief Magistrate Hofer?

BOBBY: Exactly. Chief Magistrate Hofer. When Madame Zachanassian was a girl, I was presiding judge at the criminal court of Güllen. I served there until twenty-five years ago, when Madame Zachanassian offered me the opportunity of entering her service as butler. I accepted. You may consider it a strange employment for a member of the magistracy, but the salary—

(CLAIRE bangs the mallet on the table)

CLAIRE: Come to the point.

BOBBY: You have heard Madame Zachanassian's offer. She will give you a billion marks—when you have undone the injustice that she suffered at your hands here in Güllen as a girl.

(*All murmur*)

BURGOMASTER: Injustice at our hands? Impossible!

BOBBY: Anton Schill . . .

SCHILL: Yes?

BOBBY: Kindly stand.

(SCHILL *rises. He smiles, as if puzzled. He shrugs*)

SCHILL: Yes?

BOBBY: In those days, a bastardy case was tried before me. Madame Claire Zachanassian, at that time called Clara Wäscher, charged you with being the father of her illegitimate child. (*Silence*) You denied the charge. And produced two witnesses in your support.

SCHILL: That's ancient history. An absurd business. We were children. Who remembers?

CLAIRE: Where are the blind men?

BOTH BLIND MEN: Here we are. Here we are.

(MIKE *and* MAX *push them forward*)

BOBBY: You recognize these men, Anton Schill?

SCHILL: I never saw them before in my life. What are they?

BOTH BLIND MEN: We've changed. We've changed.

BOBBY: What were your names in your former life?

FIRST BLIND MAN: I was Jacob Hueblein. Jacob Hueblein.

SECOND BLIND MAN: I was Ludwig Sparr. Ludwig Sparr.

BOBBY (*To* SCHILL): Well?

SCHILL: These names mean nothing to me.

BOBBY: Jacob Hueblein and Ludwig Sparr, do you recognize the defendant?

FIRST BLIND MAN: We're blind.

SECOND BLIND MAN: We're blind.

SCHILL: Ha-ha-ha!

BOBBY: By his voice?

BOTH BLIND MEN: By his voice. By his voice.

BOBBY: At that trial, I was the judge. And you?

BOTH BLIND MEN: We were the witnesses.

BOBBY: And what did you testify on that occasion?

FIRST BLIND MAN: That we had slept with Clara Wäscher.

SECOND BLIND MAN: Both of us. Many times.

BOBBY: And was it true?

FIRST BLIND MAN: No.

SECOND BLIND MAN: We swore falsely.

BOBBY: And why did you swear falsely?

FIRST BLIND MAN: Anton Schill bribed us.

SECOND BLIND MAN: He bribed us.

BOBBY: With what?

BOTH BLIND MEN: With a bottle of schnapps.

BOBBY: And now tell the people what happened to you. (*They hesitate and whimper*) Speak!

FIRST BLIND MAN (*In a low voice*): She tracked us down.

BOBBY: Madame Zachanassian tracked them down. Jacob Hueblein was found in Canada. Ludwig Sparr in Australia. And when she found you, what did she do to you?

SECOND BLIND MAN: She handed us over to Mike and Max.

BOBBY: And what did Mike and Max do to you?

FIRST BLIND MAN: They made us what you see.

> (*The* BLIND MEN *cover their faces.* MIKE *and* MAX *push them off*)

BOBBY: And there you have it. We are all present in Güllen once again. The plaintiff. The defendant. The two false witnesses. The judge. Many years have passed. Does the plaintiff have anything further to add?

CLAIRE: There is nothing to add.

BOBBY: And the defendant?

SCHILL: Why are you doing this? It was all dead and buried.

BOBBY: What happened to the child that was born?

CLAIRE (*In a low voice*): It lived a year.

BOBBY: And what happened to you?

CLAIRE: I became a whore.

BOBBY: Why?

CLAIRE: The judgment of the court left me no alternative. No one would trust me. No one would give me work.

BOBBY: So. And now, what is the nature of the reparation you demand?

CLAIRE: I want the life of Anton Schill.

> (FRAU SCHILL *springs to Anton's side. She puts her arms around him. The children rush to him. He breaks away*)

FRAU SCHILL: Anton! No! No!

SCHILL: No— No— She's joking. That happened long ago. That's all forgotten.

CLAIRE: Nothing is forgotten. Neither the mornings in the forest, nor the nights in the great barn, nor the bedroom in the cottage, nor your treachery at the end. You said this morning that you wished that time might be rolled back. Very well—I have rolled it back. And now it is I who will buy justice. You bought it with a bottle of schnapps. I am willing to pay one billion marks.

> (*The* BURGOMASTER *stands up, very pale and dignified*)

BURGOMASTER: Madame Zachanassian, we are not in the jungle. We are in Europe. We may be poor, but we are not heathens. In the name of the town of Güllen, I decline your offer. In the name of humanity. We shall never accept.

> (*All applaud wildly. The applause turns into a sinister rhythmic beat. As* CLAIRE *rises, it dies away. She looks at the crowd, then at the* BURGOMASTER)

CLAIRE: Thank you, Burgomaster. (*She stares at him a long moment*) I can wait.

> (*She turns and walks off*)

Curtain

Act Two

The façade of the Golden Apostle, with a balcony on which chairs and a table are set out. To the right of the inn is a sign which reads: "ANTON SCHILL, HANDLUNG."[1] *Under the sign the shop is represented by a broken counter. Behind the counter are some shelves with tobacco, cigarettes, and liquor bottles. There are two milk cans. The shop door is imaginary, but each entrance is indicated by a doorbell with a tinny sound.*

It is early morning.

SCHILL *is sweeping the shop. The* SON *has a pan and brush and also sweeps. The* DAUGHTER *is dusting. They are singing "The Happy Wanderer."*

SCHILL: Karl—

(KARL *crosses with a dustpan.* SCHILL *sweeps dust into the pan. The doorbell rings. The* THIRD MAN *appears carrying a crate of eggs*)

THIRD MAN: 'Morning.

SCHILL: Ah, good morning, Wechsler.

THIRD MAN: Twelve dozen eggs, medium brown. Right?

SCHILL: Take them, Karl (*The* SON *puts the crate in a corner*) Did they deliver the milk yet?

SON: Before you came down.

THIRD MAN: Eggs are going up again, Herr Schill. First of the month.

(*He gives* SCHILL *a slip to sign*)

SCHILL: What? Again? And who's going to buy them?

THIRD MAN: Fifty pfennig a dozen.

SCHILL: I'll have to cancel my order, that's all.

THIRD MAN: That's up to you, Herr Schill.

(SCHILL *signs the slip*)

SCHILL: There's nothing else to do. (*He hands back the slip*) And how's the family?

THIRD MAN: Oh, scraping along. Maybe now things will get better.

SCHILL: Maybe.

THIRD MAN: (*Going*) 'Morning.

SCHILL: Close the door. Don't let the flies in. (*The children resume their singing*) Now, listen to me, children. I have a little piece of good news for you. I didn't mean to speak of it yet awhile, but well, why not? Who do you suppose is going to be the next Burgomaster? Eh? (*They look up at him*) Yes, in spite of everything. It's settled. It's official. What an honor for the family, eh? Especially at a time like this. To say nothing of the salary and the rest of it.

SON: Burgomaster!

SCHILL: Burgomaster. (*The* SON *shakes him warmly by the hand. The*

---

[1] "Anton Schill, Merchandise."

DAUGHTER *kisses him*) You see, you don't have to be entirely ashamed of your father. (*Silence*) Is your mother coming down to breakfast soon?

DAUGHTER: Mother's tired. She's going to stay upstairs.

SCHILL: You have a good mother, at least. There you are lucky. Oh, well, if she wants to rest, let her rest. We'll have breakfast together, the three of us. I'll fry some eggs and open a tin of the American ham. This morning we're going to breakfast like kings.

SON: I'd like to, only—I can't.

SCHILL: You've got to eat, you know.

SON: I've got to run down to the station. One of the laborers is sick. They said they could use me.

SCHILL: You want to work on the rails in all this heat? That's no work for a son of mine.

SON: Look, Father, we can use the money.

SCHILL: Well, if you feel you have to.

(*The son goes to the door. The* DAUGHTER *moves toward* SCHILL)

DAUGHTER: I'm sorry, Father. I have to go too.

SCHILL: You too? And where is the young lady going, if I may be so bold?

DAUGHTER: There may be something for me at the employment agency.

SCHILL: Employment agency?

DAUGHTER: It's important to get there early.

SCHILL: All right. I'll have something nice for you when you get home.

SON *and* DAUGHTER (*Salute*): Good day, Burgomaster.

(*The* SON *and* DAUGHTER *go out. The* FIRST MAN *comes into* SCHILL's *shop. Mandolin and guitar music are heard offstage*)

SCHILL: Good morning, Hofbauer.

FIRST MAN: Cigarettes. (SCHILL *takes a pack from the shelf*) Not those. I'll have the green today.

SCHILL: They cost more.

FIRST MAN: Put it in the book.

SCHILL: What?

FIRST MAN: Charge it.

SCHILL: Well, all right, I'll make an exception this time—seeing it's you, Hofbauer.

(SCHILL *writes in his cash book*)

FIRST MAN (*Opening the pack of cigarettes*): Who's that playing out there?

SCHILL: The two blind men.

FIRST MAN: They play well.

SCHILL: To hell with them.

FIRST MAN: They make you nervous? (SCHILL *shrugs. The* FIRST MAN *lights a cigarette*) She's getting ready for the wedding, I hear.

SCHILL: Yes. So they say.

(*Enter the* FIRST *and* SECOND WOMAN. *They cross to the counter*)

FIRST WOMAN: Good morning, good morning.

SECOND WOMAN: Good morning.

FIRST MAN: Good morning.

SCHILL: Good morning, ladies.

FIRST WOMAN: Good morning, Herr Schill.

SECOND WOMAN: Good morning.

FIRST WOMAN: Milk please, Herr Schill.

SCHILL: Milk.

SECOND WOMAN: And milk for me too.

SCHILL: A liter of milk each. Right away.

FIRST WOMAN: Whole milk, please, Herr Schill.

SCHILL: Whole milk?

SECOND WOMAN: Yes. Whole milk, please.

SCHILL: Whole milk, I can only give you half a liter each of whole milk.

FIRST WOMAN: All right.

SCHILL: Half a liter of whole milk here, and half a liter of whole milk here. There you are.

FIRST WOMAN: And butter please, a quarter kilo.

SCHILL: Butter, I haven't any butter. I can give you some very nice lard?

FIRST WOMAN: No. Butter.

SCHILL: Goose fat? (*The* FIRST WOMAN *shakes her head*) Chicken fat?

FIRST WOMAN: Butter.

SCHILL: Butter. Now, wait a minute, though. I have a tin of imported butter here somewhere. Ah. There you are. No, sorry, she asked first, but I can order some for you from Kalberstadt tomorrow.

SECOND WOMAN: And white bread.

SCHILL: White bread.

(He takes a loaf and a knife)

SECOND WOMAN: The whole loaf.

SCHILL: But a whole loaf would cost . . .

SECOND WOMAN: Charge it.

SCHILL: Charge it?

FIRST WOMAN: And a package of milk chocolate.

SCHILL: Package of milk chocolate—right away.

SECOND WOMAN: One for me, too, Herr Schill.

SCHILL: And a package of milk chocolate for you, too.

FIRST WOMAN: We'll eat it here, if you don't mind.

SCHILL: Yes, please do.

SECOND WOMAN: It's so cool at the back of the shop.

SCHILL: Charge it?

WOMEN: Of course.

SCHILL: All for one, one for all.

(The SECOND MAN *enters)*

SECOND MAN: Good morning.

THE TWO WOMEN: Good morning.

SCHILL: Good morning, Helmesberger.

SECOND MAN: It's going to be a hot day.

SCHILL: Phew!

SECOND MAN: How's business?

SCHILL: Fabulous. For a while no one came, and now all of a sudden I'm running a luxury trade.

SECOND MAN: Good!

SCHILL: Oh, I'll never forget the way you all stood by me at the Golden Apostle in spite of your need, in spite of everything. That was the finest hour of my life.

FIRST MAN: We're not heathen, you know.

SECOND MAN: We're behind you, my boy; the whole town's behind you.

FIRST MAN: As firm as a rock.

FIRST WOMAN (*Munching her chocolate*): As firm as a rock, Herr Schill.

BOTH WOMEN: As firm as a rock.

SECOND MAN: There's no denying it—you're the most popular man in town.

FIRST MAN: The most important.

SECOND MAN: And in the spring, God willing, you will be our Burgomaster.

FIRST MAN: Sure as a gun.

ALL: Sure as a gun.

   (*Enter* PEDRO *with fishing equipment and a fish in his landing net*)

PEDRO: Would you please weigh my fish for me?

SCHILL (*Weighs it*): Two kilos.

PEDRO: Is that all?

SCHILL: Two kilos exactly.

PEDRO: Two kilos!

                    (*He gives* SCHILL *a tip and exits*)

SECOND WOMAN: The fiancé.

FIRST WOMAN: They're to be married this week. It will be a tremendous wedding.

SECOND WOMAN: I saw his picture in the paper.

FIRST WOMAN (*Sighs*): Ah, what a man!

SECOND MAN: Give me a bottle of schnapps.

SCHILL: The usual?

SECOND MAN: No, cognac.

SCHILL: Cognac? But cognac costs twenty-two marks fifty.

SECOND MAN: We all have to splurge a little now and again—

SCHILL: Here you are. Three Star.

SECOND MAN: And a package of pipe tobacco.

SCHILL: Black or blond?

SECOND MAN: English.

SCHILL: English! But that makes twenty-three marks eighty.

SECOND MAN: Chalk it up.

SCHILL: Now, look. I'll make an exception this week. Only, you will have to pay me the moment your unemployment check comes in. I don't want to be kept waiting. (*Suddenly*) Helmesberger, are those new shoes you're wearing?

SECOND MAN: Yes, what about it?

SCHILL: You too, Hofbauer. Yellow shoes! Brand new!

FIRST MAN: So?

SCHILL (*To the women*): And you. You all have new shoes! New shoes!

FIRST WOMAN: A person can't walk around forever in the same old shoes.

SECOND WOMAN: Shoes wear out.

SCHILL: And the money. Where does the money come from?

FIRST WOMAN: We got them on credit, Herr Schill.

SECOND WOMAN: On credit.

SCHILL: On credit? And where all of a sudden do you get credit?

SECOND MAN: Everybody gives credit now.

FIRST WOMAN: You gave us credit yourself.

SCHILL: And what are you going to pay with? Eh? (*They are all silent.* SCHILL *advances upon them threateningly*) With what? Eh? With what? With what? (*Suddenly he understands. He takes his apron off quickly, flings it on the counter, gets his jacket, and walks off with an air of determination. Now the shop sign vanishes. The shelves are pushed off. The lights go up on the balcony of the Golden Apostle, and the balcony unit itself moves forward into the optical center.* CLAIRE *and* BOBBY *step out on the balcony.* CLAIRE *sits down.* BOBBY *serves coffee*)

CLAIRE: A lovely autumn morning. A silver haze on the streets and a violet sky above. Count Holk would have liked this. Remember him, Bobby? My third husband?

BOBBY: Yes, madame.

CLAIRE: Horrible man!

BOBBY: Yes, madame.

CLAIRE: Where is Monsieur Pedro? Is he up yet?

BOBBY: Yes, madame. He's fishing.

CLAIRE: Already? What a singular passion!

(PEDRO comes in with the fish)

PEDRO: Good morning, my love.

CLAIRE: Pedro! There you are.

PEDRO: Look, my darling. Four kilos!

CLAIRE: A jewel! I'll have it grilled for your lunch. Give it to Bobby.

PEDRO: Ah—it is so wonderful here! I like your little town.

CLAIRE: Oh, do you?

PEDRO: Yes. These people, they are all so—what is the word?

CLAIRE: Simple, honest, hard-working, decent.

PEDRO: But, my angel, you are a mind reader. That's just what I was going to say—however did you guess?

CLAIRE: I know them.

PEDRO: Yet when we arrived it was all so dirty, so—what is the word?

CLAIRE: Shabby.

PEDRO: Exactly. But now everywhere you go, you see them busy as bees, cleaning their streets—

CLAIRE: Repairing their houses, sweeping—dusting—hanging new curtains in the windows—singing as they work.

PEDRO: But you astonishing, wonderful woman! You can't see all that from here.

CLAIRE: I know them. And in their gardens—I am sure that in their gardens they are manuring the soil for the spring.

PEDRO: My angel, you know everything. This morning on my way fishing I said to myself, look at them all manuring their gardens. It is extraordinary—and it's all because of you. Your return has given them a new—what is the word?

CLAIRE: Lease on life?

PEDRO: Precisely.

CLAIRE: The town was dying, it's true. But a town doesn't have to die. I think they realize that now. People die, not towns. Bobby! (BOBBY *appears*) A cigar.

> (*The lights fade on the balcony, which moves back upstage. Somewhat to the right, a sign descends. It reads: "Polizei." The* POLICEMAN *pushes a desk under it. This, with the bench, becomes the police station. He places a bottle of beer and a glass on the desk, and goes to hang up his coat offstage. The telephone rings*)

POLICEMAN: Schultz speaking. Yes, we have a couple of rooms for the night. No, not for rent. This is not the hotel. This is the Güllen police station.

> (*He laughs and hangs up.* SCHILL *comes in. He is evidently nervous*)

SCHILL: Schultz.

POLICEMAN: Hello, Schill. Come in. Sit down. Beer?

SCHILL: Please.

> (*He drinks thirstily*)

POLICEMAN: What can I do for you?

SCHILL: I want you to arrest Madame Zachanassian.

POLICEMAN: Eh?

SCHILL: I said I want you to arrest Madame Zachanassian.

POLICEMAN: What the hell are you talking about?

SCHILL: I ask you to arrest this woman at once.

POLICEMAN: What offense has the lady committed?

SCHILL: You know perfectly well. She offered a billion marks—

POLICEMAN: And you want her arrested for that?

> (*He pours beer into his glass*)

SCHILL: Schultz! It's your duty.

SCHULTZ: Extraordinary! Extraordinary idea!

> (*He drinks his beer*)

SCHILL: I'm speaking to you as your next Burgomaster.

POLICEMAN: Schill, that's true. The lady offered us a billion marks. But that doesn't entitle us to take police action against her.

SCHILL: Why not?

POLICEMAN: In order to be arrested, a person must first commit a crime.

SCHILL: Incitement to murder.

POLICEMAN: Incitement to murder is a crime. I agree.

SCHILL: Well?

POLICEMAN: And such a proposal—if serious—constitutes an assault.

SCHILL: That's what I mean.

POLICEMAN: But her offer can't be serious.

SCHILL: Why?

POLICEMAN: The price is too high. In a case like yours, one pays a thousand marks, at the most two thousand. But not a billion! That's ridiculous. And even if she meant it, that would only prove she was out of her mind. And that's not a matter for the police.

SCHILL: Whether she's out of her mind or not, the danger to me is the same. That's obvious.

POLICEMAN: Look, Schill, you show us where anyone threatens your life in any way—say, for instance, a man points a gun at you—and we'll be there in a flash.

SCHILL (*Gets up*): So I'm to wait till someone points a gun at me?

POLICEMAN: Pull yourself together, Schill. We're all for you in this town.

SCHILL: I wish I could believe it.

POLICEMAN: You don't believe it?

SCHILL: No. No, I don't. All of a sudden my customers are buying white bread, whole milk, butter, imported tobacco. What does it mean?

POLICEMAN: It means business is picking up.

SCHILL: Helmesberger lives on the dole; he hasn't earned anything in five years. Today he bought French cognac.

POLICEMAN: I'll have to try your cognac one of these days.

SCHILL: And shoes. They all have new shoes.

POLICEMAN: And what have you got against new shoes? I'm wearing a new pair myself.

(*He holds out his foot*)

SCHILL: You too?

POLICEMAN: Why not?

SECOND MAN: (He pours out the rest of his beer)

SCHILL: Is that Pilsen you're drinking now?

POLICEMAN: It's the only thing.

SCHILL: You used to drink the local beer.

POLICEMAN: Hogwash.

(*Radio music is heard offstage*)

SCHILL: Listen. You hear?

POLICEMAN: "The Merry Widow." Yes.

SCHILL: No. It's a radio.

POLICEMAN: That's Bergholzer's radio.

SCHILL: Bergholzer!

POLICEMAN: You're right. He should close his window when he plays it. I'll make a note to speak to him.

(He makes a note in his notebook)

SCHILL: And how can Bergholzer pay for a radio?

POLICEMAN: That's his business.

SCHILL: And you, Schultz, with your new shoes and your imported beer—how are you going to pay for them?

POLICEMAN: That's my business. *(His telephone rings. He picks it up)* Police Station, Güllen. What? What? Where? Where? How? Right, we'll deal with it.

(He hangs up)

SCHILL *(He speaks during the* POLICEMAN's *telephone conversation)*: Schultz, listen. No. Schultz, please—listen to me. Don't you see they're all . . . Listen, please. Look, Schultz. They're all running up debts. And out of these debts comes this sudden prosperity. And out of this prosperity comes the absolute need to kill me.

POLICEMAN *(Putting on his jacket)*: You're imagining things.

SCHILL: All she has to do is to sit on her balcony and wait.

POLICEMAN: Don't be a child.

SCHILL: You're all waiting.

POLICEMAN *(Snaps a loaded clip into the magazine of a rifle)*: Look, Schill, you can relax. The police are here for your protection. They know their job. Let anyone, any time, make the slightest threat to your life, and all you have to do is let us know. We'll do the rest . . . Now, don't worry.

SCHILL: No, I won't.

POLICEMAN: And don't upset yourself. All right?

SCHILL: Yes. I won't. *(Then suddenly, in a low tone)* You have a new gold tooth in your mouth!

POLICEMAN: What are you talking about?

SCHILL *(Taking the* POLICEMAN's *head in his hands, and forcing his lips open)* A brand new, shining gold tooth.

POLICEMAN *(Breaks away and involuntarily levels the gun at* SCHILL): Are you crazy? Look, I've no time to waste. Madame Zachanassian's panther's broken loose.

SCHILL: Panther?

POLICEMAN: Yes, it's at large. I've got to hunt it down.

SCHILL: You're not hunting a panther and you know it. It's me you're hunting!

(The POLICEMAN *clicks on the safety and lowers the gun)*

POLICEMAN: Schill! Take my advice. Go home. Lock the door. Keep out of everyone's way. That way you'll be safe. Cheer up! Good times are just around the corner!

(The lights dim in this area and light up on the balcony. PEDRO *is lounging in a chair.* CLAIRE *is smoking)*

PEDRO: Oh, this little town oppresses me.

CLAIRE: Oh, does it? So you've changed your mind?

PEDRO: It is true, I find it charming, delightful—

CLAIRE: Picturesque.

PEDRO: Yes. After all, it's the place where you were born. But it is too quiet for me. Too provincial. Too much like all small towns everywhere. These people—look at them. They fear nothing, they desire nothing, they strive for nothing. They have everything they want. They are asleep.

CLAIRE: Perhaps one day they will come to life again.

PEDRO: My God—do I have to wait for that?

CLAIRE: Yes, you do. Why don't you go back to your fishing?

PEDRO: I think I will.

(PEDRO *turns to go*)

CLAIRE: Pedro.

PEDRO: Yes, my love?

CLAIRE: Telephone the president of Hambro's Bank.[2] Ask him to transfer a billion marks to my current account.

PEDRO: A billion? Yes, my love.

(*He goes. The lights fade on the balcony. A sign is flown in. It reads:* "Rathaus."[3] *The* THIRD MAN *crosses the stage, right to left, wheeling a new television set on a hand truck. The counter of* SCHILL's *shop is transformed into the* BURGOMASTER's *office. The* BURGOMASTER *comes in. He takes a revolver from his pocket, examines it and sets it down on the desk. He sits down and starts writing.* SCHILL *knocks*)

BURGOMASTER: Come in.

SCHILL: I must have a word with you, Burgomaster.

BURGOMASTER: Ah, Schill. Sit down, my friend.

SCHILL: Man to man. As your successor.

BURGOMASTER: But of course. Naturally.

(SCHILL *remains standing. He looks at the revolver*)

SCHILL: Is that a gun?

BURGOMASTER: Madame Zachanassian's black panther's broken loose. It's been seen near the cathedral. It's as well to be prepared.

SCHILL: Oh, yes. Of course.

BURGOMASTER: I've sent out a call for all able-bodied men with firearms. The streets have been cleared. The children have been kept in school. We don't want any accidents.

SCHILL (*Suspiciously*): You're making quite a thing of it.

BURGOMASTER (*Shrugs*): Naturally. A panther is a dangerous beast. Well? What's on your mind? Speak out. We're old friends.

SCHILL: That's a good cigar you're smoking, Burgomaster.

---

[2] One of the principal banks of England.

[3] "City Hall."

BURGOMASTER: Yes. Havana.

SCHILL: You used to smoke something else.

BURGOMASTER: Fortuna.

SCHILL: Cheaper.

BURGOMASTER: Too strong.

SCHILL: A new tie? Silk?

BURGOMASTER: Yes. Do you like it?

SCHILL: And have you also bought new shoes?

BURGOMASTER (*Brings his feet out from under the desk*): Why, yes. I ordered a new pair from Kalberstadt. Extraordinary! However did you guess?

SCHILL: That's why I'm here.

(*The* THIRD MAN *knocks*)

BURGOMASTER: Come in.

THIRD MAN: The new typewriter, sir.

BURGOMASTER: Put it on the table. (*The* THIRD MAN *sets it down and goes*) What's the matter with you? My dear fellow, aren't you well?

SCHILL: It's you who don't seem well, Burgomaster.

BURGOMASTER: What do you mean?

SCHILL: You look pale.

BURGOMASTER: I?

SCHILL: Your hands are trembling. (*The* BURGOMASTER *involuntarily hides his hands*) Are you frightened?

BURGOMASTER: What have I to be afraid of?

SCHILL: Perhaps this sudden prosperity alarms you.

BURGOMASTER: Is prosperity a crime?

SCHILL: That depends on how you pay for it.

BURGOMASTER: You'll have to forgive me, Schill, but I really haven't the slightest idea what you're talking about. Am I supposed to feel like a criminal every time I order a new typewriter?

SCHILL: Do you?

BURGOMASTER: Well, I hope you haven't come here to talk about a new typewriter. Now, what was it you wanted?

SCHILL: I have come to claim the protection of the authorities.

BURGOMASTER: Ei! Against whom?

SCHILL: You know against whom.

BURGOMASTER: You don't trust us?

SCHILL: That woman has put a price on my head.

BURGOMASTER: If you don't feel safe, why don't you go to the police?

SCHILL: I have just come from the police.

BURGOMASTER: And?

SCHILL: The chief has a new gold tooth in his mouth.

BURGOMASTER: A new—? Oh, Schill, really! You're forgetting. This is Güllen, the town of humane traditions. Goethe slept here. Brahms composed a quartet. You must have faith in us. This is a law-abiding community.

SCHILL: Then arrest this woman who wants to have me killed.

BURGOMASTER: Look here, Schill. God knows the lady has every right to be angry with you. What you did there wasn't very pretty. You forced two decent lads to perjure themselves and had a young girl thrown out on the streets.

SCHILL: That young girl owns half the world.

(*A moment's silence*)

BURGOMASTER: Very well, then, we'll speak frankly.

SCHILL: That's why I'm here.

BURGOMASTER: Man to man, just as you said. (*He clears his throat*) Now— after what you did, you have no moral right to say a word against this lady. And I advise you not to try. Also—I regret to have to tell you this—there is no longer any question of your being elected Burgomaster.

SCHILL: Is that official?

BURGOMASTER: Official.

SCHILL: I see.

BURGOMASTER: The man who is chosen to exercise the high post of Burgomaster must have, obviously, certain moral qualifications. Qualifications which, unhappily, you no longer possess. Naturally, you may count on the esteem and friendship of the town, just as before. That goes without saying. The best thing will be to spread the mantle of silence over the whole miserable business.

SCHILL: So I'm to remain silent while they arrange my murder?

(*The* BURGOMASTER *gets up*)

BURGOMASTER (*Suddenly noble*): Now, who is arranging your murder? Give me the names and I will investigate the case at once. Unrelentingly. Well? The names?

SCHILL: You.

BURGOMASTER: I resent this. Do you think we want to kill you for money?

SCHILL: No. You don't want to kill me. But you want to have me killed.

(*The lights go down. The stage is filled with men prowling about with rifles, as if they were stalking a quarry. In the interval the* POLICEMAN's *bench and the* BURGOMASTER's *desk are shifted somewhat, so that they will compose the setting for the sacristy. The stage empties. The lights come up on the balcony.* CLAIRE *appears*)

CLAIRE: Bobby, what's going on here? What are all these men doing with guns? Whom are they hunting?

BOBBY: The black panther has escaped, madame.

CLAIRE: Who let him out?

BOBBY: Kobby and Lobby, madame.

CLAIRE: How excited they are! There may be shooting?

BOBBY: It is possible, madame.

(*The lights fade on the balcony. The sacristan comes in. He arranges the set, and puts the altar cloth on the altar. Then* SCHILL *comes on. He is looking for the* PASTOR. *The* PASTOR *enters, left. He is wearing his gown and carrying a rifle*)

SCHILL: Sorry to disturb you, Pastor.

PASTOR: God's house is open to all. (*He sees that* SCHILL *is staring at the gun*) Oh, the gun? That's because of the panther. It's best to be prepared.

SCHILL: Pastor, help me.

PASTOR: Of course. Sit down. (*He puts the rifle on the bench*) What's the trouble?

SCHILL (*Sits on the bench*): I'm frightened.

PASTOR: Frightened? Of what?

SCHILL: Of everyone. They're hunting me down like a beast.

PASTOR: Have no fear of man, Schill. Fear God. Fear not the death of the body. Fear the death of the soul. Zip up my gown behind, Sacristan.

SCHILL: I'm afraid, Pastor.

PASTOR: Put your trust in heaven, my friend.

SCHILL: You see, I'm not well. I shake. I have such pains around the heart. I sweat.

PASTOR: I know. You're passing through a profound psychic experience.

SCHILL: I'm going through hell.

PASTOR: The hell you are going through exists only within yourself. Many years ago you betrayed a girl shamefully, for money. Now you think that we shall sell you just as you sold her. No, my friend, you are projecting your guilt upon others. It's quite natural. But remember, the root of our torment lies always without ourselves, in our hearts, in our sins. When you have understood this, you can conquer the fears that oppress you; you have weapons with which to destroy them.

SCHILL: Siemethofer has bought a new washing machine.

PASTOR: Don't worry about the washing machine. Worry about your immortal soul.

SCHILL: Stockers has a television set.

PASTOR: There is also great comfort in prayer. Sacristan, the bands. (SCHILL *crosses to the altar and kneels. The sacristan ties on the* PASTOR's *bands*) Examine your conscience, Schill. Repent. Otherwise your fears will consume you. Believe me, this is the only way. We have no other. (*The church bell begins to peal.* SCHILL *seems relieved*) Now I must leave you. I have a baptism. You may stay as long as you like. Sacristan, the Bible, Liturgy, and Psalter. The child is beginning to cry. I can hear it from here. It is frightened. Let us make haste to give it the only security which this world affords.

SCHILL: A new bell?

PASTOR: Yes. Its tone is marvelous, don't you think? Full. Sonorous.

SCHILL (*Steps back in horror*): A new bell! You too, Pastor? You too?

(*The* PASTOR *clasps his hands in horror. Then he takes* SCHILL *into his arms*)

PASTOR: Oh, God, God forgive me. We are poor, weak things, all of us. Do not tempt us further into the hell in which you are burning. Go, Schill, my friend, go my brother, go while there is time.

(*The* PASTOR *goes.* SCHILL *picks up the rifle with a gesture of desperation. He goes out with it. As the lights fade, men appear with guns. Two shots are fired in the darkness. The lights come up on the balcony, which moves forward*)

CLAIRE: Bobby! What was that shooting? Have they caught the panther?

BOBBY: He is dead, madame.

CLAIRE: There were two shots.

BOBBY: The panther is dead, madame.

CLAIRE: I loved him. (*Waves* BOBBY *away*) I shall miss him.

> (*The* TEACHER *comes in with two little girls, singing. They stop under the balcony*)

TEACHER: Gracious lady, be so good as to accept our heartfelt condolences. Your beautiful panther is no more. Believe me, we are deeply pained that so tragic an event should mar your visit here. But what could we do? The panther was savage, a beast. To him our human laws could not apply. There was no other way—(SCHILL *appears with the gun. He looks dangerous. The girls run off, frightened. The* TEACHER *follows the girls*) Children—children—children!

CLAIRE: Anton, why are you frightening the children?

> (*He works the bolt, loading the chamber, and raises the gun slowly*)

SCHILL: Go away, Claire—I warn you. Go away.

CLAIRE: How strange it is, Anton! How clearly it comes back to me! The day we saw one another for the first time, do you remember? I was on a balcony then. It was a day like today, a day in autumn without a breath of wind, warm as it is now—only lately I am always cold. You stood down there and stared at me without moving. I was embarrassed. I didn't know what to do. I wanted to go back into the darkness of the room, where it was safe, but I couldn't. You stared up at me darkly, almost angrily, as if you wished to hurt me, but your eyes were full of passion. (SCHILL *begins to lower the rifle involuntarily*) Then, I don't know why, I left the balcony and I came down and stood in the street beside you. You didn't greet me, you didn't say a word, but you took my hand and we walked together out of the town into the fields, and behind us came Kobby and Lobby, like two dogs, sniveling and giggling and snarling. Suddenly you picked up a stone and hurled it at them, and they ran yelping back into the town, and we were alone. (SCHILL *has lowered the rifle completely. He moves forward toward her, as close as he can come*) That was the beginning, and everything else had to follow. There is no escape.

> (*She goes in and closes the shutters.* SCHILL *stands immobile. The* TEACHER *tiptoes in. He stares at* SCHILL, *who doesn't see him. Then he beckons to the children*)

TEACHER: Come, children, sing. Sing.

> (*They begin singing. He creeps behind* SHILL *and snatches away the rifle.* SCHILL *turns sharply. The* PASTOR *comes in*)

PASTOR: Go, Schill—go!

(SCHILL *goes out. The children continue singing, moving across the stage and off. The Golden Apostle vanishes. The crossing bell is heard. The scene dissolves into the railway-station setting, as in Act One. But there are certain changes. The timetable marked "Fahrplan" is now new, the frame freshly painted. There is a new travel poster on the station wall. It has a yellow sun and the words" "Reist in den Süden."* [4] *On the other side of the Fahrplan is another poster with the words: "Die Passionsspiele Oberammergau."* [5] *The sound of passing trains covers the scene change.* SCHILL *appears with an old valise in his hand, dressed in a shabby trench coat, his hat on his head. He looks about with a furtive air, walking slowy to the platform. Slowly, as if by chance, the townspeople enter, from all sides.* SCHILL *hesitates, stops)*

BURGOMASTER (*From upstage, center*): Good evening, Schill.

SCHILL: Good evening.

POLICEMAN: Good evening.

SCHILL: Good evening.

PAINTER (*Enters*): Good evening.

SCHILL: Good evening.

DOCTOR: Good evening.

SCHILL: Good evening.

BURGOMASTER: So you're taking a little trip?

SCHILL: Yes. A little trip.

POLICEMAN: May one ask where to?

SCHILL: I don't know.

PAINTER: Don't know?

SCHILL: To Kalberstadt.

BURGOMASTER (*With disbelief, pointing to the valise*): Kalberstadt?

SCHILL: After that—somewhere else.

PAINTER: Ah. After that somewhere else.

(*The* FOURTH MAN *walks in*)

SCHILL: I thought maybe Australia.

BURGOMASTER: Australia!

ALL: Australia!

SCHILL: I'll raise the money somehow.

BURGOMASTER: But why Australia?

POLICEMAN: What would you be doing in Australia?

SCHILL: One can't always live in the same town, year in, year out.

PAINTER: But Australia—

DOCTOR: It's a risky trip for a man of your age.

---

[4] "Travel in the South."

[5] "The Oberammergau Passion Play," portraying the suffering and death of Jesus, is performed in the south German village every ten years.

BURGOMASTER: One of the lady's little men ran off to Australia . . .

ALL: Yes.

POLICEMAN: You'll be much safer here.

PAINTER: Much!

> (SCHILL *looks about him in anguish, like a beast at bay*)

SCHILL (*Low voice*): I wrote a letter to the administration at Kaffigen.

BURGOMASTER: Yes? And?

> (*They are all intent on the answer*)

SCHILL: They didn't answer.

> (*All laugh*)

DOCTOR: Do you mean to say you don't trust old friends? That's not very flattering, you know.

BURGOMASTER: No one's going to do you any harm here.

DOCTOR: No harm here.

SCHILL: They didn't answer because our postmaster held up my letter.

PAINTER: Our postmaster? What an idea.

BURGOMASTER: The postmaster is a member of the town council.

POLICEMAN: A man of the utmost integrity.

DOCTOR: He doesn't hold up letters. What an idea?

> (*The crossing bell starts ringing*)

STATION MASTER (*Announces*): Local to Kalberstadt!

> (*The townspeople all cross down to see the train arrive. Then they turn, with their backs to the audience, in a line across the stage.* SCHILL *cannot get through to reach the train*)

SCHILL (*In a low voice*): What are you all doing here? What do you want of me?

BURGOMASTER: We don't like to see you go.

DOCTOR: We've come to see you off.

> (*The sound of the approaching train grows louder*)

SCHILL: I didn't ask you to come.

POLICEMAN: But we have come.

DOCTOR: As old friends.

ALL: As old friends.

> (*The* STATION MASTER *holds up his paddle. The train stops with a screech of brakes. We hear the engine panting offstage*)

VOICE (*Offstage*): Güllen!

BURGOMASTER: A pleasant journey.

DOCTOR: And long life!

PAINTER: And good luck in Australia!

ALL: Yes, good luck in Australia.

> (*They press around him jovially. He stands motionless and pale*)

SCHILL: Why are you crowding me?

POLICEMAN: What's the matter now?

> (*The* STATION MASTER *blows a long blast on his whistle*)

SCHILL: Give me room.

DOCTOR: But you have plenty of room.

> (*They all move away from him*)

POLICEMAN: Better get aboard, Schill.

SCHILL: I see. I see. One of you is going to push me under the wheels.

POLICEMAN: Oh, nonsense. Go on, get aboard.

SCHILL: Get away from me, all of you.

BURGOMASTER: I don't know what you want. Just get on the train.

SCHILL: No. One of you will push me under.

DOCTOR: You're being ridiculous. Now, go on, get on the train.

SCHILL: Why are you all so near me?

DOCTOR: The man's gone mad.

STATION MASTER: 'Board!

> (*He blows his whistle. The engine bell clangs. The train starts*)

BURGOMASTER: Get aboard man. Quick.

> (*The following speeches are spoken all together until the train noises fade away*)

DOCTOR: The train's starting.

ALL: Get aboard, man. Get aboard. The train's starting.

SCHILL: If I try to get aboard, one of you will hold me back.

ALL: No, no.

BURGOMASTER: Get on the train.

SCHILL (*In terror, crouches against the wall of the* STATION MASTER'S *office*): No—no—no. No. (*He falls on his knees. The others crowd around him. He cowers on the ground, abjectly. The train sounds fade away*) Oh, no—no—don't push me, don't push me!

POLICEMAN: There. It's gone off without you.

> (*Slowly they leave him. He raises himself up to a sitting position, still trembling. A* TRUCK DRIVER *enters with an empty can*)

TRUCK DRIVER: Do you know where I can get some water? My truck's boiling over. (SCHILL *points to the station office*) Thanks. (*He enters the office, gets the water and comes out. By this time,* SCHILL *is erect*) Missed your train?

SCHILL: Yes.

TRUCK DRIVER: To Kalberstadt?

SCHILL: Yes.

TRUCK DRIVER: Well, come with me. I'm going that way.

SCHILL: This is my town. This is my home. (*With strange new dignity*) No, thank you. I've changed my mind. I'm staying.

TRUCK DRIVER (*Shrugs*): All right.

> (*He goes out.* SCHILL *picks up his bag, looks right and left, and slowly walks off*)

Curtain

Act Three

Music is heard. Then the curtain rises on the interior of the old barn, a dim, cavernous structure. Bars of light fall across the shadowy forms, shafts of sunlight from the holes and cracks in the walls and roof. Overhead hang old rags, decaying sacks, great cobwebs. Extreme left is a ladder leading to the loft. Near it, an old haycart. Left, CLAIRE ZACHANASSIAN *is sitting in her gilded sedan chair, motionless, in her magnificent bridal gown and veil. Near the chair stands an old keg.*

BOBBY (*Comes in, treading carefully*): The doctor and the teacher from the high school to see you, madame.

CLAIRE (*Impassive*): Show them in.

   (BOBBY *ushers them in as if they were entering a hall of state. The two grope their way through the litter. At last they find the lady, and bow. They are both well dressed in new clothes, but are very dusty*)

BOBBY: Dr. Nüsslin and Professor Müller.

DOCTOR: Madame.

CLAIRE: You look dusty, gentlemen.

DOCTOR (*Dusts himself off vigorously*): Oh, forgive us. We had to climb over an old carriage.

TEACHER: Our respects.

DOCTOR: A fabulous wedding.

TEACHER: Beautiful occasion.

CLAIRE: It's stifling here. But I love this old barn. The smell of hay and old straw and axle grease—it is the scent of my youth. Sit down. All this rubbish—the haycart, the old carriage, the cask, even the pitchfork—it was all here when I was a girl.

TEACHER: Remarkable place.

(*He mops this brow*)

CLAIRE: I thought the pastor's text was very appropriate. The lesson a trifle long.

TEACHER: I Corinthians 13.[1]

CLAIRE: Your choristers sang beautifully, Professor.

TEACHER: Bach. From the *St. Matthew Passion.*

DOCTOR: Güllen has never seen such magnificence! The flowers! The jewels! And the people.

TEACHER: The theatrical world, the world of finance, the world of art, the world of science . . .

CLAIRE: All these worlds are now back in their Cadillacs, speeding toward the

[1] See I Corinthians 13:13: ''But now abideth faith, hope, love, these three; and the greatest of these is love.''

capital for the wedding reception. But I'm sure you didn't come here to talk about them.

DOCTOR: Dear lady, we should not intrude on your valuable time. Your husband must be waiting impatiently.

CLAIRE: No, no, I've packed him off to Brazil.

DOCTOR: To Brazil, madame?

CLAIRE: Yes. For his honeymoon.

TEACHER *and* DOCTOR: Oh! But your wedding guests?

CLAIRE: I've planned a delightful dinner for them. They'll never miss me. Now what was it you wished to talk about?

TEACHER: About Anton Schill, madame.

CLAIRE: Is he dead?

TEACHER: Madame, we may be poor. But we have our principles.

CLAIRE: I see. Then what do you want?

TEACHER (*He mops his brow again*): The fact is, madame, in anticipation of your well-known munificence, that is, feeling that you would give the town some sort of gift, we have all been buying things. Necessities . . .

DOCTOR: With money we don't have.

(*The* TEACHER *blows his nose*)

CLAIRE: You've run into debt?

DOCTOR: Up to here.

CLAIRE: In spite of your principles?

TEACHER: We're human, madame.

CLAIRE: I see.

TEACHER: We have been poor for a long time. A long, long time.

DOCTOR (*He rises*): The question is, how are we going to pay?

CLAIRE: You already know.

TEACHER (*Courageously*): I beg you, Madame Zachanassian, put yourself in our position for a moment. For twenty-two years I've been cudgeling my brains to plant a few seeds of knowledge in this wilderness. And all this time, my gallant colleague, Dr. Nüsslin, has been rattling around in his ancient Mercedes, from patient to patient, trying to keep these wretches alive. Why? Why have we spent our lives in this miserable hole? For money? Hardly. The pay is ridiculous.

DOCTOR: And yet, the professor here has declined an offer to head the high school in Kalberstadt.

TEACHER: And Dr. Nüsslin has refused an important post at the University of Erlangen. Madame, the simple fact is, we love our town. We were born here. It is our life.

DOCTOR: That's true.

TEACHER: What has kept us going all these years is the hope that one day the community will prosper again as it did in the days when were were young.

CLAIRE: Good.

TEACHER: Madame, there is no reason for our poverty. We suffer here from a mysterious blight. We have factories. They stand idle. There is oil in the valley of Pückenried.

DOCTOR: There is copper under the Konradsweil Forest. There is power in our streams, in our waterfalls.

TEACHER: We are not poor, madame. If we had credit, if we had confidence, the factories would open, orders and commissions would pour in. And our economy would bloom together with our cultural life. We would become once again like the towns around us, healthy and prosperous.

DOCTOR: If the Wagonworks were put on its feet again—

TEACHER: The Foundry.

DOCTOR: The Golden Eagle Pencil Factory.

TEACHER: Buy these plants, madame. Put them in operation once more, and I swear to you, Güllen will flourish and it will bless you. We don't need a billion marks. Ten million, properly invested, would give us back our life, and incidentally return to the investor an excellent dividend. Save us, madame. Save us, and we will not only bless you, we will make money for you.

CLAIRE: I don't need money.

DOCTOR: Madame, we are not asking for charity. This is business.

CLAIRE: It's a good idea . . .

DOCTOR: Dear lady! I knew you wouldn't let us down.

CLAIRE: But it's out of the question. I cannot buy the Wagonworks. I already own them.

DOCTOR: The Wagonworks?

TEACHER: And the Foundry?

CLAIRE: And the Foundry.

DOCTOR: And the Golden Eagle Pencil Factory?

CLAIRE: Everything. The valley of Pückenried with its oil, the forest of Konradsweil with its ore, the barn, the town, the streets, the houses, the shops, everything. I had my agents buy up this rubbish over the years, bit by bit, piece by piece, until I had it all. Your hopes were an illusion, your vision empty, your self-sacrifice a stupidity, your whole life completely senseless.

TEACHER: Then the mysterious blight—

CLAIRE: The mysterious blight was I.

DOCTOR: But this is monstrous!

CLAIRE: Monstrous. I was seventeen when I left this town. It was winter. I was dressed in a sailor suit and my red braids hung down my back. I was in my seventh month. As I walked down the street to the station, the boys whistled after me, and someone threw something. I sat freezing in my seat in the Hamburg Express. But before the roof of the great barn was lost behind the trees, I had made up my mind that one day I would come back . . .

TEACHER: But, madame—

CLAIRE (*She smiles*): And now I have. (*She claps her hands*) Mike. Max. Take me back to the Golden Apostle. I've been here long enough.

(MIKE *and* MAX *start to pick up the sedan chair. The* TEACHER *pushes* MIKE *away*)

TEACHER: Madame. One moment. Please. I see it all now. I had thought of you as an avenging fury, a Medea, a Clytemnestra—but I was wrong. You are a warm-hearted woman who has suffered a terrible injustice, and now you have returned and taught us an unforgettable lesson. You have stripped us bare. But now that we stand before you naked, I know you will set aside these thoughts of vengeance. If we made you suffer, you too have put us through the fire. Have mercy, madame.

CLAIRE: When I have had justice. Mike!

(*She signals to* MIKE *and* MAX *to pick up the sedan chair. They cross the stage. The* TEACHER *bars the way*)

TEACHER: But, madame, one injustice cannot cure another. What good will it do to force us into crime? Horror succeeds horror, shame is piled on shame. It settles nothing.

CLAIRE: It settles everything.

(*They move upstage toward the exit. The* TEACHER *follows*)

TEACHER: Madame, this lesson you have taught us will never be forgotten. We will hand it down from father to son. It will be a monument more lasting than any vengeance. Whatever we have been, in the future we shall be better because of you. You have pushed us to the extreme. Now forgive us. Show us the way to a better life. Have pity, madame—pity. That is the highest justice.

(*The sedan chair stops*)

CLAIRE: The highest justice has no pity. It is bright and pure and clear. The world made me into a whore; now I make the world into a brothel. Those who wish to go down, may go down. Those who wish to dance with me, may dance with me. (*To her porters*) Go.

(*She is carried off. The lights black out. Downstage, right, appears* SCHILL's *shop. It has a new sign, a new counter. The doorbell, when it rings, has an impressive sound.* FRAU SCHILL *stands behind the counter in a new dress. The* FIRST MAN *enters, left. He is dressed as a prosperous butcher, a few bloodstains on his snowy apron, a gold watch chain across his open vest*)

FIRST MAN: What a wedding! I'll swear the whole town was there. Cigarettes.

FRAU SCHILL: Clara is entitled to a little happiness after all. I'm happy for her. Green or white?

FIRST MAN: Turkish. The bridesmaids! Dancers and opera singers. And the dresses! Down to here.

FRAU SCHILL: It's the fashion nowadays.

FIRST MAN: Reporters! Photographers! From all over the world! (*In a low voice*) They will be here any minute.

FRAU SCHILL: What have reporters to do with us? We are simple people, Herr Hofbauer. There is nothing for them here.

FIRST MAN: They're questioning everybody. They're asking everything. (*The* FIRST MAN *lights a cigarette. He looks up at the ceiling*) Footsteps.

FRAU SCHILL: He's pacing the room. Up and down. Day and night.

FIRST MAN: Haven't seen him all week.

FRAU SCHILL: He never goes out.

FIRST MAN: It's his conscience. That was pretty mean, the way he treated poor Madame Zachanassian.

FRAU SCHILL: That's true. I feel very badly about it myself.

FIRST MAN: To ruin a young girl like that— God doesn't forgive it. (FRAU SCHILL *nods solemnly with pursed lips. The butcher gives her a level glance*) Look, I hope he'll have sense enough to keep his mouth shut in front of the reporters.

FRAU SCHILL: I certainly hope so.

FIRST MAN: You know his character.

FRAU SCHILL: Only too well, Herr Hofbauer.

FIRST MAN: If he tries to throw dirt at our Clara and tell a lot of lies, how she tried to get us to kill him, which anyway she never meant—

FRAU SCHILL: Of course not.

FIRST MAN: —Then we'll really have to do something! And not because of the money— (*He spits*) But out of ordinary human decency. God knows Madame Zachanassian has suffered enough through him already.

FRAU SCHILL: She has indeed.

(*The* TEACHER *comes in. He is not quite sober*)

TEACHER (*Looks about the shop*): Has the press been here yet?

FIRST MAN: No.

TEACHER: It's not my custom, as you know, Frau Schill—but I wonder if I could have a strong alcoholic drink?

FRAU SCHILL: It's an honor to serve you, Herr Professor. I have a good Steinhäger.[2] Would you like to try a glass?

TEACHER: A very small glass.

(FRAU SCHILL *serves bottle and glass. The* TEACHER *tosses off a glass*)

FRAU SCHILL: Your hand is shaking, Herr Professor.

TEACHER: To tell the truth, I have been drinking a little already.

FRAU SCHILL: Have another glass. It will do you good.

(*He accepts another glass*)

TEACHER: Is that he up there, walking?

FRAU SCHILL: Up and down. Up and down.

FIRST MAN: It's God punishing him.

(*The* PAINTER *comes in with the* SON *and the* DAUGHTER)

PAINTER: Careful! A reporter just asked us the way to this shop.

FIRST MAN: I hope you didn't tell him.

PAINTER: I told him we were strangers here.

(*They all laugh. The door opens. The* SECOND MAN *darts into the shop*)

SECOND MAN: Look out, everybody! The press! They are across the street in your shop, Hofbauer.

FIRST MAN: My boy will know how to deal with them.

---

[2] A kind of gin.

SECOND MAN: Make sure Schill doesn't come down, Hofbauer.

FIRST MAN: Leave that to me.

(*They group themselves about the shop*)

TEACHER: Listen to me, all of you. When the reporters come I'm going to speak to them. I'm going to make a statement. A statement to the world on behalf of myself as Rector of Güllen High School and on behalf of you all, for all your sakes.

PAINTER: What are you going to say?

TEACHER: I shall tell the truth about Claire Zachanassian.

FRAU SCHILL: You're drunk, Herr Professor; you should be ashamed of yourself.

TEACHER: I should be ashamed? You should all be ashamed!

SON: Shut your trap. You're drunk.

DAUGHTER: Please, Professor—

TEACHER: Girl, you disappoint me. It is your place to speak. But you are silent and you force your old teacher to raise his voice. I am going to speak the truth. It is my duty and I am not afraid. The world may not wish to listen, but no one can silence me. I'm not going to wait—I'm going over to Hofbauer's shop now.

ALL: No, you're not. Stop him. Stop him.

(*They all spring at the* TEACHER. *He defends himself. At this moment,* SCHILL *appears through the door upstage. In contrast to the others, he is dressed shabbily in an old black jacket, his best*)

SCHILL: What's going on in my shop? (*The townsmen let go of the* TEACHER *and turn to stare at* SCHILL) What's the trouble, Professor?

TEACHER: Schill, I am speaking out at last! I am going to tell the press everything.

SCHILL: Be quiet, Professor.

TEACHER: What did you say?

SCHILL: Be quiet.

TEACHER: You want me to be quiet?

SCHILL: Please.

TEACHER: But, Schill, if I keep quiet, if you miss this opportunity—they're over in Hofbauer's shop now . . .

SCHILL: Please.

TEACHER: As you wish. If you too are on their side, I have no more to say.

(*The doorbell jingles. A* REPORTER *comes in*)

REPORTER: Is Anton Schill here? (*Moves to* SCHILL) Are you Herr Schill?

SCHILL: What?

REPORTER: Herr Schill.

SCHILL: Er—no. Herr Schill's gone to Kalberstadt for the day.

REPORTER: Oh, thank you. Good day.

(*He goes out*)

PAINTER (*Mops his brow*): Whew! Close shave.

(*He follows the* REPORTER *out*)

SECOND MAN (*Walking up to* SCHILL): That was pretty smart of you to keep your mouth shut. You know what to expect if you don't.

(*He goes*)

FIRST MAN: Give me a Havana. (SCHILL *serves him*) Charge it. You bastard!

(*He goes.* SCHILL *opens his account book*)

FRAU SCHILL: Come along, children—

(FRAU SCHILL, *the* SON *and the* DAUGHTER *go off, upstage*)

TEACHER: They're going to kill you. I've known it all along, and you too, you must have known it. The need is too strong, the temptation too great. And now perhaps I too will join against you. I belong to them and, like them, I can feel myself hardening into something that is not human—not beautiful.

SCHILL: It can't be helped.

TEACHER: Pull yourself together, man. Speak to the reporters; you've no time to lose.

(SCHILL *looks up from his account book*)

SCHILL: No. I'm not going to fight any more.

TEACHER: Are you so frightened that you don't dare open your mouth?

SCHILL: I made Claire what she is, I made myself what I am. What should I do? Should I pretend that I'm innocent?

TEACHER: No, you can't. You are as guilty as hell.

SCHILL: Yes.

TEACHER: You are a bastard.

SCHILL: Yes.

TEACHER: But that does not justify your murder. (SCHILL *looks at him*) I wish I could believe that for what they're doing—for what they're going to do— they will suffer for the rest of their lives. But it's not true. In a little while they will have justified everything and forgotten everything.

SCHILL: Of course.

TEACHER: Your name will never again be mentioned in this town. That's how it will be.

SCHILL: I don't hold it against you.

TEACHER: But I do. I will hold it against myself all my life. That's why—

(*The doorbell jingles. The* BURGOMASTER *comes in. The* TEACHER *stares at him, then goes out without another word*)

BURGOMASTER: Good afternoon, Schill. Don't let me disturb you. I've just dropped in for a moment.

SCHILL: I'm just finishing my accounts for the week.

(*A moment's pause*)

BURGOMASTER: The town council meets tonight. At the Golden Apostle. In the auditorium.

SCHILL: I'll be there.

BURGOMASTER: The whole town will be there. Your case will be discussed and final action taken. You've put us in a pretty tight spot, you know.

SCHILL: Yes. I'm sorry.

BURGOMASTER: The lady's offer will be rejected.

SCHILL: Possibly.

BURGOMASTER: Of course, I may be wrong.

SCHILL: Of course.

BURGOMASTER: In that case—are you prepared to accept the judgment of the town? The meeting will be covered by the press, you know.

SCHILL: By the press?

BURGOMASTER: Yes, and the radio and the newsreel. It's a very ticklish situation. Not only for you—believe me, it's even worse for us. What with the wedding, and all the publicity, we've become famous. All of a sudden our ancient democratic institutions have become of interest to the world.

SCHILL: Are you going to make the lady's condition public?

BURGOMASTER: No, no, of course not. Not directly. We will have to put the matter to a vote—that is unavoidable. But only those involved will understand.

SCHILL: I see.

BURGOMASTER: As far as the press is concerned, you are simply the intermediary between us and Madame Zachanassian. I have whitewashed you completely.

SCHILL: That is very generous of you.

BURGOMASTER: Frankly, it's not for your sake, but for the sake of your family. They are honest and decent people.

SCHILL: Oh—

BURGOMASTER: So far we've all played fair. You've kept your mouth shut and so have we. Now can we continue to depend on you? Because if you have any idea of opening your mouth at tonight's meeting, there won't be any meeting.

SCHILL: I'm glad to hear an open threat at last.

BURGOMASTER: We are not threatening you. You are threatening us. If you speak, you force us to act—in advance.

SCHILL: That won't be necessary.

BURGOMASTER: So if the town decides against you?

SCHILL: I will accept their decision.

BURGOMASTER: Good. (*A moment's pause*) I'm delighted to see there is still a spark of decency left in you. But—wouldn't it be better if we didn't have to call a meeting at all? (*He pauses. He takes a gun from his pocket and puts it on the counter*) I've brought you this.

SCHILL: Thank you.

BURGOMASTER: It's loaded.

SCHILL: I don't need a gun.

BURGOMASTER (*He clears his throat*) You see? We could tell the lady that we had condemned you in secret session and you had anticipated our decision. I've lost a lot of sleep getting to this point, believe me.

SCHILL: I believe you.

BURGOMASTER: Frankly, in your place, I myself would prefer to take the path of honor. Get it over with, once and for all. Don't you agree? For the sake of your friends! For the sake of our children, your own children—you have a daughter, a son—Schill, you know our need, our misery.

SCHILL: You've put me through hell, you and your town. You were my friends, you smiled and reassured me. But day by day I saw you change— your shoes, your ties, your suits—your hearts. If you had been honest with me then, perhaps I would feel differently toward you now. I might even use that gun you brought me. For the sake of my friends. But now I have conquered my fear. Alone. It was hard, but it's done. And now you will have to judge me. And I will accept your judgment. For me that will be justice. How it will be for you, I don't know. (*He turns away*) You may kill me if you like. I won't complain, I won't protest. I won't defend myself. But I won't do your job for you either.

BURGOMASTER (*Takes up his gun*): There it is. You've had your chance and you won't take it. Too bad. (*He takes out a cigarette*) I suppose it's more than we can expect of a man like you. (SCHILL *lights the* BURGOMASTER's *cigarette*) Good day.

SCHILL: Good day. (*The* BURGOMASTER *goes.* FRAU SCHILL *comes in, dressed in a fur coat. The* DAUGHTER *is in a new red dress. The* SON *has a new sports jacket*) What a beautiful coat, Mathilde!

FRAU SCHILL: Real fur. You like it?

SCHILL: Should I? What a lovely dress, Ottilie!

DAUGHTER: *C'est très chic, n'est-ce pas?*[3]

SCHILL: What?

FRAU SCHILL: Ottilie is taking a course in French.

SCHILL: Very useful. Karl—whose automobile is that out there at the curb?

SON: Oh, it's only an Opel. They're not expensive.

SCHILL: You bought yourself a car?

SON: On credit. Easiest thing in the world.

FRAU SCHILL: Everyone's buying on credit now, Anton. These fears of yours are ridiculous. You'll see. Clara has a good heart. She only means to teach you a lesson.

DAUGHTER: She means to teach you a lesson, that's all.

SON: It's high time you got the point, Father.

SCHILL: I get the point. (*The church bells start ringing*) Listen. The bells of Güllen. Do you hear?

SON: Yes, we have four bells now. It sounds quite good.

DAUGHTER: Just like Gray's Elegy.

SCHILL: What?

FRAU SCHILL: Ottilie is taking a course in English literature.

SCHILL: Congratulations! It's Sunday. I should very much like to take a ride in your car. Our car.

SON: You want to ride in the car?

SCHILL: Why not? I want to ride through the Konradsweil Forest. I want to see the town where I've lived all my life.

FRAU SCHILL: I don't think that will look very nice for any of us.

SCHILL: No—perhaps not. Well, I'll go for a walk by myself.

---

[3] It's very smart, isn't it?

FRAU SCHILL: Then take us to Kalberstadt, Karl, and we'll go to a cinema.

SCHILL: A cinema? It's a good idea.

FRAU SCHILL: See you soon, Anton.

SCHILL: Good-bye, Ottilie. Good-bye, Karl. Good-bye, Mathilde.

FAMILY: Good-bye.

(They go out)

SCHILL: Good-bye. *(The shop sign flies off. The lights black out. They come up at once on the forest scene)* Autumn. Even the forest has turned to gold.

    *(*SCHILL *wanders down to the bench in the forest. He sits.* CLAIRE's *voice is heard)*

CLAIRE *(Offstage)*: Stop. Wait here. *(*CLAIRE *comes in. She gazes slowly up at the trees, kicks at some leaves. Then she walks slowly down center. She stops before a tree, glances up the trunk)* Bark-borers. The old tree is dying.

    (She catches sight of SCHILL)

SCHILL: Clara.

CLAIRE: How pleasant to see you here. I was visiting my forest. May I sit by you?

SCHILL: Oh, yes. Please do. *(She sits next to him)* I've just been saying good-bye to my family. They've gone to the cinema. Karl has bought himself a car.

CLAIRE: How nice.

SCHILL: Ottilie is taking French lessons. And a course in English literature.

CLAIRE: You see? They're beginning to take an interest in higher things.

SCHILL: Listen. A finch. You hear?

CLAIRE: Yes. It's a finch. And a cuckoo in the distance. Would you like some music?

SCHILL: Oh, yes. That would be very nice.

CLAIRE: Anything special?

SCHILL: "Deep in the Forest."

CLAIRE: Your favorite song. They know it.

    (She raises her hand. Offstage, the mandolin and guitar play the tune softly)

SCHILL: We had a child?

CLAIRE: Yes.

SCHILL: Boy or girl?

CLAIRE: Girl.

SCHILL: What name did you give her?

CLAIRE: I called her Genevieve.

SCHILL: That's a very pretty name.

CLAIRE: Yes.

SCHILL: What was she like?

CLAIRE: I saw her only once. When she was born. Then they took her away from me.

SCHILL: Her eyes?

CLAIRE: They weren't open yet.

SCHILL: And her hair?

CLAIRE: Black, I think. It's usually black at first.

SCHILL: Yes, of course. Where did she die, Clara?

CLAIRE: In some family. I've forgotten their name. Meningitis, they said. The officials wrote me a letter.

SCHILL: Oh, I'm so very sorry, Clara.

CLAIRE: I've told you about our child. Now tell me about myself.

SCHILL: About yourself?

CLAIRE: Yes. How I was when I was seventeen in the days when you loved me.

SCHILL: I remember one day you waited for me in the great barn. I had to look all over the place for you. At last I found you lying in the haycart with nothing on and a long straw between your lips . . .

CLAIRE: Yes. I was pretty in those days.

SCHILL: You were beautiful, Clara.

CLAIRE: You were strong. The time you fought with those two railway men who were following me, I wiped the blood from your face with my red petticoat. (*The music ends*) They've stopped.

SCHILL: Tell them to play "Thoughts of Home."

CLAIRE: They know that too.

(The music plays)

SCHILL: Here we are, Clara, sitting together in our forest for the last time. The town council meets tonight. They will condemn me to death, and one of them will kill me. I don't know who and I don't know where. Clara, I only know that in a little while a useless life will come to an end.

(He bows his head on her bosom. She takes him in her arms)

CLAIRE (*Tenderly*): I shall take you in your coffin to Capri. You will have your tomb in the park of my villa, where I can see you from my bedroom window. White marble and onyx in a grove of green cypress. With a beautiful view of the Mediterranean.

SCHILL: I've always wanted to see it.

CLAIRE: Your love for me died years ago, Anton. But my love for you would not die. It turned into something strong, like the hidden roots of the forest; something evil, like white mushrooms that grow unseen in the darkness. And slowly it reached out for your life. Now I have you. You are mine. Alone. At last, and forever, a peaceful ghost in a silent house.

(The music ends)

SCHILL: The song is over.

CLAIRE: Adieu, Anton.

(claire kisses ANTON, a long kiss. Then she rises)

SCHILL: Adieu.

(She goes. SCHILL remains sitting on the bench. A row of lamps descends from the flies. The townsmen come in from both sides, each bearing his chair. A table and chairs are set upstage, center. On both sides sit the townspeople. The POLICEMAN, in a

new uniform, sits on the bench behind SCHILL. *All the townsmen are in a new Sunday clothes. Around them are technicians of all sorts, with lights, cameras, and other equipment. The towns-women are absent. They do not vote. The* BURGOMASTER *takes his place at the table, center. The* DOCTOR *and the* PASTOR *sit at the same table, at his right, and the* TEACHER *in his academic gown, at his left*)

BURGOMASTER (*At a sign from the radio technician, he pounds the floor with his wand of office*): Fellow citizens of Güllen, I call this meeting to order. The agenda: there is only one matter before us. I have the honor to announce officially that Madame Claire Zachanassian, daughter of our beloved citizen, the famous architect Siegfried Wäscher, has decided to make a gift to the town of one billion marks. Five hundred million to the town, five hundred million to be divided per capita among the citizens. After certain necessary preliminaries, a vote will be taken, and you, as citizens of Güllen, will signify your will by a show of hands. Has anyone any objection to this mode of procedure? The pastor? (*Silence*) The police? (*Silence*) The town health official? (*Silence*) The Rector of Güllen High School? (*Silence*) The political opposition? (*Silence*) I shall then proceed to the vote—(*The* TEACHER *rises. The* BURGOMASTER *turns in surprise and irritation*) You wish to speak?

TEACHER: Yes.

BURGOMASTER: Very well.

(*He takes his seat. The* TEACHER *advances. The movie camera starts running*)

TEACHER: Fellow townsmen. (*The photographer flashes a bulb in his face*) Fellow townsmen. We all know that by means of this gift, Madame Claire Zachanassian intends to attain a certain object. What is this object? To enrich the town of her youth, yes. But more than that, she desires by means of this gift to re-establish justice among us. This desire expressed by our benefactress raises an all-important question. Is it true that our community harbors in its soul such a burden of guilt?

BURGOMASTER: Yes! True!

SECOND MAN: Crimes are concealed among us.

THIRD MAN (*He jumps up*): Sins!

FOURTH MAN (*He jumps up also*): Perjuries.

PAINTER: Justice!

TOWNSMEN: Justice! Justice!

TEACHER: Citizens of Güllen, this, then, is the simple fact of the case. We have participated in an injustice. I thoroughly recognize the material advantages which this gift opens to us—I do not overlook the fact that it is poverty which is the root of all this bitterness and evil. Nevertheless, there is no question here of money.

TOWNSMEN: No! No!

TEACHER: Here there is no question of our prosperity as a community, or our well-being as individuals—The question is—must be—whether or not we wish to live according to the principles of justice, those principles for which our forefathers lived and fought and for which they died, those principles which form the soul of our Western culture.

TOWNSMEN: Hear! Hear!

(*Applause*)

TEACHER (*Desperately, realizing that he is fighting a losing battle, and on the verge of hysteria*): Wealth has meaning only when benevolence comes of it, but only he who hungers for grace will receive grace. Do you feel this hunger, my fellow citizens, this hunger of the spirit, or do you feel only that other profane hunger, the hunger of the body? That is the question which I, as Rector of your high school, now propound to you. Only if you can no longer tolerate the presence of evil among you, only if you can in no circumstances endure a world in which injustice exists, are you worthy to receive Madame Zachanassian's billion and fulfill the condition bound up with this gift. If not—(*Wild applause. He gestures desperately for silence*) If not, then God have mercy on us!

(*The townsmen crowd around him, ambiguously, in a mood somewhat between threat and congratulation. He takes his seat, utterly crushed, exhausted by his effort. The* BURGOMASTER *advances and takes charge once again. Order is restored*)

BURGOMASTER: Anton Schill—(*The* POLICEMAN *gives* SCHILL *a shove.* SCHILL *gets up*) Anton Schill, it is through you that this gift is offered to the town. Are you willing that this offer should be accepted?

(SCHILL *mumbles something*)

RADIO REPORTER (*Steps to his side*): You'll have to speak up a little, Herr Schill.

SCHILL: Yes.

BURGOMASTER: Will you respect our decision in the matter before us?

SCHILL: I will respect your decision.

BURGOMASTER: Then I proceed to the vote. All those who are in accord with the terms on which this gift is offered will signify the same by raising their right hands. (*After a moment, the* POLICEMAN *raises his hand. Then one by one the others. Last of all, very slowly, the* TEACHER) All against? The offer is accepted. I now solemnly call upon you, fellow townsmen, to declare in the face of all the world that you take this action, not out of love for worldly gain . . .

TOWNSMEN (*In chorus*): Not out of love for worldly gain . . .

BURGOMASTER: But out of love for the right.

TOWNSMEN: But out of love for the right.

BURGOMASTER (*Holds up his hand, as if taking an oath*): We join together, now, as brothers . . .

TOWNSMEN (*Hold up their hands*): We join together, now, as brothers . . .

BURGOMASTER: To purify our town of guilt . . .

TOWNSMEN: To purify our town of guilt . . .

BURGOMASTER: And to reaffirm our faith . . .

TOWNSMEN: And to reaffirm our faith . . .

BURGOMASTER: In the eternal power of justice.

TOWNSMEN: In the eternal power of justice.

(The lights go off suddenly)

SCHILL *(A scream)*: Oh, God!

VOICE: I'm sorry, Herr Burgomaster. We seem to have blown a fuse. *(The lights go on)* Ah—there we are. Would you mind doing that last bit again?

BURGOMASTER: Again?

THE CAMERAMAN *(Walks forward)*: Yes, for the newsreel.

BURGOMASTER: Oh, the newsreel. Certainly.

THE CAMERAMAN: Ready now? Right.

BURGOMASTER: And to reaffirm our faith . . .

TOWNSMEN: And to reaffirm out faith . . .

BURGOMASTER: In the eternal power of justice.

TOWNSMEN: In the eternal power of justice.

THE CAMERAMAN *(To his assistant)*: It was better before, when he screamed "Oh, God."

(The assistant shrugs)

BURGOMASTER: Fellow citizens of Güllen, I declare this meeting adjourned. The ladies and gentlemen of the press will find refreshments served downstairs, with the compliments of the town council. The exits lead directly to the restaurant.

THE CAMERAMAN: Thank you.

(The newsmen go off with alacrity. The townsmen remain on the stage. SCHILL *gets up)*

POLICEMAN *(Pushes* SCHILL *down)*: Sit down.

SCHILL: Is it to be now?

POLICEMAN: Naturally, now.

SCHILL: I thought it might be best to have it at my house.

POLICEMAN: It will be here.

BURGOMASTER: Lower the lights. *(The lights dim)* Are they all gone?

VOICE: All gone.

BURGOMASTER: The gallery?

SECOND VOICE: Empty.

BURGOMASTER: Lock the doors.

THE VOICE: Locked here.

SECOND VOICE: Locked here.

BURGOMASTER: Form a lane. *(The men form a lane. At the end stands the* ATHLETE *in elegant white slacks, a red scarf around his singlet)* Pastor. Will you be so good?

(The PASTOR *walks slowly to* SCHILL*)*

PASTOR: Anton Schill, your heavy hour has come.

SCHILL: May I have a cigarette?

PASTOR: Cigarette, Burgomaster.

BURGOMASTER: Of course. With pleasure. And a good one.

(*He gives his case to the* PASTOR, *who offers it to* SCHILL. *The* PASTOR *lights the cigarette. The* PASTOR *returns the case*)

PASTOR: In the words of the prophet Amos—

SCHILL: Please—

(*He shakes his head*)

PASTOR: You're no longer afraid?

SCHILL: No. I'm not afraid.

PASTOR: I will pray for you.

SCHILL: Pray for us all.

(*The* PASTOR *bows his head*)

BURGOMASTER: Anton Schill, stand up!

(SCHILL *hesitates*)

POLICEMAN: Stand up, you swine!

BURGOMASTER: Schultz, please.

POLICEMAN: I'm sorry. I was carried away. (SCHILL *gives the cigarette to the* POLICEMAN. *Then he walks slowly to the center of the stage and turns his back on the audience*) Enter the lane.

(SCHILL *hesitates a moment. He goes slowly into the lane of silent men. The* ATHLETE *stares at him from the opposite end.* SCHILL *looks in turn at the hard faces of those who surround him, and sinks slowly to his knees. The lane contracts silently into a knot as the men close in and crouch over. Complete silence. The knot of men pulls back slowly, coming downstage. Then it opens. Only the* DOCTOR *is left in the center of the stage, kneeling by the corpse, over which the* TEACHER's *gown has been spread. The* DOCTOR *rises and takes off his stethoscope*)

PAINTER: Is it all over?

DOCTOR: Heart failure.

BURGOMASTER: Died of joy.

ALL: Died of joy.

(*The townsmen turn their backs on the corpse and at once light cigarettes. A cloud of smoke rises over them. From the left comes* CLAIRE ZACHANASSIAN, *dressed in black, followed by* BOBBY. *She sees the corpse. Then she walks slowly to center stage and looks down at the body of* SCHILL)

CLAIRE: Uncover him. (BOBBY *uncovers* SCHILL's *face. She stares at it a long moment. She sighs*) Cover his face.

(BOBBY *covers it.* CLAIRE *goes out, up center.* BOBBY *takes the check from his wallet, holds it out peremptorily to the* BURGOMASTER, *who walks over from the knot of silent men. He holds out his hand for the check. The lights fade. At once the warning bell is heard, and the scene dissolves into the setting of the railway station. The gradual transformation of the shabby town into a thing of elegance and beauty is now accomplished. The railway station glitters with neon lights and is surrounded with garlands, bright posters, and flags. The townsfolk, men and women, now in brand new clothes, form themselves into a group in front of the station. The sound of the approaching train grows louder. The train stops)*

STATION MASTER: Güllen-Rome Express. All aboard, please. (*The church bells start pealing. Men appear with trunks and boxes, a procession which duplicates that of the lady's arrival, but in inverse order. Then come the* TWO BLIND MEN, *then* BOBBY, *and* MIKE *and* MAX *carrying the coffin. Lastly* CLAIRE. *She is dressed in modish black. Her head is high, her face as impassive as that of an ancient idol. The procession crosses the stage and goes off. The people bow in silence as the coffin passes. When* CLAIRE *and her retinue have boarded the train, the* STATION MASTER *blows a long blast)* 'Bo—ard!

(*He holds up his paddle. The train starts and moves off slowly, picking up speed. The crowd turns slowly, gazing after the departing train in complete silence. The train sounds fade)*

The curtain falls slowly

POEMS

Richard Cory

E. A. Robinson

Whenever Richard Cory went down town.
We people on the pavement looked at him:
He was a gentleman from sole to crown.
Clean favored, and imperially slim.

And he was always quietly arrayed.
And he was always human when he talked;
But still he fluttered pulses when he said,
'Good-morning,' and he glittered when he walked.

And he was rich—yes, richer than a king—
And admirably schooled in every grace:
In fine, we thought that he was everything
To make us wish that we were in his place.

So on we worked, and waited for the light,
And went without the meat, and cursed the bread;
And Richard Cory, one calm summer night.
Went home and put a bullet through his head.

In a Station of the Metro

Ezra Pound

The apparition of these faces in the crowd;
Petals on a wet, black bough.

Sonnet 73

William Shakespeare

That time of year thou mayst in me behold
When yellow leaves, or none, or few, do hang
Upon those boughs which shake against the cold.
Bare ruined choirs where late the sweet birds sang.
In me thou see'st the twilight of such day
As after sunset fadeth in the west.
In me thou see'st the glowing of such fire.
What on the ashes of his youth doth lie
As the deathbed whereon it must expire,
Consumed with that which it was nourished by.
This thou perceivest, which makes thy love more strong,
To love that well which thou must leave ere long.

Sonnet 116

William Shakespeare

Let me not to the marriage of true minds
Admit impediments. Love is not love
Which alters when it alteration finds,
Or bends with the remover to remove:
O, no; it is an ever-fixèd mark,
That looks on tempests and is never shaken:
It is the star to every wandering bark,
Whose worth's unknown, although his height be taken.
Love's not Time's fool, though rosy lips and cheeks
Within his bending sickle's compass come;
Love alters not with his brief hours and weeks,
But bears it out even to the edge of doom.
  If this be error and upon me proved.
  I never writ, nor no man ever loved.

ACKNOWLEDGMENTS

Sherwood Anderson, "Death in the Woods," published in the *American Mercury*, September 1926. Copyright 1926 by The American Mercury, Inc. Renewed 1953 by Eleanor Copenhaver Anderson. Reprinted by permission of Harold Ober Associates Incorporated.

John Cheever, "The Swimmer," from *The Brigadier and the Gold Widow* by John Cheever. Copyright © 1964 by John Cheever. Reprinted by permission of Harper & Row, Publishers.

Friedrich Duerrenmatt, "The Visit," adapted by Maurice Valency. © Copyright 1956, by Maurice Valency, as an unpublished work entitled "The Old Lady's Visit" adapted from *Der Besuch Der alten Dame*, by Friedrich Duerrenmatt. © Copyright 1958 by Maurice Valency. Reprinted by permission of Random House, Inc.

Moliere, "Tartuffe," translated by John Wood, from *Misanthrope and Other Plays*; reprinted by permission of Penguin Books Ltd.

Flannery O'Connor, "A Good Man Is Hard to Find." Copyright 1953 by Flannery O'Connor; renewed 1981 by Mrs. Regina O'Connor. Reprinted from *A Good Man Is Hard to Find and Other Stories* by Flannery O'Connor by permission of Harcourt Brace Jovanovich, Inc.

Ezra Pound, "In a Station of the Metro," from *Personae*. Copyright 1926 by Ezra Pound. Reprinted by permission of New Directions Publishing Corporation.

E. A. Robinson, "Richard Cory," from *Children of the Night* by Edward Arlington Robinson. Copyright protected under the Berne Convention. Reprinted with permission of Charles Scribner's Sons.

Sophocles, "Antigone," translated by T. H. Banks. © 1956 by Theodore Howard Banks, from *Three Theban Plays*. Reprinted by permission of Oxford University Press.

Eudora Welty, "A Worn Path." Copyright 1941, 1969 by Eudora Welty. Reprinted from her volume *A Curtain of Green and Other Stories* by permission of Harcourt Brace Jovanovich, Inc.

Edith Wharton, "The Eyes," from *The Ghost Stories of Edith Wharton*, edited by William R. Tyler. Copyright 1910 Charles Scribner's Sons; renewal copyright 1938 William R. Tyler. Copyright protected under the Berne Convention. Reprinted by permission of Charles Scribner's Sons.